Why does comedy matter? Is it celebratory or subversive? What makes it flourish, and which creative forces resist it? *English Comedy* addresses these and related questions by invoking a variety of works from Aristophanes to Walt Disney, while focussing on the traditions of comic writing in England. Poetry, the novel and (above all) drama are examined to assess the constrictions and liberations of genre, the negotiations or divergences between comic practice and theory, and the dynamics of theatrical language. Ranging from medieval and Renaissance drama through Romantic poetry to twentieth-century literature and philosophy, *English Comedy* makes a valuable contribution to our understanding of the heritage of comic writing.

ENGLISH COMEDY

ENGLISH COMEDY

EDITED BY

MICHAEL CORDNER

University of York

PETER HOLLAND

Trinity Hall, Cambridge

JOHN KERRIGAN

St John's College, Cambridge

CAMBRIDGE
UNIVERSITY PRESS

Published by the Press Syndicate of the University of Cambridge
The Pitt Building, Trumpington Street, Cambridge CB2 1RP
40 West 20th Street, New York, NY 10011-4211, USA
10 Stamford Road, Oakleigh, Melbourne 3166, Australia

First published 1994

Printed in Great Britain at the University Press, Cambridge

A catalogue record for this book is available from the British Library

Library of Congress cataloguing in publication data

English comedy / edited by Michael Cordner, Peter Holland, and John
Kerrigan.
p.   cm.
Includes index.
ISBN 0 521 41917 4 (hardback)
1.   English drama (Comedy) – History and criticism.   I. Cordner,
Michael.   II. Holland, Peter, 1951–   .   III. Kerrigan, John.
PR631.E54   1994
822'.052309 – dc   20   93–8125 CIP

ISBN 0 521 41917 4 hardback

To Anne Barton

Contents

Illustrations

Notes on contributors

JONAS BARISH taught from 1954 to 1991 at the University of California, Berkeley. Since 1991 he has been Professor Emeritus of English. He has published *Ben Jonson and the Language of Prose Comedy* (1960), *The Antitheatrical Prejudice* (1981), and various essays chiefly on Renaissance and later drama. He is currently at work on a study of closet drama.

JONATHAN BATE is King Alfred Professor of English Literature at the University of Liverpool and a former Fellow of Trinity Hall, Cambridge. He is the author of *Shakespeare and the English Romantic Imagination* (1986), *Shakespearean Constitutions* (1989), *Romantic Ecology* (1991) and *Shakespeare and Ovid* (1993).

RICHARD BEADLE is a Lecturer in English at the University of Cambridge and a Fellow of St John's College. He has recently edited, with Toshiyuki Takamiya, *Chaucer to Shakespeare: Essays in Honour of Shinsuke Ando* (1992), with Rosamond McKitterick, the *Catalogue of the Pepys Library at Magdalene College, Cambridge: Medieval Manuscripts* (1992) and the forthcoming *Cambridge Companion to Medieval English Theatre*.

GILLIAN BEER is a Professor of English at Cambridge University and a Fellow of Girton College. Among her books are *The Romance* (1970), *Darwin's Plots: Evolutionary Narrative in Darwin, George Eliot and Nineteenth-Century Fiction* (1983) and *Arguing with The Past: Essays on Narrative from Woolf to Sidney* (1989).

MARTIN BUTLER is a Lecturer in the School of English, University of Leeds. He has written *Theatre and Crisis 1632–1642* (1984) and *Ben Jonson's 'Volpone': A Critical Study* (1987), and has edited Volume II of *The Selected Plays of Ben Jonson* (1989).

MICHAEL CORDNER is a Senior Lecturer in the Department of English, University of York. He has published editions of plays by Farquhar, Etherege and Vanbrugh and is General Editor of the forthcoming World's Classics Drama Library for Oxford University Press, for which he is co-editing a collection of *Four Restoration Marriage Plays*. He is also working on a book on English comedy, 1660–1720.

JOHN CREASER is Hildred Carlile Professor of English Literature at Royal Holloway, University of London, and Executive Secretary of the Malone Society. His publications on Renaissance drama include an edition of *Volpone* (1978) and several essays on Ben Jonson. He is currently writing a study of Milton's earlier work.

BARBARA EVERETT, who teaches and lectures at Oxford University (Somerville College), has also held appointments at Cambridge (Newnham College) and at the University of Hull. Her most recent books are *Poets in Their Time: Essays on English Poetry from Donne to Larkin* and *Young Hamlet: Essays on Shakespeare's Tragedies*.

ERIC GRIFFITHS teaches English at Trinity College, Cambridge. He is the author of *The Printed Voice of Victorian Poetry*.

PETER HOLLAND is Judith E. Wilson Lecturer in Drama in the Faculty of English at Cambridge and a Fellow of Trinity Hall. Among his publications are *The Ornament of Action: Text and Performance in Restoration Comedy* (1979), editions of the plays of Wycherley (1981) and of *A Midsummer Night's Dream* (1994), collections of essays (as contributing editor) on *The Play Out of Context* (1988) and *Reading Plays* (1991) as well as many articles on Chekhov, Shakespeare and Shakespearean production.

JOHN KERRIGAN is a Fellow of St John's College, Cambridge and a University Lecturer in English. He has edited, among other texts, Shakespeare's *Sonnets and 'A Lover's Complaint'* and published numerous essays on English poetry and drama.

STEPHEN ORGEL is the Jackson Eli Reynolds Professor of Humanities at Stanford University. His books include *The Jonsonian Masque, The Illusion of Power* and, in collaboration with Roy Strong, *Inigo Jones*. He has edited Ben Jonson's masques, the poems and translations of Christopher Marlowe and, for the Oxford Shakespeare, *The Tempest*.

ADRIAN POOLE is a Fellow of Trinity College, Cambridge and a University Lecturer in English. Among his publications are *Gissing in Context* (1975), *Tragedy: Shakespeare and the Greek Example* (1987) and a study of Shakespeare's *Coriolanus* (1988).

RICHARD ROWLAND is Lecturer in English Literature at St Anne's College, Oxford. He has edited *Edward II*, for the new *Complete Works* of Marlowe (Oxford English Texts), and co-written an Introduction for *The Tragedy of Mariam* (Malone Society, 1991). He is currently working on an edition of the two-part Elizabethan history play *Edward IV*, which is to be published by The Malone Society in 1996.

JONATHAN WORDSWORTH is a Fellow of St Catherine's College, Oxford and University Lecturer in Romantic Studies. He is the author of *William Wordsworth: The Borders of Vision* and editor of the forthcoming Longman *Annotated Selections* of Wordsworth (with Nicola Trott and Duncan Wu) and the Cambridge *Complete Poetry and Prose*. He is also general editor of the Woodstock Facsimile series *Revolution and Romanticism*.

Introduction

Michael Cordner, Peter Holland and John Kerrigan

On the title-page of *The Double-Dealer* (1694), Congreve placed a motto from Horace's *Ars Poetica*: 'Interdum tamen, & vocem Comœdia tollit' ('Sometimes however comedy too raises its voice', line 93). As Anne Barton has noted, Congreve is plainly hinting here at 'the dark strain in the play which the Theatre Royal audience had found perplexing', while seeking 'to claim classical sanction for its stridence'.[1] Comedy often seems to feel obliged to warn its readers, even apologise to them, whenever it is going to deal with serious matters, as if the false opposition between the comic and the serious had some element of truth in it. Whenever comedy raises its voice – or puts its head over the parapet – it usually expects to be shot at for arrogantly rising above its literary station.

For comedy to claim to matter has often been considered pretentiousness. For criticism to turn its attentions to comedy has often been considered aberrant. Though Aristotle appears to have had no doubt that comedy mattered and probably spent a significant part of the lost second book of the *Poetics* analysing it, the body of comic theory is notoriously slim by comparison with its non-identical twin, tragedy. Umberto Eco's brilliant fantasy in *The Name of the Rose* of the lost treatise's suppression as a subversive text underlines the dangerousness of comedy in some moods, but evades considering other causes for the paucity of comic theory: above all the conventional hierarchy that places tragedy at the peak of cultural achievement and insists on a lowly status for comedy. Despite the contributions of philosophers and literary generalists from Bergson to Northrop Frye, and the (usually more illuminating) remarks of practitioners from Dryden through Meredith to Barry Humphries, writing about comedy continues to seem less prestigious and culturally significant than writing about tragedy.

I

Perhaps, though, the critical impulse to stand aside from comedy – to let it go about its mischief unmolested – pays prudent tribute to the mode's antipathy to generalisation and prescription. For the most part dedicated to flouting norms and frustrating expectations, comedy has an ingrained antagonism to rules. When rules are proposed for its own conduct, it sets out to mock or break them, engaging in reflexive literary satire and wilful generic imperialism. This is where plays like *The Critic* flourish, while such scripts as *Bartholomew Fair* and *A Tale of a Tub* show comedy planting its flag in areas of experience marked off as belonging to tragedy ('Hero and Leander' performed by puppets) or court masque (In-and-in Medlay's device). Mention of Jonson is salutory, however, in reminding us of the complexity with which some comic writers combine prescription and subversion. The strains created in *Every Man Out Of His Humour* between satirical action and sardonic, or laughable, commentary, show comedy being pushed so far that, as John Creaser remarks later in this book, the result is 'crammed with judgment' yet impossible to 'take on trust'. In this, as in other respects, Jonson defines an extreme. More often, comedy acknowledges rules in order to establish its freedom.

This collection has no pretentions to filling up the space that might be occupied by a theory of comedy, a space that should perhaps be called 'a much-needed gap in the literature'. But Congreve's appeal to classical authority in his choice of epigraph is part of comedy's recurrent awareness of having its own traditions. Jokes need the trigger of novelty (which is why we usually start them by asking 'Have you heard the one about...?'), even though, as Eric Griffiths points out in the closing essay of this book, 'it is the old jokes we go back to'. Comedies, however, tend to accept (and signal) their belonging to a continuum of written and theatrical practice. Their unruliness is compatible with an awareness of traditional resources. While the exclusivity of high tragedy results in historical and social lacunae, periods and cultures that are conventionally demeaned by not having generated tragedies, comedy has fewer breaks in its fossil record. Like the works which they discuss, the essays in this volume are aware of (without attempting to provide 'coverage' for) the traditions of comic writing in England. In argument they often take their bearings from the work of Anne Barton, a critic whose remarkable explorations in Classical, Renaissance, Restoration and Romantic literature have frequently – as most recently in *The Names of Comedy* (1990) and *Byron: 'Don Juan'* (1992) – gravitated to comedy. The collection has been produced to accompany and mark the publication, by Cambridge University Press, of a selection from her writings on drama: *Essays, Mainly Shakespearean*. Some of the authors included in *English Comedy* were Anne Barton's students, some were or are her colleagues in Cambridge and Oxford.[2] The pages which follow are offered as a reflection on and tribute to her work on comedy.

Recent critical iconoclasm has made merry with 'the cult of Shakespeare'. A lot of politically knowing laughter has been directed at the excesses of Victorian and Edwardian Bardolatry, as well as more up-to-date manifestations of Bardbiz. Yet the works which we call 'Shakespeare' – perhaps especially the comedies – have reconstituted themselves rather successfully in the culturally relativist and verbally ludic milieu of post-structuralist criticism. Is this yet another endorsement of the 'myriad-minded' timelessness of the man from Stratford, or does it owe more to sustaining continuities within English comic writing? Almost from the outset, those comedies which were gathered in the Folio of 1623 were subject to adaptation: cartoon versions are only the latest twist given to a kaleidoscope which has been turning since Davenant's rewrite of *The Tempest* (starting-point of Peter Holland's essay on Noël Coward) and Purcell's *The Fairy Queen*. Whatever explains the phenomenon, the lasting vitality of Shakespearean comedy is a central theme of this collection. And the opening group of essays establishes in relation to Shakespeare many of the criteria and concerns which will recur throughout: the constrictions and liberations of genre, the negotiations or divergences between comic drama and theory, the operation of comic language, and the need to revalue and redefine the nature of difficult or undervalued work.

From its beginnings, Western comedy has been interested in animality. Had the second book of Aristotle's *Poetics* survived, it would doubtless have reiterated his dictum – announced in *De anima*, and ringingly endorsed in the epigraph to *Gargantua* – that it is laughter which distinguishes humanity from the animals. Aristophanes has his frogs, wasps and birds, giving him comic access to the livelier properties of that political animal, man. But if comedy has traditionally enjoyed presenting human behaviour as more like that of animals than society might care to admit, it can also make animals more directly part of its scope. In the first essay of *English Comedy*,

Richard Beadle traces the long pedigree of Crab, Lance's dog in *The Two Gentlemen of Verona*. Examining the use of dogs and their masters (usually gleemen, *joculatores*, clowns) on the medieval and Renaissance stage, he sheds light not only on the kinds of laughter roused by Shakespeare's play but on threatening hints of depravity associated with the recalcitrant Crab. Different comic possibilities from those which now obtain were available when man met dog in the sixteenth century, and Shakespeare (like all playwrights) worked in culturally available materials. Reweighting the balance between theatrical and literary analysis, the essay reminds us that Shakespeare's sources are as likely to be the traditions of dramatic practice as the accidents of his reading.

Even in Aristophanes, characters are more often human than animal. But how human is a character? Stephen Orgel's essay begins by correcting, on grounds as historical as Beadle's, our urge to define Renaissance comedy by polarising it against tragedy, but then proceeds to question character itself. Reminding us of the fondness of early modern plays for 'scenes of writing' and 'handwritten discourse as the mode of action', he indicates some of the consequences which flow from character possessing that quality of writtenness of which Crab is blissfully unaware. Orgel is interested in the witty ambiguities created by written documents in tragedies and histories (as when Marlowe's Edward II is killed by Mortimer's duplicitous Latin) as well as in generic comedy. But he is also concerned to establish a larger relationship between the confined scriptedness of roles and their life beyond the limits of plays. By analysing illustrations and scholarly commentary, Orgel redefines our sense of Shakespearean character, and indicates how performance style remodels the past. This argument is pursued into the verbal minutiae of *The Tempest* and *The Winter's Tale*, showing how details of the 'late' comedies have been manipulated by editors not (as one might expect) to make Shakespeare their contemporary but to deflect attention away from what remains troubling in the plays.

Textual details also attract Jonas Barish and Barbara Everett. The former is drawn to those moments of transition (sometimes missed by editors) when Shakespearean comedy moves between verse and prose. What does the dramatist signal by these shifts? What potentials of comic meaning can be found there? Barish established his reputation with a pioneering study of *Ben Jonson and the Language of Prose Comedy* (1960). In his contribution to *English Comedy*, he gauges the artistry of Shakespearean prose (with its 'verbal hijinks, verbal fireworks, and verbal filigree') against the foil provided by a verse which 'serves more often as the vehicle for the nuts and bolts with which the actions and passions of the plot are spun'. Everett's essay on *Much Ado About Nothing* starts with a more local crux. From the editorial problem posed by a few words of Leonato in Act 5, she moves out to the tonal difficulties of a play which has not (compared with Shakespeare's romantic comedies) had its critical due. Admirers of Everett's work will recognise, in this manoeuvre, a tactic resourcefully deployed in her *Young Hamlet: Essays on Shakespeare's Tragedies* (1989). And it is towards the more sombre, paradoxical, tragi-comic features of *Much Ado* that her present discussion devolves. For her, Messina is a world in 'which some version of the political, the power-issue, is serious: a world which defers to Courtship and to social hierarchy'. This sounds like the language of new historicism, but Everett is less interested in glancing context (and political moralising) than in defining the play's 'special, almost novelistic sense' of reality.

Adrian Poole completes the opening group of essays by relating memory and forgetfulness to the dynamics of Shakespearean comedy. To characterise the social texture and structural properties of *Much Ado*, Barbara Everett invokes Restoration comedy, Oscar Wilde, *Pride and Prejudice* and *Vogue* magazine. Poole's initial pages ring with authorities far more cosmopolitan – Kundera, Baudelaire, Borges, Giordano Bruno, Freud, Montaigne, Bergson and Charles Péguy – because, like other contributors to the volume (John Kerrigan and Eric Griffiths most obviously), he finds it impossible to talk about particular, English varieties of comedy without invoking strands in European culture generally. Poole's central concern is with 'the ways and means and kinds of forgetting' in the comic parts of Shakespeare, but he shows how this relatively limited subject cannot be unpacked without investigating links between hilarity, vertigo and self-forgetfulness, the mnemonic authority of father figures, the emotional difficulty of forgiving, and the ambiguities (especially where mourning is involved) of oblivion. Noting, with Scots detachment, Peter Burke's observation that 'The English seem to prefer to forget' – and that they can afford to do so because of their success in winning wars – he ends his essay by reflecting on cultural amnesia.

From Shakespeare the next group of essays turns to other English Renaissance writers. If Shakespearean comedy is protean, then

Jonsonian comedy is, in John Creaser's view, enigmatic. At times too 'audacious' in the theatrical demands he made, Jonson alienated audiences and reacted against their displeasure with notorious displays of scorn. Yet to think of Jonson as essentially a prickly and difficult artist is to prevent ourselves registering how far his 'dramaturgy is founded not on distrust but on confidence in the audience'. The dramatist's defiant reaction against those who misunderstood him can be taken as evidence of disappointed trust. Creaser sets out to show how deeply Jonson is speaking for himself when he remarks, in *The Masque of Queens*, 'A *Writer* should always trust somewhat to the capacity of the *Spectator*.' Examining the author's 'artistic greediness', his variety and inventiveness, Creaser finds in the plays a 'radical elusiveness' not unrelated to Renaissance ideas of perspective and habits of dialogue, but having the potential to make Jonson appear the possessor of just that '*Negative Capability*' which Keats famously found in Shakespeare.

In his sympathy for the more flexible, Shakespearean features of Jonson, Creaser is close to Anne Barton. Like the author of *Ben Jonson, Dramatist* (1984), he also has a liking for the early and late works of a playwright who has too often been regarded as the creator of only four, Jacobean masterpieces. The problem has always been that, until scholarship makes some sort of case for neglected plays, they have little chance of gaining the performances which generate critical interest. Yet the qualities which deserve to rescue comic drama from neglect are (even more than is the case with tragedy or history) likely to become fully apparent only in production. A cheering example of interaction between the academy and the theatre is provided by the resurgence of interest in Jonson's *The New Inn*. Revalued in *Ben Jonson, Dramatist*, in the light of 'Elizabethan nostalgia' under Charles I, the comedy was (in direct response to Barton's advocacy) successfully revived by the RSC. Those parts of the script which had been condemned as undramatic – Lovel's long speeches on love and valour, the formidably improbable dénouement – held audiences spellbound.

The next two essays in *English Comedy* deal with a pair of Caroline comedies which have been, like *The New Inn*, misconstrued. Thanks to its commanding central figure, Sir Giles Overreach, *A New Way to Pay Old Debts* has, at least since Kean, held a place in the repertory. But, as Martin Butler reminds us, its 'grimness' has troubled critics. Rather in the style of Anne Barton's work on late Jonson (though with different ideological priorities), Butler returns *A New Way* to the politics of the mid-1620s, establishes with fresh clarity the social position of Sir Giles, identifies Lovell as (historically speaking) his 'real opponent', and, in short, adjusts our sense of the entire play. The result is a comedy of politically, as well as dramatically, vivid 'grimness' – certainly not a script which needs the 'pervasive jollying up' of its last RSC production (1983). Starting from the suggestion that Heywood's *The English Traveller* was written in partial response to Massinger (notably to the 'scepticism' of *The Roman Actor*), Richard Rowland sets out to make a case for this neglected play. While Butler's essay is sensitive to social pressures outside the theatre, Rowland supports his systematic reassessment with telling cross-reference to travel books, classical drama, obscure Stuart plays and other works by Heywood to provide reasons for revaluing a work which, in his view, 'uncovers wisdom, generosity and loyalty in the unlikeliest places'. Theatre directors should note: it is time for *A New Way to Pay Old Debts* to be reconnected to the energies of its historical moment, and time for *The English Traveller* to follow *The New Inn* into the repertory.

Many of the most influential twentieth-century accounts of post-Restoration comedy have spotlit major figures while largely ignoring the bulk of the period's comic output. When the evidence is examined thus selectively, Etherege's *She Would If She Could* stands out as, in the words of John Palmer, 'the first finished example of the new comedy of manners'[3] and therefore, in effect, the prototype for all significant subsequent experiments in the mode. This version of playwriting history has by now been thoroughly discredited, but at least it offered a confident explanation of why, in Thomas Shadwell's words, 'some of the best Judges in *England*' deemed *She Would If She Could* 'the best Comedy... written' since 1660.[4] No generally accepted alternative account has been devised to replace it, and, in the process, re-situate Etherege's comedy more confidently in relation to the varied comic output of the late 1660s playhouses. Michael Cordner's contribution takes a fresh look at *She Would*, the difficulty it caused its first audience, and some of the grounds for the attempted rebuilding of its reputation after the failure of its premiere. He discerns in the play an intricate exploitation of audience expectations, linked to an ambitiously experimental use of a single plot structure. This is a reading which, by implication, makes *She Would* a natural companion piece to the vigorous canvassing of the relative merits of multiple and single plots in Dryden's *Essay of Dramatick Poesy*, published earlier in the same winter in which Etherege's play was premiered.

Comedies, then, can be 'grim', generically ambivalent, or (like *She Would*) sophisticatedly frustrating of what audiences anticipate. But the comic can also be traced into the smallest particularities of poetic language. In 'Rhyming as Comedy' Gillian Beer 'investigates how rhyme gets under the guard of reason and teases words out of their autonomy, doubling, dissolving, and playing across the rim of meaning'. As a result, her concern is not with rib-tickling verbal consonance but 'with rhyme as dialogue, quarrel, and undersong and with the helpless excess of possibility that poises it always on the brink of comedy'. Far from being arid word-lists, rhyme dictionaries are revalued in her essay as gardens of beautifully useless information, in which 'Familiar and arcane terms jostle each other and fall nonchalantly into the ear's agreement.' Working examples from Herbert and Pope, she shows how rhyme deflects and transfigures. Her reading finds nuances in, and around, lyrics (such as Hardy's 'The Voice') which are far from comic in their subject matter. But rhyme's forcing together of different (often differently spelled) concepts, like 'moon' and 'June', registers, as Beer points out, a dialogic potential. In Bakhtinian language, 'The licensed licence of rhyme…displays "carnivalesque" qualities – tousling language, overturning the hierarchies of signification, locking together terms from disparate linguistic registers.' Hers is an account in which, rather than providing harmonious containment, 'The comedy of rhyme lies in its refusal of established categories.'

The comic resources of Romanticism are explored in the next two essays. Jonathan Wordsworth shows that, although Sterne and Burns anticipate features of 'Wordsworthian comedy', there is, in such poems as *The Idiot Boy*, an unprecedented intermixture of the sublime and the direct, the tersely rhymed and genially relaxed. Shelley accused Wordsworth of being 'solemn' and mocked him for it in *Peter Bell the Third*. Jonathan Wordsworth admits that his poet can be 'a trifle solemn' when justifying his work, but maintains that the verse has different properties. Through patient attention to the shape of passages and timing of lines, to ballad form, mock-epic and 'conversational styles', he shows how much wit, charm and tact there is in early Wordsworth. A context for this defence is provided by Jonathan Bate's 'Apeing Romanticism'. Invoking Byron's cry, 'The days of Comedy are gone, alas!', Bate reminds us that literature of the late eighteenth and early nineteenth century often resisted the comic. Jonathan Wordsworth's analysis of *Peter Bell* as 'a comedy of the workings of the mind' becomes the more striking when set against Bate's insistence that the impulse to fantasy and transcendence in Romantic verse usually required insulation from the deflating effects of comedy. By means of an extended comparison between Wordsworth and Byron, Bate identifies a strain of 'anti-Romanticism'. Against the gaunt, abstemious solitaries of *Lyrical Ballads* and *The Excursion* he sets the sociable, sensuous, celebratory figures of that 'anti-Romantic manifesto', *Don Juan*. Even the virtuosity of Byron's technique is found to be integrally comic. In a way that recalls Gillian Beer's account of rhyme as tacitly sexual and playful, Bate argues that rhyming in *Don Juan* joins realms of experience 'promiscuously': not so much (as Yeats said of tragedy) a drowner but a bridger of dykes.

If, for Richard Beadle, dogs command the stage, Jonathan Bate introduces us to a veritable menagerie. He starts with bears, advances to geese and parrots, takes in 'a fox – & two new mastiffs' (from Byron's letters) plus 'a Persian cat and kittens' (from *Don Juan*) while dilating on monkeys and apes, and finishes his essay with Sir Oran Haut-ton (cf. orang-utan) in Peacock's *Melincourt*. Links between the animal and human contribute, similarly, to John Kerrigan's essay on noses. His piece belongs (with those by Peter Holland and Eric Griffiths) to the group of three which rounds off *English Comedy* by starting from, or centering in, late nineteenth and twentieth-century work while ranging widely through comical history. Quoting the pseudo-Aristotelian *Physiognomonica*, Kerrigan establishes the antiquity of those theories which classify personal character by resemblance to animal features. His discussion of determinism and stereotyping leads him through Lavater to the Victorian novel; but at the centre of his attention lie those varieties of exaggerated, performative comedy which (though branch-lines run through Sterne and Gogol) naturally belong on stage, in *commedia dell'arte*, at the Punch and Judy show. This is an essay which puts on a comic nose and follows it about. As a result, it touches on topics – such as racism, psychoanalysis and urban drainage – which, if human nature were better, would not seem comic at all.

Interested in peculiar organs, in noses which set people apart, Kerrigan's essay tests the boundary between comedy and isolation. He is interested in the pathos of Cyrano de Bergerac, the laughter-surrounded loneliness of H. G. Wells's 'man with a nose'. By contrast, Peter Holland's 'Noël Coward and Comic Geometry' takes the reader back to social interactiveness, but concentrates on those systems of partnering and re-partnering in love which can develop into the equivalent of a round-dance or quadrille. Taking a long view of his subject, he shows that a geometrical patterning of relationships holds good across much comedy from Plautus to Joe Orton. These erotic permutations are displayed most lucidly in farce (Marivaux's *La Dispute*) and opera (Mozart's *Così Fan Tutte*). But they also contribute structurally to comedies of social and emotional depth, such as *A Midsummer Night's Dream*. The danger must always be that patterning of this sort will evoke stock responses from an audience, reactions of recognition which limit comedy's ability to challenge the norm. Holland argues that in Coward's plays, however, and especially *Design for Living*, received geometrical schemes can undergo remarkable transformations, until the 'quadrilateral' of stable desire and the 'triangle' of unstable desire merge in civilised subversion.

English Comedy ends with the apparently unlikely conjunction of Ludwig Wittgenstein and comedy. Ever since Aristophanes' damaging misrepresentation of Socrates in *The Clouds*, philosophy and comic laughter have regarded each other with suspicion. Eric Griffiths sets out to demonstrate, however, that a cultivated sense of absurdity contributed to the work of the greatest English-speaking philosopher of this century. Arguing that Wittgenstein's emphasis on the 'surroundings' of linguistic acts gives his later writings a peculiar affinity with (and relevance to students of) comic drama, Griffiths shows how philosophically informed criticism can elucidate the 'lustrous, swift enigmas' of plays like *The Comedy of Errors*. In dealing with comical 'errors', how far does Shakespeare resemble a philosopher? Developing a distinction implicit in Wittgenstein, Griffiths shows how superficial misapprehensions ('mistakes') differ from more 'deeply' erroneous misalignments of judgement – 'errors' which are likely to have their own cogency. This can shed much light on certain kinds of drama, if we recognise that *All's Well That Ends Well* (for example) is not so much 'a parable of Bertram's mistakes, and how he is rid of them' but a demonstration of 'error's reluctance in several people, especially Helena'. In his closing pages, Griffiths justifies the claim that Wittgenstein 'is a philosopher of genius who understands, depicts (and suffers under) an inward sense of what is funny in philosophising'. Evidence can be found in his method:

parallels may be drawn between the comic techniques of Chaplin and Wittgensteinian explanation, and between 'animated cartoons' and his use of metaphor. But there is also a resemblance in the scope of expected outcomes. As Griffiths soberingly observes, 'his philoso-phising resembles comic practice...as Lichtenberg portrayed it: "Comedy does not effect direct improvement, and perhaps satire does not do so either: I mean one does not abandon the vices they render ludicrous. What they can do, however, is to enlarge our horizons and increase the number of fixed points from which we can orientate ourselves in all the eventualities of life more quickly"'.

The essays in *English Comedy* set out to 'enlarge...horizons' and 'orientate' readers in a vast field of comedy and cultural life. 'Enlargement' comes from recognising that, granted the influence of French farce, Italian *commedia* and the like, English comedy is as hybrid in its pedigree as Crab. But it also comes from acknowledging that Thalia's patronage extends over works which are generically unstable, 'grim', or lyrically concerned with loss, as well as those which are 'festive' and ribald. It follows, given this range of production, that to 'orientate' ourselves as audiences and readers cannot be a single act. To grapple with the kinds of comedy is to address the possibilities of life. It is to enquire into that process of 'experimentation' with 'different roles' and 'half imaginary, half real' potentialities which – as Anne Barton points out, in defence of Heywood's *Foure Prentises of London* (*c.* 1600) – even the most minor (and eccentric) comedy can offer to its public.[5]

NOTES

1 'Introductory note' to Scolar Press facsimile (Ilkley, 1973) of William Congreve, *The Double-Dealer*.
2 The book was also helped by the editorial guidance of Sarah Stanton, at Cambridge University Press, by Nick de Somogyi (who did some checking) and by Peter Kerrigan (who kindly made the index).
3 *The Comedy of Manners* (London, 1913), 75.
4 Preface to *The Humorists* (1671).
5 'London Comedy and the Ethos of the City', *The London Journal*, 4 (1978), 175–6 (rpt in *Essays, Mainly Shakespearean* (Cambridge, 1994)).

Crab's pedigree

Richard Beadle

Should the dog Crab in *The Two Gentlemen of Verona* ever be presented as a pedigree animal? Lance and others may call him a cur, but such a term was not always applied in a spirit of derogation. The category of tinker's cur, which is where Crab would be placed in John Caius's elaborate taxonomy *Of Englishe Dogges* (1576),[1] is mentioned honourably for its long-suffering and fidelity, and these are significant matters in the human drama going on around him. The pedigree of any given Crab may not necessarily be distinguished, but of the theatrical ancestry of his kind there is much to be said, for it is longer than that of any other figure who appears in the play, excepting his master, the clown, whose companion in performance he has been through more than one millennium. Nowadays, the presence of a real dog on stage in a production of *The Two Gentlemen* tends to hold little more than novelty or charm for most in the audience. Crab's behaviour is the unpredictable extempore of a natural and (mostly) silent comedian *sans savoir*, given to unscheduled entrances and exits, visits downstage to stare at the audience, more or less embarrassing scratchings, sniffings and lickings, and maybe worse. Reviews of modern productions seldom fail to comment on his antics, and in truth such scene-stealing can be a welcome relief from a main plot sadly over-determined by the fantastic and etiolated conventions of *fin amour* and the friendship cult – if nothing else, every Crab can be guaranteed to yawn at some point in the proceedings. In the twentieth century, the music-halls were almost the last refuge of clown-and-dog acts, though they are not impossible to find to this day. When *The Two Gentlemen* was new, however, the clown with a dog walked on to the stage as a familiar image drawn from an everyday world of largely sub-literary popular entertainment, whose roots in medieval and antique comic tradition ran deep. It was an image rich in association and implication, and in creating a confrontation between the new world of elaborately scripted professional theatre and these ancient improvisatory figures, Shakespeare happened to distil a significant moment in the history of comic drama. Unexpectedly, the dog is not called upon to perform any tricks (though Lance does specify his urinating on the leading lady as a 'trick' of sorts), and there is a curious insistence on the fact that he will not weep. Whilst his master the clown was triumphantly assimilated, to be re-incarnated in a series of celebrated comic roles, the dog had no more part to play in the new synthesis, and in some ways his presence was more than this particular comedy could bear.

The date of *The Two Gentlemen of Verona* remains conjectural, but there is little doubt that in Lance we have Shakespeare's first fully-fledged attempt to write 'the clown's part' – to *write*, that is, a part which had traditionally been largely extemporised. Though it is Lance who ostensibly leads Crab on a string, it is a string that effectively ties the clown to this emblem of his forebears, the proverbial gleeman's, tinker's or fiddler's bitch, of the late antique and medieval *mimi* and *joculatores*. Such dogs could readily be trained to perform tricks, or even to take part in plays, but their role was equally likely to be such as Crab's, the mute stooge going about his 'improvised' doggy life regardless of his master's sufferings. The clown's part was first perfected in the 1570s and 1580s by Richard Tarlton, who, as we shall see, retained the popular entertainer's traditional affinity with dogs, and was remembered as working with one. He died in September 1588, and his immense celebrity in life was instantly translated into a posthumous reputation which far exceeded that of any other performer of his time, perhaps of any time. It has recently been suggested that *The Two Gentlemen* (along with other early plays of Shakespeare) could date to just within Tarlton's lifetime, but there are reasons to suspect that it was probably composed, perhaps in more than one phase, sometime during the years which followed shortly upon the great clown's death.[2] If this was so, then the part of Lance would surely have been taken by William Kempe, 'Iestmonger and Vice-gerent generall to the Ghost of Dicke Tarlton' as Nashe was to call him in *An Almond for a Parrat* (1590) – one of a spate of conceits on Tarlton's return in spirit form at the time.

The structural and organic weaknesses of *The Two Gentlemen* have long been recognised.[3] Though Lance and Crab are effective in reflecting aspects of the main plot and the principal characters in a parodic or ironic light, they are strictly speaking inessential to the structure, and were almost certainly not part of the original scheme of the play. If they were some sort of afterthought, we do not know whether it was prompted primarily by aesthetic or other considerations. Either way, the management of their entrance was bound to be peculiarly significant. The way it is made to happen is pregnant with suggestion of many things, both recent and much older in comic tradition, about clown and dog alike. Not far into the second act comes the strange, short scene – barely twenty lines – of the ambiguous troth-plighting and rather unsatisfactory parting of the young lovers Proteus and Julia:

PROTEUS The tide is now – nay, not thy tide of tears;
    That tide will stay me longer than I should.
    Julia, farewell.
                [*Exit Julia*]
                What, gone without a word?
    Ay, so true love should do; it cannot speak,
    For truth hath better deeds than words to grace it.
        [*Enter* PANTINO]
PANTINO Sir Proteus, you are stayed for.
PROTEUS Go; I come, I come.
    [*Aside*] Alas this parting strikes poor lovers dumb.
                    Exeunt (2.2.14–21)[4]

Whether or not they were originally designed to do so, the admirable Julia's tears and silence, thus glossed by the less estimable Proteus's romantic clichés and half-hearted wordplay, cue Lance and Crab for a leavetaking of a rather different character:

LANCE Nay, 'twill be this hour ere I have done weeping; all the kind of the Lances have this very fault. I have received my proportion like the prodigious son and am going with Sir Proteus to the imperial's court. I think Crab, my dog, to be the sourest-natured dog that lives: my mother weeping, my father wailing, my sister crying, our maid howling, our cat wringing her hands, and all our house in a great perplexity; yet did not this cruel-hearted cur shed one tear... (2.3.1–8)

The way Lance goes on to dramatise this lachrymose leavetaking, casting his staff, hat, and shoes severally as the members of his family to constitute a play-within-the-play, has its ultimate origins in the impromptu repertoire of the itinerant popular entertainer with his dog. The anthropomorphic–cynanthropic turn was always going to be a primary device: 'I am the dog. No, the dog is himself, and I am

1 Tarlton, the Elizabethan clown

the dog. O, the dog is me, and I am myself. Ay, so, so.' (18–19). We shall look presently at a much older version of this kind of impersonated monologue which suggests that the device was at least three hundred years old when Shakespeare took it up. Lance, imagining himself as a prodigal son, kneels before his father to receive his blessing, takes his leave, and so the little improvised drama ends: 'Now the dog all this while sheds not a tear nor speaks a word. But see how I lay the dust with my tears. [*Enter* PANTINO]' (26–7). *Why* Crab should be expected to say anything, or, more to the point, weep – and his failure to shed a tear is rather carefully emphasised again here at the close – is a question which seems not to have attracted much interest. The mere idea of a dog in tears no doubt possesses sufficient comic incongruity to account for Lance's impromptu, but as we shall see the significance of the question lies in an aspect of the popular comic tradition to which he and Crab belong. Pantino urges Lance to ship, and he departs in a flurry of puns rather better than those of his master: 'you'll lose the tide' (30) prompts an elaborate grammatical quibble on Crab as 'the [one who is] tied', lending verbal as well as visual emphasis to the bond between clown and dog mentioned above; and finally Lance earns himself a kick in the pants after indelicately imputing to Pantino one of the less attractive canine habits:

[PANTINO] ...why dost thou stop my mouth?
LANCE For fear thou shouldst lose thy tongue.
PANTINO Where should I lose my tongue?
LANCE In thy tale.
PANTINO In thy tail! [*Kicking him*] (38–42)

The comic substance of this scene needs to be viewed in perspectives both short and long. Whilst the actors get on with their work, Crab's unscripted and unpredictable antics, varying from performance to performance, are the most obvious manifestation of a distinctly physical presence, which is reinforced both through Lance's improvised dramatic monologue, and in the language of his banter with Pantino. But before turning to the nature of this more ancient presence, we should attend first to that of Tarlton. Our best current conjectures serve to suggest that the memory of his death was still green whilst the play was being written, and it is relevant to consider why and how, in these circumstances, Shakespeare might have chosen to venture for the first time upon a scripted clown's role as an addition to the text.

It is no part of the purpose here to suggest that in Lance Shakespeare intended anything so naive as an attempt to reincarnate Tarlton – lesser talents were already busy failing to resist the obvious in this regard. There are however grounds for thinking that with Crab so demonstratively tied to him, and in the particular role in which he casts himself in his impromptu domestic comedy, there is an oblique and allusive placing of Tarlton's type of genius at a point of suspense between an old world of popular comic entertainment, and the nascent realm of professional stage comedy. Indeed, given even what little we know of Tarlton, it is difficult to imagine how anyone could attempt to write a clown's part shortly after 1588 without some sense of his presence. Both contemporary witness and modern accounts of him agree that he was the first actor to achieve national acclaim, and that his reputation in life and afterwards has exceeded that of any successor.[5] The ways in which the nation at large chose to venerate him were many and various, perhaps the most indicative being inn signs carrying his image, one of which survived in London to the end of the eighteenth century; though at the same time it has to be said that there was also a tradition of using his picture to designate the door behind which the jakes was to be found. One of the first nursery rhymes which we still teach our children (in the form of 'The Grand Old Duke of York') began its documented life in the seventeenth century as 'Old Tarlton's Song'. His death on 3 September 1588 was followed by a string of publications, mostly ballads and jest-books, invoking his name in some conceit upon his demise, usually in a form implying reincarnation: *Tarlton's Farewell* appeared a matter of three weeks after his death, and was soon followed by *Tarlton's Recantation* (1589), *Tarlton's Repentance*, and *Tarlton's Ghost and Robin Goodfellow* (1590), all ballads or songs, and all apparently lost.[6] Likewise in 1590, Robert Wilson, Tarlton's fellow comedian in the Queen's Men, published a revised version of one of their pieces (*The Three Ladies of London*, 1584), in tribute to his dead colleague, *The Three Lords of London*. Also extant are the quasi-biographical jest-books *Tarlton's News out of Purgatory* (1590), attributed to the 'adopted son' to whom Tarlton is said to have promised his 'clown's suit', Robert Armin, and the two instalments of *Tarlton's Jests* (?1590 and 1600, reprinted together 1613 and subsequently). Wilson's *Three Lords* seems to mention Tarlton under a stage name or popular soubriquet, 'Willy', making him a likelier candidate than most for the recently deceased 'pleasant Willy' mentioned by Spenser in the Thalia section of *Teares of the Muses* (1590). Later, Tarlton's ghost was impersonated in William Percy's play *Cuck-Queans and Cuckolds Errants* (1601). The real extent of Shakespeare's acquaintance with Tarlton and his work can never be known, but the great clown's influence upon him (the nature of which has recently been ably reviewed by David Wiles)[7] has never been doubted. Tarlton's role as the clown Derick in the version of *The Famous Victories of Henry V* staged in the 1580s has naturally led to suggestions that the conception of Falstaff owes something to him, and Hamlet's discovery of Yorick's skull is traditionally believed to have provided the opportunity for specific tribute.[8]

Tarlton's Jests[9] contains a mixture of biographical facts (which can be verified or supported from other sources), apocryphal anecdotes, and older jest-book material foisted on him to pad the book out. It would appear that a good part of Tarlton's informal act consisted of jokes told against himself in the persona of a *faux-naïf* rustic 'clown' like Lance, though taking care to have the last word. The following, unusually elaborate in its action and dialogue, has an entirely authentic ring:

How *Tarltons* Dogge lickt vp six pence

Tarlton in his travaile had a Dogge of fine qualities, amongst the rest, he would carry six pence in the end of his tongue, of which he would brag often, and say, Never was the like. Yes, saies a Lady, mine is more strange, for he will beare a French crowne in his mouth: no, saies *Tarlton*, I thinke not: lend me a Frenche crowne, saies the Lady, and you shall see: truly Madame, I haue it not, but if your dog will carry a crackt English crowne, here it is: but the Lady perceiued not the iest, but was desirous to see the dogs trick of six pence. *Tarlton* threw down a teaster [*6d. coin*], and said, Bring Sirra: and by fortune the Dog took vp a Counter, and let the money lie: a Gentlewoman by, seeing that, askt him how long he would hold it? An houre, saies *Tarlton*: that is pretty, saied the Gentlewoman, let's see that: meane time she tooke vp the sixe pence, and willed him to let them see the money againe: when he did see it, it was a Counter, and he made this Rime.

> Alas, alas, how came all this to passe?
> The worlds worse then it was:
> For silver turns to brasse.

I, sayes the Lady, & the dog hath made his master an Asse: but *Tarlton* would never trust his Dogs tricks more. (E3–E3v)

The statement that '*Tarlton* in his travaile had a Dogge of fine qualities', and that after this incident (whether truly or not) he 'would never trust his Dogs tricks more', suggest that the sight of him working with a dog was likely to have been a familiar one. One way and another, dogs (as well as other performing animals, such as Banks's celebrated horse) feature largely in *Tarlton's Jests*. Like his silver screen successor W. C. Fields, he seems to have possessed an undue and not always welcome attraction for them in both professional and private life.[10] One of the *Jests* records how he acquired another of his comic accoutrements, his deformed nose (see below, p. 244), parting dogs and bears that had got into a fight. His favoured position at court gave rise to the following episode, record of which is found in the State Papers, Domestic, about a month before his death:[11]

How Tarlton played the God Luz with a flitch of bacon at his back, and how the Queen bade them take away the knave for making her to laugh so excessively, as he fought against her little dog, Perrico de Faldas, with his sword and long staffe, and bade the Queen take off her mastie...

Fighting with mastiffs was a form of entertainment which also served the purpose of keeping them in training as guard dogs, as John Caius explained.[12] It was a skill practised by the kind of itinerant entertainer portrayed by Robert Armin in the *History of the Two Maids of More-clack* (1609). A suitor, Toures, enters disguised 'in a tawny coate like a tinker', calling for his dog:[13]

HUMIL Indeede whats a tinker without's wench, staffe and dogge.
LADY Is this the tinker you talke on?
HUM. I madam of Twitnam, I haue seene him licke out burning fire brands with's tongue, drinke two pense from the bottome of a full pottle of ale, fight with a Masty, & stroke his mustachoes with his bloody bitten fist, and sing as merrily as the sobrest Querester.
MADGE Come tinker, stop, mend.
TOUR. Ile tickle your holes.

The role which Lance imagines for himself as 'the prodigious son', taking leave of his father in lachrymose vein and kneeling to receive a blessing, is peculiarly reminiscent of parts said to have been performed by Tarlton in what appear to have been scripted plays. In *Tarlton's Jests*, 'A Iest of an Apple hitting *Tarlton* on the face' describes him in precisely the same posture as Lance portrays himself as he leaves on his journey:

Now I come to my father; [*Kneels*] 'Father, your blessing'. Now should not the shoe speak a word for weeping. (2.3.20–1)

Tarlton hauing flouted the fellow for his Pippin which he threw, hee thought to be meet with *Tarlton* at length, so in the Play *Tarlton's* part was to trauell, who kneeling downe to aske his Father blessing: the fellow threwe an Apple at him, which hit him on the cheeke: *Tarlton* taking vp the Apple, made this Jest.

> Gentlemen, this fellow with his face of Mapple,
> Instead of a Pippin hath throwne me an Apple:

But as for an Apple he hath cast a Crab,
So in stead of an honest woman God hath sent him a Drab.

The people laughed heartily, for he had a Queane to his Wife. (B2–B2v)

It is tempting to reflect that there could be more than meets the eye here in the apple-thrower's intervention rebounding on him as a sour (crab/?Crab) joke, but be that as it may, Tarlton's part in another play which was clearly a variant on the 'prodigious son' theme (inasmuch as this prodigal was not in the habit of returning) was recollected by Henry Peacham, who described it in *The Truth of Our Times* (1638):[14]

I remember when I was a School-boy in *London*, *Tarlton* acted a third sons part, such a one as I now speake of: His father being a very rich man, lying upon his death-bed, called his three sonnes about him, who with teares, and on their knees, craved his blessing, and to the eldest sonne, said hee, you are mine heire, and my land must descend upon you, and I pray God blesse you with it: The eldest sonne replyed, Father I trust in God you shall yet live to enjoy it yourself. To the second sonne, (said he) you are a scholler, and what profession soever you take upon you, out of my land I allow you threescore pounds a year towards your maintenance, and three hundred pounds to buy you books, as his brother he, weeping answer'd, I trust father you shall live to enjoy your money yourselfe, I desire it not, &c. To the third, which was Tarlton, (who came like a rogue, in a foule shirt without a band, and in a blew coat with one sleeve, his stockings out at heels, and his head full of straw and feathers) as for you sirrah (quoth he) you know how often I have fetched you out of *Newgate* and *Bridewell*, you have beene an ungracious villaine, I have nothing to bequeath to you but the gallowes and a rope: *Tarlton* weeping and sobbing upon his knees (as his brothers) said, O Father, I doe not desire it, I trust in God you shall live to enjoy it yourselfe. There are many such sons of honest and carefull parents in *England* at this day. (102–5)

Peacham was probably born in 1576, and presumably saw this play sometime in the mid-1580s. Given the comic and didactic potential of St Luke's 'he wasted his substance in riotous living', it is not surprising that the prodigal son theme appears in a number of sixteenth-century plays, mostly of an academic or pedagogic character,[15] though the role was already old even then, appearing as early as the thirteenth century in the Old French farce *Courtois d'Arras*.[16] Tarlton's clowning and weeping in the part on the popular stage find an appropriate analogue, if not a reminiscence, in Lance's.

Tarlton set a precedent for weeping clown-prodigals, and Lance weeps likewise, but Crab does not, and we have already asked why he should be expected to do so. To begin to construct an answer involves looking far back beyond Tarlton and any dog he performed with 'in his travaile'. The inclusion of animals in plays, whether more formal varieties of drama or unscripted entertainments, had a long history before Crab took the stage. The mode favoured was commonly the comic, and the species involved were those which lent themselves to training, usually dogs, but sometimes bears.[17] Contemplating the (apparently real) bear which pursues Antigonus off the stage in Act 3 of *The Winter's Tale*, Anne Barton has remarked how the presence of animals in plays can effect a displacement of the audience's habitual engagement with the dramatic illusion. It expresses itself characteristically as bewilderment concerning the level of 'reality' to which the creature belongs:[18] the stage dog seems to hover uncertainly between the illusory realm of the play, and the audience's world of everyday reality. Animals can appear either incidentally, or with a functional value which both dramatist and actor can exploit for a variety of effect. The horses, camels, calves, donkeys, sheep, squirrels, rabbits and various kinds of bird, for example, which were introduced *à l'occasion* as the biblical narrative unrolled in the later medieval religious drama, were usually, but not always, little more than props.[19] The introduction of a real bear in *The Winter's Tale* seems, on the other hand, to be of a piece with a variety of studied modulations in stage illusion characteristic of Shakespeare's late plays.

Crab was a stealer of puddings, and his remotest recorded ancestor was possibly Labes ('Grabber'), the dog arraigned for stealing and devouring a cheese in one of Aristophanes' weirdest comic fantasies, the trial scene in *The Wasps*.[20] Authorities differ as to whether a real dog or merely a mute actor in a dog mask actually appeared in the dock, though it may be remarked that the scene's comic and satiric thrust against the loathed Cleon, the 'rabble's dog' whose surrogate in the play is the principal accuser, would have been sharpened by a hyper-ridiculous confrontation with the real thing. Somewhat over four centuries later, between 69 and 79 A.D., Plutarch saw a dog in a play at Rome. He described its performance in the section of the *Moralia* devoted to 'The Cleverness of Animals', which Philemon Holland translated into English for the first time in 1603:[21]

Yet can I not conteine my self, but I must needs in this place recite unto you one lesson that I my selfe saw a dogge to take out, when I was at *Rome*: This dog served a plaier who professed to counterfeit many persons, and represent sundry gestures; & among sundry other prety tricks which his master taught him, answerable to divers passions, occasions and occurrences represented upon the stage, his master made an experiment on him with a drogue or medicine which was somniferous indeed and sleepie, but must be taken and supposed deadly; who tooke the piece of bread wherein the said drogue was mingled, and within a little while after he had swallowed it downe, he began to make as though hee trembled, quaked, yea and staggered, as if he had beene astonied, in the end he stretched out himselfe, and lay as stiffe as one starke dead, suffering himselfe to be pulled, haled, and drawen from one place to another, like a very blocke, according as the present argument and matter of the place required; but afterwards, when hee understood by that which was said and done, that his time was come, and that he had caught his hint, then beganne he at first to stirre gently by little and little, as if hee had newly revived or awakened, and started out of a dead sleepe, and lifting up his head, began to looke about him too and fro; at which object all the beholders woondered not a little; afterwards he arose upon his feet, and went directly to him unto whom he was to goe, very jocund and mery: this pageant was performed so artificially, I cannot tell whether to say or naturally, that all those who were present, and the emperour himselfe (for Vespasian the father was there in person, within the theater of *Marcellus*) tooke exceeding great pleasure, and joied woonderfully to see it.

Plutarch's 'plaier who professed to counterfeit many persons, and to represent sundry gestures' with his dog was a forebear of the wandering *mimi*, *scurrae*, *histriones*, or *joculatores* execrated by generations of Christian moralists in the post-classical centuries, and what little we know of their activities comes largely from incidental remarks in episcopal prohibitions and the like. Some fuller glimpses are given here and there in the eleventh-century Latin romance of *Ruodlieb*,[22] a text whose author was very familiar with the repertoire of the mimes. As well as the activities of performing bears and birds, a dog is described performing a full-scale variety act as entertainment at a courtly feast. Amongst other things, he singles out a thief in the company (much as Banks's horse is said to have walked over to Tarlton when asked to pick out the greatest fool (*Tarlton's Jests*, c3–c3v)), and one of his accomplishments is to give an impression of weeping: 'Qui se prostrauit caput inque pedes sibi ponit / Et ueluti fleret ueniam poscens ululauit' (x, 93–4). (He stretched out on the ground and placed his head between his paws, and as though he were weeping, he whined and begged pardon.) Such performing dogs, weeping or not, were effectively an everyday feature of the later medieval scene. They are numerous amongst the grotesques that begin to swarm in the margins of illuminated manuscripts from the thirteenth century,[23] and Langland obviously assumed that readers of *Piers Plowman* would know what he meant when he described Gluttony reeling out of an alehouse, weaving proverbially hither and thither 'lik a glemannes bicche' (B version, V, 346), a minstrel's dog trained to walk on its hind legs.

The involvement of dogs in more formal varieties of drama can also be traced from the time that scripted plays begin to appear. Of the so-called Latin elegiac comedies which suddenly became popular amongst the leisured and sophisticated clergy of the northern French and English cathedral schools in the late twelfth century, at least one, *Babio* (which is probably of English origin), looks likely to have been presented *par personnages*.[24] The action consists of a series of cruel but farcical deceptions practised upon Babio, a foolish *senex amans*, by members of his family and household. He grieves in unrequited lust for his stepdaughter, and his isolation as the butt of the comedy is emphasised by the intervention of a dog, Melampus, whose Ovidian name (after Actaeon's hound) compounds the joke. Like Crab, Melampus is indifferent to his master's grief, and merely barks at him:

> Accedat propius... Est canis! Ecce latrat.
> Care Melampus, tace. Stipis hesternae memor esto.
> Babio sum. Latra, care Melampe, minus.
> Ecce canis transit; sed adhuc dolor ille remansit.   (14–17)

(Someone's coming... It's the dog! How he barks. Do be quiet, dear Melampus. Think about yesterday's bones. It's me, Babio. Dear Melampus, don't bark so much. The dog has gone, but grief remains here still.)

Such functional inclusion of dogs in plays resurfaces occasionally, alongside their appearance for incidental purposes, in both texts and records of performance down to Shakespeare's time. A characteristically obscure farcical scene in John Skelton's *Magnificence* (?1520–2)[25] involves Folly (a real fool) in protracted negotiations for the exchange of his dog for a bird (either an owl or a hawk), owned by Fancy, who is also dressed as a fool at this point (1042ff.). Folly's dog is a 'pilled [*mangy*] cur', and seems to be part of the play's dangerous and therefore cryptic polemic against Cardinal Wolsey, the butcher's son from Ipswich, whose policies had earned him nicknames like 'The mastif Curre bred in Ypswitch towne' and 'the Bocher's Curr'. As the publication of plays became commoner towards the end of the sixteenth century, one learns more about the appearances of animals on the stage. Usually there is no more motive behind their introduction than a touch of literalism in the tradition of the medieval religious drama mentioned above: if the story involves a hunter, then he should have dogs. When a version of the *Hippolytus* was staged at King's College, Cambridge in 1552, two shillings and sixpence was laid out in hiring 'canes venatici' from a local country worthy.[26] A lost play of *Narcissus* in 1571 made similar provision, but took the dogs' role to a logical extreme:[27]

John Tryce for mony to him due for Leashes, & dog-hookes, wt staves, and other necessaries; by him provided for the hunters that made the crye after the fox (let loose in the Coorte) with theier howndes, harnes, and hallowing, in the play of Narcissus. wch crye was made of purpose even as the woorde then in utterance in the parte then played, did Requier... xxjs. viijd.

Incidental appearances of dogs in Elizabethan and Jacobean plays are not uncommon – instances will be found in *Jacob and Esau* (1568), *Clyomon and Clamydes* (1599), Peele's *Old Wives' Tale* (1595), and *The Roaring Girl* of Middleton and Dekker (1611). Apart from Shakespeare, however, Ben Jonson seems to have been the only dramatist of the time to have brought dogs on stage for more than incidental effect, and he plays with them in a rather different way. Two, Block and Lollard, appear towards the end of *The Staple of News* (1625), in a scene intended to exhibit the insanity of Pennyboy senior (5.4). He puts the dogs on trial in a scene ostensibly modelled on the arraignment of Labes in *The Wasps*, though Coleridge found them, in this role, uncomfortably and gratuitously reminiscent of Tray, Blanch and Sweetheart.[28] The anonymous dog in *Every Man Out of His Humour* (1599), undoubtedly Crab's closest relative on the contemporary stage, is given considerable prominence as the principal objectification of the quixotic Puntarvolo's fantastic humour.[29] Jonson's attitude towards this animal is unsentimental, which is no doubt characteristic of an age when dogs were simply killed when they had outlived their use,[30] and it again leaves an uncertain taste in the mouth. Macilente contrives to poison the dog, and visibly kicks it off the stage, as unfortunate stage-directions in the quartos reveal (*Hee throwes off the dogge... Kicks him out*, 5.1). It is finally reported as being a long time a-dying in the wood-yard, and Puntarvolo, robbed of this harmless component of his delusions, is left in tears. How far this episode was intended by Jonson as some sort of comment on Crab and his tearful master can only be a matter for speculation,[31] but it returns us to Lance's insistent association of his dog with grief.

Stories of human beings, usually women, metamorphosed into

dogs which howl or weep for their sufferings are ancient and widespread. The emblem of extreme human grief inherited from classical legend was Hecuba, the mobled queen, eventually transformed by suffering into Euripides' 'bitch of Cynossema', having taken her appalling revenge on Polymestor:

> locus extat et ex re
> nomen habet, veterumque diu memor, illa malorum
> tum quoque Sithonios ululavit maesta per agros

(The place still remains and takes its name [the Dog's Tomb] from this incident, where she long remembering her ancient ills, still howled mournfully across the Sithonian plains.)[32]

There was a strong urge to interpret the apparent expression of grief by a dog in terms of a metempsychosis, and it is doubtless for this reason that the most widespread of such tales, usually known as 'The Weeping Bitch', is generally taken to have originated in the East, where it first appears in early Sanskrit writings. The basic form of the story, the breadth of whose dissemination in medieval and early modern Europe it would be difficult to exaggerate,[33] never varies, and may be represented by a fifteenth-century English version, which stands midway between Shakespeare and the early Middle English dramatisations of it we shall look at in a moment:

Petrus Alphonsis tellis how som tyme þer was a wurshupfull man þat went on pylgramege, and he had a gude wyfe and a chaste. So þer was a yong man þat luffid hur passandly, & wolde hafe giffen hur grete giftis to hafe had his luste on hur, and sho wolde not on no wyse. So at þe laste he fell seke for sorow at he mot not spede, & lay in his bed. So þer come in ane olde wyfe & vysitt hym & askid hym what was þe cauce at he was seke for. And he oppynd his herte vnto hur & tolde hur all þat hym aylid. And sho said hym þurte [*he need*] not be seke her-for, sho cuthe help hym well enogh. And he promysid hur a gude rewarde to helpe hym. So sho had a little bykk whelpe, & sho held it fastand ij dayes. So on þe iij day sho made a cake of mustard & mele & gaff it, & it ete it. And for byturnes of þe musterd it began hugelie to grete [*weep*], & þe een þerof to ryn. So sho went vnto þis gude wyfe hows, and þis whelpe folowid hur. And sho, becauce she was ane olde wyfe, welcomyd hur fayre, & gaff hur meat and drynk. So at þe laste sho askid hur what þis whelpe aylid to wepe þus. And sho answerd & said, 'Dere Dame, it is no mervell if I make sorow & wepe, for þis whelpe was my doghter, & was a full leall maydyn, & a gude & a fayr. And becauce sho wolde not consent vnto a yong man þat luffid hur, þus sho was shapen to be a biche whelpe.' And with þat sho lete as sho swownyd & wepid sore. So þis gude wyfe made mekull sorow, & said, 'What mon I do? Allas! for I am in þe

same cace, for a yong man luffis me & I hafe dispysid hym, and I am aferd
þat I sall oght [*utterly*] be mysshapend.' And þan þe olde wyfe answerd &
cownceld hur to consent vnto hym, late hym hafe his liste at sho wer not
forshapyn & made a byche whelpe. & sho prayed hur to go for hym, and sho
did & fechid hym vnto þis womman, & þer he had his luste & his desyre; &
þis false alde when [*crone*] had a gude reward of ather partie.[34]

Though this tale must have been popular in oral tradition, its
circulation in written form occurred mainly as a sermon *exemplum* in
such widely used collections as the *Disciplina Clericalis* of Petrus
Alphonsi (twelfth century, from which the foregoing Middle English
version was translated), and the *Gesta Romanorum* (thirteenth century), which continued to be reprinted in numerous editions in the
sixteenth and seventeenth centuries.[35] However, the tale's moral
application was by no means invariably pursued, and, inasmuch as it
contained the necessary ingredients of a crafty trick and illicit sex, it
furnished an equally useful motif for vernacular fabliaux.

It was probably from this sort of source that two Middle English
versions of the 'The Weeping Bitch' were derived. The earlier, *Dame
Sirith*, is found in a manuscript miscellany including other popular
and entertaining texts, datable to the 1270s and copied in Worcester-
shire. Slightly later (and alas a fragment only) is the text entitled
Interludium de Clerico et Puella, probably set down around 1300, in
Lincolnshire dialect, on a long narrow roll of parchment which gives
every appearance of having been an itinerant performer's copy.
These two texts are the only surviving early English representatives
of a once large repertoire of popular dramatic entertainments. To
judge by incidental references and Continental analogues, it consisted
mostly of short farces based on plots like those of the fabliaux, put on
either by small groups of performers, or by a single *joculator* who
mimicked all the parts.[36] As is well known, one element found its way
on to the professional stage in Shakespeare's time, in the first place
through Tarlton's agency, as the clown's jig found as an *entr'acte* or
tail-piece to the main play on the bill. *Dame Sirith* and the *Interludium*,
though they appeared at much the same time in different parts of the
country, represent independent derivates from a lost vernacular
narrative version. Evidently the story of the bawd and her dog was
seen as having dramatic potential for either a small troupe or a solo
performer who possessed a biddable animal. Such adventitious
survival, in two distinct versions, from a period whose ephemeral
drama is otherwise almost entirely lost, suggests that 'The Weeping

Bitch' was a common enough entertainment in the later thirteenth and fourteenth centuries. Later, versions of it appear to have been seen in Grimsby (1431) and York (1447). That it continued to be known through the fifteenth and into the sixteenth is indicated by the English adaptation of *Calisto and Melebea*, published by John Rastell *c.* 1525, where the translator introduces the dog motif (in the form of a dream) to represent the bawd Celestina's temptation, on Calisto's behalf, of the chaste Melebea. A Danish Shrovetide farce of the same period, *Den Utro Hustru*, also dramatises the story.[37]

The *Interludium*, as its title suggests, gives 'The Weeping Bitch' in a form arranged for performance *par personnages*, but the episode involving the dog itself is in the section of the text that has been lost.[38] *Dame Sirith*, which could be performed either by a single *joculator* or a troupe of three and a dog, makes the action clear.[39] The young man Wilekin, having failed in his suit to the merchant's wife Margeri, bribes Dame Sirith to intercede for him. She (or the mime in her voice) responds with

> Neren neuer pones beter biset
> Þan þes shulen ben!
> For I shal don a iuperti
> And a ferli maistri
> Þat þou shalt ful wel sen. (274–8)

(Never was money better spent than this shall be, for I shall contrive a trick, and a cunning stratagem, as you will see.)

Then, without pausing, she turns from Wilekin and addresses another 'Þou', hitherto unmentioned in the text, but visible throughout to the audience:

> Pepir nou shalt þou eten;
> Þis mustart shal ben þi mete,
> And gar þin eien to rene.
> I shal make a lesing
> Of þin heie renning –
> Ich wot wel wer and wenne. (279–84)

(Now you shall eat pepper, and this mustard shall be your food, to cause your eyes to run. Out of your watery eyes I shall contrive a falsehood – where and when I know well.)

Wilekin responds:

> Wat! nou const þou no god!
> Me þinkeþ þat þou art wod –
> Ʒeuest þou þe welpe mustard? (285–7)

(Hey, this is foolish, It seems to me you're mad – are you giving the dog mustard?)

and the weeping dog is shown to the suggestible Margeri:

> ... þenne bigon þe clerc to wiche,
> And shop mi douter til a biche.
> Þis is mi douter þat Ich of speke:
> For del of hire min herte brekeþ.
> Loke hou hire heien greten;
> On hire cheken þe teres meten. (354–9)

(... then the clerk cast spells, and turned my daughter into a bitch. This is my daughter, about whom I speak – my heart breaks out of grief for her. Look how her eyes weep – on her cheeks the tears mingle.)

Upon her return, the bawd reports her success to her client, and encourages him in coarse terms to take full advantage of the situation:

> ... loke þat þou hire tille
> And strek out hire þes. (440–1)

(Make sure you plough her and stretch out her thighs.)

Though the audience and Margeri might be expected to content themselves with imagining a tearful dog, the deictic texture of the writing at the relevant points quoted above leads one to suspect, or fear, that the process described in the *exemplum* was carried out to the letter – that the mime starved the dog for a couple of days, then fed the animal bread soused in mustard and pepper in the course of the show.[40] Either way, given the appeal of the play suggested by the incidence of survival, and the durability of the corresponding folk-tale, fabliau, or *exemplum*, it would have been difficult in late medieval and early modern Europe *not* to have known the story of the go-between with a weeping dog.

Lance also takes on the role of go-between to Silvia on behalf of Proteus, but his dog (as we have been firmly told) does not weep. Unfortunately for his master, the dog is very much himself, and at the point where Dame Sirith's dog exhibits tears before the desired lady, Crab is guilty of producing a watery discharge of another kind, which we shall be obliged to consider in a moment. This episode is the sole and slender thread which connects Lance and Crab to the main plot concerning the lovers. Lance's errand to Silvia from Proteus is to present her with a love-token. This happens to be another dog, a lap-dog, which is stolen *en route*. Lance, as we learn from another play-within-the-play constituted by his second solo appearance with his dog (4.4.1–22), substitutes Crab. Crab disgraces himself, stealing a capon from Silvia's plate, farting beneath the dinner table, and urinating over her farthingale, upon which she rejects what she is given to understand was Proteus' love-gift. The clown's *spiel* through which Lance portrays this scene has naturally tended to deflect attention from thought about its implications, in favour of the more comfortable image of Crab before the audience's eyes, 'The first onstage dog... the kind of reliable creature that can be counted upon to do little worse than sit on the boards and smile and thump his tail–' '...life itself standing at the centre of the comedy wagging its tail'.[41]

The errand upon which Proteus sends Lance is but a small part in that gentleman's larger programme of deceit, especially in sexual matters, the true colours of which are eventually revealed in his undisguised attempt to rape Silvia (5.4.58–9). As we have seen, the use of a go-between with a dog in transactions of this kind was a very ancient motif, the part played by the dog being to represent to the victim the retributive consequences of a failure to co-operate with agent's plans for sexual conquest. Proteus seeks to present a lapdog, which he refers to rather obscurely, and perhaps with overtones, as 'my little jewel' (4.4.39).[42] This is the animal which is stolen from Lance, as he puts it in an ominous phrase, 'by the hangman's boys in the market place' (4.4.46). Crab assumes the role of Proteus' love-token, and though Lance's description of what happens next is very funny, the dog's outbreak of feral behaviour upon coming into Silvia's presence also deserves serious attention. As good a starting-place as any is Freud's observation of the paradox that though the dog is man's best friend, its name is also the source of his most widespread term of abuse, since it is not revolted by excrement, nor is it ashamed to display its sexual functions.[43] Crab 'thrusts me', as Lance chooses to put it,[44] amongst the gentlemanlike dogs beneath the Duke's table, and is only there 'a pissing while' before the odour which presages his excrement creates a stir. The overtly sexual significance of his grosser offence in urinating upon Silvia's clothing is in part decently displaced in Lance's clowning ('When did'st thou see me heave up my leg...'), but it is there plainly enough in our everyday experience of dogs, as well as in literary tradition. Illustrating a variety of lecher amongst the seven deadly sins in *The Parson's Tale*, Chaucer used the image of 'an hound when he comth by the roser [*rose bush*] or by othere beautees, though he may nat pisse, yet wole he heve up his leg and make a countenaunce to pisse', and it is found again about a century later in a bawdy passage in Dunbar's *Tua Mariit Wemen and the Wedo*.[45] The association of dogs with sexual pollution generally is deep-seated in Judaeo-Christian imagery,[46] and though Crab is only doing what comes naturally, the context of his behaviour in the human drama unfolding around him has shadowy implications which the slight framework of the play seems unable to sustain.

The idea that Lance and Crab were a later addition to a draft or earlier version of *The Two Gentlemen*, in part as an ironic counterpoint to character and action in the main plot, is fairly recent. Not many years ago a critic thought himself adventurous to be 'hinting a comparison of Proteus with Crab' in the 'want of sensibility to old ties and to his friend Launce's feelings'... 'As a present for Silvia, Crab resembles the love that Proteus proffers her'.[47] This is fair comment as far as it goes, but – as it should be in real comedy – the situation is more fraught. Crab's diverting but gross parting shot is the last and most offensive of the gestures which cause Silvia to reject him as an unacceptable gift from an unwelcome suitor, and its pollution of her person has a sinister premonitory air. Her subsequent preference for being eaten by a lion, rather than be rescued from outlaws and left alone in the woods with the predatory Proteus (5.4.33–5), turns out to be amply founded.

Contemplation of his pedigree tends to suggest that Crab may be a more pungent and corrosive presence in *The Two Gentlemen of Verona* than most would care to think. As we have seen, dogs were introduced into plays for both incidental and functional reasons from early times, but compared with other examples Crab somehow appears to fall into both categories simultaneously. He is ultimately descended from the solo mime's performing dog, best known in dramatic tradition from the erotic farce of 'The Weeping Bitch', though Shakespeare's immediate exemplar for a clown-dog act was probably that of Richard Tarlton. Tarlton was the popular comedian who had managed a brilliant transition from improvised entertainment to professional stage comedy, an achievement for which the creation of Lance might well be thought to stand as an apt memorial. There is also appropriateness in the fact that though the clown first appears with his ancient companion tied to him, he is later prepared to give the dog away, for in theatrical terms Crab is a thing of the past, whilst Lance contains the potential for development. Crab, emphatically dry-eyed, performing no tricks, appears superficially to be nothing more than himself, and in this incidental, tail-wagging, winsome, scene-stealing part, he appeals irresistibly to a very English, post-Romantic attitude towards dogs,[48] in theatre audiences and critics alike. In his shadowier functional role, which it is just as well we do not see, but receive refracted through Lance's droll impersonated monologue, he appears in a very different light: the heir to an ancient line in sexual conquest through farcical deception, the excremental emblem of lust and defilement. This is the fitting prolepsis to a violation of fundamental human relations on Proteus's part which is infinitely more serious than any offence against *fin amour* or the friendship cult, those no doubt necessary fictions of fine breeding, could ever be. Crab is perhaps best not presented as a pedigree animal. His is a long story, a mongrel's tragi-comedy, and it serves to disclose a dog beneath the skin.

NOTES

I am most grateful to the editors and to Professor Jill Mann for helpful comments upon an early draft of this essay, and I am particularly indebted to Dr Richard Axton, who has been more than generous in sharing his thoughts on stage dogs with me since my undergraduate days.

1 Johannes Caius, *Of Englishe Dogges* (English translation by Abraham Fleming, STC 4347) (London, 1576), 29–30.
2 *The Two Gentlemen of Verona*, ed. Clifford Leech (London, 1969), xxi–xxxv. For the recent conjecture of a date as early as 1587, see E. A. J. Honigmann, *Shakespeare's Impact on his Contemporaries* (London, 1982), 88.
3 Stanley Wells, 'The Failure of *The Two Gentlemen of Verona*', *Shakespeare Jahrbuch*, 99 (1963), 161–73; *Two Gentlemen*, ed. Leech, xviii–xxi.
4 Quotations are from *The Two Gentlemen of Verona*, ed. Kurt Schlueter (Cambridge, 1990).
5 The best-documented account of Tarlton is to be found in E. Nungezer, *A Dictionary of Actors and of Other Persons associated with the Public Representation of Plays in England before 1642* (New Haven, 1929), s.n.
6 E. Arber, *A Transcript of the Registers of the Company of Stationers of London 1554–1640 A.D.*, 5 vols. (London, 1875–7), II, 500, 526, 531, 559.
7 David Wiles, *Shakespeare's Clown: Actor and Text in the Elizabethan Playhouse* (Cambridge, 1987), Ch. 2.
8 J. A. Bryant, Jr, 'Shakespeare's Falstaff and the Mantle of Tarlton', *Studies in Philology*, 51 (1954), 149–62; B. Nicholson, 'Kemp and the Play of *Hamlet*. Yorick and Tarlton', *New Shakespeare Society Transactions*, 1880–6, 57–64.

9 Quoted from STC 23683.3, rather than the modernised (and bowdlerised) edition by J. O. Halliwell (London: Shakespeare Society, 1844).

10 See R. L. Taylor, *W. C. Fields, His Follies and Fortunes* (London, 1950), *passim*.

11 Cited in C. R. Baskervill's valuable account of Tarlton in *The Elizabethan Jig and Related Song Drama* (Chicago, 1929), 95–105 (98).

12 Caius, *Of Englishe Dogges*, 25–6.

13 Facsimile in: Robert Armin, *Collected Works*, ed. J. P. Feather, 2 vols. (New York and London, 1972), II, C3v–C4.

14 STC 19517.

15 F. P. Wilson, *The English Drama 1485–1585*, ed. G. K. Hunter (Oxford, 1969), 96–101.

16 *Medieval French Plays*, trans. by Richard Axton and John Stevens (Oxford, 1971), 137–64.

17 See *The Scriptores Historiae Augustae*, Loeb Classical Library, 3 vols. (London and New York, 1932), III, 446–7, for bears acting in a late Roman farce.

18 Anne Barton, '"Enter Mariners, wet": Realism in Shakespeare's Last Plays', in *Realism in European Literature: Essays in Honour of J. P. Stern*, eds. Nicholas Boyle and Martin Swales (Cambridge, 1986), 28–49 (43–4).

19 *The Staging of Religious Drama in Europe in the Later Middle Ages: Texts and Documents in English Translation*, eds. Peter Meredith and John E. Tailby (Kalamazoo, 1982), 117–20.

20 Aristophanes, *The Wasps*, lines 836ff.

21 *The Philosophie, commonlie called, the Morals written by the learned Philosopher Plutarch of Chaeronea* (London, 1603); STC 20063.

22 *Ruodlieb: Faksimile-Ausgabe des Codex Latinus Monacenisis 19486 der Bayerischen Staatsbibliothek München und der Fragmente von St Florian*, vol. II, Kritischer Text, ed. Benedikt Konrad Vollmann (Wiesbaden, 1985).

23 Lillian M. C. Randall, *Images in the Margins of Gothic Manuscripts* (Berkeley and Los Angeles, 1966), 91–4.

24 *Commedie Latine del XII e XIII Secolo*, vol. II, *Babio*, ed. Andea Dessi Fulgheri (Genoa, 1980); *Babio: A Twelfth Century Profane Comedy*, ed. M. Brennan (Charleston, 1968).

25 John Skelton, *Magnificence*, ed. Paula Neuss (Manchester, 1980), 40–1.

26 *Records of Early English Drama: Cambridge*, ed. Alan H. Nelson, 2 vols. (Toronto, 1989), I, 180.

27 Quoted by Louis B. Wright, 'Animal Actors on the English Stage before 1642', *Publications of the Modern Language Association of America*, 42 (1927), 656–69 (658), who also gives further details of the dogs in plays during the years 1568–1611 which follow.

28 As cited in Ben Jonson, *The Staple of News*, ed. Anthony Parr (Manchester, 1988), 245n.

29 Cf. Anne Barton, *Ben Jonson, Dramatist* (Cambridge, 1984), 71–2. Puntarvolo also has a cat, supposedly kept in a bag or confined to its

chamber owing to a cold. Professor Barton suggests that 'Jonson, obviously, did not want to cope with it on stage.' A cat did, however, achieve an on-stage role in *Gammer Gurton's Needle* (?1563) (accused of swallowing the needle), and Wright, 'Animal Actors', 667, quotes an account of some early nineteenth-century performing cats from the *Memorials of Bartholomew Fair*. In the modern theatre, Harold Pinter has provided a singularly tricky role for the actress who is obliged to hold a cat throughout most of *The Collection*.

30 Keith Thomas, *Man and the Natural World: Changing Attitudes in England 1500–1800* (London, 1983), 102.

31 Barbara Everett, 'The Fatness of Falstaff', *Proceedings of the British Academy*, 76 (1991), 109–28 (112).

32 Ovid, *Metamorphoses*, XIII, 569–71, Loeb Classical Library, 2 vols. (London and Cambridge, Mass., 1916). See also Euripides, *Hecuba*, lines 259–73.

33 See the mass of references assembled in Stith Thompson, *Motif-Index of Folk Literature*, 6 vols. (Copenhagen, 1955), K 1351, 'The Weeping Bitch', and D 141.1, 'Transformation: woman to bitch'. The story first appears in written form in Oriental romances such as the Sinbad cycle in the Arabian Nights' Entertainments. It seems to have found its way to the West through Hebrew channels, notably the *Disciplina Clericalis*, a widely circulated collection of moralised tales by the twelfth-century Spanish convert Petrus Alfonsi (Moshe Sefaradi), personal physician to Henry I of England; see H. Schwarzenbaum, 'International Folklore Motifs in Petrus Alfonsi's "Disciplina Clericalis"', *Sefarad*, 21–3 (1961–3), ii, 24–8.

34 M. M. Banks, ed., *An Alphabet of Tales*, Early English Text Society, 126–7 (1904–5), no. 537.

35 For post-medieval editions of the *Gesta Romanorum* see STC 21286.2–21290a. Further to Thompson (n. 32 above), numerous other citations for the tale in medieval collections of *exempla* will be found in F. Tubach, *Index Exemplorum: A Handbook of Medieval Religious Tales* (Helsinki, 1969), no. 661, 'Bitch, weeping'.

36 Richard Axton, *European Drama of the Early Middle Ages* (London, 1974), 17–19, draws together some of the scattered evidence for this phenomenon.

37 Ian Lancashire, '"Ioly Walte and Malkyng": a Grimsby Puppet Play in 1431', *Records of Early English Drama Newsletter*, 1979: 2, 6–8; Richard Axton, 'Folk Play in Tudor Interludes', in *English Drama: Forms and Development*, eds. Marie Axton and Raymond Williams (Cambridge, 1977), 15–18, and *Three Rastell Plays*, ed. Richard Axton (Cambridge, 1979), 17. I am grateful to Professor Graham Caie for the reference to the Danish version: *Fastelavnsspillet i Denmarks senmiddelalder: om Den utro hustru og fastelavnsspillets tradition*, ed. Leif Søndergaard (Odense, 1989).

38 *Dame Sirith* and the *Interludium* are respectively nos. vi and xv in *Early Middle English Verse and Prose*, eds. J. A. W. Bennett and G. V. Smithers (2nd edn, Oxford, 1968).

39 Richard Axton, *European Drama*, 21, suggests that *Dame Sirith*, which contains introductory narrative passages, could have been performed by a solo mime with a dog, though the text would seem to be readily adaptable to different modes, and was doubtless intended to be so.

40 Alternatively, irritant eye-drops, like those used by modern film and television actors called upon to weep, might have been used.

41 Everett, 'Fatness of Falstaff', 113.

42 'Jewel' has a capital J in the Folio, which has led to the suggestion (not generally accepted) that Proteus might be using the dog's name. Bawdy senses of 'jewel' are 'maidenhead', and in the plural (via 'stone') 'testicles'. Note Speed's equivocatory advice to Proteus earlier in the play as to the gifts he might offer the supposedly hard-hearted Julia: 'Give her no token but stones...' (1.1.132).

43 Sigmund Freud, *Civilization and its Discontents*, ed. J. Strachey, trans. J. Riviere (rev. edn, London, 1963), 37n.

44 One of the effects of the ethical dative, frequently a device of oral storytelling, is to reinforce the action of the verb whilst keeping the narrator's presence in the foreground. 'Thrust' has the obvious clown's resonance for Lance. Earlier, he bawdily described Speed as 'an unmannerly knave, that will thrust himself into secrets', at the end of the scene where they recite the vulgar catalogue of his mistress's qualities (3.1.360).

45 *Parson's Tale*, line 857. Where I have retained 'beautees' (*sc.* 'objects of beauty') above, most editions substitute the emendation '[bushes]', though such a reading is not found in the manuscripts. The source of the image has recently been noted in a thirteenth-century insular abridgement of Chaucer's basic source for the *Parson's Tale*, the *Summa de vitiis* of William of Peraldus: 'Sed stulti leccatores sunt similes cani, qui transiens per rosetum vel virgultum, si maculare illud non potest, tibiam levat et signum facit'; see S. Wenzel, 'A Source of Chaucer's Seven Deadly Sins', *Traditio*, 30 (1974), 351–78 (374). For Dunbar, see *The Tua Mariit Wemen*, lines 185–7 (of a husband who rates himself highly as a lover, but performs poorly): 'He dois as a dotit [*silly*] dog, that damys [*pisses*] on all bussis, / And liftis his leg apone lofte, thoght he nought list pische'.

46 The chaste and well-bred anchoresses addressed by their spiritual guide in the *Ancrene Wisse* (*c.* 1225) are warned that temptation to lechery will come as a fawning 'dog of hell', sneaking up to them with his 'bloody fleas of stinking thoughts'; Bennett and Smithers, xviiib, 363ff. The association of the dog with the devil, evil, temptation, and damnation was very strong in both Old and New Testament thought, flowing from texts like the Psalmist's 'Deliver my soul from the sword; My darling from the power of the dog' (Ps. 22. 20), and St John's closing words in

the Apocalypse: 'Without are the dogs and the sorcerers, and the fornicators, and the murderers, and the idolaters, and everyone that loveth and maketh a lie' (Rev. 22. 15).

47 Harold F. Brooks, 'Two Clowns in a Comedy (to say nothing of the Dog): Speed, Launce (and Crab) in "The Two Gentlemen of Verona"', *Essays & Studies 1963*, 91–100 (99), and further, *Two Gentlemen*, ed. Leech, lv–vi, lxi, lxix.

48 Thomas, *Man and the Natural World*, 108.

The comedian as the character C

Stephen Orgel

I am taking the term comedy here in its Renaissance sense, not simply as the opposite of tragedy but as the largest condition of drama. This is a sense that persisted in English through the eighteenth century: Johnson defines 'comedian' as 'a player in general, a stage player'; *comédien* is still a generic term for actor in French, as *commediante* is in Italian. When the Swiss traveller Thomas Platter visited the Globe theatre in 1599, he reported that he 'saw the tragedy of the first Emperor Julius [Caesar] with at least fifteen characters very well acted. At the end of the comedy', he continued, 'they danced according to their custom...'[1] Comedy, for this Renaissance spectator, included tragedy. There is, even for modern audiences, a generic truth in the traditional terminology: the tragic purgation of the state and the spirit and the reassertion of norms that is the end of tragedy leave us in the world of comedy. Tragedy is what makes comedy possible – or, to put it another way, comedy is the end of tragedy – and the Renaissance liked to emphasise this aspect of tragedy by concluding its tragedies, as the performance of *Julius Caesar* Platter saw concluded, with a jig. This is something that is all but inconceivable to modern audiences; and when critics discuss the emotional effects of plays like *King Lear* or *Macbeth*, they invariably forget about the jig. But comedy and tragedy were not a dichotomy in the Renaissance; Scaliger's *Poetics* places many plays in both categories, and to the performing tradition, at least, comedy was an essential element of tragedy.[2] I have not, therefore, limited my discussion to plays that modern taxonomy calls comedies. My argument begins with tragedy, but it is largely concerned with comic issues, and concludes with those Shakespearean comedies that we have found so problematic generically that since the time of Dowden we have redefined them as romances.

36

When Coriolanus angrily rejects Rome with the words 'There is a world elsewhere', he imagines a space outside his play, a world he can control. He declares his intention, in effect, of writing his own script, invokes to himself the power of the playwright. The remainder of the play is in every sense designed to prove him wrong, designed to prove that no character can escape his play. The world Coriolanus unsuccessfully rejects is an all-encompassing and quite particular place, defined, indeed, overdetermined: Coriolanus' drama, like all drama, begins with, depends on, and cannot escape its script.

But what does it mean to say that every drama depends on a script – how is this more than a self-evident commonplace, even a tautology? To begin with the most practical and material consideration, the term implies that the essence of drama is a text, and more specifically, one written by hand. Scripts, however, eventuate in plays, which are performances, not texts. I begin with an observation of Jonathan Goldberg's, and my opening remarks are a free fantasia on themes elucidated by that remarkable book *Writing Matter*:[3] Renaissance plays seem compulsively to turn to scenes of writing, to letters and documents, to handwritten discourse as the mode of action. Thus transpires everything from crucial revelations:

> *A letter falleth.*
> What's here? A letter? Tush, it is not so!
> A letter written to Hieronymo!
> 'For want of ink, receive this bloody writ.
> Me hath my hapless brother hid from thee.
> Revenge thyself on Balthazar and him,
> For these were they that murderèd thy son.'[4]

to amorous declarations:

> Doubt that the stars are fire,...
> But never doubt my love,[5]

to the damning evidence, in writing, of Falstaff's ha'pennyworth of bread compared with his intolerable deal of sack.

But letters also suppress evidence:

They met me in the day of success; and I have learned by the perfect'st report they have more in them than mortal knowledge... Whiles I stood rapt in the wonder of it, came missives from the king, who all-hailed me

Thane of Cawdor, by which title, before, these weird sisters saluted me, and referred me to the coming on of time with 'Hail, king that shalt be!'[6]

Macbeth's letter to his 'dearest partner of greatness' faithfully reflects the royal hand which has entitled him 'Cawdor'; but it omits the crucial witness Banquo, and the 'more than mortal' knowledge that he would be 'lesser than Macbeth, and greater', and that his progeny would inherit Macbeth's throne. Missives both represent and misrepresent.

Writing in all these cases is a potent mode of dramatic action, a mode perhaps most fully exemplified when Hamlet throws off his melancholy, saves his life, grapples with the pirates, usurps his uncle's authority and by implication his throne, and performs all these acts not through heroic combat, but by forging a royal letter and then writing Horatio a letter about it. On the stage, moreover, these events are conveyed simply by Horatio reading the letter aloud, as if to remind us of the essential subtext of all drama, that what actors do is, in the end, not perform actions but recite scripts: is it mere coincidence that the speaker's name is an aspirated – a living, breathing – oratio?

If the writing of documents is endemic to Renaissance drama, the forging of documents is its essential corollary. Hamlet's forgery of Claudius' letter apparently depends not on his ability to imitate his uncle's hand, but to imitate that of a scribe – he 'wrote it fair', something that 'statists' – statesmen – consider 'a baseness.'[7] In this case the deception depends on Hamlet's willingness both to conceal his social class by writing in the hand of a functionary, and to manipulate his heritage by employing his father's signet to represent himself as his uncle: the instrument of authentication, the royal seal, does not distinguish between kings.

Hamlet himself, however, is easily identified by his handwriting. 'Know you the hand?' Laertes asks, at least considering the possibility that the ominous letter Claudius receives upon Hamlet's return is inauthentic, and Claudius replies, 'Tis Hamlet's character.'[8] The character, indeed, was the hand, or rather the letters formed by it, until well into the seventeenth century. Transferred uses in Shakespeare relate to other equally external marks of inner worth – the face, the comportment:

> I will believe thou hast a mind that suits
> With this thy fair and outward character,[9]

Viola says, determining – correctly as it turns out, but the wilfulness is apparent – to trust the ship's captain who, in Shakespeare's source, *Apollonius and Silla*, has betrayed her. The dangers of such certainty are evident in the Duke's equally unquestioning assumption in *Measure for Measure* that Angelo's 'character...to th' observer doth thy history | Fully unfold.'[10] Considering the ease with which Hamlet imitates other hands, Claudius' confidence may seem to be similarly misplaced; but the reliance on handwriting for identification was, in dramatic contexts, all but absolute. Gloucester simply substitutes Edgar's forged handwriting for everything he knows about his son, what we would call his character – in effect, the character itself can be forged:

GLOUCESTER You know the character to be your brother's?
EDMUND If the matter were good, my lord, I durst swear it were his; but in respect of that, I would fain think it were not.
GLOUCESTER It is his.[11]

And Polonius, employing Reynaldo slanderously to misrepresent Laertes' character in Paris, urges him to 'lay what forgeries you will' upon his son.[12] The parental stratagem is particularly unsavoury precisely because Reynaldo's forgeries are all but certain to be believed: authenticity is scarcely ever an issue in assessing the reports and documents of Renaissance drama. The most unlikely missives command implicit belief – nobody ever sees through a forgery.[13] It is apparently not even necessary to read the letter oneself. Gloucester, though he can read, unquestioningly relies on Edmund to identify Edgar's handwriting; but judging from the evidence of the many analogous moments on Shakespeare's stage, the outcome would be no different if he had done his own reading. Malvolio contemplating a love letter supposedly from Olivia considers himself a trained graphologist:

By my life, this is my lady's hand. These be her very C's, her U's and her T's; and thus makes she her great P's. It is, in contempt of question, her hand.[14]

The forgery produces an obscene orthography, but Malvolio is as ignorant of what he speaks as he is of what he reads. He is, moreover, being gulled here far more significantly by the playwright than by the mischievous Maria: the salutation that is his text, 'To the unknown beloved, this, and my good wishes', contains neither C nor P. The first, essential forgery is the script.

The terminally ambiguous letter by which Mortimer orders the death of Edward II is handwriting at its most duplicitous:

> *Edwardum occidere nolite timere bonum est*
> Fear not to kill the king, 'tis good he die.
> But read it thus, and that's another sense...
> Kill not the king, 'tis good to fear the worst.[15]

This is designed both to authorise the execution and to exculpate its author, but the judicious and judicial Edward III, succeeding to his father's throne, ignores the machiavellian syntax and condemns Mortimer simply upon his admitting to the handwriting – unexpectedly, in this world of misrepresentation, the truth for once shines through the character:

MORTIMER 'Tis my hand. What gather you by this?
EDWARD III That thither thou didst send a murderer.[16]

Justice here is a function of illiteracy. Mortimer is executed not for the debatable meaning of his letter, but for its indubitable consequences; and therefore to acknowledge the hand is to admit everything.

The hand is everything; what it writes is nothing – or rather, no one thing. Troilus, tearing up the letter Cressida has sent to protest her continuing love, observes that 'Th'effect doth operate another way': if the hand is Cressida's, the letter, whatever it says, is 'mere words'[17] – as in the case of Mortimer, to know the hand is to know everything. But even in the best of characters, meanings are ambiguous, intentions unknowable. The blushes that the Friar in *Much Ado* reads as evidence of Hero's innocence are taken by Claudio and Leonato to confirm her guilt. King Duncan testifies to the radical uncommunicativeness of surfaces:

> There's no art
> To find the mind's construction in the face;
> He was a gentleman on whom I built
> An absolute trust,[18]

he says of Cawdor, as he nevertheless prepares to make the same mistake with Macbeth. Cymbeline, in fact, articulates the ultimate impenetrability of forgery for the age, the impossibility of doubting the character as it presents itself. When his queen's evil nature is finally revealed, he observes that

> Mine eyes
> Were not in fault, for she was beautiful,

Mine ears that heard her flattery, nor my heart
That thought her like her seeming. It had been vicious
To have mistrusted her.[19]

The character is nothing but what one sees, what one reads. Whether
it is true or false, it is all there is.

II

The critical issue underlying all these cases, what is implicitly
credible, is handwriting; and whatever this says about the realities of
Renaissance social psychology, it is obvious that in drama, the
character is the script – Laertes even calls Ophelia 'a document in
madness'.[20] For characters within the drama, there are no options
about whether or not the script is trustworthy: the script is the play.
To the playwright, therefore, the greatest, the most anarchic danger
is the unwritten, improvisation, Hamlet's fear lest the clowns 'speak
more than is set down for them', take control of the character, and
thereby pre-empt 'some necessary business of the play',[21] making the
plot subservient to the character, and more dangerously, the
dramatist subservient to the actor.

But actors are, if they wish to be, free agents – it was, indeed, the
playwright in the Renaissance theatre who was the employee, the
actors the employer. Hamlet's complaint makes sense only because
he is a royal playwright, and therefore (in this respect like
Shakespeare) his own boss. The more profoundly subversive notion
that the characters too are not a mere function of the script, but are,
as Coriolanus imagines himself to be, somehow trapped in it, and
might therefore free themselves, enter or create 'a world elsewhere',
contrive to act independently of the playwright – the basic conceit of
Prospero's epilogue to *The Tempest*, of *Rosencrantz and Guildenstern are
Dead*, *Six Characters in Search of an Author*, *The Purple Rose of Cairo* – is
one that has been, for most of the history of drama, either a
contradiction in terms, or simply unimaginable.

Unimaginable, that is, by playwrights. But figures like Hamlet and
Falstaff have, almost from the beginning, had a life outside their
plays; and there was a time when supplying Shakespeare's heroines
with girlhoods was not only a reasonable undertaking, but a recipe
for a best seller. These are, for us, relatively unthreatening examples,
from which we have, for the past fifty years or so, managed to keep a
comfortable distance. They are, however, more deeply implicated in

2   *The wits* (1660), frontispiece

3   Henry Peacham(?), a scene from *Titus Andronicus*, 1595

the history of theatre than we can easily perceive from where we stand.

Plate 2, for example, from a volume only a generation removed from Shakespeare, shows a collection of favourite comic characters from the pre-Restoration stage, the subjects of burlesque skits performed during the Commonwealth. The two Shakespearean ones are Falstaff and Mistress Quickly, downstage left – Mistress Quickly is identified only as 'Hostes', and is present as a foil for Falstaff. The other characters who entertained the public during the puritan interregnum are Antonio from *The Changeling*, feigning madness in a bishop's mitre upstage left; Bubble the clown from *Greene's Tu Quoque*, emerging through the curtains and uttering the words that identify him, 'Tu quoque'; a figure labelled 'Simpleton', from Robert Cox's *Simpleton the Smith*, the only character from a Commonwealth skit; a French dancing master from William Cavendish's *The Variety*; and Claus, the beggar king from Fletcher's *Beggar's Bush*.[22] This plate assumes that characters are both the essence of their dramas, and, paradoxically, independent of them.

Plate 3 is a much more famous survival, from Shakespeare's own time, the so-called Peacham sketch of *Titus Andronicus*. These figures are all to be found in the play, and they are certainly engaged in the performance of a scene; the scene, however, is not in the play. The drawing is valuable in a number of ways: it reveals a great deal about the construction of character for the Elizabethan spectator, but it also tells us something Shakespeare's texts do not about how he constructed his fictive world; and in a still larger sense, it bears on the relation between Shakespeare's text and its performance, not only in the Elizabethan theatre, but on any stage, and in the mind of the spectator.[23]

At the centre of the scene stands Titus, attended by two soldiers. Queen Tamora, on her knees, pleads for the lives of her two sons, who kneel behind her guarded by Aaron the Moor – the caption reads, 'Enter Tamora pleading for her sons going to execution.' This is, as I say, not quite a scene from the play. There is a passage in 1.1 that accords with the personnel of the scene depicted, but it also requires a coffin onstage; so to begin with, a necessary prop has been omitted by the artist. A larger problem is that at this point in the play, Aaron is a prisoner, and there is no way of accommodating the cautionary figure with drawn sword to the text that has survived. Because of this and some other small inconsistencies, it is now usually assumed that the drawing is not a sketch of an actual performance in progress, but a recollection of one, an imaginative reconstruction by an Elizabethan of the Shakespearean stage in action – this is the way one of Shakespeare's contemporaries remembered a Shakespeare play in the theatre.[24]

It is a commonplace to say that Shakespeare imagines everywhere to be England, but if the Peacham sketch is our evidence, this is obviously untrue. It does allow us, however, to consider what limits there were to the imagination of otherness for him, and what place character had in the world elsewhere. Titus is in Roman dress, and Tamora is in generalised royal garments, vaguely medieval – certainly neither Roman nor Elizabethan. Aaron and the son on the right are in costumes that, judging from the sleeves, are Elizabethan, though their pants could be either Roman military bases or Elizabethan puff-pants. The son on the left wears the same sort of sash as Titus, which is clearly intended to be Roman. The guards on the far left, however, are fully fledged Elizabethan soldiers. The scene is an image of here and elsewhere, now and then, us and them.

The sketch, with its obvious inconsistencies, looks oddly primitive to us, but it embodies something essential about Renaissance drama, which classicists like Sidney complained of: the fluidity of its action, and its fondness for, and indeed, reliance on, anachronism. This

4   A scene from *Eunuchus*, from *P. Terentii Afri...Comoediae*, Paris 1552

drawing is true to Shakespearean conceptions of drama, which is characteristically inconsistent because its reality is infinitely adjustable. The costumes here are designed not to mirror a historical moment, but to indicate the characters' roles and relationships; as I have written elsewhere, what Renaissance drama offers the viewer is not a coherent, consistent world but what the Renaissance would have recognised as an *argument*. This is what critics from Horace to Castelvetro and Sidney mean when they say that mimesis is only the means of drama, not its end. Its end is the same as the end of poetry and the other verbal arts: to persuade.[25] This is the respect in which the Peacham sketch is in fact internally consistent. It does not mime a world, it expresses an action, and it does so by indicating to the viewer the significance, position, status, relationships of its figures. Its elements fit together not like a logical proposition but like a rhetorical argument; which is to say that the essential element in their structure is the way they enable an audience to interpret and understand them.

    I want to deconstruct this image now, to give a sense of why both the primacy of character and that rather casual attitude toward anachronism, that apparent blindness to temporal inconsistency (which is almost a defining feature of the Renaissance as we construct

5 *Oedipo Tyranno* as performed at the Teatro Olimpico, Vicenza, 1585; detail of a fresco in the theatre

it), is not seen as a weakness, and indeed might even be conceived as a virtue.

Illustrations of the earliest printed drama, such as that in Plate 4, show the characters in contemporary dress; there is no attempt to indicate the Romanness of the play through costume or decor. Terence was performed in Humanist academies, and this plate indicates performance practice in the period. There is no anachronism here because there is no sense of history: the play's history is irrelevant to its function, which is moral and educational; it teaches both the lessons of comedy and the language of learning. Terence is conceived in the fullest sense as contemporary.

The preference for this performing style cannot be ascribed to ignorance: the age knew perfectly well from descriptions in ancient texts how Terence appeared in Roman theatres. There are even illustrated manuscripts of Terence as late as the twelfth century showing the actors wearing masks and togas; there is no question that an awareness of authentic performing practice did in fact survive.[26] But clearly, authenticity was considered inappropriate, or even irrelevant, to the performance of classical plays.

In contrast, when the most famous classical play, *Oedipus*, opened Palladio's Teatro Olimpico in Vicenza in 1585, it was costumed according to the same principles as *Titus Andronicus* in the Peacham drawing (Plate 5). The actors do not wear togas, but they do not wear modern dress either; they wear dignified ceremonial robes, with only a bit of drapery around the king's shoulders to suggest the historical era. Explicitly anachronistic details are used to establish roles: the priests surrounding Oedipus wear bishops' mitres and copes. The Teatro Olimpico, unlike Shakespeare's stage, was consciously undertaking a historical enterprise. But the re-creation of the past nevertheless requires the semiotics of the present.[27]

And therein lie the limitations on the imagination of otherness: these images tell us that our sense of the other depends on our sense of its relation to ourselves; we comprehend it insofar as it differs from us, and conversely, we know ourselves only through a knowledge of what we are not – we construct the other as a way of affirming the self. These operations are, obviously, not unique to Shakespeare's theatre or to the Renaissance.

Here, to take only a single example, is the frontispiece for *Henry VIII* in the first illustrated Shakespeare, edited by Nicholas Rowe in 1709 (Plate 6). The scene shows Henry VIII, Wolsey and two

6　*Henry the Eighth*, frontispiece from the play in Nicholas Rowe's Shakespeare, 1709

courtiers. The King's identity is established by making him a living version of Holbein's famous portrait; he is not merely in historically appropriate Tudor dress, but the embodiment of an authorised, historically authentic image. But the court milieu is also an essential element of the play, and the courtiers therefore wear court fashions of 1709, including curled wigs and frock coats. Wolsey's ecclesiastical garb, with its lace-trimmed surplice, is similarly modern. The conventions of costuming in Vicenza in 1585 and in London in 1595 remain valid for the stage of Dryden and Addison.

In fact, they are still in force today, though since they are our conventions rather than those of the Renaissance or the eighteenth century, they tend to be invisible. Films on historical subjects will often exhibit an archaeological fidelity to period styles of costume, but the hair styles and makeup of the stars are almost invariably our own. This is essential if the stars are to look glamorous. Thus, although (for example) Sam Waterston's hair in *The Great Gatsby* and Michelle Pfeiffer's makeup in *Dangerous Liaisons* were strictly modern, they did not register as anachronistic, and will not do so until fashions change sufficiently for them to appear dated. Anne Hollander reproduces a remarkable example from Zeffirelli's *Taming of the Shrew*, with modern hair styles for Michael York's Lucentio and his Bianca Natasha Pyne, and historically correct hair for an unglamorous extra attending them.[28]

None of this, obviously, is controlled by the text. It has to do with how we realise the characters and extend them beyond what the text gives us, and in particular, where we choose to locate them in relation to ourselves. Nor is it, as a way of conceiving drama, limited to the world of the playhouse.

III

I suggest that the assumptions behind *The Girlhood of Shakespeare's Heroines* in fact have been and remain the controlling models for our treatment of Renaissance drama; that the independence of characters from their texts has in fact been for several centuries a commonplace of critical and editorial practice – so commonplace, indeed, as to render it and its implications all but invisible.

Let us begin with a famous crux in *The Tempest*: when Caliban appears, he is bitterly attacked first by Prospero –

> Thou poisonous slave, got by the devil himself
> Upon thy wicked dam[29] –

and then by Miranda –

> Abhorred slave,
> Which any print of goodness will not take, etc.[30]

From Davenant's and Dryden's Restoration revision until the 1940s, editors consistently reassigned the latter speech to Prospero, on the grounds that it was out of character for Miranda. We have in recent years developed a number of ways of dealing with the perceived inconsistency of Shakespearean character: we argue that Renaissance notions of psychology differed from ours; that the Renaissance self was not an inner reality but a set of roles, often contradictory; that drama was not a novelistic picture of life but a rhetorical or oratorical structure, and characters therefore changed not according to any inner motivation but according to the demands of the developing argument; that characters are not people but elements of the plot; and so forth. Contemporary criticism has little reason to expect consistency from the persons of drama, and recent editors have usually allowed Miranda her outburst, though in performance the speech is still more often than not given to Prospero. (As it was in Peter Greenaway's *Prospero's Books*; the revision seemed to me particularly striking in this case, an indication of how basically conventional a reading of the play the film was, despite all the nudes and the ravaged Claribel and Prospero's wife and the opulent inventiveness of the presentation. The textual change, moreover, was basically pointless since Prospero was speaking everyone else's lines anyhow.)

But why is the speech considered inconsistent or out of character? It is true that 'Abhorred slave...' does not suit a Miranda who is all innocence and passivity; but in fact there is a good deal in the role as it transpires in the folio text that is neither innocent nor passive. The speech, for example, is not at all inconsistent with Miranda's conduct toward Ferdinand, which is nothing if not active and forthcoming, nor with her immediate assumption that when Prospero accuses Antonio of unbrotherly behaviour, he is therefore implying that his mother had committed adultery. Miranda's defence of her grandmother at this moment, whatever we imagine its source to be, cannot be evidence of innocence and passivity.[31]

The decision to reassign the speech, then – unquestioned for almost three centuries – derives not from a recognition of inconsistency or textual corruption, but from a desire for a different Miranda, or perhaps more deeply, from a conviction about what kind of model

Shakespeare ought to be providing for young women. This is not, in itself, an argument against the emendation: so long as theatre is a living art, every age will create the Shakespeare it requires. It is worth remarking, however, that such a revision does assume that Miranda has a reality independent of her lines in the text, and that the lines, therefore, in order to produce the 'real' Miranda, can be adjusted to accord with whatever that character is conceived to be. But what is Miranda's character other than the lines she speaks? To revise the lines in accordance with the character is to fall into the most circular of hermeneutic circles.

Let us take another case. Leontes is a far more complex character than Miranda, and the editorial desire to produce a comprehensible psychology out of the folio text of *The Winter's Tale* has, since the early eighteenth century, been irresistible. After the first sudden access of jealousy, his altered demeanour is noticed by Hermione and Polixenes:

POLIXENES   What means Sicilia?
HERMIONE He something seems unsettled.
POLIXENES   How, my lord?

to which, in the folio, Leontes replies,

What cheer? How is't with you, best brother?[32]

From Hanmer's edition on, heavy weather has been made of this. Isn't Leontes recovering too quickly? Doesn't the line properly belong to Polixenes? This emendation, unlike the reassignment of Miranda's attack on Caliban, has attracted recent editors, most notably Pafford and Bevington.

But here too, the problem is not one of a perceived inconsistency. Mercurial changes are of the essence of Leontes' character; the reply is disconcerting not because of the change of mood, but because it makes Leontes out to be not only paranoid but hypocritical as well. The two conditions are, however, surely not incompatible. Here the editorial desire has been to render the character less complex and more rational, just as editors often argue that Leontes may in fact have perfectly good grounds for his jealousy, that Hermione, though innocent, may have presented the appearance of impropriety. Directors, following suit, sometimes give Hermione and Polixenes a suspiciously intimate pantomime to justify Leontes' outburst 'Too hot, too hot.'[33]

These, of course, are not neutral assumptions, and have consequences for the play as a whole. If Leontes' jealousy is reasonable, an honourable mistake, ought he to be as severely punished for it as he is? Nobody within the play, nobody except editors and critics, undertakes to exculpate Leontes. Imagine a version of the play in which Camillo responded to Leontes's charges against his wife with 'I see why you might think that, but...', and the lesson Paulina was concerned to impress upon him was that you mustn't believe everything you see. This is not an inconceivable reading of *The Winter's Tale*, but it is hardly the reading to which most editors would admit that they subscribe.

Now for a case with broader implications. When Camillo tries to argue Leontes out of his mad fantasy, he says,

> I cannot
> Believe this crack to be in my dread mistress,
> Sovereignly being honourable. I have loved thee –

and Leontes, in a fury, interrupts him with

> Make that thy question, and go rot![34]

This has occasioned much debate. Theobald objected that Camillo could not call his sovereign 'thee', and gave the line to Leontes. Johnson concurred in the alteration, as did Warburton. Most subsequent editors down to the present day have agreed that the pronoun is a problem, though since the eighteenth century the line has generally not been reassigned. Dover Wilson found the issue significant enough to resolve it with an emendation: 'T'have loved the –'; and Leontes's interruption thus prevents Camillo from naming the king of Bohemia. Ingenious as this is, it proved unpersuasive, and now looks preposterous; and editors continue to worry the question.

But why is it assumed that Camillo cannot call Leontes 'thee'? Paulina calls him 'thee', and much worse, in 3.2; the notion that Leontes cannot be addressed in this way depends on anachronistic attitudes towards kingship. The question of how to address the king was in fact quite an open one in the period: James I complained constantly that he was not treated with enough respect, and one of the major innovations of Charles I was the reform and codification of court protocol. But in a larger sense, the debate depends on an assumption that the court of legendary Sicilia is a literal reflection of actual court practice; and here it is sufficient to observe that if James I had decided to have his daughter Elizabeth exposed in infancy, he would not have been permitted to do so.

There is, no doubt, no way of preventing ourselves from seeing

Shakespeare in our own image. Even the most radically historicised Shakespeares depend on a history that is constructed, and that will change with every generation. Stephen Greenblatt's Shakespeare, richly informed as it is by Renaissance politics and culture, is obviously as much a creature of our own age as William Poel's authentically Elizabethan stage productions were of the 1890s. But the striking thing about the editorial practices I have been considering is that they do not show us revising Shakespeare's characters to act as we act. On the contrary, what is suppressed in them is precisely our deepest convictions about the constitution of our own psychology, our insistence on the pre-rational, irrational, libidinous and unconscious sources of human behaviour. This is what we do not want our Shakespeare to mirror. No one with any experience of fifteen-year-old girls believes that they are, as a class, passive and non-sexual. Many critics have observed that Leontes' jealousy, violent and unsubstantiated, is in fact realistic, far more true to human experience than Othello's super-rationalised passion, which has a villain for its agent. To render Miranda an innocent and rationalise Leontes's jealousy is not to make *The Tempest* and *The Winter's Tale* more true to life, but to distance and sentimentalise them.

Finally, to emend or argue away the directness of Camillo's address to his sovereign, to assume that the relation of subject to ruler is necessarily one of circumspection and concessiveness, is to rewrite the nature of authority and the question of what is owed to it, arguably the central issue in *The Winter's Tale* – as it has been a central issue for our own time. And perhaps this is the real point: the editorial process has worked not to keep Shakespeare our contemporary, but to deflect Shakespearean drama from our deepest concerns.

NOTES

Note: some of this material has appeared in my essay 'Knowing the Character', *Zeitschrift für Anglistik und Amerikanistik*, 2.2 (1992).

1 Quoted in E. K. Chambers, *The Elizabethan Stage* (Oxford, 1923), II, 365.
2 For a fuller discussion of the issues involved, see my essay 'Shakespeare and the Kinds of Drama', *Critical Inquiry*, 6: 1 (Autumn, 1979), 107–23.
3 *Writing Matter: From the Hands of the English Renaissance* (Stanford, 1990).
4 Thomas Kyd, *The Spanish Tragedy*, 3.2.24ff.
5 *Hamlet* 2.2.115–19.

6 *Macbeth* 1.5.1–8.

7 *Hamlet* 5.1.32–4.

8 4.7.52.

9 *Twelfth Night* 1.2.51–2.

10 1.1.27–9.

11 *King Lear* 1.2.66–71.

12 *Hamlet* 2.1.20.

13 Partial exceptions: the Duchess of Malfi realises that the images she is shown of her dead children are in fact wax effigies, and Titus Andronicus sees through Tamora's claim to be the figure of Revenge. Neither of these is a document.

14 *Twelfth Night* 2.5.80–2.

15 Christopher Marlowe, *Edward II* 5.4.10.

16 5.6.47–8.

17 *Troilus and Cressida* 5.3.109.

18 *Macbeth* 1.4.11–14.

19 *Cymbeline* 5.5.62–6.

20 *Hamlet* 4.5.178 – the only instance of the word 'document' in Shakespeare.

21 3.2.36ff.

22 The plate is discussed in detail by R. A. Foakes, *Illustrations of the English Stage 1580–1642* (London, 1985), 159–61.

23 The drawing appears at the top of a page that also includes a passage from the play; the passage combines speeches from Acts 1 and 5, but even so does not really fit the scene illustrated, and apparently represents an unsuccessful attempt by someone other than the artist to match text to the drawing. In the margin of the text is the signature Henricus Peacham, and a date that is unclear but is generally read as 1595.

24 For a summary of the arguments relating to the drawing, see Foakes, *Illustrations*, 48–51.

25 'Shakespeare Imagines a Theater', in *Shakespeare, Man of the Theater*, eds. Kenneth Muir et al., (Newark, 1983), 44.

26 See, for example, the beautiful manuscript reproduced in Cesare Molinari, *Theatre Through the Ages* (New York, 1975), 113.

27 For a fuller discussion of the utility of anachronism to historical re-creation on the stage, from which some of the present discussion is taken, see my essay 'Counterfeit Presentments: Shakespeare's *Ekphrasis*', in *England and the Continental Renaissance*, eds. Edward Chaney and Peter Mack (Woodbridge, 1990), 177–84.

28 *Seeing Through Clothes* (New York, 1978), 310.

29 1.2.319–20.

30 1.2.350ff.

31 1.2.118–20.

32 1.2.146–8.

33 1.2.108.

34 1.2.321–3.

Mixed verse and prose in Shakespearean comedy
Jonas Barish

Prose and verse interlink, interlock, and interinanimate each other so
often and so densely in Shakespeare's comedies that it seems useful to
explore at least briefly some of the points of conjunction between the
two, and to identify some of the chief tactics by which Shakespeare
moves from one to the other, as well as to understand, where possible,
the uses and purposes of such juxtapositions.

Frequently, of course, the two forms alternate in cleanly defined
blocs, for example from one scene to another, when the stage has been
cleared and new characters enter; or for self-evident purposes within
a scene, as when a new character arrives to join others already there,
or a key character departs; or when two or more speakers address
each other each clinging to his or her preferred medium; or when the
tone of a scene changes, whether abruptly or gradually, between one
speech and another.

Of these possibilities, the first is the most obvious, least interesting,
and (no doubt) least in need of illustration. Even a cursory glance at
the act and scene division of the 1623 Folio will show an abundance
of instances in which a new scene coincides with a shift from prose to
verse or its opposite, as new characters, new topics of discourse, a new
social milieu, or a new emotional climate, come into view.

More worthy of notice would be those occasions when the language
of a scene already under way changes with the arrival of a new
character, as when the usurping Duke Frederick, in *As You Like It*,
storms in to banish Rosalind, in angry blank verse, intruding into the
prose being spoken up to that point by Rosalind and Celia themselves,
who, once he has left the stage, do not revert to their former chit-chat
but continue, with heightened anxiety, in the medium he has
initiated. Another angry Duke, Vincentio, in the last scene of *Measure
for Measure*, his cowl plucked off by Lucio, drops the prose he has been
speaking in his guise as Friar, and proceeds to final judgement in

55

'ducal' verse. In this case of course the new character does not so much enter as throw off an assumed role, with the effect of obliterating that role (Friar Lodowick) and substituting the 'actor' behind it (Vincentio).

Certain characters confine themselves entirely, or almost entirely, to one or the other mode. Launcelot Gobbo, in *The Merchant of Venice*, never uses verse, never submits to the metrical style of his interlocutor – whether Jessica, Shylock, Bassanio, or Lorenzo – though occasionally he converts them to *his* style. *The Merchant* being composed chiefly in metre, Launcelot's prose forms a dissenting, oppositional, somewhat subversive voice whenever he speaks. In this he differs from such loosely comparable clowns as the two Dromios, or Grumio, who although for the most part equally prosaic, are also more malleable, ready to respond in kind to the verse of others, to fill out metrically incomplete lines, or supply rhyming lines in order to complete couplets initiated by other speakers, or else, like Bottom, or Feste, to break into songs or snatches from old plays. Unlike these, Launcelot maintains a kind of flinty obduracy that preserves his separateness and psychic independence quite irrespective of his servile social position.

In *The Merry Wives of Windsor*, with its extremely high quotient of prose, the opposite situation obtains. Only two characters talk in verse, but they do so with close to a hundred per cent regularity, whatever others may be doing: Pistol rarely departs from his fustian iambics, and Fenton almost never from his blank verse romancing of Anne Page, so that each in his own way provides a running contrast to the homelier idiom of the rest, one by way of parody, the other by way of a change in emotional register.[1]

There are moments also when two characters stubbornly persist in speaking to each other each in their separate idioms even when these may be heard to clash. The lovestruck Titania, bewitched by Puck's magic flower-juice, woos Bottom in rhymed verse, mostly pentameter couplets, while Bottom replies to her, as to her attendants, only in his own brand of clumsily courtly prose (937–1020, 1511–58). The amusement for us lies in the contrast, the incommensurability, between her urgent endearments and his awkwardly prosaic responses. A similar dialogue of the deaf takes place in *Twelfth Night* when Sebastian, mistaken for Cesario by Feste, addresses the latter entirely in blank verse, while Feste responds with equal insistence in prose. When Sir Toby and Sir Andrew appear on the scene the same opposition persists, Sebastian sticking doggedly to his blank verse, the others just as insistently challenging him in prose. In this case the contrast involves a distinct element of conflict, reaching an exchange of blows, but as in the encounter between Bottom and Titania, the incomprehension between the opposing parties is heightened, or at least underscored, for us, by their incompatible rhythmic languages.

A related though not identical effect occurs in the finale of *A Midsummer Night's Dream*. There the rhymed verses spoken by the Prologue, by Wall, Lion, and Moonshine in the 'Pyramus & Thisbe' playlet, are punctuated by dry satiric asides, in prose, from the noble onlookers, speaking not to the players but to each other, so as to embody a sophisticated and in any case altogether different reaction to the lamentable tragedy before them from whatever its putative authors and clownish performers wish to convey. Prose is also the form to which the rustic players themselves must resort when put out of their parts by the heckling from their audience. This would illustrate what I believe to be a more general proposition, that alternations between verse and prose in the plays usually have more to do with local contrast, in rhythm or tone, than with any fixed principle such as social degree, sex, or presumed level of politeness. Up to this point in this play, the aristocratic characters, the Duke and his circle, have spoken either blank verse or couplets, while the mechanicals have used prose. In the present scene, with the latter performing a play that purports to be high tragedy, they turn appropriately to rhymed verse, which means that for contrast the court must (or in any case does) turn to prose. Verse, we quickly discover, can be made to sound quite as absurd as the most clownish prose. Nothing intrinsic to either medium requires its employment in any given dramatic context.

To turn to even more momentary kinds of alternation: the final scene of *The Two Gentlemen of Verona* is composed entirely in blank verse, with one significant and startling exception. Valentine's offer to yield his claim in Silvia to the repentant Proteus prompts the disguised Julia to swoon with a cry, 'Oh me vnhappy' (TLN 2208),[2] and with that cry to provoke a flurry of prose, leading to her disclosure of her true identity, by which time, only a few moments later, we are firmly back in the realm of blank verse. In this case the sudden lurch into prose, indicative of the breakdown of the speaker's consciousness, is totally unplanned and unpurposed, comparable in that regard to the much more agonizing moment of Othello's fall into epilepsy, rendered in a totally fragmented and chaotic – as well as nonmetrical – word-jumble.

In *Love's Labour's Lost*, after much blank verse persiflage among the Princess of France and her ladies on their first appearance, all the ceremonial flourish of the King's greeting, 'Faire Princesse, welcom to the Court of *Nauar*', is dashed by the icy water of the Princess's prose reply: 'Faire I giue you backe againe, and welcome I haue not yet: the roofe of this Court is too high to bee yours, and welcome to the wide fields, too base to be mine' (585–9), where the stinging antitheses have the effect of scuttling the King's dignity while underlining that of the Princess. In this case, as not infrequently, the shift from one medium to another, designed to produce a sharp change of tone, is confined to a single speech, following which we return to the momentarily dominant form.

The changeover may also involve a move in the opposite direction, from prose into verse, to mark an emotional heightening. When Viola, in the person of Cesario, woos Olivia for the first time, their dialogue starts in prose; a playful Viola matches wits with a drily mocking Olivia. After her request, however, to see her interlocutor's face, when Olivia unveils, Viola, startled and troubled by the gen- uineness of Olivia's beauty, shifts decisively into verse: 'Excellently done, if God did all' (527). This she really means; she is no longer simply spinning words. Knocked out of her assigned part, she now begins to play it in earnest and with increasing intensity. Olivia for a moment pursues her own bantering vein in prose, until Viola's fervour draws from her, also in verse, a tepid enumeration of Orsino's merits, followed by a slow access of warmth and wonderment, concluding with the embarrassed request that the new go-between return to plead his master's cause. Finally, alone, Olivia confesses – still in verse – that she herself has caught 'the plague', though not, curiously, from Cesario's eloquence but from his 'perfections', which 'creepe in at [her] eyes' (593).

Throughout this scene, as throughout generally, the shifts between verse and prose offer hints and opportunities to actors, to assist them in activating theatrically the dynamics of feeling, the starts and stops, the ceaseless ebbs and flows of it of which Shakespearean dialogue is so characteristically composed. In the scene in question, the shift into verse on Viola's part registers the sudden shock on her of Olivia's unveiled beauty, affording the player a variety of possible ways to represent it. Clearly a change of tone is involved, but what exactly is the new tone? Multiple possibilities present themselves, among which it is the player's obligation, and challenge, to choose.

All these instances represent decisive shifts between one medium and another, where little doubt arises as to which of the two we are dealing with, though there are plays, especially *Love's Labour's Lost* and *A Midsummer Night's Dream*, where the patterning and the alternations not only between verse and prose, but among the various sorts of verse – blank verse, pentameter couplets, interlinked couplets, octosyllabics, stanzaic forms, all interweaving and intertwining – can become bewilderingly intricate, and where Shakespeare is obviously aiming to offer us an abundance of auditory pleasures, to sing and speak to us, like Viola to Orsino, in many sorts of music.

But the prose of the comedies, in addition, has its own stretches of what in an earlier essay I referred to as 'indeterminacy', where Shakespeare seems 'to be composing in a kind of intermediate zone between verse and prose, to be drifting... in a misty mid-region or no-man's-land between [the two] fixed poles'.[3] Though such stretches seem fewer here than in the tragedies, they also seem more often to serve deliberately as transitions from one mode to the other, with verse in the process of losing its metrical precision and disintegrating, so to speak, into prose, or prose tightening up its implicit rhythmicality – realising its full rhythmic potential, one might say – and taking on the stricter, more systematic pulsations of metre.

One such transition occurs in *The Two Gentlemen of Verona*, where the irreverent Speed has been explaining the symptoms of true love to Valentine, in prose. Valentine has been confessing his infatuation with Silvia. When Silvia makes her first appearance, he salutes her with a certain stiff formality: 'Madam & Mistres, a thousand good-morrows.' Speed, scornfully, and, no doubt, aside, responds: 'Oh, 'giue ye-good-ev'n: heer's a million of manners.' Silvia replies to Valentine's greeting in terms similar to his own: 'Sir *Valentine*, and seruant, to you two thousand', prompting another belittling aside from Speed: 'He should giue her interest: & she giues it him.' This last might perhaps be heard as a rough trochaic hexameter before Valentine, finally, moves unequivocally into blank verse: 'As you inioynd me; I haue writ your Letter / Vnto the secret, nameles friend of yours', &c. (489–95). Here the tentative approaches to rhythmic regularity in the initial greetings, and in Speed's second aside, seem to lead into the blank verse that crystallises, at length, with Valentine's report on his letter-writing assignment.

The return to prose a moment later, following Silvia's departure, seems to be accomplished by way of another bridge passage (526–32), as Speed breaks out into a series of tumbling couplets. These tear the blank verse fabric to shreds and form a natural avenue of decomposition through which the language loses its metrical exactness and takes on the irregularity of prose. The passage illustrates another frequent feature of Shakespeare's comic writing: he often uses tumbling verse, loose ragged couplets lacking a fixed or distinct system of stresses, to modulate from prose into verse, by introducing rhyme, or else from verse into prose, by blurring the firmness of the metrical pattern.

Speed, in the first of these stretches, is obviously commenting, like the Athenian courtiers at the playlet, without intending to be overheard by those on whom he is commenting – at least at first. But the clash between verse and prose can also resemble a direct contest of wills, a confrontation in which one character ultimately succeeds in imposing *his* speech habit onto a more compliant one, or one of lower social rank. In *The Taming of the Shrew*, when Petruchio wrangles with the hapless Tailor over the instructions for Katherina's gown, his servant Grumio steps in to second his master. Petruchio having railed at the Tailor in comically furious blank verse, the Tailor, mindful of his self-respect, first defends himself in the same measure: 'Your worship is deceiu'd; the gowne is made / Iust as my master had direction: / *Grumio* gaue order how it should be done.' At this point, I believe, a transition to prose becomes audible. Grumio chimes in in prose to challenge the Tailor's claim: '*Gru.* I gaue him no order, I gaue him the stuffe.' The Tailor, still in blank verse, protests: 'But how did you desire it should be made?' To which Grumio, in prose once more, 'Marrie sir with needle and thred.' The Tailor struggles to preserve his dignity by persisting in the more 'elevated' medium: 'But did you not request to haue it cut?' To which Grumio, now prosing more emphatically, retorts, 'Thou hast fac'd many things.' At this point the Tailor himself collapses into prose, 'I haue' (2101–9), in which manner they continue, through the reading of the 'note of fashion', and Grumio's threat of a duel, until Petruchio moves to settle the question by re-establishing the iambic beat, 'Well sir in breefe the gowne is not for me.'

Grumio, at this point, still in prose, supports his master (or rather, pretends to do so while impudently taking this last statement in the wrong sense): 'You are i'th right sir, 'tis for my mistris.' Petruchio, continuing in blank verse, orders the Tailor to 'Go take it vp vnto thy masters vse', producing another antic intervention, and a last prose outburst, from Grumio, this time feigning to correct his master: 'Villaine, not for thy life: Take vp my Mistresse gowne for thy masters vse [!]', before subsiding finally (more or less) into verse himself (2138–42). Here we have an instructive instance of one character (Grumio) forcing the rhythm of another character (the Tailor) to his own conceit, into prose, and then, having done so, being himself forced back into verse by the pressure of a third character, Petruchio. There is nothing here, surely, which could not be made to sound distinctly by skilled actors.[4]

Generally, in the forest scenes of *As You Like It*, Rosalind and Celia address each other and Orlando in prose. Verse makes its appearance chiefly with Silvius and Phebe, as an instrument of parody. Thus in 4.3, Rosalind's prose complaint about Orlando's tardiness is cut short by the arrival of Silvius, who launches into his doleful pentameters, and is answered in kind by Rosalind. Having read Phebe's versified letter aloud, Rosalind comments scathingly on it and on Silvius's pusillanimity, in prose. The entrance of Oliver with the bloody napkin then introduces a sequence in blank verse, but this too is cut short by Rosalind's swooning (like Julia) into prose, though not without at least one moment of indeterminacy (2318–20): '*Oli.* Be of good cheere youth: you a man? / You lacke a mans heart. / *Ros.* I doe so, I confesse it:' The indeterminacy here may be judged by the fact that three recent editors have treated it in three different ways. Riverside (Evans), following F, prints it as verse; New Arden (Latham) not only prints it all as prose, but does the same with the unmistakably blank verse line that precedes it, '[*Cel.*] I pray you will you take him by the arme' (2317). Pelican (Sargent) does best, I think, with 2317 as verse and 2318–19 as prose.

Further indeterminacy occurs at the climax of the mock duel in *Twelfth Night* (3.4.310–90), preparations for which have reached crisis point when Antonio enters to defend Viola, whom he takes for Sebastian, and is pursued moments later by the arresting Officers. Toby has goaded Sir Andrew to the attack, in prose (with assurances that his terrible opponent has promised not to harm him), to which the terror-stricken Sir Andrew exclaims, 'Pray God he keepe his oath', a three-foot iambic line followed by Viola's blank verse confession, 'I do assure you 'tis against my will', leading into Antonio's first speech, also in blank verse (1826–31). Seconds later,

the Officers having arrested Antonio, again in prose, Antonio, like Sir
Andrew a moment before, responds with a three-foot iambic reply,
'You do mistake me sir', directly followed by the Officer's blank
verse, 'No sir, no iot: I know your fauour well', &c. (1845–46). In
both cases the fragmentary metrical line serves as a bridge from prose
into verse, making the transition less abrupt.

We might note, further, that in the conclusion of this scene, the
dialogue among Sir Toby, Sir Andrew, and Fabian has been so
thoroughly infected by the verse rhythm of Viola's speech concerning
her likeness to her brother that that continues to sound in their own
language. Sir Toby's first words after her exit – 'A very dishonest
paltry boy, [/] and more a coward then a Hare' – are readily heard
as two nearly perfect iambic tetrameters; Sir Andrew's 'Slid Ile after
him againe, and beate him' as an almost perfect 'headless'
pentameter; and Sir Toby's final statement – 'I dare lay any money,
twill be nothing yet' – as a flawless hexameter (1906–16). Despite the
slightly more prevailing prose feel of this little interchange, the
iambic drum does seem still to be beating in it, even as the characters
are doing their best, one might say, to anticipate M. Jourdain and
talk prose.

To turn now to a somewhat different consideration, having to do
with the differences between prose and verse: I am struck, in the case
of the more extended prose speeches, by how highly structured they
often are compared to their verse counterparts. They seem to utilise
visible and audible rhetorical or syntactical patterns as a way of
compensating for the absence of metrical structure. If, for example, in
The Merchant of Venice, we look at Shylock's dialogue with Antonio in
1.3 (following the usual scene division) in the ancecdote about
Jacob's sheep, or in Shylock's reminder of how Antonio has spat on
him, spurned him, and reviled him as a dog, we find the language to
be familiar, lifelike, and conversational, without obvious artificiality.
The blank verse creates a strong rhythmic current which is, however,
unobtrusive; it works on us without in any way requiring our
conscious attention to it.[5]

When we come to his central speech in the play, however, in which
Shylock turns in rage against his tormentors, Solanio and 'Salarino',
we find something very different, something highly patterned,
stamped with unmistakable artifice, a procession of five impassioned
parisonic series. Antonio has '[1] disgrac'd me, and hindred me halfe

a million, laught at my losses, mockt my gaines, scorned my Nation, thwarted my bargaines, cooled my friends, heated mine enemies, and what's the reason? I am a *Iewe*: [2] Hath not a *Iew* eyes? hath not a *Iew* hands, organs, dementions, sences, affections, passions, [3] fed with the same foode, hurt with the same weapons, subiect to the same diseases, healed by the same meanes, warmed and cooled by the same Winter and Sommer as a Christian is: [4] if you pricke vs, doe we not bleede? if you tickle vs, doe we not laugh? if you poison vs doe we not die? and if you wrong vs shall we not reuenge? If we are like you in the rest, we will resemble you in that. [5] If a *Iew* wrong a *Christian*, what is his humility, reuenge? If a *Christian* wrong a *Iew*, what should his sufferance be by Christian example, why reuenge? The villanie you teach me I will execute, and it shall goe hard but I will better the instruction' (1266–83). Each of these series, with its own inner intricacies, such as the various antitheses, 'laught at my losses, mockt my gaines', 'cooled my friends, heated mine enemies', &c., or the anaphora on 'if' in series 4 and 5 – thus leads to its own local climax, and the whole sequence to a towering summary climax.

What we find on this occasion, as often in Shylock's prose, is not metrical regularity, but a form of syntactic regularity, always shifting slightly – very much as metre, skilfully handled, always shifts slightly from off dead centre so as not to sound mechanical. It is played with, interfered with in small details so as to forestall rigid symmetry, but nevertheless offering as insistent a pattern for the ear and mind as rhyme or metre, if not more so. To be sure, Shylock in the first scene is in a self-confident, expansive mood, being earnestly sued to for the desired loan by an enemy who has momentary need of him. Under the circumstances he is at peace with himself and sure of himself. In the later scene he has been tormented by Jessica's flight and enraged by the theft of his casket, so that he is nearly wild with grievance, on top of which salt is being rubbed into his wounds by the jeers of the two 'Gentlemen'. Shakespeare has chosen to cast his despairing fury into this overwrought prose outburst, in which the very ostenta-tiousness of the rhetorical structure serves as an index to the intensity of the speaker's anguish.

In the same play, the opening dialogue between Portia and Nerissa, in prose, is marked by a highly visible logicality. The language swarms with logical devices, such as the explanatory particle 'for', and the clincher 'therefore', in addition to formulae like 'as...as', 'if x then y', 'more x than y', 'neither x nor y'. These often appear in combination, as in 'If I could bid the fift welcome with so good heart as I can bid the other foure farewell, I should be glad of his approach: if he haue the condition of a Saint, and the complexion of a diuell, I had rather hee should shriue me then wiue me' (318–22), where, again, the syntactic skeleton is elaborated and underscored by the parisonic correspondences. Yet if we look at Portia's verse speeches, such as that on the quality of mercy, or those she addresses to Bassanio or Lorenzo at Belmont, we find not an absence of logic, certainly, but rather that the logical pattern is so muted, so fully absorbed into the texture of the verse that it never forces itself into our consciousness as it does in these prose passages.

In the scene following, in which Shylock talks to Bassanio about Antonio's scattered ships, including the 'rats' that threaten them, and about the ways in which he, Shylock, will or will not consort with the Christians, structure is provided by quite different means, by what we may recognise as a peculiarly Shylockian vein of iteration, the repetition of the same phrase-ending in successive phrases ('epistrophe'), those phrases further stiffened by parison: 'I will buy with you, sell with you, talke with you, walke with you, and so following: but I will not eate with you, drinke with you, nor pray with you' (359–61).

Launcelot Gobbo's first speech, an extended soliloquy (568–95), displays its own structure in another way, in the competing voices through which Launcelot dramatises the conflicting impulses in his mind, allocating one voice to his conscience, one to the devil, and one to a third party, 'himself'.

From the Falstaff of *The Merry Wiues of Windsor* we hear still a further sort of prose structure in the knight's recital of his late misfortunes, cast into the chill Thames along with Mistress Ford's foul linen: 'Haue I liu'd to be carried in a Basket like a barrow of butchers Offal?... The rogues slighted me into the riuer with as little remorse, as they would haue drown'de a blinde bitches Puppies... my bellies as cold as if I had swallow'd snow-bals, for pilles to coole the reines' (1683–1700). A few moments later, expostulating on the same theme to 'Master Brook': 'I suffered the pangs of three seuerall deaths: First, an intollerable fright, to be detected with a jealous rotten Bell-weather: Next to be compass'd like a good Bilbo in the circumstance of a Pecke, hilt to point, heele to head [i.e., bent double like a flexible sword]... And then to be stopt in like a strong distillation with stinking Cloathes... thinke of that, that am as subiect to heate as butter; a man of continuall dissolution, and thaw...more then halfe stew'd in grease (like a Dutch-dish) to be throwne into the Thames, and coold, glowing-hot, in that serge like a Horse-shoo; thinke of that; hissing hot' (1774–88).

What distinguishes Falstaff's speech here is the abundance and vitality of his figurative language, the outpouring of picturesque similes with which he laments the outrage to his flesh and the vulnerability of his corporeal being: 'like a barrow of butchers Offal', 'with as little remorse as they would haue drown'de a blinde bitches Puppies', 'as cold as if I had swallow'd snow-bals', 'detected with a iealious rotten Bell-weather', 'compass'd like a good Bilbo in the circumference of a Pecke', 'like a strong distillation with stinking Cloathes', 'as subject to heate as butter', 'stew'd in grease (like a Dutch-dish)', 'coold, glowing-hot...like a Horse-shoo...hissing hot', etc.

Most often, then, it is the prose speeches that seem not merely to utilise but to luxuriate in patterning. Even in much briefer and more local instances, we often find the same phenomenon. From a scene already discussed, we might contrast the striking rhetorical structure of some of Viola's initial prose speeches to Olivia – e.g., 'I bring no ouerture of warre, no taxation of homage; I hold the Olyffe in my hand; my words are as full of peace, as matter' (502–4); or 'The rudenesse that hath appear'd in mee, haue I learn'd from my entertainment. What I am, and what I would, are as secret as maiden-head: to your eares, Diuinity; to any others, prophanation' (507–10) – where we even hear an elaborate syntactic inversion ('the rudeness...haue I learn'd') of a sort often thought of as 'poetical' – with her verse speeches a moment later following the revelation of Olivia's beauty: 'Lady, you are the cruell'st shee aliue, / If you will leade these graces to the graue, / And leaue the world no copie' (532–4), &c. – so striking in its simplicity and naturalness, its total absence of flourish.

Finally, in a perhaps slightly more ambiguous example, we may turn to the two speeches of Prince Hal that frame his initial appearance in *1 Henry 4*: First, his opening reply to Falstaff's question concerning the time of day: 'Thou art so fat-witted with drinking of olde Sacke, and vnbuttoning thee after Supper, and sleeping vpon Benches in the afternoone that thou hast forgotten to demand that truely, which thou wouldest truly know. What a diuell hast thou to do with the time of the day? vnlesse houres were cups of Sacke, and minutes Capons, and clockes the tongues of Bawdes, and dialls the signes of Leaping-houses, and the blessed Sunne himselfe a faire hot Wench in Flame-colour'd Taffata; I see no reason, why thou shouldest be so superfluous, to demaund the time of the day' (116–26). This comic onslaught so bristles with structure, with its tight logical framework and its figures of climax, that it has lent itself more than once to being cited and diagrammed, by way of contrast to a more realistic kind of prose, and as a superlative instance of high symmetricality combined with flexibility.[6] One might almost describe it as a demonstration piece in how language can be used with improvisatory aplomb while at the same time adopting, and flaunting, many of the prized devices of schoolbook rhetoric.

Hal's verse soliloquy at the end of the same scene, by contrast, a more premeditated address to his tavern mates, the audience, and himself, shows some of the same traits as the verse speeches of Shylock and Portia: despite a firm logical substructure, and despite its grave formality, it totally lacks the swagger, the gaudiness and boister-ousness of the address to Falstaff. In his initial speech, Hal is rubbing Falstaff's nose, and ours, in his mastery of language. He is deliberately making language *perform*. The words come tumbling forth, and they do his bidding. In the soliloquy, on the other hand, this bravura element is lacking. While giving us the fruit of prior reflection and pondered planning, Hal maintains a steady, quiet focus on the plan itself, its purposes and its hoped-for effects. He is not, this time, making language turn handsprings, or engaging in performative acrobatics for our amusement.

Clearly none of the effects just mentioned is in itself peculiar to prose. With any of the prose passages from Shylock mentioned above, for example, we might compare Shylock's refusal to accept the repayment of his loan from Antonio: 'Ile haue my bond, speake not against my bond, / I haue sworne an oath that I will haue my bond (1690–1); or again, 'Ile haue my bond, I will not heare thee speake, / Ile haue my bond, and therefore speake no more' (1698–99). Here we have the same harping on a single key word that we sometimes find in his prose speeches, only now in metrical guise. The difference lies chiefly in the greater elaborateness and extensiveness of the repetitions in the prose.

I think we must conclude then that Shakespeare's prose neither obeys nor does it illustrate Roman Jakobson's distinction between prose and verse, according to which verse is based on metaphor, on

likenesses between things, and prose on metonymy, on the connections and contiguities between things.[7] To me it seems rather that
prose is used, much oftener than verse, as the medium for verbal
hijinks, verbal fireworks, and verbal filigree, while verse serves more
often as the vehicle for the nuts and bolts with which the actions and
the passions of the plot are put together. The fact however that
counter-examples may nearly always be found to discredit hard-and-
fast distinctions serves chiefly to remind us that no matter how
cleverly we may think we have driven Shakespeare into a corner and
made him abide our question, he always manages to find a loophole
through which to wriggle free and mock our efforts.

NOTES

1 The fact that Pistol's speeches are sometimes misprinted as prose (in Q,
a bad quarto) or mislineated (in F), and the fact that he is mimicking the
rant he has picked up in the theatre, does not alter the more overriding
fact that most of his dialogue remains 'relentlessly iambic'. We can
refuse to call it 'poetry' if we so decide, but there seems no way to
withhold the less honorific, more neutral label 'verse'. But see on this
point George T. Wright, *Shakespeare's Metrical Art* (Berkeley, 1988),
110–11.

2 Citations from Shakespeare will be to *The Norton Facsimile: The First
Folio*, ed. Charlton Hinman (New York, 1968), with parenthetical line
references keyed to Hinman's through-line numbering.

3 Jonas Barish, 'Mixed Prose–Verse Scenes in Shakespearean Tragedy',
Shakespeare and Dramatic Tradition: Essays in Honor of S. F. Johnson, eds.
W. R. Elton and William B. Long (Newark, Del., 1989), 41.

4 I realise that one might perhaps hear Grumio's first two answers as
scannable tetrameters, the first with an iamb followed by three anapests
– 'I gaue him no order, I gaue him the stuffe' – the second lacking the
unstressed upbeat in the first foot – 'Marrie sir with needle and thred'
– and ending with an anapest – but both these imperfectly metrical lines
collide with and jar against the Tailor's grave regularity rather than in
any way complementing it or harmonising with it. The upshot is that
Grumio's prose retorts wreck the Tailor's blank verse, unless the actor is
determined to have it otherwise, and so wrenches it.

5 On iambic pentameter as the 'most speechlike' of English metres, see
Wright, *Shakespeare's Metrical Art*, 1–16.

6 Jonas Barish, *Ben Jonson and the Language of Prose Comedy* (Cambridge,
Mass., 1960), 45–6; Brian Vickers, *The Artistry of Shakespeare's Prose*
(London, 1968), 91–2.

7 'Two Aspects of Language and Two Types of Aphasic Disturbances', in
Krystyna Pomorska and Stephen Rudy, eds., *Language in Literature*
(Cambridge, Mass., 1987), 95–114.

Much Ado About Nothing: *the unsociable comedy*

Barbara Everett

Social workers sometimes speak of people 'falling through the net'. That's what it can seem that *Much Ado About Nothing* has done, critically speaking. Audiences and readers rarely like it quite as much as the two comedies by Shakespeare which follow it, *As You Like It* and *Twelfth Night*: they feel that by comparison it lacks some sort of magic. Professional critics can take this vague disappointment much further, almost echoing the nineteenth-century charge that the heroine Beatrice is an 'odious woman'. In case it appears that we have changed all that, it may be worth mentioning that what is probably still the only full-length handbook on the play describes Beatrice (at least in her earlier unreformed phase) as 'self-centred', 'the embodiment of pride', a person who '*cannot love*', 'a crippled personality, the very antithesis of the outgoing, self-giving character [Shakespeare] values most highly'. Nor is this study by J. R. Mulryne exceptional. A leading paperback edition cites it approvingly and itself describes both Benedick and Beatrice as 'posing', 'showing themselves off as a preparation for mating'; and it regrets that this pair of lovers fails to 'arouse in an audience the warmth of feeling' evoked by a Portia or a Rosalind. The writer of this Introduction, R. A. Foakes, can only conclude that 'The contrast between [Claudio and Hero] and Beatrice and Benedick was surely designed in part to expose the limitations of both couples.'

'This lookes not like a nuptiall', Benedick murmurs helpfully as the catastrophic Wedding Scene of *Much Ado* gets under way: and the reader of the play's criticism can often feel the same. Particularly given that we are considering a love-comedy by Shakespeare, the remarks I have quoted all seem to me to be startling judgements. For opinions to differ so much can provoke useful thought. Perhaps Shakespeare's mature comedies, once recommended literary fodder

for school-children on the grounds of their charming pure-minded
simplicity, are – whatever their other characteristics – not so simple
after all. When Shakespeare first staged *Much Ado*, fairly certainly in
1598 or '99, he was coming to the end of a decade of extraordinary
achievement and invention. The first Tragedies, the earlier Histories
and Comedies lay behind him, *The Merchant of Venice* immediately
preceded *Much Ado*, and Shakespeare had probably written most of
both parts of *Henry IV*. The dramatist of *The Merchant of Venice* and
Henry IV was in no way unsophisticated or unambitious. If he gave
the three comedies we now choose to call 'mature' his most
throwaway titles, they aren't throwaway plays. Possessed as they are
of a profound sense and vitality which suggest the popular audience
they were written for, their lightness nonetheless recalls that
'negligent grace' (*sprezzatura*) which the aristocratic culture of the
Renaissance aspired to. The very unpretension of *Much Ado About
Nothing*, its affectionate straightforward transparency have been
invented to deal with human experience dense enough and real
enough to produce notably different reactions from given human
beings.

These comedies have become so familiar that it can be hard to
think of them freshly. I want therefore to begin by approaching *Much
Ado* from a slightly unexpected angle – because sometimes, when we
are surprised, we see things more clearly. I'm going to start by
thinking about one of the comedy's textual cruces, involving a few
words spoken by Leonato in the first scene of Act 5. An interestingly
shaped play, whose structural rhythm the dramatist was to use again
in *Othello* (a fact which alone may say something about the work's
seriousness), *Much Ado* has its main plot's climax, which turns out to
be a pseudo- or anti-climax, in Act 4: in the big, bustling, peopled
and very social Wedding Scene, which sees the gentle Hero, unjustly
shamed by the machinations of the villains, publicly humiliated and
jilted by her courtly fiancé Claudio – though the fidelity to her of her
witty though here grieving cousin, Beatrice, brings to Beatrice's side
her own lover, the humorous Benedick.

In marked contrast, Act 5 opens with a quiet scene between two
suddenly aged men, Hero's father Leonato and his brother Antonio.
Critics have often thought it the most feeling moment in a drama they
otherwise find cool. Leonato rebuffs his brother's philosophical
comfort; he will be stoical, Leonato says bitterly, only if so advised by
one who has suffered precisely as, and as much as, himself:

> If such a one will smile and stroke his beard...
> Patch griefe with proverbs, make misfortune drunke
> With candle-wasters: bring him yet to me,
> And I of him will gather patience.

I have edited this, cutting out a line which both the early texts, the 1600 Quarto and the 1623 Folio, are agreed on, but which the great late-Victorian New Variorum edition fills two and a half of its large minutely printed pages of Notes discussing: and which all modern editors emend, in various slightly unconvincing ways. In the authentic texts, Leonato says that his despised comforter would be one to

> stroke his beard,
> And sorrow, wagge, crie hem, when he should grone,
> Patch griefe with proverbs

— and so on.

I want to talk for a few moments about what I think Leonato really said (which is not quite what modern editors make him say). It's necessary to add that, as the New Variorum records in its textual apparatus, fortunately or unfortunately an excellent American scholar named Grant White printed in his edition of 1854 the emendation I'm going to propose: but, since he dropped the emendation in his second edition, and didn't explain or gloss it in the first place, the field remains reasonably clear. He thought, and I too had thought independently, that Leonato describes his would-be comforter angrily as 'sorrow's wagge' – 'And, sorrow's wagge, crie hem, when he should grone': a compositorial mistake very easy to account for; for, in the old Secretary hand which Shakespeare had learned to write in, the terminal letter 's' to a word was written as a kind of scrawled loop very like a topped comma. Let the comma lose its top because of a shortage of ink and the text reads just as in the Quarto and Folio.

It's an interesting fact that the editor of the New Variorum, the scholar Furness, urges us to find these early texts 'irredeemably corrupt' – not even to try, that is, to emend their version of the line. And he does so because the line shocks him as it stands. No editor, however authoritative (he says) 'can ever persuade me that Shakespeare put such words, at this passionate moment, into Leonato's mouth. There is a smack of comicality about "wag" which is ineffaceable.'

There is indeed. But perhaps Shakespeare put it there. The seriousness, even the genius of *Much Ado* may be to bring in precisely that 'smack of comicality' where we least expect it – just as its dramatist invents peculiarly English constables for his Sicilian play, to stumble fat-headedly into arresting the villains and bringing about the play's happy ending. A 'wag' is a word and a social phenomenon that is nearly obsolete now, though I can remember my own mother using it drily, with something of Furness's rebuke. A wag is or was a person who habitually, even desperately, tries to be funny. But in Shakespeare's time the word hadn't progressed to this degraded condition – it had not, so to speak, grown up: it remained the 'little tine boy' of Feste's song. For the most familiar colloquial usage of 'wag' in the poet's own day was in the tender phrase, 'Mother's wag'. The word denoted a mischievous small prankster, amusingly naughty as little boys often are. Only a few years before *Much Ado*, Greene in his *Menaphon* has, 'Mothers wagge, prettie boy' – and Falstaff calls Hal his 'sweet Wagge' in Part I of *Henry IV*.

Leonato says that the father who, having lost a child, could still find or accept words of comfort would be 'Sorrow's wagge': he means the man would be himself a child, immature. And the phrase has an element of oxymoron that defines his shock and outrage. Like Furness after him, this decently conventional, hierarchical, even conservative old man thinks that certain conjunctions of what they would have called the grave and the gay, of grief and humour, are 'irredeemably corrupt'.

Before we agree with them both, we ought perhaps to pause and ask whether Shakespeare has not shaped this encounter of the two old men so as to prevent us doing just that. The 'passionate moment' which the Victorian editor points to is surely something odder than passionate – and is odd in a way that is relevant. For (and this is my chief topic here) *Much Ado About Nothing*'s real achievement may be to make us think very hard indeed about this quality of the 'passionate' in human beings.

In this scene, Leonato and Antonio wear something that is easy to call, at sight, the dignity of the bereaved; and they wear it consciously. But this is odd because, though Hero may be disgraced, she is certainly not dead. And both Leonato and Antonio know it. Moreover, we in the audience know that even Hero's disgrace is rapidly melting into air: for the grieving scene is linked to the Church Scene by, and is immediately preceded by, the comic bridge-scene in which the ludicrous constables – the more senior proclaiming, with something of Leonato's own self-important fury, that he 'hath had losses' – have apprehended the villains and are at this moment hotfoot bringing a full disclosure to Leonato.

Later in this Fifth Act, Don Pedro and Claudio will make solemn acknowledgement at the quasi-tomb of Hero. This action has its own meaning – the moment's music allows the gesture a dimension of the symbolic: the scene mutedly articulates some sadness which all grown-up 'understanders' of this highly civilised, social comedy know to be intrinsic to most passion seeking social embodiment. In the very preceding scene, 5.2, Benedick has lightly told Beatrice that she doesn't live in 'the time of good neighbours', if it ever existed; that 'if a man doe not erect in this age his owne tombe ere he dies, hee shall live no longer in monuments, then the Bels ring, & the Widdow weepes' – i.e., not long. But symbols are one thing, and facts another, even in our greatest poetic dramatist. Hero still isn't dead. And the fact that she isn't, and that we know that she isn't, and that her family, too, know that she isn't, turns this grieving ceremony at the tomb into something like the masked dances which characterise this sophisticated comedy: an art, a game, a pretence – a deception exonerated by having been proposed in good faith and by a man, so to speak, of the cloth.

Much Ado's tomb-trick may in short be considered as not unlike those bed-tricks in the two later, much darker comedies, *Measure for Measure* and *All's Well That Ends Well*. Greater, much more intense, these two plays tell us far more about Shakespeare's interest in the tragi-comic – though neither they, nor any other play written by him is truly identifiable with the genre as the Continental aristocracy of the period knew it. But *Much Ado* shares one striking characteristic with them. It has the tragi-comic concern with love in society, a society for which some version of the political, the power-issue, is serious: a world which defers to Courtship and to social hierarchy. From this point of view, the tomb-trick is like the bed-tricks in working as a special kind of 'good deceit' or virtuous untruth, a device of worldly accommodation in a light but moral art. The clever courtiers, with Don Pedro at their head, have descended on Leonato's provincial family, and have done these simpler if still socially aspiring people some harm. Now the tables are pleasingly turned, the foolers are fooled, and Leonato and Antonio regain something of their lost honour merely by the silent superiority of knowing what they know.

But if this is conceded, something else must follow. The tomb-trick is peculiarly like those forms of wise comfort (and the word comfort actually means 'self-strengthening') angrily rejected in the grieving scene by the passionate Leonato. The music of the tomb-scene, shortly after, though saying nothing true, can still both calm and resolve. It thus performs the act at first denied by Leonato in the scene I started from: it can, like the wag's wisdom, 'Charme ache with ayre, and agony with words'. While the old man scorns sorrow's wags, something wise in the play embraces them.

I have used the word 'embrace' here deliberately – and not only because it is a love-comedy we are concerned with. For Elizabethans, the chief image of Love itself was as a 'wag': as the Puck-like armed baby, Cupid – naughtily dangerous, even disturbing to the coolly rationalistic eye of the Renaissance, yet in these comedies also the medium of great good. Puck himself is, after all, in the service of Oberon the King. Yet Puck moves in the night, 'Following darkenesse like a dreame', and the wood where the lovers wander is a distressing and frightening place. These complexities make Shakespeare's Love, and love's Happiness, a pair of twins, springing from the circumstances of sorrow: sorrow's wags.

I am hoping to suggest that in this casual phrase, a local crux in the text of a light comedy, we have some suggestion of the kind of rich complexity, of fruitful half-paradox, which gives *Much Ado* the vitality and depth by which it now survives. The comedy's Italian director, Franco Zeffirelli, once referred to it as a 'very dull play'. And *Much Ado* is indeed simple if we compare it, for instance, to its predecessor *The Merchant of Venice*. But that play's fascinating intellectual battles, its energy of contrasts embodied in Portia and Shylock, the market-place and Belmont, leave behind at the end a disquieting dissatisfaction, a sense of something unjust or unresolved. This is a subject I shall return to. For the moment I want only to suggest that *Much Ado* may have chosen to be a 'very dull play', to be simple to the eye.

But its simplicity is a solidity. Shakespeare uses the *novelle* sources from which he has taken his main plot to generate a special, almost novelistic sense of the real, of a world where people live together to a degree that is socially and psychologically convincing, and new in the poet's work. And this realistic, even novelistic comedy deepens itself by containing, indeed we may say, with Leonato in mind, by *embracing* contradictions everywhere beneath its smooth and civil surface. If there is, to Leonato's mind, a troubling indecorum, an unconventionality in the juxtapositions, momentarily glimpsed by him, of sorrow with joy and of play with love, then it has to be said that such vital oppositions pervade the play, and are its life. Let me touch on one famous passage. At one point Don Pedro finds himself proposing marriage to Beatrice. He does not love her, nor she him. He has been led into it by his belief in the kindness of his own impeccable manners: a self-defeating trap from which he is released by Beatrice, who of course has led him into it in the first place, with the neat licentious speed of some brilliant Court Fool. Panting slightly, the courtly Don Pedro tells Beatrice that she was 'born in a merry howre'. She wins again, both wittily and touchingly: 'No sure my Lord, my Mother cried, but then there was a starre daunst, and under that was I borne.' This nicely hints at some of the reasons why this (to my mind) superb heroine has been and can still be disliked by a whole host of male scholars, both past and present. She is Shakespeare's true heroine, woman as 'wag', the sharp and comical child of sorrow.

Beatrice does something far more waggish than merely walking along a razor's edge of good behaviour with a visiting grandee. Indecorum is embodied in the fact that she and her story, which a formal criticism calls 'the sub-plot', take over the play, edging aside the main-plot story of Claudio and Hero. It's well known that Charles I wrote against the title of his text of the play 'Benedik and Betrice', and the sympathy of most succeeding readers has agreed with him. But the high originality of this comic structure can leave editors behind. Much in accord with the New Penguin Introduction which I quoted earlier, the New Arden confronts as the chief critical problem the question, 'What can or should be done to balance the play?' and proposes as answer: 'Hero and Claudio can gain in prominence; Benedick and Beatrice can be less salient.' But perhaps the comedy has its own balance, which can only be impaired by these adjustments: and this balance has to do with the delicate poise of energies suggested by the phrase, 'sorrow's wag'. I have lingered over this conceit because of all it can suggest about the essential principles involved in a Shakespearean comedy: principles necessitating both light and dark, both seriousness and laughter.

It can be a struggle to explain why these romantic comedies carry the value that they do – why, seeming to be 'About Nothing' (as their ironic or nonchalant titles suggest) they nonetheless evoke from those who truly like them, words like 'true' or 'brilliant' or 'profound'. The 'Nothing' of the *Much Ado* title is now, of course, somewhat undercut by our understanding that Elizabethans could pronounce 'Nothing' as 'Noting'. The plot of the comedy certainly turns on what this pun implies: note-taking, spying, eavesdropping. No other play in Shakespeare introduces so much eavesdropping – each new turn of the action depends on it. The confusions of Don Pedro's wooing of Hero for his protégé Claudio, the machinations by which his bastard brother Don John deceives Claudio into believing Hero unchaste, the trick by which Beatrice and Benedick are persuaded that each loves the other, the discovery of the villains by the comic constables – all these are effected by the incessant system of eavesdropping. Yet underneath the noting there is nothing. The play's first act is filled by a flurry of redoubled misunderstanding which scholars often assume to be textual confusion or revision. This seems to me a mistake. The dramatist plainly wanted his comedy to be this way: he wanted the world he had invented to be swept through by these currents of pointless energetic bewilderment. Later, after all, he almost unwinds the villainy of the mainplot before our eyes, by having the pretend-Hero address her villainous lover as 'Claudio', a naming which would have left the heroine all but guiltless. Shakespeare's change of all his sources in this main plot is important here: what they presented as evidence, he converts to mere inference. An editor once complained that the omission of the 'Window Scene' does an injustice to Claudio. Perhaps; but it was meant to. And this stress in Shakespeare's play on the insecurities of mere social inference even touches the other lovers. In the last scene, the obdurately individual Beatrice and Benedick show signs of being as near as makes no matter to a readiness to back out of each other's arms: loving each other 'no more then reason', 'in friendly recompence', taking each other 'for pittie', yielding 'upon great perswasion'.

Much Ado About Nothing reminds us, both as title and play, that, though life is indeed serious, most human beings pass much of their time in little things, unseriousness; that the ordinary, social fabric of life can be very thin, made up of trivia, and we can often feel a kind of real nothingness underneath ('hee shall live no longer in monuments, then the Bels ring, & the Widdow weepes... an hower in clamour and a quarter in rhewme'). Benedick's light definition of human void is a striking one, peculiarly apt in the theatrical world which has produced it, where revels are always 'now...ended'. He evokes it in a context congenital to Shakespearean comedy, that of the presence or absence of real human feeling: love in a world which is defined as recognisably *not* 'the time of good neighbours', and in which the sound of the bells is short, of weeping even shorter.

Shakespeare's comedies are a 'Nothing' concerned with serious things: and these serious things are the principles of true human feeling, in a world in which a wise man knows that so much is nothing. To be at ease in such reflections demands at once ironic detachment and feeling participation. Consonantly, if we are trying to describe the power, the real survival-value of even the poet's earliest comedies, it has to do with his ability to bring laughter together with tenderness. We think of Launce and his dog in *The Two Gentlemen of Verona*; of the tough slapstick of *The Taming of the Shrew*, resolving into Katherine's sober devotion; or the weeping of the angrily jealous Adriana in the brilliant fast farce of *The Comedy of Errors*. The coolest and most intellectual of aristocratic revues, *Love's Labour's Lost* ends with a father dead and Berowne sent, in the name of love, to 'move wilde laughter in the throate of death'; and it includes the memory of a girl, Katherine's sister, who died of love: 'He made her melancholy, sad, and heavy, and so she died: had she beene Light like you, of such a merrie nimble stirring spirit, she might a bin a Grandam ere she died.' Titania, similarly, in *A Midsummer Night's Dream*, tells of her loyalty to the friend who died in childbirth, like so many Elizabethan women:

> she being mortall, of that boy did die,
> And for her sake I doe reare up her boy,
> And for her sake I will not part with him.

I quoted Beatrice's 'No sure my Lord, my Mother cried.' Immediately after, with Beatrice sent out of the room, Leonato tells that, by Hero's report, Beatrice has 'often dreamt of unhappinesse, and wakt her selfe with laughing'. Something very similar might be said of Shakespeare's comedies in themselves: their character from the beginning has to do with finding a way of being 'sorrow's wag'. His art recognises the interdependence of the dark and the light in life, especially at those points of love and friendship where feeling is most acute, and often most complex. The mature comedies seek to perfect a style or condition in which happiness exists not just despite unhappiness but through it, because of it, yet charitably and sympathetically, like Patience smiling at grief. There must in the end be the co-existence, the smiling and the grief. In *The Merchant of Venice*, for all its brilliance, there is no final co-existence: something has been sacrificed to the desired achievement of extreme contra-rieties, of the play of light and dark. As the sociable Bassanio has to use the lonely loving Antonio, so in the end the golden Portia must destroy the embittered, dark-housed Shylock, the greatest personage in the comedies.

It's in the art of co-existence that *Much Ado's* supremacy lies: this, the first of Shakespeare's mature comedies in which very different human beings believably live together. Its 'dullness' (to quote Zeffirelli) is only the prosaic quality of the novel as against the poem. Yet this temperate, equable and witty world Shakespeare has created has surprising resonances, depths and possibilities. If prose is the comedy's dominant medium, the work's very coherence and inven-tiveness is a poetic achievement of a high kind.

That creativity is first manifested by Shakespeare's making of 'Messina'. That the dramatist calls his play's setting Messina, and makes his elderly Leonato, father to Hero and uncle to Beatrice, Governor of it, does not have to be taken too seriously – seriously in the sense of literally. 'Messina' is any romantic place lived in by rich and relatively important people. But, off the literal level, 'Messina' has extraordinary self-consistency and convincingness. The fantasy-place also functions as the grounding of the real; and, immediately below the surface, things hold together. I will give one small example from the first lines of the play: it says something about the way the poet's imagination has worked on his fantasy-place, and may even give some hint as to why Shakespeare chose this Sicilian port as his locality. *Much Ado* begins with the descent of grand visitors, heralded by formal letter and Gentleman-Messenger, on the excited and grateful Leonato: the visitors being the well-born and triumphant young warriors, Don Pedro and friends. The stage 'Messina' is thus flooded by a desired and aspired-to standard of Court behaviour, one evidenced in the battle just won (the chief occupation of a Court culture was warfare); and also in the good manners everywhere, the formal wit, the letters, the vivid sense of worldly hierarchies.

But directly this Court standard is initiated, we feel its ambiguity. Don Pedro brings with him the brother he has just defeated, the villainous Don John. The opening words of the drama speak of the distinguished visitor by his Spanish title – he is '*Don Peter* of *Arragon*';

and his brother Don John's title can hardly fail to remind an Elizabethan audience of that Don John of Austria who was similarly a Spaniard, a natural son of Philip II. Oddly enough, it was at the port of Messina that the fleets gathered before the great battle of Lepanto, where 'Don John of Austria' rode 'to the wars'. Catholic Spain was at Lepanto the defender of what Renaissance Christians held to be true civilisation against the barbarian hordes of the East. But she was also the lasting, unchanging threat to English supremacy at sea – and she represented a Church thought by many of Protestant Elizabeth's subjects to be wickedly authoritarian: a double face, as the play's courtliness will shift between light and dark.

For, though Leonato welcomes Don Pedro's visit as a high honour, Don Pedro brings with him the bastard brother, Don John, the at least nominal source of all the play's troubles, his dark, surly, lonely ill-nature an interesting shadow to Don Pedro's all-too-glittering sociality. And young Claudio, Don Pedro's friend, is as amiably disagreeable as he is conventional. It is entirely unsurprising that he should later indicate his interest in Hero by making certain that she is her father's heir; that his deception by the villains should be as rapid as his consequent repentance; and that the girl he readily accepts at Leonato's hand as second bride should be 'Another Hero'. In the triviality of their love is the necessary stability of their society.

The story of his two independent individualists, Beatrice and Benedick, Shakespeare seems to have invented for himself. But the main Hero-and-Claudio plot of his play he took from the great stock of international Renaissance romance. These facts are perhaps suggestive: they may tell us something about the kind of world Shakespeare saw himself creating in this comedy of 'Much Ado'. 'Messina' is a figure for the most courtly, most worldly aspirations of ordinary people. The society of 'Messina' is governed by decorum, convention and fashion. Its only alternative, bred within itself, is the hostile isolationist Don John, the lawless brother who has determined 'not to sing in my cage'. Everyone else does sing in the cage – the cage being Leonato's great house with its arbour-full of secrets for a garden, a world of spiky high-level chatter where formal compliments intertwine with informal insults. It's not surprising that the comic policemen get the impression that the villains are led by one Deformed, a man of some fashion. Even Shakespeare himself sings in his cage: amusedly inventing at one point the babble of *Vogue* magazine, telling us that Hero's wedding-dress will be worth ten of the Dutchesse of Millaine's 'cloth a gold and cuts, and lac'd with silver, set with pearles, downe sleeves, side sleeves, and skirts, round underborn with a blewish tinsel'.

'Messina' is tinsel itself, and yet very real. It can't be satirised or politicised out of existence, nor even assumed to be a mere preserve of the rich. The constables who enter the play in its third act to resolve the problems of their nominal superiors are just as much given to chat and argument as anyone else in Messina, and as interested too in social status. They are rustic, obdurately English instead of Sicilian, and often very funny ('We will rather sleepe than talke, wee know what belongs to a Watch' – 'Nothing' operates here, too). 'Messina' represents a mundane if aspiring social reality which we recognise at sight: that social world which is, as Wordsworth remarked, the 'world/Of all of us', and in it, we 'find our happiness, or not at all'. When Benedick resolves to marry, he remarks briskly that 'the world must be peopled', and we all (of course) laugh. Yet he is serious too; and this is what *Much Ado* portrays in 'Messina' – the world of people that 'must be peopled'.

This wonderfully real and recognisable world Shakespeare brings alive in the very style and structure of his comedy. 'Messina' talks a fine and formal, conversational yet mannered prose, which in the genuinely intelligent becomes admirably flexible. Only those who are unusually deeply moved (Beatrice in love, Hero's family in and after the Church Scene) speak in verse, and that not often. The play is a very Elizabethan work, yet it sometimes sounds to the ear almost like Restoration Comedy, at moments even like Wilde. Its structure has the same tacit expressiveness. The action falls naturally into Messina's large crowded scenes of social encounter – the opening arrival of the soldiers, the evening dance in mask, the church wedding, the final celebration. It is because of these thronged and bustling scenes that the moment when Benedick and Beatrice speak their love to each other, left alone on the stage after the interrupted marriage, has such startling effect.

Despite the eventfulness of what we call the main plot, nothing really happens to the more social characters of the play, who are precisely defined as people to whom nothing can happen (hence, 'Another Hero'). Late in the play, after Hero has been cruelly rejected on her wedding-day and is believed to be dead by all but her family and friends, there is a decidedly subtle and embarrassing encounter between the young men, as Don Pedro and Claudio think to take up again their old verbal teasing of Benedick, and can't realise by how much he has now outgrown it. This unawareness is the continuity of the social, the process by which it survives: 'Messina' lives in a perpetual present, where salvation depends on the power to forget. It has all been, after all, 'Much Ado About Nothing'. And yet there is of course an exception to this. Beatrice and Benedick do change. And the index of this change, their falling in love, is the great subject of the comedy.

Beatrice and Benedick are most certainly inhabitants of Messina. Hero's cousin and Claudio's friend, they belong in their world, possessed by a social realism summed up in Beatrice's 'I can see a Church by daylight.' Moreover, there is a real sense in which we are glad to see the cousins and friends join hands again at the end of the play, with a sensible patient warmth foreshadowing that romantic yet worldly wisdom which keeps the families joined, if at some distance, at the end of *Pride and Prejudice*.

Yet Beatrice and Benedick do still change. Modern Shakespeareans who work assiduously to banish this change, to work the hero and heroine back into those borders of the action from which they come, seem to me to be in serious error, and to be breaking the back of a work of art. *Much Ado*'s very originality of action and structure, that power of mind which animates Shakespeare's lightest comedies, here depends on the growing importance of two people who, though their intelligence gives them authority from the beginning, are socially on the margins of the action, subordinate in interest to the possibly younger Hero and Claudio. But, where the trick played on Claudio by Don John destroys his shallow love for Hero, Don Pedro's fooling only releases real depths of feeling in Beatrice and Benedick, the two unsociable individuals who think themselves determined to resist the enforcements of matrimony.

There has been in much recent criticism a comparable resistance to the originality of *Much Ado* itself, one evidenced by the repeated insistence that Beatrice and Benedick do not change and fall in love in the course of the play: they are (the argument goes) in love when it begins. Again, I have to say that I find this near-universal assumption entirely mistaken. Despite all the sophisticated techniques of the modern psychological novel, the analysis of actual human feeling often lags far behind Shakespeare still. Beatrice and Benedick begin their play attracted to each other, but not in love. Both are children of 'Messina'; both play its games; both belong to a social world for which such attraction is an ordinary datum of experience. 'Messina' assumes that men and women are always after each other and always betraying each other: 'Men were deceivers ever'; and Benedick joins in with Leonato's social by-play of distrusting his own child's legitimacy.

But both from the first see beyond, and through, the merely social, as Benedick really prefers 'my simple true judgement' to what he is 'professed' or supposed to think. This soldierly preference for sincerity suggests that he might similarly like to be truly in love with Beatrice. But he isn't. When he finally does fall, he is honest enough – in a fashion both comic and heroic – to tell her how 'strange' he finds it to feel so much. Earlier, though, what has angered Beatrice is this sense of a mere conditionality in Benedick, which might never have become fact. With an allusive dimension of past and future which distinguishes the two senior lovers from the rest of timeless Messina, Beatrice has two curious references to time past which have puzzled critics. She tells of the moment when Benedick 'challeng'd Cupid at the Flight', and was in turn challenged by Leonato's fool. This narrative anecdote works, I believe, as a conceit of analysis, a definition for a pre-psychological age: she is saying that Benedick may think his resistance to love so clever and aristocratic, but really it is just stupid. This is Beatrice the 'odious woman', descended from Katherine the Shrew; but Shakespeare has deepened the moment and justified the rudeness. With a touch of Lear's Fool in her, Beatrice is the true human heart, struggling against the mere manners of Messina.

And this becomes plainer in her Second-Act answer to Don Pedro, who tells her she has 'lost the heart of Signior *Benedicke*':

Indeed my Lord, hee lent it me a while, and I gave him use for it, a double heart for a single one, marry once before he wonne it of mee, with false dice, therefore your Grace may well say I have lost it.

This is less private history than a fine open act of analysis. Beatrice describes what the courtly Don Pedro, without knowing it, means by 'heart': a world of mere lending and borrowing, a scene of mere winning and losing. The dice are false. Charmingly, wittily and sometimes politely, Beatrice is looking for something else again. Her brisk, tough and cool character belongs – and this is Shakespeare's profound insight, in the most psychologically interesting romantic comedy he has yet written – to one of the most romantic and idealistic of human beings. But she isn't intending to discuss her heart in Messina, a world which is, in her own words, 'civill as an Orange, and something of a jealous complexion'.

With these views, Beatrice may well, as she knows herself, 'sit in a corner and cry, heigh ho for a husband'. And Benedick is as true an individual as herself. Despite the friendly effervescence of his successful social being, there is another Benedick who is most himself when he 'sits in a corner'. In a curious small scene (2.3) he complains of the change in Claudio: and his soliloquy is prefaced, in a way that editions don't explain, by his sending of his boy to fetch the book 'in my chamber window' for him to read 'in the orchard'. The vividness of this is on a par with the thorough realism elsewhere in *Much Ado*: and it throws up a sudden image of the solitude of the real Benedick, whom we see when no one else is there. The book in the hand is for Elizabethans a symbol of the solitary.

In short, here are two people who could easily have remained divided from each other, in a state of irritated or quietly melancholy resentment at themselves and at life. This Elizabethan comedy brings alive what we may think of as a datum of peculiarly modern experience, the randomness, the accidentality of existence: the fact that many things in the life of feeling remain 'a perpetual possibility / Only in a world of speculation'. Attraction starts up socially but there need be no happy endings; there is only 'Much Ado About Nothing', a waste of wishes and desires.

The two difficult lovers owe much to the courtiers for bringing them together, a debt which justifies the forgivingness of the last scene. Yet neither Beatrice nor Benedick is precisely dependent on the tricks of a trivial milieu for their feeling. Orthodox Elizabethans believed that God indeed made 'Much' out of 'Nothing', the Creation out of Void. The change of these two intelligent and principled lovers asks to be comparably explained. They come together over the quasi-dead body of Hero, at the end of the Church Scene. They are, that is to say, drawn together by their shared sympathy for the wronged girl. It is this tertium quid outside themselves that permits Benedick to say at last, 'I do love nothing in the world so well as you, is not that strange?' and Beatrice to answer, 'As strange as the thing I know not, it were as possible for me to say, I loved nothing so well as you.'

I am hoping to suggest that there is a paradox here not far from the oddity of 'sorrow's wag'. The moment is so romantic because not romantic – or not so in the Messina sense; it is the true romanticism of the real. Benedick is at heart a kind man, which to Elizabethans meant 'kinned', 'brotherly'. He is deeply grateful to Beatrice, and besides can't bear to watch her crying. All this, on top of her usual attraction for him. She responds in precisely the same way, not merely changing the subject when she says firmly: 'I am sorry for my cousin.' It's as if she were drawing up the rule-book for the rest of their lives. Both Beatrice and Benedick are individuals who have feared love because it means so much to them; when they do lose their heart, as here, it won't be a 'double' one, in the sense of *dishonest*. What brings them together at last is neither trick nor fluke, but the conjunction of shared principle – a principle which depends on their independence, even their loneliness as human beings. As a result, their professions of love are deep with risk and danger, which is why their bond is involved with a girl in some sense dead, and why Beatrice must ask Benedick to 'Kill *Claudio*'. He doesn't, and it's as well that he doesn't obey the whim of a wildly angry woman. But he's ready to. There is therefore a kind of death in their love, for both of them. 'Sitting in the corner' is the posture of a prizefighter or duellist; when the two advance to the centre, someone may lose, and something must die. There is a delightful, comic, humorous charm and truth in the fact that, as soon as the trick is afoot and love declared, both start to feel terrible: Benedick gets toothache and Beatrice a fearful cold. Many critics assume a pretence on their part, but I think not.

When Shakespeare borrowed his immensely widely disseminated main-plot story from many sources, he did something strange to it. He used a legend that turned on strong evidence of infidelity, and he took the evidence away. There is no 'Window-Scene' in our comedy. The poet has thereby transformed a tale of jealousy into something much nearer to a definition of love, which asks the question: 'How in the world do we ever *know*?' The answer of *Much Ado* is: 'By whatever we take to be the dead body of Hero' – a character whose very name is suggestive. Leaving aside the Leander-loss, we may say that in *Much Ado About Nothing* one kind of hero and heroine is replaced by another. Comparably, one kind of social, winning-and-losing false-dicing love finds itself quietly upstaged by something quite different: a feeling intensely romantic, because involving real individuals, yet grounding itself on something as sober, or we could even say 'dull', as an extreme and responsible human kindness. And the true lovers are kind, to each other and others, because they are aware that life necessitates it even from the romantic. They are both, that is to say, sorrow's wags.

Beatrice and Benedick, 'sitting in the corner' of life, each resent marriage because they are helplessly individual beings. But their very independence and individuality, their corner-view, gives them what no one else in the comedy really has – truth of feeling. Their thinking and feeling for themselves has as its high-water-mark that famous moment, already quoted, at which Beatrice, always quick off the mark, thinks almost too much for herself. As she weeps angrily in the church after Hero's rejection, Benedick makes his vital move – he lets Don Pedro's party leave without him, and stays to comfort Beatrice, asking gently if he can help her. Yes, she says, he can; he can kill Claudio. The play is a comedy precisely because Benedick, always the sounder in sizing up the mark he is being asked to get off, doesn't have to kill Claudio; and we can hardly regret the fact that 'Messina' survives. Here is a co-existence we can like as well as finding likely. But we can't regret either the two individuals who are, as Benedick says, 'Too wise to wooe peaceablie'. The comedy needs their wisdom, just as it needs the constables' folly. Intensely romantic, therefore, as well as consistently funny, *Much Ado* is serious in its concerns while always wearing the air of being entertainingly 'About Nothing'.

Laughter, forgetting and Shakespeare

Adrian Poole

August 1991 will be remembered as the month that Lenin waved goodbye. In the Lithuanian capital of Vilnius an elated crowd awaited the duel between his thirty-foot statue and a motorised crane. It was a disappointment. The old man had always been hollow inside, so he gave up the ghost all too easily. His mighty torso sailed up into the sky, its once imperial arm now tilted into a gesture of farewell, before being lowered onto a lorry and carted off. *The Times* correspondent noted that his trousers put up more of a fight, and 'only collapsed after persistent nudging by the crane'.[1] This may not be enough to obliterate him from human memory. History is littered with mortal monuments. The vices of the Emperor Heliogabalus prompted Shakespeare's contemporary John Speed to designate him 'this *Superlative Monster*'; he records the resolution of the Roman Senate 'that his name should be obliterated out of all monuments...so odious was the remembrance of this *Image of Ignominy*'.[2] Such images of fame and infamy get nudged in and out of collective memory, for better and worse.

In *The Book of Laughter and Forgetting* Milan Kundera recalls the rapturous laughter that greeted the advent of Communist rule in his country.[3] In the spring of 1948 everyone danced in a ring. Two years later most of them were still dancing, but some like Kundera himself had been expelled from the magic circle. The nature of the laughter had changed now that there were enemies of the state to be punished and executions to celebrate. Laughter is hard put to remain innocent of prepositions – laughing at, laughing with, laughing for, laughing off. At least outside of paradise, on earth or wherever, when the Psalmist predicts that 'the valleys also shall stand so thick with corn, that they shall laugh and sing' (LXV, 5.14). Human laughter would seem to require the obliteration of a something or somebody, not merely to be derided but to be laughed out of existence.

85

Baudelaire recalls with admiration the more openly violent hilarity inspired by an English pantomime he once witnessed. It was the embodiment, he says, of extravagance, excess, abandon: 'le vertige d'hyperbole', 'une ivresse de rire'. He remembers in particular the intoxicating power of the show's beginning, the entry into 'le vertige', when a fairy's wand abruptly transforms Pierrot and Harlequin and Columbine from sober citizens, just like members of the audience, into possessed madmen. 'Tous leurs gestes, tous leurs cris, toutes leurs mines disent: La fée l'a voulu, la destinée nous précipite, je ne m'en afflige pas; allons! courons! élancons-nous!'[4] This is in other terms the ecstasy of Dionysiac possession, an orgy of self-forgetting. We find a milder version of it in *A Midsummer Night's Dream* and a more savage one in *The Bacchae*.

Exactly what or whom do we need to forget or get forgotten? There is the mutinous laughter of the underdog and the triumphant laughter of the topdog, but they mirror each other's fear and desire. Kundera imagines a comic fable that summarises many theories of the origins of laughter in the will to power. He supposes that initially laughter is the province of the Devil, a means of contesting the authorised versions of meaning. It offers a welcome relief from the burden of belief they impose, but its goal is nihilism. The angels retaliate by hijacking the Devil's invention and entirely transposing its meaning. 'Whereas the Devil's laughter pointed up the meaninglessness of things, the angel's shout rejoiced in how rationally organised, well conceived, beautiful, good and sensible everything on earth was.'[5] Yet outside the realm of fable, it may be hard to separate the angels from the devils. One may turn into the other; one may even be a bit of both. The governess of James's *The Turn of the Screw* would like to think of herself as an angel, yet she may well be the devil addressed by Miles's famously indeterminate last words, 'Peter Quint, you devil!'

Shakespeare's stage is thronged with people who claim they are on the side of the angels and vice-versa. Titania mistakes Bottom's singing for an angel's and Romeo pretends to mistake Juliet's voice for that of a 'bright angel', but only erotic passion can excuse such willing abasements. Angels are more frequently invoked for the special protection they afford, usually at moments of more or less mortal danger, when the limits of human power are most blatant. 'Angels and ministers of grace defend us!' cries Hamlet. Angelo is neither angel nor devil but he holds the power of life and death over

Isabella's brother Claudio. Isabella flies into a generalisation that seeks to contrast man's use of power with heaven's. She says that the thunderbolt strikes the oak but leaves the myrtle; in other words it discriminates in punishing the lofty or exceptionally vicious, but spares the ordinary or commonplace. This distinctly pagan argument puts her on shaky theological ground, and it is possible to believe that she knows it. She goes on:

> but man, proud man,
> Dress'd in a little brief authority,
> Most ignorant of what he's most assur'd
> (His glassy essence), like an angry ape
> Plays such fantastic tricks before high heaven
> As makes the angels weep; who, with our spleens,
> Would all themselves laugh mortal.
>
> (*Measure for Measure* 2.2.117–23)

Isabella is trying to exploit the familiar idea of a double contrast between angels and men and men and apes. Man stands between the gods and the beasts or the angels and the apes, and as we look down on the apes, so the angels look down on us. As man laughs at the fantastic tricks of the apes, so the angels would laugh at the fantastic tricks of man, if they were human – but they are not human and so they weep instead. It would certainly be a neat division of labour, if angels just wept, men laughed and apes got angry.

But laughter is rarely if ever unshadowed by grief and anger. Isabella shares the ape's sense of impotence in the face of superior power. But she also feels the sense of injustice such as we suppose the ape to be incapable of feeling, and this is why her anger is coloured both by tears and derision. She is herself at once angry and grieving and laughing because she can see the scene in triplicate. It includes victim (herself, Claudio, the ape) and oppressor (Angelo, man), but also the third and superior figure of an audience. She is asking Angelo to imagine the scene from this loftier perspective and view 'Angelo' (and Claudio and Isabella) as the 'angels' do. To see the world as theatre would be to remember the real nature of man's place between the angels and the apes, neither one nor the other but composed partly of both. Yet far from resolving Angelo's dilemma, Isabella's appeal will only exacerbate it. For if he is to surrender to the memory of the ambivalent humanity he shares with Claudio (and Isabella), he must forget the authority with which he has been invested, however briefly, and vice versa.

Outside of fable and fantasy, remembering and forgetting can no more be purged of each other than can the angelic and the diabolic. Borges has a little fable about a man who can forget nothing. Paralysed by a fall from a horse, Ireneo Funes awakes from the dream that screens ordinary mortals from their own perceptions. His memory preserves not only the difference of every leaf of every tree, but of every occasion on which he perceives or imagines each different leaf. His mind can escape neither into the diffusion of sleep nor the abstraction of thought. He is at the mercy of absolute detail, 'the solitary and lucid spectator of a multiform, instantaneous and almost intolerably precise world'.[6] Such a man could never laugh, save perhaps from furious chagrin, for to laugh you must be free to forget. As soon as the double process of remembering and forgetting is coerced, whether by the frailties of the body or the forces of the state, we realise what a precious liberty it is, and like all liberties, how laughably precarious. And how insidiously we collude in its exploitation.

Kundera has compiled a personal dictionary of sixty-three words that are particularly important to him and his writing. The entry on 'Forgetting' is helpful.[7] He notes that a remark made by Mirek, one of the characters in *The Book of Laughter and Forgetting*, has often been taken as the novel's message. It certainly has a memorable ring to it: 'The struggle of man against power is the struggle of memory against forgetting.' Kundera does not disparage the apophthegm but he suggests that readers should not be too impressed by it. Everyone recognises a thought which after Orwell has passed into the collective wisdom of late twentieth-century Western man. It is a commonplace. Kundera goes on to observe that for him the originality of Mirek's story lies elsewhere. Mirek and his friends are struggling against the forces of the totalitarian state to ensure that they are not forgotten, but at the same time Mirek is desperate to make people forget the ex-mistress of whom he is ashamed. The will to forget is certainly a political issue, but it is also what Kundera calls an 'anthropological' one. It is something we cannot escape; we can only study with the appropriate amusement and horror the various forms it takes, overt and furtive, in the weaving and unweaving of our lives. It has become the particular province of the novel to explore the theme of forgetting, Kundera believes, an exploration that 'has no end and no conclusion'. In a striking, summary paradox he describes forgetting as 'absolute injustice and absolute solace at the same time'.[8]

Like the waywardness of laughter, the waywardness of memory outrages the desire for total mastery. In *The Art of Memory* Frances Yates offers to trace the alluring tradition of artificial memory from classical antiquity to the end of the seventeenth century.[9] The story she tells reaches its climax in the extraordinary 'memory theatres' of Giulio Camillo and above all of Giordano Bruno. These dream-constructions are close to nightmare, with their insane ambition to grasp the inner secrets of the universe. We can hear a similarly eery exhilaration in Freud's ostensibly sober prose. In *The Psychopathology of Everyday Life* he ponders some of the complex mechanisms behind our everyday forgettings and false rememberings, but as usual his writing is triumphant with the sense of its own mastery.[10] Where forgetting was, there recollection shall be, at least for the seer who can retrace all the lost paths and recompose the mind's labyrinthine design.

Such pretensions will themselves become the target for derision and rightly so. Bruno's vision of imperial sway over the realm of memory finds its contemporary antidote in Montaigne's abject figure of impotence. The fool that Montaigne makes of himself is richly deliberate, never more so than in some passages of the essay 'On Presumption'.[11] His memory, he tells us, is no more obedient than the mutinous members of his body that seem to have a will of their own. The more he seeks to master it, the more unco-operative it becomes. A comic little scene flares up as master and servant get entangled in a classic sequence of misunderstandings. (Florio's translation compounds the mystification by its uncertain way with pronouns.)

Or, plus je m'en defie, plus elle se trouble; elle me sert mieux par rencontre, il faut que je la solicite nonchalamment: car, si je la presse, elle s'estonne; et, depuis qu'elle a commencé à chanceler, plus je la sonde, plus elle s'empestre et embarrasse; elle me sert à son heure, non pas à la mienne.

And the more I distrust it, the more it troubleth me. It serveth me better by chance, and I must carelessly sollicite her, for if I urge her, she is astonished; and if it once beginne to waver, the more I sound her, the more entangled and intricate she proveth. She wil wait upon me when she list, not when I please.[12]

The 'art of memory' sought to build a fabric of its own, perfectly proportioned, over which it exercised an absolute sway. The menace in these ambitions comes through many of the illustrations that Yates reproduces, not least the weirdly vacant stages of Robert Fludd's *Ars memoriae.*[13] By contrast Montaigne affects despair at the way his charmingly nonchalant memory cannot be trusted to cross a courtyard without forgetting its errand. It is no good expecting his memory to help him find the book he thinks of reading in the library at the far end of the house; the message is bound to escape en route, so he has to entrust it to a more reliable servant. But then things are always escaping the grasp of the man who confesses: 'Je m'eschape tous les jours et me desrobe à moy.'[14] He cannot remember his servants' names and will surely end up by forgetting his own. Out of his own experience there flowers the aphorism, as shrewd as it is muted, that 'Je m'aide à perdre ce que je serre particulièrement.'[15]

Three centuries later Henri Bergson would not have disagreed that memory has a mind of its own, and the theory of comedy he expounds in his essay *Le Rire* is heavily dependent on his ideas about the relations between memory and matter previously developed in his weightier book, *Matière et mémoire.*[16] He argues that of the two kinds of memory that we enjoy, one serves our interests in the struggle for physical survival along with the other animals. It is a neuro-physiological phenomenon and we might do better to call it 'habit'. The other kind of memory distinguishes us from the apes and affiliates us to the angels, in that it gives us access to the realities of time, spirit, and freedom.

Coextensive à la conscience, elle retient et aligne à la suite les uns des autres tous non états au fur et à mesure qu'ils se produisent, laissant à chaque fait sa place et par conséquent lui marquant sa date, se mouvant bien réellement dans le passé définitif...[17]

The human being who lived only by habit would be 'a man of impulse', and one who surrendered to pure memory would be 'a dreamer'. (Or madman, we might add, such as Borges's Ireneo Funes or the aspirant magus who would master or be mastered by Yates's 'art of memory': 'leaving to each fact its place and... marking its date'.) Bergson's arguments are not free from confusion, but Mary Warnock observes with justice that physiology and even psychology would seem to confirm Bergson's central claim 'that, in some sense, everything is remembered, and that forgetfulness is nothing but an inhibition of memory'.[18]

The main thrust of Bergson's theory of comedy is that we laugh at human beings when they forget themselves and start behaving with the mindlessness of animals or machines.

Là où la matière réussit ainsi à épaissir extérieurement la vie de l'âme, à en figer le mouvement, à en contrarier enfin la grâce, elle obtient du corps un effet comique. Si donc on voulait définir ici le comique en le rapprochant de son contraire, il faudrait l'opposer à la grâce plus encore qu'à la beauté. Il est plutôt raideur que laideur.[19]

Laughter serves to make us remember the spirit in the body, and thus to revive the suppleness that is the body's 'grace'. In fact there is a surprising rigidity to the strictness with which Bergson associates the propensity of human beings towards rigidity with their anti-social tendencies. Comedy begins, he says, with what might be called 'le raidissement contre la vie sociale', and laughter serves to correct this dissident impulse.

Est comique le personnage qui suit automatiquement son chemin sans se soucier de prendre contact avec les autres. Le rire est là pour corriger sa distraction et pour le tirer de son rêve.[20]

This aptly describes one of laughter's motives, but Bergson seems deaf to its other possibilities. The dreamer might be obeying an excellent impulse in trying to escape from the automatic behaviour of his fellow-beings. He or she might be drawn, self-forgettingly, towards the embodiment of a more vital idea of fellowship or company or society, an idea of love. Like Shakespeare's Romeo and Juliet, for instance, whose passion for each other indeed makes them 'distracted', and helps to separate them from the banefully formulaic behaviour that governs the rest of their world. But in *Le Rire* Bergson reduces the relations between individual and social being to a single model, forgetting some of his own more complex thoughts on the matter, thoughts that eventually get developed at length in his last major work, *Les Deux Sources de la morale et de la religion* (1932).

The trouble with Bergson's ideas about matter and memory and laughter is that they lack an adequate sense of the collective and social dimensions of their subjects. This was the insufficiency that Charles Péguy attempted to redress in taking over and transforming many of Bergson's ideas.[21] Some of the possible implications of Péguy's extensions can be glimpsed from his comments on the failure of the Russian revolution of 1905. The handful of intellectuals who tried to spark the revolution off had not taken sufficient account of the body of the people. Thinkers, dreamers, theoreticians, speculators,

[ils] avaient fini, – avant de commencer, – par totalement méconnaître, par *oublier* totalement, (je me sers à dessein de ce terme de psychologie de la mémoire), la lourdeur du corps qu'ils traînaient derrière eux. La mémoire avait oublié la matière.[22]

One might say that history is composed of the infinite ways in which memory and matter, in the sense that Péguy uses them, try to forget each other. From a different political perspective Walter Benjamin notes the estrangement from history entailed by Bergson's theory of memory, and the thing it seems to forget: death.[23]

The comedy that Bergson is concerned with is only partly and uncertainly artistic. 'Elle n'est pas désintéressée comme l'art pur', he says.[24] But in so far as he is thinking of a literary tradition, it is centred on Molière and the ethos of critical, ironic, or satirical comedy. He is oblivious to the ethos of Aristophanic or Rabelaisian laughter, to the idea of laughing 'with' rather than, or as well as, laughing 'at'. And hence of course he has no real thought of Shakespeare.

The theatre is a place in which people partly forget themselves together, on stage and in the audience. The gathering is important for relieving the fear that you might be the only one to remember or forget. Everyone loves the moment when Bottom comes out of his dream and shares the impossibility of deciding what exactly he has got to forget or remember and whether he will be up to it. Antony and Cleopatra make everyone feel better, for the time being, by assuring us that you do not have to remember everything to be remembered by everybody. Octavius Caesar never understands this. Shakespeare makes Hotspur doomed but likeable by the way he cannot remember the name of the place where he first met Bolingbroke and then forgets the map he needs for his scene with Glendower. Hal has got the mastery of his memory that Hotspur lacks, and we are meant to believe Warwick when he repeats Hal's self-steeling claim that he has never really forgotten who he is and must be. All his fraternising with the mischief-makers will serve Hal in the future when 'their memory / Shall as a pattern or a measure live, / By which his Grace must mete the lives of other' (*Henry IV, Part II* 4.4.75–7). But patterns and measures, bounds and clocks, monuments and records and scutcheons, the name of any thing that seeks to outlive the extant moment, anything that smells of a noun, all this is what the mischief-makers want to commit to oblivion.

Fathers positively reek of nouns, and they are certainly one of the things the young lovers of the comedies need to put behind them before they find a self they will be able to remember. They need to defy gravity and play the truant from the weighty patterns and measures prepared for them, like the Hal whom Falstaff, playing his father, pretends to reprove with the question: 'Shall the blessed sun of heaven prove a micher and eat blackberries? a question not to be ask'd' (*Henry IV, Part I* 2.4.407–9). The answer is a resoundingly temporary 'yes'. But there are ways and means and kinds of forgetting and the plays are distinguished from each other by the different backlogs they create and the different ways in which these are worked and played off.

Fathers and father-figures are certainly prone to believe their words have an absolute power to record and erase. But there is a hollow ring to the Duke's pronouncement of general amnesty at the end of *The Two Gentlemen of Verona*: 'Know then, I here forget all former griefs, / Cancel all grudge, ...' (5.4.142–3). Easier said than done. There is a more obviously ominous levity to the way Richard II tells the feuding Bolingbroke and Mowbray to 'Forget, forgive, conclude and be agreed' (*Richard II* 1.1.156). Jesters might be distinguished into those who never forget a grudge, such as Thersites, and those who can never remember one, such as Falstaff, whom we are told was 'ang'red ... to the heart' by a withering joke of Hal's only to be told in the next breath that 'he hath forgot that' (*Henry IV, Part II* 2.4.8–9). The relations between forgiving and forgetting are at the heart of *All's Well That Ends Well*, and there is a calculated untimeliness to the King's premature assurance to the Countess that he has 'forgiven and forgotten' her son Bertram's errors: 'Let him not ask our pardon, / The nature of his great offense is dead, / And deeper than oblivion we do bury / Th' incensing relics of it' (5.3.22–5). But it is not in a king's gift to consign things to oblivion. By the time of *All's Well* the role played by remembering and forgetting in the relations between parents and children has become rich and strange and looks forward to the late romances.

The words of the fathers can carry more weight than this and not only in tragedy. One may think of the very different roles, baneful and benign, played by Egeus in *A Midsummer Night's Dream* and Leonato in *Much Ado*, by Portia's dead father and Jessica's living one in *The Merchant of Venice*, by the dead fathers of Helena and Bertram and their living surrogates, the Countess and the King, in *All's Well*. In *As You Like It* Orlando has the durable old Adam to inspire him with the thought of his father and address him as, 'O you memory /

Of old Sir Rowland' (2.3.3–4); in *Love's Labour's Lost* the news of the
King's death intrudes with magnificent abruptness into the young-
sters' frolicking to breathe a welcome sense of the need for endurance;
in *Twelfth Night* brother and sister recognise themselves and each
other by the mole upon the brow of the father who died on Viola's
thirteenth birthday: 'O, that record is lively in my soul' (5.1.246). It
is not necessarily all grief and grudge that the past bequeaths to the
future.

But death and bereavement and mourning are decisive in the
forgetting and remembering in which Shakespearean comedies
interest themselves. That relentless devotee of oblivion, Sir Toby
Belch, makes his first entrance sullenly whingeing: 'What a plague
means my niece to take the death of her brother thus? I am sure care's
an enemy to life' (*Twelfth Night* 1.3.1–3). There are sunnier ways of
putting this, but death is certainly the thing that comedians try to get
forgotten, as Falstaff gently rebukes Doll Tearsheet for gently
reminding him: 'Thou whoreson little tidy Bartholomew boar-pig,
when wilt thou leave fighting a' days and foining a' nights, and begin
to patch up thine old body for heaven?' 'Peace, good Doll, do not
speak like a death's-head, do not bid me remember mine end' (*Henry
IV, Part II* 2.4.231–5). Fortunately Doll underestimates Falstaff's
resources when she implies that he can muster nothing more to while
away the time than fighting and foining.

Liquid plays a large part in Falstaff's composition, and forgetting
seems to require a kind of liquefaction, though strong liquor is not
necessarily the best or only means to it. From classical antiquity
onwards forgetting is associated with liquid, with the drugged wine
that Helen serves Menelaus and their guest Telemachus in *Odyssey
IV*, with the 'river of unmindfulness' at the end of Plato's *Republic*,
and the river Lethe of Virgil's *Aeneid VI*, from which souls must drink
before they achieve reincarnation.[25] (Rosalind darts a dazzling, self-
deprecating glance at her own capacity for magical re-embodiments,
when Orlando's verses excite her to the exclamation: 'I was never so
berhym'd since Pythagoras' time, that I was an Irish rat, which I can
hardly remember' (*As You Like It* 3.2.176–8).) Ovid locates the river
of forgetfulness at the cave of Sleep to which Iris is sent to beg a dream
(*Metamorphoses XI*).

Before Lethe became a river Hesiod made her the daughter of *eris*
or 'strife' (*Theogony* 226–7), and most of the occasions in Shakespeare
when Lethe makes an appearance (there are seven in all) involve the

imminent pressure of violent grudge: when Richard III tempts Queen Elizabeth with the thought of forgetting the wrongs he has done her (*Richard III* 4.4.251), when Antony indicates the bloody hands that have murdered Julius Caesar (*Julius Caesar* 3.1.206), when the new King Henry V confronts the Lord Chief Justice who imprisoned him when he was heir to the crown (*Henry IV, Part II* 5.2.72), and when the Ghost obliquely menaces Hamlet with the suggestion that he might not be 'apt' for revenge (*Hamlet* 1.5.33). Sextus Pompeius welcomes the thought that Antony may have irretrievably sunk himself in 'a Lethe'd dullness' (*Antony and Cleopatra* 2.1.27), but Pompey joins the other world-leaders in succumbing to the charm of temporary oblivion, when they all respond to Antony's call to steep their sense 'In soft and delicate Lethe' (2.7.108). Soft and delicate, and in these particular circumstances, potentially lethal.

It is in *Twelfth Night* that Lethe enjoys its happiest associations with sleep, dream, drink, fancy, and love. Sebastian responds to Olivia's miraculously unsought attention by wondering to himself:

> What relish is in this? How runs the stream?
> Or I am mad, or else this is a dream.
> Let fancy still my sense in Lethe steep;
> If it be thus to dream, still let me sleep! (4.1.60–3)

Sleeping and dreaming provide a regular chance to forget, and the characters who are most haunted by memories bear eloquent witness to the forfeit of this common blessing, such as Henry IV and Macbeth. But sleep can also allow memories to return looking even uglier than in their waking shapes. The idea of total oblivion can be a source of horror or solace no less than the idea of total recollection, but the forms of forgetting and remembering that the comedies make their inhabitants learn to endure are more awkwardly changeable and incomplete. *Twelfth Night* is especially rich in the liquid undercurrents it blends of weeping, drowning, drinking, singing and dreaming. Olivia vows to preserve the love of her dead brother 'in her sad remembrance' (1.1.31), but his memory will melt into the new likenesses of Cesario and then Sebastian. The liquefying Lethe into which characters sink can dissolve the very difference itself that we had supposed to exist between remembering and forgetting. Sebastian's 'Lethe' certainly has a magical and romantic aura to it, but his 'steep' provides an everyday complement. 'Steeping' is something you do or did to salt meat and barley and flax, to tired or wounded flesh and limbs, and all too commonly to the sense that needs to be deadened. With its own kind of poetry the *O.E.D.* recalls the idea at the root of the word, 'of softening, altering in properties, cleansing, or the like, or for that of extracting some constituent'. In Shakespeare's histories and tragedies the liquid in which things get regularly 'steeped' is of course blood and the action hardens memory into indelible griefs and grudges. In the comedies the predominant liquids are clearer, they enter and leave the body more freely in the form of water and wine and tears and sweat, and their action dissolves memory into new forms of readiness.

At the end of *Romeo and Juliet* the fathers finally decide to forget their ancient grudge by commissioning statues of the dead lovers. Statues are always matter for memory, along with trophies, tombs and monuments. Hermione's statue is a rare kind of likeness, being 'Lonely' (or 'Lovely'), 'apart', especially reserved for Leontes (*The Winter's Tale* 5.3.18). But memorials and mementos and monuments have difficulty in retaining their privacy. Once you commit your memory to matter, it runs the risk of public exposure and circulation. Lovers may exchange 'remembrances', as Proteus and Julia do in *The Two Gentlemen,* and Desdemona, like Ophelia, receives 'remembrances' from the man she loves, but these can easily fall into the wrong hands. In *All's Well* the reckless Bertram gives his 'monumental ring' away to Diana.

This is all very well if it ends well – much virtue in 'if' – and there may be a wisdom in forgetting to try and master the forms of memory, just letting them take their own sweet way. But this is not a tactic that will commend itself to the forces of authority, and the Shakespearean theatre inspects the efforts they make to control the forms of what modern historians call collective or social memory.

At the top end of the political scale we can see one form of 'remembrance' embodied in the sword of justice that Henry V commits to the hands of the Lord Chief Justice. We can hear another in the endless strife of the history plays over the preservation and interpretation of past events. Hotspur calls Henry IV 'this forgetful man' for his failure to remember his debt to the men who helped him to the throne, and Worcester relentlessly reminds Henry of the oath he swore at Doncaster. But, dearly as he might wish to, Henry cannot forget his dependence on the memories he shares with others, not only with the other barons but also with the rest of his shattered nation. He knows how much is at stake in advising his son and heir to busy giddy minds with foreign quarrels, 'that action, hence borne out, / May waste the memory of the former days' (*Henry IV, Part II* 4.5.214–15). *Henry V* displays his successor's greater confidence in the power to produce the shapes of collective memory. This Henry calls the pedigree that he sends the French King 'this most memorable line' – the word 'memorable' occurs in no other play of Shakespeare's, but in this, four times – and we see him stamping history with the signature of his own myth. The play colludes with this myth, but to read it as merely doing so is to forget the care with which it anatomises the ways that myths get made. This is also true of what, in their different ways, the Roman plays are up to.

At the other end of the scale the most important form taken by collective memory is that of commonplace, of proverbial wit and wisdom. Needless to say, these resources stand in a permanently ironic relation to the efforts of official history to persuade the body of the people that particular events and individuals and stories are uniquely significant. The long and complex 'popular tradition' recollected by Robert Weimann, the tradition of clowning and parody and commentary, may be said to represent the rearguard action of a collective memory determined to resist the lessons of official history that its would-be masters seek to instil.[26] Near the end of *Henry IV, Part II*, as the time of carnival draws to its close, Justice Silence bursts into popular song – 'Do nothing but eat, and make good cheer', and so on (5.3.17ff.). The peculiar pathos of such a moment has nothing to do with the singer himself, whom we presume to have had as good a run for his money as his colleague, the less reticent Shallow: they are *Justices*, after all. Nor is it to do with the sentiments of the lyrics, which are exactly as forgettable as those of any popular song, then or now. It is simply a matter of rhythm and timing such as we can recognise in any terminal cadence. The party is virtually over. This is Shakespeare's way of giving the kind of historical articulation to the past that Walter Benjamin imagined when he wrote of the need 'to seize hold of a memory as it flashes up at a moment of danger'.[27] This is just such a moment of danger, though Silence and Shallow and Falstaff are oblivious to it, or try to be.

Earlier on the recruiting scene has provided a more obvious 'moment of danger', such as many members of Shakespeare's first audience would have recognised all too clearly. Unlike Bullcalf and

Mouldy, Feeble announces that he will not try and bribe his way out of the war.

> By my troth I care not; a man can die but once, we owe God a death. I'll ne'er bear a base mind. And't be my dest'ny, so; and't be not, so. No man's too good to serve 's prince, and let it go which way it will, he that dies this year is quit for the next. (3.2.234–8)

In his Arden edition A. R. Humphreys makes the just and kindly comment that Feeble 'shows his admirable spirit in a volley of proverbs and tags'. We may smile or even laugh at the way Bullcalf and Mouldy save their own skins, though even here there is a nice distinction between them, for the 'old dame' whom Mouldy pleads as his excuse, even if she is a fiction, sounds a shade more solid than the pathetically vague 'friends' from whom Bullcalf does not want to be parted. But Feeble's resolute self-forgetfulness raises a warmer kind of laughter, as we recognise the strength of the commonplace in which he takes refuge and finds a kind of courage.

'The English seem to prefer to forget', Peter Burke pithily remarks. Not that this is the way they like to think of themselves. (I write as a Scot.) Burke is pondering the reasons behind the differing weight and intensity with which cultures recall their own pasts. He continues:

> It is often said that history is written by the victors. It might also be said that history is forgotten by the victors. They can afford to forget, while the losers are unable to accept what happened and are condemned to brood over it, relive it, and reflect how different it might have been.[28]

Shakespeare can serve to remind the English, and some others, that remembering and forgetting are as inseparable from each other as winners and losers. And that it is not always easy to tell which is which.

NOTES

All references to Shakespeare are to *The Riverside Shakespeare*, ed. G. Blakemore Evans et al. (Boston, 1974).

1 Anatol Lieven, *The Times*, 24 August 1991, 3.
2 John Speed, *The History of Great Britaine* (1611), VI, xxvi, 235.
3 Milan Kundera, *The Book of Laughter and Forgetting*, trans. Michael Henry Heim (London, 1983), 65ff.
4 Charles Baudelaire, 'De l'essence du rire', *Curiosités esthétiques* (1868), in *Oeuvres complètes*, II (Paris, 1976), 541.
5 Kundera, *The Book of Laughter and Forgetting*, 62.

6 Jorge Luis Borges, 'Funes the Memorious', in *Labyrinths*, eds. Donald A. Yates and James E. Irby (Harmondsworth, 1970), 94.

7 Milan Kundera, *The Art of the Novel*, trans. Linda Asher (London and Boston, 1988), 130.

8 Kundera, *The Art of the Novel*, 130.

9 Frances A. Yates, *The Art of Memory* (London and Henley, 1966).

10 Sigmund Freud, *The Psychopathology of Everyday Life*, trans. Alan Tyson, The Pelican Freud Library, vol. v (Harmondsworth, 1975).

11 Michel de Montaigne, *Essais*, livre II (Paris, 1969), 295–324.

12 Montaigne, *Essais*, II, 312; *The Essayes of Michael Lord of Montaigne*, trans. John Florio (London and Toronto, 1928), II, 376.

13 Yates, *The Art of Memory*, illustrations 17, 18a and b.

14 Montaigne, *Essais*, II, 305.

15 Montaigne, *Essais*, II, 314.

16 Henri Bergson, *Le Rire: essai sur la signification du comique* (1900), and *Matière et mémoire: essai sur la relation du corps à l'esprit* (1896), in *Oeuvres complètes* (Genève, 1946). Available translations are *Laughter: An Essay on the Meaning of the Comic*, trans. C. Brereton and F. Rothwell (London, 1911), and *Matter and Memory*, trans. N. M. Paul and W. S. Palmer (New York, 1991).

17 Bergson, *Matière et mémoire*, 157.

18 Mary Warnock, *Memory* (London and Boston, 1987), 31.

19 Bergson, *Le Rire*, 30.

20 Bergson, *Le Rire*, 88.

21 See A. E. Pilkington, *Bergson and His Influence: A Reassessment* (Cambridge, 1976), 27–98.

22 Pilkington, *Bergson and His Influence*, 56.

23 Walter Benjamin, *Charles Baudelaire: A Lyric Poet in the Era of High Capitalism*, trans. H. Zohn (London, 1973), 51.

24 Bergson, *Le Rire*, 108.

25 For a useful account of memory and forgetting in classical Greek writing and thought, see Michele Simondon, *La Mémoire et l'Oubli dans la pensée grecque jusqu'à la fin du Vᵉ avant J.-C.* (Paris, 1982).

26 Robert Weimann, *Shakespeare and the Popular Tradition in the Theater: Studies in the Social Dimension of Dramatic Form and Function*, ed. Robert Schwartz (Baltimore and London, 1978).

27 Walter Benjamin, 'Theses on the Philosophy of History', in *Illuminations*, ed. Hannah Arendt and trans. Harry Zohn (London, 1973), 257.

28 Peter Burke, 'History as Social Memory', in *Memory: History, Culture and the Mind*, ed. Thomas Butler (Oxford, 1989), 106.

Enigmatic Ben Jonson

John Creaser

If Shakespeare resembles the artist according to Stephen Dedalus –
'invisible, refined out of existence, indifferent, paring his fingernails'
– Ben Jonson jabs a long finger-nail at us, chivvying and belligerent.
His works are experienced through the assertive presence of their
author.

Unlike Shakespeare, Jonson took command of his texts. He
presented them as classics, with the quality of printing, the lay-out
on the page and the supporting matter of learned works of art.
He carefully established his literary canon as the work of a man who
is kept before us as a real and formidable off-stage presence, or
through obtrusive critical paraphernalia. Within the plays, moreover, there is a strong sense of the 'implied author'. Even in *The
Alchemist* – which, for all its brilliance, is relatively orthodox in
narrative technique – we perceive the author as the ultimate alchemist, the virtuoso who can transmute filth into theatrical gold. The
increasing confusion of the characters flourishes under the masterly
control of the author.

One result of Jonson's assertion of self is the contempt he expresses
for audiences and readers, apart from a discriminating few. Despite
his success, he was a vulnerable and insecure man, an assertive Stoic
in reaction to the subversive volatility of his temperament. His
anxieties were no doubt exacerbated by the ambivalence of his social
position, as a bricklayer educated at Westminster School and a
branded felon moving in courtly circles. The proudly independent
author and moral arbiter was hungry for approval and praise, and
the most bizarre moment of many recorded by Drummond in the
Conversations is this: 'Of all stiles he loved most to be named honest,
and hath of that ane hundreth letters so naming him.'[1] A failure to
approve him and his work was angrily dismissed as the expression of
ignorance or envy, and aggression and disdain are naked in the

apologias accompanying those plays which, in a long and erratic career, had not been popular successes.

Jonson was, or sought to become, what Richard Helgerson has termed a self-crowned laureate, 'the great poet as the anointed spokesman of the nation', or, in Jonson's own terms, 'he which can faine a *Common-wealth*[,] ... can governe it with *Counsels*, strengthen it with *Lawes*, correct it with *Judgements*, informe it with *Religion*, and *Morals*'.[2] But despite his laureate ambitions, Jonson's genius was for non-laureate forms: for satire, comedy, court entertainment, and epigram rather than for epic and high tragedy. He therefore sought to establish the literary seriousness of his endeavours. The *Epigrams*, for example, become in their dedication 'the ripest of my studies'.

This involved distancing himself from the everyday business and standards of commercial theatre, from the audiences and the playwrights of the very theatres for which he wrote. The prologue to the Folio version of *Every Man In His Humour*, a prologue to the whole volume, is typical in its disdain both for the audience – 'you, that have so grac'd monsters' – and for the plays they had praised, with their elastic sense of time and place and their primitive sensationalism of effect.

Jonson's ready disdain was heightened by his touchiness at failure, since it is expressed inversely to the success of the play. Flops such as *Catiline* and *The New Inn* generate particularly forthright condemnations of the popular audience. It is tempting to withhold sympathy from an author of such keen susceptibility here, since by and large the reactions of those original audiences have been borne out by theatrical tradition. The hits have remained hits whenever Jonson has held the stage, and the flops have rarely been thought worth the risk of revival.

Yet Jonson's most popular plays, *Volpone* and *The Alchemist*, are also the easiest to enjoy, because they offer the orthodox excitement and reward of strong plotlines and the sharp dramatic focus which such plotting encourages. Where it is possible to be at all specific about the reasons for Jonson's contemporary failures, it seems that he was merely being too daring and unorthodox for his audiences. One result of this is that several fine plays have been neglected largely because they are less fine than *The Alchemist*. The most notorious of his failures was *The New Inn*, and consequently the play was neglected for centuries. Yet John Caird's rich production for the Royal Shakespeare Company in 1987 was a complete vindication of the play's stageworthiness. The character now known as Pru was at the heart of the trouble. The original audience sneered so much 'because the Chambermaid was named *Cis*' that Jonson changed her name, while Owen Felltham in his riposte to Jonson's outraged 'Ode to Himself' scorned the playwright for having put 'Before a Chamber-maid / Discourse so weigh'd, as might have serv'd of old / For Schools, when they of Love and Valour told'.[3] This suggests that the 1629 audience fell short of that unorthodox generosity of mind with which Jonson puts the self before the status and gives moral pre-eminence to a chambermaid.

Similarly, we know from the preface to *Catiline* that audiences objected to the length of Cicero's oration in Act 4. But there is no intrinsic reason why long speeches should be undramatic, as many Volpones have shown in the mountebank scene and as John Carlisle's 'commanding and eloquent Lovel' demonstrated at Stratford, where 'his long orations on love and valour were spell-binding in the theatre'.[4] Jonson takes a great risk with Cicero's oration, because, I suggest, his aim is to show its comparative ineffectiveness. His fundamental perception throughout the play is the precariousness of order. Cicero is a skilful politician, yet his success even with the reckless Catiline gang depends on extreme good fortune, and he lacks the nerve to tackle the real danger to the state, the controlled threat of Caesar and Crassus. Even the oration, where he is apparently at the height of his powers, is presented with ironic reservations. Catiline is not silenced, and, more to the point, the oration fails in its primary aim, which is to flush Catiline's followers out into the open – a failure later acknowledged before the Senate (5.122–3). The more the self-regarding Cicero puts into the oration, the more he fails. A good production might be able to put across the tense dynamics of the scene.

It seems that in 'failures' such as these – or in the appearance at the end of *Every Man Out Of His Humour* of the Queen's image, which 'many seem'd not to rellish'[5] – Jonson was being too audacious for his audiences. The insertion of the note 'To the Readers' before Act 3 of *The Staple of News*, informing them that the absurd news is meant to be absurd, shows that Jonson was indeed at times the victim of naive misinterpretation.

Nevertheless, I suggest that Jonson's dramaturgy is founded not on distrust but on confidence in the audience. Jonson was certainly angered by particular audiences which failed to meet the demands of certain plays, but his disdain is reserved for those audiences rather than the role he gives the audience. As he says in *The Masque of Queens*: 'A *Writer* should alwayes trust somewhat to the capacity of the *Spectator*' (lines 105–6). Despite the arrogant and touchy presentation of his texts, the plays as scripts for performance assume a flexible and sophisticated response, the very response which his laureate ambitions and personal susceptibilities prevented him from acknowledging as even possible in the popular theatre of the day.

I differ here from those many critics who, taking Jonson at his word, find his plays to be acts of aggression towards an audience which is disdained and put on trial. For example, Douglas Duncan, in *Ben Jonson and the Lucianic Tradition*, writes most perceptively of Jonson's resourceful and unpredictable 'art of teasing', yet finds a pervasive 'scorn' and 'distrust of the audience', a 'contemptuous distance' from it, and he stresses that Jonson's attitude to the audience is 'inquisitorial'. The error, I suggest, lies in applying Stanley Fish's elementary model of 'intanglement', which assumes readers and audiences to be so obtuse that they continually fall into the same authorial traps, however well they know a work.[6]

Jonson's teasing or challenging of the audience is in practice provocative rather than aggressive. It is true that he is ready to deceive the audience. The re-emergence of Hermione, which is so unexpected in Shakespeare, would be less uncharacteristic in Jonson, who conceals the identity of Macilente, Epicoene, Pennyboy Canter and of everyone who lives at the New Inn. But while Jonson does not take the audience into his confidence, he has confidence in the audience. The ending of *The New Inn*, for example, is preposterous on a literal reading, with fantastic revelations crowding one after the other. Although an ancient and apparently stable genre, comedy is always in its more adventurous writers a genre at odds with itself. Its most obvious convention, the happy ending, is compatible neither with the bitterness of mocking laughter nor with the sadness at human realities which pervade the genre. The happy ending is a conscious unreality, and *The New Inn* takes this to the limit. Even so, the deeper mood here is poignant rather than flippant or ironic, since the verse keeps hinting that the miraculous denouement is no more, and no less, than a 'dream of beauty'. As Anne Barton puts it,

the ending…is indeed the stuff of fantasy and dream, as Jonson was entirely aware. In real life, lords do not marry chamber-maids, lost children have a way of staying lost…Jonson…handles it…as a poignant wish-dream, a

palpable but highly charged fiction that gains strength from the very
honesty of its admission that this is how we should all like the world to be,
but know it is not.[7]

Such an ending assumes a subtle and patient audience, which can
laugh with rather than at the revelations. The absurdities brought on
at the removal of an eye-patch reveal both the preciousness and the
unreality of this 'brave new world' in Barnet. Such an audience,
guided by sensitive performance, was found at the Swan in 1987,
even though it was absent from the Blackfriars in 1629.

Jonson does not condescend to write down to the alleged limits of
his audience. He suspected that the unprecedented severity of the
ending of *Volpone* could cause difficulty – and this was a reasonable
fear, since critics have often simplified the episode – but he left it as it
was, even while affirming he might easily have 'varied it'.[8] Jonson
respects his audience as good teachers respect their pupils, by setting
and requiring high standards. His plays make unremitting demands.
Even *A Tale of a Tub*, generically his most stable play, requires a
triple perspective, encompassing the affectionate portrayal of rural
life, the genial burlesque of Inigo Jones's pretensions, and a critical
nostalgia which by implication sets this image of community against
the divisiveness within Caroline England.[9]

Where Jonson trusts, he tries. Characteristically, he challenges the
audience to a duel of understanding and to make sense of outrageous
and unpredictable stratagems. Just how bizarre and extreme Jonson's
demands can be has often been obscured by the neo-classical guise in
which he presents his texts. 'From no needfull rule he swerveth',
claims the Prologue to *Volpone*, yet he ignores the crucial rules even in
his most assertively neo-classical plays: for example, the unity of
action in *Volpone* itself, and the unities of time and place in *Sejanus*.
The language of decorum with which the plays are thrust at us is
there primarily, I suggest, for the sake of Jonson's aspiration towards
laureate status. Writing in what was still for conventional minds a
despised form of popular entertainment, and deeply in need of being
heard with that seriousness which he both desired and deserved,
Jonson adopts erudition as a defensive armature.

But from the ethic of moderation issues an art of excess. By
affirmation, Jonson is a lord of limit, practising a dogmatic art of
containment, stressing the virtues of the 'gather'd self'.[10] The beings
celebrated authoritatively in his poems and assertively in his earlier
plays live 'at home' in their own bosoms; they are figures of self-

sufficiency and integrity even when eminent in society. In the plays, however, virtue is insipid and imagination is lavished on the Bobadils and Mammons.

Such characters' vivid excess is oddly in rapport with their maker, for it epitomises what is exuberant, unruly, and iconoclastic in the plays' creative energies, answering to the violence and idiosyncrasy of the man himself, 'oppressed with fantasie' and 'passionately kynde and angry'.[11] In practice, Jonson's conservative theorising merely emphasises the multitudinous inventiveness of his work, as a plumb-line reveals how a wall is out of true. The studied moderation of principle underlines the outrageousness of practice, as Jonson pushes his plays to the extreme. Even *The Case is Altered*, that early and unacknowledged work written when Jonson was still strongly influenced by New Comedy, crams two Plautine plays into one complex action, has five men in pursuit of the same woman, and leaves several characters unattached and disconsolate at the end, while verging on tragedy in Count Ferneze's nineteen years of pain and in the perversion of Jaques' love and generosity into an obsession with gold.

T. S. Eliot, in 'Four Elizabethan Dramatists' had Webster, Tourneur, Middleton and Chapman in mind when he wrote of 'their artistic greediness, their desire for every sort of effect together, their unwillingness to accept any limitation and abide by it'.[12] What might Eliot, who baulked at even the presence of the Weird Sisters and Banquo's ghost in the same play (p. 116), have made of that classical gallimaufry, the last act of *Poetaster*? The greatest figures of Augustan Rome are drawn into a petty modern quarrel, and an elevated celebration of *The Aeneid* is put in the shade. Jonson's irrepressible backbiter Tucca sits beside Maecenas and Gallus; Augustus and Virgil look on as a Lucianic emetic is administered to Crispinus/Marston, and the whole is rounded off with a song.

Jonson's theatrical diversity here is much closer to the despised *Antonio* plays of Marston than to a classical decorum. Such 'artistic greediness' pervades his work, in an immoderate piling of speech on speech, character on character, effect on effect. The sheer bulk, huge cast, and maze-like intricacies of *Bartholomew Fair* are as characteristic as the accumulations of absurdity in *Cynthia's Revels* and *Every Man Out*. In some ways the modern artist closest to Jonson is Fellini: the slumming courtiers of *Poetaster* resemble the fashionable dissolutes of *La Dolce Vita*, and the duel in etiquette between the god Mercury and the fantastic traveller Amorphus (*Cynthia's Revels*, 5.4) is a weird forerunner of the mannequin parade of ecclesiastical attire in Fellini's *Roma* – monstrous displays of vulgarity, overwhelming in energy and exhilarating in their sheer confidence. Jonson's drama moves continually between the two poles of 'licence', from precedent and authority to licentious outrage. The opposites are continually attracted to one another; Jonson's fantasists, such as Bobadil and Amorphus, are often sticklers for formality, while his figures of authority, from Clement to Chanon Hugh, feel themselves licensed to behave licentiously.

The greediness and wild theatrical inventiveness are most pronounced in the underrated early works where Jonson is still sporting with follies rather than crimes. Yet they remain present even in tragedy, in the audacity, for example, with which Jonson juxtaposes the bitchiness of the women's world in Act 2 of *Catiline* and the melodramatic horrors of Act 1. In Dryden's *Essay of Dramatic Poesy*, Lisideius complains that each of Jonson's tragedies is an 'oleo' of a play, an 'unnatural mixture' and 'ill mingle' of 'scenes admirable in their kind', and in his neo-classical terms he is right.[13] Jonson is everywhere audacious, even in the genial and unassuming *Tale of a Tub*. That play ends with a scene at once absurd and captivating. It is a wedding supper where the marriages are lower-class, and the guests include wooers from the gentry who have had to come to terms with loss. The wedding entertainment is a masque celebrating the bewildering events of the day which have led to the unexpected marriages, and the masque is a shadow-play where some Heath Robinson device parodies the splendours of Inigo Jones. Those idealisations of royalty at Whitehall become here a touching celebration of communal well-being, as the characters witness a kindly version of their exploits, and as characters and audience join in amused delight at the theatrical ingenuities.

Jonson's art is always taking risks, and never rests in generic norms. His fundamental audacity is what Eliot termed 'skill in doing without a plot',[14] though strictly speaking the skill lies in not *depending* on plot, for some of the plays are strongly plotted and all have intricately interwoven series of events. Despite the authority of Aristotle and centuries of dramatic and critical precedent, Jonson requires the audience to free itself from centring on narrative. This realignment is emphatic in the earlier work, for the *Humour* duo and *Cynthia's Revels* are plays where, outdoing *Godot*, nothing happens three times. *Every Man In*'s echoing of New Comedy is there to prise the audience away from conventional expectations. The young hero with the 'blocking figure' of a father, the *servus delusus* of Brainworm, the *miles gloriosus* of Bobadil, and the ultimate marriage to a sketchy heroine – all these allude to the norms of New Comedy, yet here the marriage is not the mainspring of the events. It only begins to emerge at 4.3.30–1 (3.4.189–90 in the Quarto), when Bridget acknowledges that she finds Ed Kno'well attractive. Moreover, New Comedy plotting has already been parodied, in Kitely's account of that most unromantic foundling, Thomas Cash (2.1.15–23).

The plotlessness of so many of the plays – or the lack of 'story' within the elaborate stasis of the plot – is apt for 'having every sort of effect together'. It means that anything can happen at any moment. Even where Jonson uses stronger narratives, these are unfamiliar, and are unpredictable in outcome. It is not only *Volpone* which might have ended differently. Liberated from the obligatory betrothals of romantic comedy and the routine ingenuities of New Comedy, Jonson has a whole repertoire of manoeuvres and endings made possible by the *galère* of rogues and fools. The audience is kept on the *qui vive*; it rarely knows where it is, or what to expect, and can never settle down.

The epitome of Jonson's wild inventiveness is *Every Man Out*, the play which – to the credit of the early audience – made his reputation and which is now his most underrated work. Here is a play for the Globe which (in the Chorus to Act 3 Scene 6) rejects the traditions of popular romantic comedy, and asks the fundamental question: *Quid sit Comoedia?* The answer is an appeal to classical standards, especially the definition attributed to Cicero: *Imitatio vitae, Speculum consuetudinis, Imago veritatis*. Yet the play is as radical a re-thinking of classical comedy as it is of the popular theatre. Its provocative lack of all but short-term traces of plotting distances it from the fantastic logic of Aristophanes, let alone the stereotypes of New Comedy.

Although a heavily verbose text on the page – and although it is now presumably beyond revival, since its relentless display of folly has long lost topical piquancy – it makes an endearingly imprudent script of rampant theatricality. The whole action is a play within a play, devised by Asper. It progresses through a series of *coups de théâtre*, starting with the dramatised critical theory of the Induction – leading into dizzying shifts of perspective as the earnest Cordatus becomes the butt of the Prologue and Jonson himself of his own creation, Carlo Buffone – and continuing until an image of the Queen is brought on to purge Macilente of his envy, and Asper is revealed within Macilente.

Every Man Out is also a play crammed with judgement, from the innovatory Theophrastan Characters to the theorising of Asper to the commentary of Cordatus to the incessant placing of the other characters by Macilente and Carlo to innumerable incidental judgements by others. Yet amid all this judgement, nothing can be taken on trust (except that Cordatus is a more shrewd neo-classical critic than Mitis). The Asper of the Induction is a much less balanced figure than the Asper of the Characters, and this alone is enough to deprive us of secure judgement in what is to come. Much of the action is presented by Macilente and Carlo, and their 'squint-eyed sight' inevitably distorts. Macilente's eventual transformation from malice to pity implies that every single judgement he has uttered requires re-thinking, and the re-emergence of Asper makes it possible that the whole play within a play has been a purgation of his own moral aggressions. Nor is there guidance for us in the action itself, since it has blatantly lacked poetic justice: miseries are heaped onto the fopperies of Fastidious Brisk, while the rancid Carlo has merely a token punishment.

The 'artistic greediness' and the apparent chaos of this play – Jonson's first manifesto – are signs of his testing of the audience and of his trust in it. Re-thinking the implications of the Ciceronian *Imitatio*, *Speculum*, and *Imago*, Jonson gives some coherence to his experimentation by putting the stress throughout on perception. The most resonant word of the play – and it remains important through-out the oeuvre – is 'observe'. Once Asper has been roused from his fury and has 'observ'd' the presence of the spectators (Induction, 51), he offers it a 'mirrour' (118) in which he will reveal deformity, and invites Cordatus and Mitis to 'observe what I present' (154). The action proper begins with Macilente in fury at what he has 'observ'd' in the world, wishing 'the organs of my sight were crackt' (1.1.19 and 25). Such language echoes throughout, particularly in Act 3, when for the first time Jonson has characters parading in London. It is a world where characters come to see and be seen. To see is to make a judgement, and a judgement is an 'observation' (3.3.17).

The insistent language of perception, in this verbose and yet so visual play, alerts the audience to the need for judgement. The association of observation and independent judgement is enforced from the start, when Mitis asks Cordatus: 'Does he observe all the lawes of *Comedie*?', and Cordatus replies of the standard rules listed by Mitis: 'O no, these are too nice observations' (Induction, 235 and 242). Jonson floods the audience with what, in a good contemporary performance, must have been an overwhelming and yet exhilarating tide of perceptions and judgements, leaving no ground for the audience which is firm and dry, except the comments of Cordatus which prove that the author knows what he is doing. From first to last, the work is enigmatic. The genial dedication to the Inns of Court presents the play as a carnival relaxation for when 'the Lord of liberty raignes' (20–1), whereas the classicism of the Characters and the prolonged Induction suggest more ambition and moral strenuousness. The emergence of both pity and Asper within Macilente at the end suggests that the abrasive judgement which the play has seemed to encourage is misplaced. The open-endedness is explicit in Cordatus's refusal to make any closing comment (5.11.67).

Every Man Out is a pioneering work; it anticipates something of Jonson's great decade which is still undervalued: the enigmatic nature of the comedies. I do not have in mind here the formal enigmas of the emblem books, although these do occur.[15] Instead I mean the radical elusiveness of which this apparently most dogmatic and forthright of dramatists is capable. Time and again Jonson makes what seems to be a definitive statement, or presents a character in a definitive posture, only for the definitive to become enigmatic. What initially seems clear turns out to be equivocal, or teasingly elusive, or, in the most developed form, insoluble in significance.

Major Shakespearean figures rarely come on stage and declare themselves in definitive words or action. Typically, one grows into awareness of them, because they live and grow in time; understanding, say, Orsino or Bertram or Shylock requires the whole play. Antonio the merchant begins enigmatically because a recent change has made him an enigma to himself: 'In sooth, I know not why I am so sad.' But even the more complex of Jonson's figures tend to be definable, seen in a state of arrested development. Their speeches generate little sub-text, except as intrigue. Bobadil, Corbaccio, Subtle, Mammon, Ursula, even Mosca – these are the same from first to last.

Yet Jonson is a much more devious author than this simplified (rather than simple) mode of characterisation might suggest.

Especially throughout the great decade, a character or a situation or even a whole play can tantalise us with its enigmatic variations. The first instance comes with Thorello's last speech at the close of *Every Man In*. Here we have a major character uttering apparently definitive words – a poem inset and italicised in the text – summing up his cleansing from jealousy and his commitment to his wife:

> *See what a drove of hornes flie in the ayre,*
>   *Wingd with my cleansed, and my credulous breath:*
> *Watch them suspicious eyes, watch where they fall,*
>   *See see, on heades that thinke they have none at all.*
> *Oh what a plentuous world of this will come,*
>   *When ayre raynes hornes, all men be sure of some.*

(5.3.418–23)

The passage is both a repudiation of jealousy, and, implicitly, a repudiation of that repudiation, since the cleansing breath is 'credulous', and since all men can be sure of horns. Seen one way, this is a strong statement by a confident character, as he impudently blows his horns out over all the men in the audience. Seen another, it reveals a neurotic unable to purge himself. The speech stands out all the more strikingly in the shortened Folio ending, where Kitely adds a prose gloss: 'I ha' learn'd so much verse out of a jealous mans part, in a play' (5.5.82–3). The actor seems here to be taking leave of his part in what could be either an insolent or a placatory way. Kitely, however, seems now all the more trapped in his role. The only words he has to disavow jealousy are borrowed words, and even these restore the jealousy he dismisses.

Although a speech like this – multi-faceted and more than ambivalent, irreducible to even a complex single interpretation – reads oddly in the relatively lucid world of *Every Man In*, it introduces versions of enigma which pervade *Every Man Out* and become steadily more challenging in the four great comedies, culminating in *Bartholomew Fair*. For example, *Volpone*, a play filled with unreliable judgements and doubtful touchstones, is teasingly elusive throughout. The opening prayer to gold is blasphemy at first sight, and more like parody with hindsight, once we have felt Volpone's lust for performance and lack of avarice. The Epilogue insolently appeals beyond 'the lawes' which have punished Volpone to the theatrical pleasure he has given. The play holds two essential orders of value in tense and precarious opposition – the histrionic realm where vir-

tuosity is king, and the realm of moral virtue – and the epilogue
leaves us with an insoluble problem made explicit.

What kind of drama is *The Alchemist*? Although it presents the
Blackfriars of 1610 with a meticulously contrived realism, does not
the very concentration of distinctive individuals and happenings into
one house and one day create an impression of fantastic unreality?
Does the play offer the moral insight of satirical comedy or the moral
holiday of farce? Is Lovewit's conscious waiving of moral proprieties
a guide to our response, or a warning against corruption and folly?
The play is an enigma because Jonson never shows his hand. As
conflicting traditions of critical interpretation demonstrate, each of
these bifocal readings is possible at any point, yet the two are
incompatible.

In *Epicoene*, the very action is a puzzle, which Jonson and Dauphine
keep unsolved till the end, and this epitomises the lack of authorial
guidance. To a remarkable degree for a comedy, the eventual
disposition of rewards is no guide to merit. The cold and predatory
Dauphine ends up with the money and the women. The nitwits La
Foole and Daw are repeatedly humiliated, while the equally fatuous
collegiate ladies go unscathed, since they must be kept available for
Dauphine. There could not be a more transparent name than
'Truewit', yet this loquacious and forthright young man is the most
secretive person in a play full of voluble characters with something to
hide. He puzzles even his friends, troubling Clerimont with a display
of '*Stoicitie*' (1.1.66), and making Dauphine wonder how he has
'come forth so sudden and absolute a courtling' (4.1.129–30). The
dazzling surface play of his contradictory speeches leaves it unknowable what, if anything, lies beneath, and some 'irritable
reaching' after certainty is understandable. I recall a performance at
Oxford in the late 1960s in which the actor found his clew to unravel
the whole character in words spoken while Dauphine is advising his
friends to visit public gatherings: 'In these places a man shall find
whom to love, whom to play with, whom to touch once, whom to
hold ever' (4.1.61–2). The actor drew out the last phrase, making it
a revelation of sincere yearning; the dandy dropped the mask for a
moment, and was shown to be a nice guy underneath. Jonson makes
such a reading possible by the way he adapts Ovid here: *Illic invenies
quod ames, quod ludere possis, / Quodque semel tangas, quodque tenere velis.*[16]
The 'ever' added to Ovid's 'hold' turns an open-ended affair into
permanence. Yet the actor's drastic simplification of the character

was not a service to the play. Jonson's paraphrase tantalisingly brings the possibility of lasting love into the cynical virtuosity, but perhaps merely to create an elegant apposition: 'whom to touch once, whom to hold ever'.

This is in keeping with Jonson's enigmatic vision in the play. *Epicoene* is unprecedented in its total lack of an embodied positive; there is not even a Celia, or Arruntius, or Cordatus to give at least sincerity to any affirmation of value. Instead, as in *Troilus and Cressida*, we are led to perceive the characters in terms of values to which they allude. But judgement is more elusive still than in Shakespeare's play, for there some characters do at least aspire in their imperfect way towards the values of love and honour which they profess. In Jonson's cold play – 'making a little winter-love in a darke corner'[17] – the humane values are only glancingly present, as in Truewit's 'whom to hold ever', or in Clerimont's lyrically heartless complaint against Lady Haughty's cosmetics that the 'adulteries of art...strike mine eyes, but not my heart' (1.1.101–2). Jonson leaves us to fend for ourselves in this play. For once there is little consciousness of an authorial presence. The only response is to be as agile as Truewit himself, sifting sense and nonsense, perceiving for ourselves those positives for evaluation which are neither stated nor embodied.

But the ultimate Jonsonian enigma comes with the stark dichotomy of *Bartholomew Fair*. This has often been read, and performed, as a genial and saturnalian play, an urban festive comedy of benign immersion in an alien setting. Equally often, however, it has been read and performed as a harsh and satirical exposure of carnality and cupidity.[18] These viewpoints are at once incompatible and equally valid. Like the trick perspective paintings in which the age delighted – 'Though he be painted one way like a Gorgon, / The other way's a Mars' – the play presents one face when viewed from one perspective and quite a different face when viewed from another.[19]

Uniquely among Jonson's plays, *Bartholomew Fair* is an 'occasional' work. The Induction locates the play at the Hope Theatre on 31 October 1614, while the next night, All Saints' Day, the play opened the winter season at court, with a prologue and epilogue addressed directly to the King. The enormous cast and unprecedented length of the play suggest that it was not written for the standard repertory, and no contemporary performances are known but these two. In writing it, Jonson must have had the court as well as the Hope in mind, since there seems no precedent for such an immediate transference from the public stage to the court. Writing with both performances planned, Jonson will have had two distinct audiences in mind. Among the dirt and stink of the Hope, *Bartholomew Fair* is a popular work open to all comers. At the court, it is addressed to an elite.[20]

The two venues direct attention to the pair of incompatible perspectives from which the play invites scrutiny. At the court, the play is a mellow festive comedy, as the audience looks from above onto a series of piquant sights and amusing moral aberrations. At the Hope, the play is intimate, realistic, satirical, and sour; Bartholomew Fair is Vanity Fair.

At court, the *Fair* is genial saturnalia, where the ruling elite condescends to watch a radical mockery of rule. As Ian Donaldson puts it, the play 'is a comic parable upon the...gospel text: *Judge not, that ye be not judged*'. The play turns on the ambivalence of 'licence': fair-folk and visitors alike feel licensed by authority or social position to behave licentiously.[21] The denouement is unequivocally benign. Aggressive moralists are deflated, and uneasy consciences are purged. The keynote is the reminder to Overdo that he is 'but *Adam*, Flesh, and blood! you have your frailty' (5.6.97), and his acceptance of this by inviting his 'good friends all' (108) home to supper. No harm is done, and the play ends with marriage, reconciliations, and festivity.

From a courtly perspective, a coherent view can be developed on these lines. But changing the perspective changes the underlying conventions, and the comedy is transformed. The mellow view proposes that the major visitors to the Fair are representatives of authority, and that these would-be reformers are themselves re-formed.[22] Yet Overdo and his fellow authoritarians are only pretenders to authority – they are found wanting by orthodox standards – and their actual conversions are perfunctory. For example, although Dame Purecraft eases her conscience by confessing her frauds to the supposed madman, she has no thought of abandoning her gains, or apparently her practice. In a more realist atmosphere, the marriage of self-seeking Winwife and self-righteous Grace Wellborn seems a travesty of romance. Characters undergo the retribution of remaining themselves.

The play's duality of vision is epitomised in the phrase where Quarlous recommends a sense of proportion to Overdo: 'And no enormities' (5.6.109). As a mellow reminder of the pettiness of the wrongdoing which Overdo has self-importantly observed, this is healthy. Yet the play has also uncovered a series of genuine 'enormities': the fraud of Purecraft and Busy; the threatened misalliance of Grace; the madness of Trouble-all; the ensnaring of two apparently respectable wives. Moreover, Quarlous himself is as implicated in 'enormity' as anyone. Against all his early advice to Winwife, he has married an elderly widow for her criminal gains. Having expediently acquired the wardship of Grace, he is permitting her to marry his friend Winwife only if she pays Quarlous heavily for the privilege. Coming from a decent character, the interjection 'And no enormities' would unequivocally bear out a mellow reading, but from Quarlous it implies that 'enormity' is to be laughed out of court because the case of Quarlous does not bear looking into. Such irreconcilable 'duplicity' in the text is found throughout. From one angle the puppet-play is an innocent and amusing image of the theatre itself, and from the other a foul travesty of art and festivity.

Bartholomew Fair is all the more tantalisingly enigmatic because it conveys a strong sense that the author is in control. It combines the multitudinousness of the comical satires with the strict ordonnance of the greater comedies. The multiplicity of the action and the huge spread of the text are an act of authorial daring. Moreover, form is clearly imposed onto the apparently sprawling life of the play by means of act-divisions, which at this date, and in a company which had merged with the Children of the Queen's Revels, would have been indicated by musical interludes. An audience perceiving the play as a series of acts would have a sense of symmetry: each act begins with a new character (or with Leatherhead in a new role); each is divided into six scenes, and during each act the stage tends to become more crowded and noisy. Scholars have located numerous internal symmetries.[23]

Faced with a play which is so radically ambivalent, so gargantuan in scope and yet so commandingly presented, the audience is brought to a state of bewildered admiration. Authority rests with the author; judgement and comprehension seem always beyond our reach. The comedies of reconciliation which follow this climax of enigmatic art are more relaxed in mood, and enigmatic qualities are occasional and genial. In the *Fair*, however, there is no balance, let alone synthesis, and it is an exhilarating although troubling experience to have our expectations and judgement jolted in this way. Jonson questions authority by conceding the accuracy but implying the inadequacy of a unifying, orthodox viewpoint. In a cast of unprecedented fullness and vitality, all the characters except Trouble-all assert their 'licence' and authority. We, on the other hand, lack both the security and the blinkers of a clear guiding authority and perspective, even though we are so conscious of the playwright's presence.

Paradoxically, Jonson is here abandoning power even as he flourishes it, and he uses his control of the situation to relinquish didacticism. Since he is teasing the audience out of thought, he cannot also be telling it what to think. Instead he pays the high compliment of trusting us to be enlightened by uncertainty.

Jonson is taking to an extreme those arts of insoluble dichotomy found in diverse authors in the later sixteenth and seventeenth centuries. For example, recent criticism sees the plays of Lyly as perspective puzzles, deftly patterned diagrams of enigma, inviting and eluding resolution.[24] Similarly, there is no balance or reconciliation in the drama of Marlowe, whose mind (in the words of William Empson) 'erected absolutely opposed ideals' so that the heinous sin becomes '*the proper thing to do*'.[25] *Tamburlaine* is both an amoral, exultant celebration of an heroic prodigy *and* a humane critique of such a protagonist: 'Applaud his fortunes as you please'. John Ford's somewhat different approach in *Perkin Warbeck* is to baffle the sceptical judgement by making rational explanations of the pretender seem petty. Perkin is too authentic to be pretending, and has too fine a humanity to be merely deluded. The royalty of his spirit triumphs over the letter of his social origins, whatever they may be. As Anne Barton has written of 'The Earl of Rochester's Conference with a Post Boy': 'It manages simultaneously to magnify and deflate *both* its subject and the orthodox values by which that subject is being judged, to invite belief and to undercut it.'[26] Several of Rochester's other poems are profoundly two-faced in this way, inviting rational analysis only to show the limits of analysis.

Jonson's strategy here descends from the pervasive rhetorical culture of the sixteenth century in which minds were trained to argue *in utramque partem*, on both sides of any question. At its best, as Joel B. Altman maintains, it allows 'that suspension of commitment which life does not usually afford, but is one of the things that fiction is for' and 'not only gives shape and voice to the vast jumble of undiscriminated moral notions circulating in the human mind, but also makes us respond emotionally to them, test the validity and provenance of our responses as the viewpoints grind with murderous innocency one against another, and finally compels us to weigh the value and the limitations of each'.[27]

But Jonson's explorations are more radical than the Tudor drama examined by Altman, for there 'the play is fashioned around a central question or questions, and the plot constitutes proof and counter-proof in a progressive argument toward a solution'.[28] Enigmatic art like Jonson's is more searching and more openly disquieting, for there is no resolution; he undermines intellectual security by bringing home the partiality of judgement. It need not be – and in Jonson it certainly is not – an expression of relativism. But it insists with a humbling ingenuity on how baffled and limited the judgement may be. This approaches what Altman terms 'dark comedy', where the play's resolution is inadequate to the human problems that have been revealed (p. 394). In Jonson, however, the tone is not necessarily dark, for normally the audience is conscious of the drama as an artefact, of the playwright's teasing but exhilarating display of authorial dexterity and moral agility.

As so often, the tendency of Jonson's art is here the converse of Shakespeare, where (to use terms from Wallace Stevens) comedy moves towards images of 'expressible bliss' which are 'too ripe for enigmas, too serene'.[29] Even so, although the belligerent Jonson may seem pre-eminently an artist of the 'egotistical sublime', the openness and patience required by his enigmatic art are Shakespearean in tendency. It is, in its way, an art requiring '*Negative Capability*, that is when man is capable of being in uncertainties, Mysteries, doubts, without any irritable reaching after fact & reason'.[30]

NOTES

1 Lines 631–2, in C. H. Herford and Percy and Evelyn Simpson, *Ben Jonson*, 11 vols. (Oxford, 1925–52), I, 150, cited below as *Works* and the source of all quotations from Jonson.

2 Helgerson, *Self-Crowned Laureates: Spenser, Jonson, Milton, and the Literary System* (Berkeley, 1983), 7; *Discoveries*, 1034–7, *Works*, VIII, 595.

3 Lines 29–30, *Works*, XI, 339.

4 Martin Butler, ed., *The Selected Plays of Ben Jonson* (Cambridge, 1989), II, 302.

5 *Works*, III, 602.

6 Douglas Duncan, *Ben Jonson and the Lucianic Tradition* (Cambridge, 1979). Quotations are from 115, 213, 233, and 164 respectively. The debt to Stanley Fish is acknowledged on 6 and 232, and is evident, *inter alia*, on 151, 156, 160, and 163.

7 *Ben Jonson, Dramatist* (Cambridge, 1984), 280–1.

8 Epistle, line 113.

9 See Anne Barton, *Ben Jonson*, 321–37.

10 A phrase from *Epigram* 98 cited by Thomas M. Greene, 'Ben Jonson and the Centered Self', *Studies in English Literature*, 10 (1970), 325–48, reprinted by Greene in *The Vulnerable Text: Essays on Renaissance Literature* (New York, 1986), 194–217.

11 From Drummond's summary in *Conversations*, 692 and 687, *Works*, I, 151.

12 T. S. Eliot, *Selected Essays* (London, 3rd edn, reprinted 1966), 116.

13 John Dryden, *Of Dramatic Poesy and Other Critical Essays*, ed. George Watson (London, *Everyman*, 1962), I, 49.

14 *Selected Essays*, 155.

15 See, for example, Jackson I. Cope, '*Bartholomew Fair* as Blasphemy', *Renaissance Drama*, 8 (1965), 127–52, and John Creaser, 'The Popularity of Jonson's Tortoise', *Review of English Studies*, n.s. 27 (1976), 38–46.

16 'There will you find an object for passion or dalliance, something to taste but once, or to keep, if so you wish' (*Artis Amatoriae*, 1.91–2, *Loeb Classical Library* translation by J. H. Mozley).

17 *Discoveries*, 59, *Works*, VIII, 565.

18 For brief surveys of the critical and theatrical diversity of interpretation, see Frances Teague, *The Curious History of Bartholomew Fair* (Lewisburg, 1985), esp. 14–15 and 108–9, and ch. 7, esp. 137. For a compact listing of major academic studies, see Richard A. Burt, '"Licensed by Authority": Ben Jonson and the Politics of Early Stuart Theater', *ELH*, 54 (1987), 557 n. 17.

19 *Antony and Cleopatra*, 2.5.116–17. Some of the techniques of such paintings are outlined by Ernest B. Gilman, *The Curious Perspective: Literary and Pictorial Wit in the Seventeenth Century* (New Haven, 1978), 34ff., who in passing cites passages which reveal Jonson's familiarity with such methods, notably *Every Man Out of His Humour*, 4.3.91–93, and the sonnet '*In Authorem*' prefaced to Nicholas Breton's *Melancholic Humours*.

20 On the dual occasions and audiences, see Ian Donaldson, *The World Upside Down* (Oxford, 1970), 46–77, and William Blissett, 'Your Majesty is Welcome to a Fair', *The Elizabethan Theatre IV*, ed. George Hibbard (Ontario, 1974), 80–105.

21 *The World Upside Down*, 77 and 50.

22 For influential examples, see Jonas A. Barish, *Ben Jonson and the Language of Prose Comedy* (Cambridge, Mass., 1960), 187–239, especially the closing pages, and 'Feasting and Judging in Jonsonian Comedy', *Renaissance Drama*, n.s. 5 (1972), 3–35, esp. 28–9.

23 For example, Richard Levin, 'The Structure of *Bartholomew Fair*', *PMLA*, 80 (1965), 172–9, and Guy Hamel, 'Order and Judgement in *Bartholomew Fair*', *University of Toronto Quarterly*, 43 (1973), 48–67.

24 See, for example, Leah Scragg, *The Metamorphosis of Gallathea* (Washington, D.C., 1982), 4ff.

25 Cited in Judith O'Neill, ed., *Critics on Marlowe* (London, 1969), 119, from a book-review in *The Nation*, 163 (1946), 444–5.

26 'John Wilmot, Earl of Rochester', *Proceedings of the British Academy*, 53 (1967), 52.

27 *The Tudor Play of Mind: Rhetorical Inquiry and the Development of Elizabethan Drama* (Berkeley, 1978), 87 and 62.

28 *Tudor Play of Mind*, 229. For similar statements, see also 25–6, 69, 147, 194, 200, 256, 390, 391, and 393.

29 Phrases from 'Notes towards a Supreme Fiction' and 'Credences of Summer', *The Collected Poems of Wallace Stevens* (London, 1955), 404 and 374. An exception to such resilient serenity (which has often to absorb a good deal of melancholy) is of course *The Merchant of Venice*, which Altman cites as a 'dark comedy' (394).

30 Hyder E. Rollins, ed., *The Letters of John Keats 1814–1821*, 2 vols. (Cambridge, Mass., 1958), I, 193.

A New Way To Pay Old Debts: *Massinger's grim comedy*

Martin Butler

The fate of Philip Massinger has been a curious one for a major writer of comedy. *A New Way to Pay Old Debts* and *The City Madam* are arguably the most enduring comic achievements to have been produced between *Bartholomew Fair* and *The Country Wife*, and they almost alone have kept Massinger's name alive, yet in recent times his reappraisal has been made largely on the basis of his strengths in non-comic genres. The range and solidity of his work are perhaps more highly regarded now than they ever have been: most notably, Anne Barton's classic essay 'The Distinctive Voice of Massinger' makes a compelling case for the clarity of his language, the integrity of his dramaturgy, and the coherence of his political preoccupations.[1] But while the tragedies and tragicomedies are in the ascendant, the comedies continue to be dogged by a conviction that they are just not comic enough. The trouble is they are really not terribly funny, and from some angles their humour feels rather grim, even unpleasant, not to say distasteful. T. S. Eliot may have praised Massinger as a master of sombre comedy,[2] but later critics have found his humour uncomfortable, too nakedly a compound of fears, anxieties and insecurities. Even in the nineteenth century, when *A New Way* was barely ever off the boards, its popularity arose not from its comedy but from its melodrama, Edmund Kean having discovered that Sir Giles Overreach was a part to tear a cat in. Kean's audiences attended less for the laughs than for the more dangerous pleasures of being reduced to hysterical fainting fits by his 'Richard III of common life' and the towering passions and thrilling violence which he exhibited.[3] The RSC revival of 1983, with its pervasive jollying up of the original, was only the latest instance of this conviction that as a comic dramatist Massinger left a great deal to be desired.[4]

It is self-evident that this difficulty with Massinger arises from a discomfort with his historical positioning: his humour is over-

shadowed by history. Nowhere is this more apparent than in the
emphatically *ex post facto* considerations that invariably intervene
into readings of *A New Way to Pay Old Debts*. A comedy in which an
embattled aristocratic elite circumvent the will to power of an
upwardly mobile citizen who challenges the hegemony of the 'true
gentry' (2.1.89),[5] *A New Way* has usually seemed an embarrassingly
unmediated rehearsal of the looming crisis of mid-century – a
perception enshrined in the RSC revival, which opened with a
ragged waif laboriously chalking the numbers '1642' onto the floor.
Given this postulate, the comedy of *A New Way* inevitably seems
anything but carefree. In the notorious Leavisite reading by R. A.
Fothergill, the play is a vile lampoon on a class-enemy: Massinger, a
grovelling forelock-tugger of the Faithful Retainer variety, provided
a declining aristocracy with the repellent but futile satire that it
wanted.[6] Current accounts of the play have left such value-laden
judgements behind, but they still sound the note of historical regret.
Michael Neill has analysed the patriarchal ideology encoded in the
play and identified episodes in which that ideology seems to come
into question, but though these moments hint at potential transformations within an otherwise conservative comedy for Neill they do
not come into coherent focus: Massinger's overriding commitment to
old stabilities prevents him from working through the awkward
questions to which he is provoked.[7] And in Philip Edwards's reading
of the play, sensitive though it is to niceties of social placing, the
thwarting of Overreach's ambitions still seems like wish-fulfilment for
the sake of a disappearing class, and Massinger an exorcist who isn't
quite on planet Earth. The shrewdness of Massinger's perception of
change is contaminated by an 'atavistic belief (shared by those who
participated in court masques) in the value of dramatic performances
as a means of warding off disaster'.[8] From here it is only a short step
to the RSC revival with its portentous hint that however amusing
these people might be, they were already on the wrong side of history.
    Grim comedy indeed: with 1642 looming ahead, Massinger must
have been whistling in the dark to keep his spirits up. But it is pretty
obvious that in all of these readings the local historical embeddedness
of the comedy has been subordinated to a long-term and largely
tendentious teleology: the magnetism of that mystical number 1642.
Writing at the very outset of Charles's reign – indeed, within the first
six months – Massinger was in no position to predict upheavals that
were seventeen years hence, and which he would not himself live long

enough to see. Of course the argument runs that although Massinger could not foretell the future his play was still registering the developing transformation of its times, and testifying unconsciously to changes which it could not address save as a barely apprehensible nightmare. And yet if that is the case, the issue is one of defining those transformations in ways that are historically meaningful. Beneath the doom-laden reading of *A New Way* lie the intertwined assumptions that the period constituted the 'Crisis of the Aristocracy' and that the Civil War represented an assault on an outmoded elite by the forces of modern economic individualism. Tempting though these assumptions are as glosses on *A New Way*, neither would cut much ice with today's historians, who have long abandoned Whiggish models of progressive crisis, and who have found a vastly more active role for the aristocracy to play in bringing down the monarchy. Indeed, in one recent scenario, it's the old aristocracy who in the 1640s are to be found on the other side of history, managing resistance to the 'evil counsellors' of Charles Stuart.[9] This view has been hotly contested, but whatever the truth of its details it does have the merit of reminding us that the role of at least some sections of the aristocracy in this period was oppositional, and that their resistance to change was far from equivalent to defeatism. More crucially, the teleology that telescopes 1642 into 1625 does so at the risk of radically misconstruing the developing alignments that were in fact in play around the comedy. If *A New Way* was engaged with the politics of its moment, it's worthwhile establishing the nature of that engagement before concluding too eagerly that Massinger's politics were historically futile. This may not make the comedy much less grim, but at least it won't look quite as defensive.

Certainly the play is preoccupied with preserving the status quo. Sir Giles's dreams about having great ladies kowtow to his daughter are demolished, and status is restored to those young scapegraces who had forfeited their rank as gentlemen: the prohibition on ambition coerces even Lord Lovell who, in refusing to wed Margaret Overreach, rejects her father's offer to buy him an earldom (4.1.144). At the same time, the play assumes that rank will out and birth confers inherent privileges. This is clearest in the case of Welborne, whose lapse into prodigality is really only generosity by another name (4.2.108–9), and who despite his rags is mortally offended by a charitable hand-out from Alworth (a mere page). Everybody assumes that hierarchies are in-born and natural, and even Overreach shares this general fetish, his ambitions seeming so unsettling precisely because he too believes he can never be a legitimate gentleman. Holding that there is 'a strange Antipathie / Betweene vs, and true Gentry' (2.1.88–9), he testifies to the resilience of the boundaries over which he leaps. His ambitions seem so transgressive because he is so firmly convinced that rank can never safely be disregarded.[10]

But although the play is a paean to birth, it does not ignore the facts of change. Though leaving the ladder of rank firmly in place, Massinger does allow a limited movement up and down it. His Nottinghamshire may be quiet, but it is not static. At the bottom, Tapwell is hoping that his alehouse will lift him into the village elites. Already he has the menial office of scavenger in view, and more may follow (1.1.67–8). At the top, similarity of status makes Lovell and Lady Alworth a marriageable pair ('Our yeares, our states, our births are not vnequall' he tells her), but marriage to a lord *is* promotion for this gentleman's widow, and she is properly over-whelmed by the 'great fauour' which it involves (5.1.45, 62). And in between, accommodations have been licensed between the poorer gentry and their wealthier competitors, despite Lovell's distaste for an 'issue / Made vp of seuerall peeces, one part skarlet / And the other *London*-blew' (4.1.224–6). Margaret Overreach may not end up a countess, but she does enter the orbit of gentility, albeit in the reduced opening of wife to Alworth (page to Lord Lovell but son to a once wealthy gentleman). This connection is hedged around with all kinds of provisos, notably Lovell's insistence that marriage with anyone as lowly as Margaret would 'adulterate my blood' (4.2.223), but the restoration of impoverished gentlemen to their estates has involved voting with the pocket book, and some controlled mis-cegenation turns out to be inevitable. Massinger doesn't exactly represent his gentlemen as an Open Elite; notwithstanding, the ability of the English aristocracy to accommodate themselves to money was a factor which would help them to retain their social hegemony well into the nineteenth century,[11] and Massinger's prediction of their adaptability is something which the grim reading significantly marginalises.

Of course, the element of control is critical here: the play permits money to be tacked on to blood without the hereditary elites feeling it has damaged their authority. We are not shown structural change but the absorption of competitors into a hierarchy in which the mystique of birth continues to dominate, and those with cash are accepted only if they defer to the social pre-eminence of those whose overdrafts they are bailing out. Margaret is a legitimate marriage for Alworth because she is a walking mouthpiece for the ideology of deference, shame-faced when she has to order the impoverished Lady Downefalne about (3.2.49–52), and so upset about her father's insanity at the end that she is putty in her husband's hands. On the other hand, these are not terms to which Sir Giles will agree, and since he cannot be brought within a gradualist accommodation he has to be made to self-destruct. This appears to be a damaging gap in the play's social analysis, artificially limiting as it does the one character who seems seriously to challenge normative values. However, it is needful to look at just what Overreach's challenge amounts to.

Overreach isn't of genteel birth. 'I come from the Cittie', he tells Marrall, and he thinks in terms of the 'Fewde' between men of wealth and 'such whose Fathers were Right worshipful' (2.1.81–8). He might be assimilated to Luke Frugal in *The City Madam* – another power-hungry citizen who delights in enslaving aristocratic creditors[12] – or to the usurer Lucre in Middleton's *A Trick to Catch the Old One*, but there are significant differences, not the least of which is the distance that Overreach has already covered by migrating to Nottingham's shady groves. This is more than a matter of geography. Sir Giles may have arrived in provincial society only recently but he is not a simple interloper: the locals object to his exploitation of widows and orphans, but he already has a foothold in their community which conditions their dealings with him. They may complain that his chicanery is undermining the neighbourhood, but he is already exhibiting some of the *de facto* marks of gentility, and although related to the stereotype of the Middletonian citizen he cannot be equated with it exactly.

Sir Giles's dignity is damaged by his associates. Justice Greedy's insatiable hunger is a demystified version of his own ambition, and he is badly let down by Marrall, who slurps the soup at Lady Alworth's table, provoking much supercilious comment from her servants about the slovenliness of lawyers (2.2.118–32). But although the despicable Marrall is clearly non-U, the contrast underlines how much more genteel Sir Giles actually is. He would have known how to behave, as he is sensitive to nuances of compliment and insult. He dismisses Marrall's tale about having been entertained by the lady

with absolute incredulity – it's a 'most incredible lye' by an
'Impudent Varlet' (2.3.87–94) – because his sense of the proprieties
is so outraged by it, and although Lovell tactfully rebukes Lady
Alworth for her patronage of Welborne, it is Sir Giles to whom her
derogation feels positively monstrous (3.3.26, 4.1.238). When Welborne insults him with the bare title 'Sir' (5.1.114), it is with a finely
calculated sense of how painful to him such casual disrespect will be.
Such considerations would be absurd in Lucre and downright
irrelevant to Luke Frugal, but they show how much Sir Giles already
is a part of the society which he affects to despise, how delicately he
has been positioned on the border between belonging and exclusion.

Were it not for Marrall at his side, Sir Giles might well seem a
gentleman. He has a knighthood, and no one ever thinks this is
inappropriate. He has ties in the locality, since his wife was sister to
old Sir John Welborne, and twice his 'friends' here are spoken of,
though they never actually come into view (2.1.56, 5.1.313). He tells
Marrall that great countesses' doors have flown open to him
(2.3.88–90), and as a suitor to Lady Alworth he has free access to her
house (1.3.1–33). He is sufficiently entrenched in the shire to join the
magistracy if he wanted to, and sufficiently comfortable to refuse for
the sake of more nefarious considerations (2.1.10–22). More crucially,
he affects the lifestyle of a gentleman, and however much others are
troubled by it, it does not strike them as inherently ridiculous. Says
Lady Alworth's cook:

> this Sir *Giles* feedes high, keepes many seruants,
> Who must at his command doe any outrage;
> Rich in his habit; vast in his expences;
> Yet he to admiration still increases
> In wealth, and Lordships.   (2.2.110)

Overreach rebukes Greedy for being more interested in food than in
making money, but he doesn't himself behave like 'a vsurer that
starues himself' (2.2.106). He is more a Volpone than a penny-
pincher, and he spends high when he needs to do so, welcoming
Lovell with a great display of plate, linen, viands and perfume, and
dismissing Marrall's complaint that ''Twil be very chargeable'
(3.2.1–10). Most striking of all, he wears a sword – the symbolic
badge of gentility – and threatens repeatedly to use it.

The violence of Sir Giles was intrinsic to Kean's interpretation –
his Overreach was remembered as 'the most terrific exhibition of

human passion' that the stage had ever seen[13] – but even without
Kean the intensity of Overreach's rages will always unsettle any
naively comic reading of the play. His violence is a political thing,
since it is the means by which he expresses his power. Its principal
beneficiaries are Marrall (who is in physical fear of him throughout)
and Margaret (whose eyes he threatens to dig out), and it links him
to Welborne (who opens the play by beating up Tapwell). But as
matters accelerate, Sir Giles develops a startling propensity to
challenge people to duels. He is outraged at Margaret's suggestion
that Lovell might take advantage of her, then forsake her:

> Doe I weare a sword for fashion? or is this arme
> Shrunke vp? or wither'd? does there liue a man
> Of that large list I haue encounter'd with,
> Can truly say I e're gaue inch of ground,
> Not purchas'd with his blood, that did oppose me?
> Forsake thee when the thing is done? he dares not.
> Giue me but proofe, he has enjoy'd thy person,
> Though all his Captaines, Eccho's to his will,
> Stood arm'd by his side to iustify the wrong,
> And he himselfe in the head of his bold troope,
> Spite of his Lordship, and his Collonelship,
> Or the Iudges fauour, I will make him render
> A bloody and a strict accompt, and force him
> By marrying thee, to cure thy wounded honour;
> I haue said it.   (3.2.140–54)

This is not mere bravado or bluster. Overreach may not know his
daughter but he has no illusions about lords (it's worth recollecting
that even Massinger's 'puritanical' patron, the Earl of Pembroke,
had two illegitimate children by Lady Mary Wroth), and Lovell,
who has fought overseas, would be a considerable opponent. Further,
Overreach's society understands and respects the ethos of duelling:
Welborne's most pressing claim on Lady Alworth is that he had
seconded her husband in all his duels (1.3.103–4). Overreach's
threats here are directed at his daughter, but they establish his ability
to compete within the aristocratic arena on aristocratic terms: he
may appear a bad man to his enemies, but his boldness for his
'honour' is a quality which means they have to take him seriously.
Subsequently we find him telling Lovell that 'with mine own sword
/ If call'd into the field, I can make that right, / Which fearefull
enemies murmur'd at as wrong' (4.1.118–20) and in the final scene
he repeatedly responds to bafflement by calling out the supposedly

honourable men whom he rightly sees have defeated him by trickery. He draws on Welborne and wants to take him 'single in the field' (5.1.149); only swords can keep him from Marrall; and his culminating action is a public challenge to Lovell. Welborne derides this, but Overreach's retort that only 'coward hunters' brave the lion from behind the safety of numbers is the kind of insult that knows the people against whom it is directed (5.1.299–311; and compare 'cowards' at 5.1.241). The gesture which in his final insane speech symbolically disqualifies him from gentility is his impotent failure to draw his sword out of its scabbard.

My point in drawing out these underemphasized aspects of Overreach's character is that although he challenges the Nottinghamshire gentry he does not embody a rival ideology with which their ideology of rank is in collision. He is not a Luke Frugal, a miserly citizen who longs to sit in solitude amidst his store. Rather, he has internalised the values of the class to which he aspires, and once entrenched amongst the aristocrats he would outstrip them at their own game. Conspicuous consumption holds no terrors for him. He tells Lovell that as his father-in-law he will shower him with cash and 'ruine / The Country' for the sake of keeping up the 'port' and 'riotous wast' which goes hand in hand with being a nobleman: the marriage gives him more pleasure than Lovell will have 'In spending what my industry hath compass'd' (4.1.105–9, 138). Overreach is not a plebeian revolutionary whose victory would be the end of the world as we know it. On the contrary, it would continue as the old aristocratic world, but with a new man at the top. What he desires is power, expressed in terms of enslaving all men to his personal will. He would be 'the grand incloser / Of what was common, to my priuate vse': he would have 'all men sellers, / And I the only Purchaser', and his daughter waited on by decayed ladies since ''tis my glory, though I come from the Cittie, / To haue their issue, whom I haue vndone, / To kneele to mine, as bond-slaues' (2.1.32–3, 81–3; 4.1.124–5). Plainly the element of status anxiety is strong here – it is the social elites whom Overreach's ambitions hit hardest – but his ambitions paradoxically reinforce hierarchies of rank since they depend for their satisfaction on outrageous acts of subordination, and once Overreach has wed Margaret to Lovell he intends to raise her husband to yet higher dignities (4.1.142–4). Overreach is not a leveller but a tyrannical megalomaniac, striving to reduce the whole of the nation to his private will. It's not surprising that the man who thought 'the whole world' was 'Included in my selfe' should end the play in a strait-jacket (5.1.355–6).

So *A New Way* does not rehearse a coming crisis as the '1642' model supposes it to do. Although Massinger has labelled Overreach as an arriviste, we do not see a city challenge to aristocratic ideologies so much as an attempt to hijack the hierarchies of rank by someone acting out of radically private motives, a rabid individualist who will be defeated by the resistance of society as a whole to domination by the will of a single person (Overreach's schemes depend on the willingness of other people to cooperate – especially Margaret and Marrall – and since they won't his ambitions are doomed to frustration). An ideological conflict is being represented here, but it is not between an ideology of rank and the bourgeois ideology which Massinger is purported to have been so very anxious about. Rather, what we are witnessing are tensions within the ideology of deference itself, which are articulated as competition *between* members of the ruling elites and which are resonant of the political divides of the 1620s rather than the 1640s. By which I mean that Overreach's real opponent is not Welborne but Lovell, and that these two competitors embody what in 1625 were coming to emerge as rival perceptions of the character of political obligation.

Lovell gets short shrift in most accounts of the play, probably because he's assumed to be boringly conventional. Actually, the entire play is really a victory for him. In this world of orphans and absent fathers, in which Sir Giles hopes by marrying himself to Lady Alworth and his daughter to Lovell to become the patriarch of a nightmarish anti-family, Lovell eventually emerges as the ideal father restored. His marriage engrosses the play's social prestige, and everyone ends in situations of political obligation to him. Margaret weds his devoted page, who promptly turns Overreach's estates over to *his* disposal (5.1.387–8); Welborne will redeem his honour by fighting overseas in Lovell's regiment. Overreach had nurtured a fantasy in which Lovell would be subordinated to him: Lovell would be his son-in-law and the next Lord Lovell a grandson dancing on his knee (4.1.99–103). As things turn out, Overreach is demolished and power is returned to the hands of the one person whose claim to precedence rests on hereditary birthright.

Massinger gives Lovell a highly unusual colouring: he's middle-aged, he's an aristocrat, and he's a soldier. As a romantic hero he's more like a father than a lover, and age qualifies him for social leadership as much as amatory success. As an aristocrat, he's very carefully positioned, above everybody else in the play but not quite at the top of the social tree: his lack of ambition for the higher status that Overreach would purchase for him labels him in a significantly oppositional way. From the mid-1610s James had been selling titles for ready money, and Buckingham's relatives had been amongst those most conspicuously profiting from the fluidity of status, but Lovell has no truck with this sort of thing. His honour has been 'By vertuous wayes atchieu'd, and brauely purchas'd' (4.1.195), and his willingness to let his name die rather than preserve it through a connection with Margaret expresses a contempt both for city wealth and for the unmerited honour that the crown was happy to sell for cash. It is on the field of battle that he (and Alworth and Welborne) see honour as being truly established.

We have to take the war context seriously to understand what Massinger is getting at. In the Oxford edition Philip Edwards disparages the military angle by relating the play to the disastrous expedition led to the continent in 1624 by the German general Ernst von Mansfeld, and in a more recent essay he links Lovell to Kenelm Digby's quixotic privateering around the Mediterranean in 1627–9 and implies that these 'chivalric notions of military honor' were out of touch with reality.[14] But the situation was more complex than this. After the collapse of the Spanish Match late in 1623, England was swept with war fever, as a nation tired of James's appeasement of Spain embraced the prospect of renewed military action. Mansfeld's expedition was a fiasco, but this was due to bad organisation by a mercenary more interested in his money than his men, and to the fact the King hobbled it by forbidding Mansfeld to take any direct action against Spain, thus preventing him from relieving the siege of Breda, the one thing that might have been strategically significant (a failure still lamented by Lady Alworth's cook (1.2.26–8)). But James died in March 1625 and was replaced by a youthful king eager for honour abroad. Virtually Charles's first action was to fit out a fleet against Spain, the first act of warfare to be promoted by the crown since the days of Elizabeth.[15]

In the event, Cadiz was a disaster, but Massinger was writing before the news got home,[16] and even afterwards enthusiasm survived for the right kind of war. In 1625, besides Mansfeld's dwindling army and the new troops raised for Cadiz, there were plans for an attack on the Spanish privateers at Dunkirk (an action to which Marrall refers, 5.1.231–3),[17] and four British regiments were in action under the Prince of Orange in the Low Countries. These troops had been raised in 1624 to fulfil the terms of an alliance with the Dutch, and they had a high public profile. Since they were volunteers (not conscripts like Mansfeld's troops), they evoked the days of Leicester and Sidney, when English soldiers had defended Dutch liberty against Spain, and at court there was fervent competition for officers' places. The companies were eventually led overseas by four popular noblemen, the Earls of Essex, Oxford and Southampton and Lord Willoughby; Oxford and Southampton would both die in the service. Essex went on to Cadiz, then returned in 1626 with a new body of volunteers for Germany. These men were still in Holland, though much reduced, in 1627.[18]

After years of appeasement and failure to fight for Protestantism, great expectations attached to these initiatives. In the pamphlet *Honour in his Perfection*, by Gervase Markham (like Massinger, a Pembroke client), fulsome praise is heaped on the companies and their aristocratic leaders. Markham argues that their glory will inspire emulation in gentlemen left behind: 'Nor was this done so much to extol and renowne them, as to quicken and set on fire the noble hearts of many others, which now like some of the Statues or the Monuments in Westminster lye sleeping on their Elbowes'.[19] For Arthur Wilson, who accompanied Essex to Holland, the Earl's campaigns embodied the best of English honour, in contrast to soldiery associated with the Duke of Buckingham, whose navy was humiliated at Cadiz and who would preside over an even greater debacle at the Isle of Rhé. Whereas Buckingham seemed a flamboyant and self-serving commander, Essex was a 'gallant voluntier', his companions 'daring Spirits' whose careers validated the honour of their ancestors. These were men who had been at odds with James's pacific court, and even under the warlike Charles such popular nobles would still be distrusted. Essex, said Wilson, was someone 'who ever affected...a naturall and just freedom of the subject', and he was sent to Cadiz to 'sweeten the business', 'being a man beloved of the people, and the people not likeing [Buckingham's] exorbitant power'.[20] Wilson wrote with hindsight, but at the time it was seen that the popularity of such officers brought in volunteers, and that war usefully got troublesome aristocrats out of the country. In the 1640s Essex would fight the King, as general for

parliament; in Thomas Scott's *Robert Earl of Essex his Ghost* (1624) he
was already being mythologised as the successor to his father's
Elizabethan heroics.

It is this kind of soldiering – an army of patriots, officered by
gentlemen and generalled by popular nobles – that I suspect we are
to associate with Lovell.[21] Lovell's soldiery is discussed at some
length, and it is underlined that he is the 'gallant minded, popular
Lord Louell, / The minion of the peoples loue' (2.1.69–70). Not only
does he command soldiers but

> what's rare is one himselfe,
> A bold, and vnderstanding one; and to be
> A Lord, and a good leader in one volume,
> Is granted vnto few, but such as rise vp
> The Kingdomes glory.   (3.2.78–82)

Overreach assumes Lovell is just like all the other gaudy court
cavaliers. He tells Margaret to expect him to take liberties with her
since he is 'a Courtier, and a Soldier, / And not to be trifl'd with'
(3.2.106–7), and Alworth plays up to this false image, boasting that
his lord will celebrate his marriage 'at Court' with all pomp and
ceremony (4.3.95–7). Remarkably, Alworth has his own doubts
about Lovell, and agonises over his fear that when presented with
Margaret Lovell will take her and forget about his page. He describes
it as a test of his patron's military character, describing Margaret as
a cannon whose bullets will so fiercely assault the bulwarks of Lovell's
'rebellious Passions' that he will be unable to defend himself
(3.1.60–71). In fact, of the four aristocratic colonels, Oxford had just
this kind of reputation as a debauched cavalier. When he went to war
in Germany in 1620, one wag wrote that 'Sir Horace Vere / Hath
caried the earle of Oxford where, / He neither shall have wine nor
whore, / Nor Hercules himself could do no more'.[22] But Lovell turns
out to be a responsible soldier who will not betray his dependant
(3.1.37–41) and who easily keeps his appetites under control. He is,
in fact, a kind of aristocratic puritan.

War, as Lovell and company see it, is the proving-ground for an
ethos of sobriety, duty and obligation:

> it is a schoole
> Where all the principles tending to honour
> Are taught if truly followed: But for such
> As repaire thither, as a place, in which
> They doe presume they may with licence practise

> Their lusts, and riots, they shall neuer merit
> The noble name of souldiers. To dare boldly
> In a faire cause, and for the Countries safety
> To runne vpon the cannons mouth vndaunted:
> To obey their leaders, and shunne mutenies;
> To beare, with patience, the winters cold,
> And sommers scorching heate, and not to faint,
> When plenty of prouision failes, with hunger,
> Are the essential parts make vp a souldier,
> Not swearing, dice, or drinking. (1.2.100–14)

This opposition between cavalier debauchery and disciplined soldiery Welborne will have to learn, and he promises finally to redeem
his riots by following the wars. Further, these values have political
spin-offs, since good captains keep their words to their men, and
Lovell's honour is seen as bound up with his sincerity and sense of
obligation. Unlike Overreach, who is deceitful, who enjoys being
served by slaves, and who supposes that riotous living is the
incontrovertible prerogative of greatness, Lovell insists on his
contempt for 'Great men' whose sense of superiority makes them
treat 'all such as follow 'em, / Without distinction of their births, like
slaues' (3.1.22–5). As a patron he is 'more like a Father to [Alworth]
than a Master', and his word is his bond, in contrast to the 'othes
bound vp with imprecations, / Which when they would deceive, *most
Courtiers* practize' (3.1.30, 44–5, my emphasis). There is an antithesis
here, crystallising around the wartime politics of the 1620s, which
invests Lovell in the character of patriotic and selfless aristocrat,
aware of his obligations to his dependants and his role in the service
to his country, and opposes him to Overreach. With his desire to
enslave just about everyone Overreach offends against this code, and
provokes rebellions in Margaret and Marrall. His tyranny is
inevitably thwarted by the benevolent aristocratic paternalism for
which Lovell is the figurehead.

Doubtless there is a great deal of evasion involved here. Massinger's
ideological assumptions oblige him to idealise Lovell, and to restrain
the potentially subversive elements of his action within a constitutionalist frame. Margaret's and Marrall's rebellions against
Overreach are hardly acts which liberate them, since she is just as
powerless in the new community as she was in the old, and once he
has betrayed his old master he is destroyed forever with the new.
Lovell's outlook is not remotely democratic, and in acknowledging

him as a father who knows the 'fitting difference' between footboy and gentleman (3.1.27) Alworth reinforces the ladder of deference off which no one ever steps. But the crucial point is that Massinger is not idealising the aristocracy per se but a particular section within the aristocracy, and the values to which they were coming to be attached. A middle-aged soldier, Lovell invokes older notions of heroism, the ethos of the earl of Essex (and his father) rather than that of the present favourite Buckingham. A Caroline nobleman, he is also a kind of Elizabethan, and this at a time when disasters at Cadiz and Rhé were demonstrating the failure of Charles and his favourite to live up to patriotic expectations. For all that the play propels a citizen upstart against the entrenched elites, it is a split within the ideology of the elites that it rehearses. Its antithesis between a traditional aristocracy, concerned for sobriety, patriotism, social order and political obligation, and a parvenu who lives high and answers to no one for his actions, speaks eloquently of the anxieties of the 1620s – and it does so by no means from a position of withdrawal.

Inevitably, it is difficult not to feel that Buckingham is the missing link here, and that his combination of unchallenged influence and grand living was very much at stake. As everyone knows, Overreach was a fantasia on a member of his family, Sir Giles Mompesson, the monopolist impeached by the 1621 parliament, whose Christian name he shares and whose extortion of money from innkeepers is echoed in 1.1 and 4.2. This chimes with the play's broadly oppositional colouring. Monopolies were a special grievance in James's last decade, and Pembroke chaired the Lords committee that considered Mompesson's crimes. More particularly, they were an embarrassment to Buckingham, given that Mompesson was a client and that two of his brothers were deeply involved in other offensive monopolies.[23] But one can take this too far: Overreach's outlines don't correspond at all to Mompesson's, who was old Wiltshire gentry,[24] and by 1625 the heat was off monopolies, which had been brought under statute in 1624. In any case, the play doesn't raise monopolies as a grievance, and personal caricature would have been extremely hazardous.

The real relevance of Mompesson lies in the anxiety which he had exposed amongst the parliamentary gentry about the erosion of their local powers. Ostensibly his actions had hurt provincial innkeepers, but he struck a parliamentary nerve by seeming to undermine the autonomy of justices of peace. His patent entitled him to reform an abuse by regulating unlicensed inns, but in practice he sold licenses for cash and legalised innkeepers left and right that local magistrates had already banned. In parliament this provoked a storm of constitutionalist protest about London-based patentees interfering in local affairs, but the outrage was also motivated by social considerations. Sir Edward Coke fulminated that the patent did a 'great dishonour to the Justices of peace, and a great indignitie'; Sir Thomas Wentworth said justices 'ought not to be made subject to every petty patentee, which is a slavery makes men weary of the office'; and Sir Robert Phelips protested that though 'the king hath referred a great part of the government of this kingdom to the justices of the peace, this disheartenenth them, for it maketh a justice of peace to be buffeted by a base alehousekeeper. I never knew government receive so great a wound.' It was deemed especially offensive that Mompesson had written 'insolent' letters to some justices, as this 'would make inns to curb justices of the peace'.[25] Understandably, Mompesson fled rather than face impeachment, but his punishment in absentia had a strong social element. Beside a massive fine, imprisonment and banishment, he was degraded from his knighthood, declared unfit for future office, and sentenced to ride along the Strand with his face to the horse's tail, and to be forever held an infamous person. Evidently his offence was not only greed, but his unsettling impact on inherited interests and loyalties.

This parliamentary overreaction helps to substantiate the particular nightmare that Massinger's Welborne is living, a gentleman who has lost not only lands but status and who, in the course of the play, is threatened with all kinds of exquisitely shameful humiliations – the stocks, hanging, loss of his ears. But Mompesson also shows how intimately at this time the developing political polarisations were bound up with more inchoate fears of social transformation, fears which (though expressed conservatively) helped to give emotional force to issues that otherwise involved challenges to royal authority. Over monopolies, James embraced the cause of reform and MPs were relieved to find that their complaints were not construed as subversion. But at a time when the crown was using the sale of aristocratic titles as a means of raising cash; when the Earl of Suffolk had recently been accused of corruption so extensive that he was said to have turned the Exchequer into a shop and his deputy into 'the prentice that cried "What do you lack?"';[26] and when one of the articles of impeachment against Buckingham was that his family had engrossed honours out of all proportion to their services to the crown;[27] then a concern to retain things in their older order was hardly devoid of more unsettling implications. Once the crown became perceived as the innovator, then resistance to change amongst the elites had consequences that could not easily be kept within the old sphere of conservatism. The gulf that opened up between 'new ways' and 'old debts' in the parliaments of the later 1620s – even if it was not a step on some hypothetical road to civil war – marked the emergence of polarisations that were helping to make conflict all the more likely.

I do not wish simply to replace one teleology with another. In 1625 such developments were still in the future and Massinger can send Welborne abroad to do 'seruice / To my King, and Country' without much sense of strain between the two terms (5.1.398–9). And yet the tensions which Massinger has to efface in order to reach this conclusion are eloquent testimony to the erosion of consensus in the mid-1620s. There is a glaring contradiction (for example) between Welborne's high spirits, which are allowed so long as they stay on this side of prodigality, and Lovell's sobriety: this contradiction within the aristocratic ethos exposes the problems in an ideology in which one group of aristocrats are constructed as oppositional figures yet which continues to assume that society is notwithstanding premised on the social hegemony of the aristocracy at large. Conversely, the disturbing similarities which Overreach manifests to the people who eject him from their ranks advertise the difficulties involved in defining him as the unwanted Other, when to a very considerable extent he already belongs. (In this regard it is Margaret in the last scene – who marries her gentleman but breaks down because the marriage kills her father – who measures most overtly the tensions in Massinger's resolution.) Such inconsistencies demonstrate that the play's investments were both in change and in keeping things as they always had been, and they define the limits to Massinger's ability to imagine solutions to his age's emergent crisis. And while Massinger's aristocrats may not be able to predict the future, it should be clear by now that they are not in retreat, but are gearing themselves up to encounter it. It still may not be very funny to see Overreach destroyed by his peers and superiors, but at least we can better understand why his thwarting should have been felt to be a historical necessity.

NOTES

1 *The Times Literary Supplement*, 1977, 623–4; reprinted in Douglas Howard, ed., *Philip Massinger: A Critical Reassessment* (Cambridge, 1985), 221–32. For some other recent reappraisals, see Albert Tricomi, *Anti-Court Drama in England, 1603–1642* (Charlottesville, 1989); and Lawrence Venuti, *Our Halcyon Dayes: English Prerevolutionary Texts and Postmodern Culture* (Madison, Wis., 1989), 55–98.

2 *Selected Essays* (London, 1932), 216.

3 Robert Hamilton Ball, *The Amazing Career of Sir Giles Overreach* (Princeton, 1939), 64–8.

4 This revival is described with excellent detail by H. Neville Davis, '*A New Way to Pay Old Debts*: Massinger and the RSC', *Critical Quarterly*, 26 (1984), 47–56.

5 Citations are to *The Plays and Poems of Philip Massinger*, eds. Philip Edwards and Colin Gibson, 5 vols. (Oxford, 1976).

6 R. A. Fothergill, 'The dramatic experience of Massinger's *The City Madam* and *A New Way to Pay Old Debts*', *University of Toronto Quarterly*, 43 (1973–4), 68–86.

7 Michael Neill, 'Massinger's Patriarchy: *A New Way to Pay Old Debts*', *Renaissance Drama*, n.s. 10 (1979), 185–213.

8 Philip Edwards, 'Philip Massinger: Comedy and Comical History' in A. R. Braunmuller and J. C. Bulman, eds., *Comedy from Shakespeare to Sheridan* (Cranbury, N.J., 1986), 179–93 (184).

9 I refer to the work of John Adamson: see especially 'The Baronial Context of the English Civil War', *Transactions of the Royal Historical Society*, 5th series, 40 (1990), 93–120; and 'Parliamentary Management, Men of Business, and the House of Lords, 1640–49' in Clive Jones, ed., *A Pillar of the Constitution* (London, 1989), 21–50. For the hot contesting, see the amazing exchange between Adamson and Mark Kishlansky: Kishlansky, 'Saye What?', *Historical Journal*, 33 (1990), 917–37, and Adamson, 'Politics and the Nobility in Civil-War England', *Historical Journal*, 34 (1991), 231–55.

10 On this point, see Gail Kern Paster, 'Quomodo, Sir Giles, and Triangular Desire: Social Aspiration in Middleton and Massinger', in Braunmuller and Bulman, *Comedy from Shakespeare to Sheridan*, 165–78.

11 See Lawrence Stone and Jean Fawtier Stone, *An Open Elite? England 1540–1880* (Oxford, 1984); and David Cannadine, *The Decline and Fall of the British Aristocracy* (New Haven, 1990).

12 See Martin Butler, 'Massinger's *The City Madam* and the Caroline Audience', *Renaissance Drama*, n.s. 13 (1982), 157–87.

13 Ball, *The Amazing Career of Sir Giles Overreach*, 68.

14 Edwards, 'Philip Massinger: Comedy and Comical History', 185. There is an altogether more positive appraisal of Kenelm Digby's privateering by Kenneth R. Andrews in *Ships, Money and Politics:*

Seafaring and Naval Enterprise in the Reign of Charles I (Cambridge, 1991), 106–27.

15 The background to this whole period has been brilliantly treated by Tom Cogswell in *The Blessed Revolution* (Cambridge, 1989).

16 News of Cadiz reached England in December 1625 (*Calendar of State Papers*, Venetian series [*CSPV*] *1625–1626*, 244, 253, 269).

17 The Dunkirk privateers were a perennial source of irritation to both English and Dutch operations in the North Sea. A blockade of Dunkirk was broken by a storm in November 1625, and discussions took place between the English and Dutch concerning the fitting out of a new fleet to suppress the Dunkirkers. See *CSPV 1625–1626*, 213, 223, 230: and Samuel Rawson Gardiner, *History of England...1603–42*, 10 vols. (London, 1883–4), V, 325, VI, 35.

18 Cogswell, *The Blessed Revolution*, 256, 274–8; Vernon F. Snow, *Essex the Rebel* (Lincoln, Ne., 1970), 118–24, 158–65; A. T. S. Goodrick, *The Relation of Sydnam Poyntz* (Camden Society, 1908).

19 Gervase Markham, *Honour in his Perfection* (London, 1624), sigs. A2^v–3^r.

20 Arthur Wilson, 'Observations of God's Providence, in the Tract of my Life' in Philip Bliss ed., *The Inconstant Lady* (Oxford, 1814), 119, 122–3, 127; and *The History of Great Britain* (London, 1653), 135–6 (speaking of the 1620 campaign). See also Snow, *Essex the Rebel*.

21 Other noblemen active at sea and on land against Catholic forces in these years included the Earls of Warwick, Buccleuch and Danby.

22 John Chamberlain, *Letters*, ed. N. E. McClure, 2 vols. (Philadelphia, 1939), II, 314–15.

23 On Mompesson, see Gardiner, *History of England*, IV, 1–44, 84; Gardiner, 'On Four Letters from Lord Bacon to Christian IV of Denmark', *Archaeologia*, 41 (1867), 219–69; Stephen K. Roberts, 'Alehouses, Brewing, and Government under the Early Stuarts', *Southern History*, 2 (1980), 45–71: Keith Wrightson, 'Alehouses, Order and Reformation in Rural England, 1590–1660', in Elizabeth Yeo and Steven Yeo, eds., *Popular Culture and Class Conflict 1590–1914* (Brighton, 1981), 1–27; Peter Clark, *The English Alehouse* (London, 1983); Menna Prestwich, *Cranfield: Politics and Profits under the Early Stuarts* (Oxford, 1966), 278–9; Robert Zeller, *The Parliament of 1621* (Berkeley, 1971); Conrad Russell, *Parliaments and English Politics 1621–1629* (Oxford, 1979), 98–108; and Elizabeth R. Foster, 'The Procedure of the House of Commons against Patents and Monopolies, 1621–1624', in W. A. Aiken and B. D. Henning, eds., *Conflict in Stuart England* (London, 1960), 57–85.

24 Sir Richard Colt Hoare, *The Modern History of South Wiltshire*, I (London, 1822), 2, 218–19.

25 Foster, 'Procedure of the House of Commons', 79; and Wallace Notestein, Helen Relf and Hartley Simpson, eds., *Commons Debates 1621*, 7 vols. (New Haven, 1935), II, 109–10, 112, VI, 257.

26 Prestwich, *Cranfield*, 221.

27 Roger Lockyer, *Buckingham* (Harlow, 1981), 322.

'*Thou teachest me humanitie*': Thomas Heywood's The English Traveller

Richard Rowland

At the Blackfriars theatre in 1626 the King's Men gave several performances of Philip Massinger's tragedy *The Roman Actor*, a play which Anne Barton has rightly characterised as 'more pessimistic about the power of art to correct and inform its audience than any other play written between 1580 and 1642'.[1] It seems likely that as avid a playgoer as Thomas Heywood would have made the short trip from his home in Clerkenwell to see it. If he did, the experience may have been a disconcerting one. He would have heard Joseph Taylor as the eponymous hero defending the theatre, eloquently and at length, with arguments about its moral efficacy which were closely modelled on those Heywood himself had advanced in *An Apology for Actors* (1612).[2] He would then have witnessed the play's systematic annihilation of both the arguments and the man who courageously expounds them. In *The Roman Actor* theatre itself is out of control; comedy entrenches rather than reforms folly, noble love stories incite not veneration but lust, and 'real' violence masquerades as tragic fiction. It is the contention of this essay that Heywood's own most theatrically self-conscious play, *The English Traveller*, might be considered as a thoughtful response to Massinger's scepticism, conducted on two fronts: first, when he composed and brought the play to the stage of the Cockpit, probably in the following year; and second, when he decided to publish it six years later, at a time when the theatre was again under attack, and when ideological divisions in the literary world were edging Heywood closer to Massinger himself.

To suggest that Heywood ever made a considered response to anything is of course to fly in the face of a tradition of critical abuse which began, while Heywood was still alive to read it, when the compiler of *Witts Recreations* (1640) urged him to refrain from 'groveling on the stage'.[3] Some thirty years later the charmless cataloguer Francis Kirkman, anticipating Dryden's 'Mac Flecknoe' by more than a decade, wrote contemptuously about the 'mean' quality of plays which, he added unpleasantly, were all composed 'in Taverns'.[4] Interestingly, the piece of Heywood's writing which above all aroused Kirkman's antipathy, and which has incurred the ridicule of theatre historians ever since, occurs in the preface to *The English Traveller*: Heywood's nonchalant boast that he has 'had either an entire hand, or at the least a maine finger' in two hundred and twenty plays.[5] While this probably outrageous claim has achieved a certain notoriety, and while posterity has been scrupulous in affording Heywood his wish, expressed later in the same 'address', that he should not be 'Volumniously [sic] read', the remarkable play which follows has received little attention, and most of that has been derisive.[6]

Although the play was probably written when the Queen Henrietta's company was in its infancy (1626–7) it remained, like much of Heywood's earlier work, unprinted until 1633. By this time the adornment of playtexts with dedications, and with definitions or castigations of current theatrical tastes had become almost obligatory but Heywood's preliminaries here are unusually suggestive about the kind of achievement he believed *The English Traveller* to be. He hopes, for instance, that the 'bare Lines' of his verse will sustain a play in which he has, unusually for him, deployed neither 'Drum, nor Trumpet, nor Dumbe show', and which even eschews 'Song, Dance' and 'Masque' (Prologue, A3ᵛ). The printed text, moreover, Heywood now sees as an appropriate gesture of defiance to that 'Separisticall humorist' William Prynne, and his recent scurrilous attack on playwrights and players.[7] Lastly, the reader is told, the play is a 'Tragi-Comedy', containing 'Some Mirth, some Matter, and perhaps some Wit'.

For Heywood to classify his play generically in this way is in itself a new departure. He knew the theory underpinning the genre thoroughly; the *Apology* has an informed discussion of the commentaries of 'Donatus', which praised Terence for his mediation between the extremes of low comedy and high tragedy, and there are also the requisite obeisances to Aristotle's strictures on style and decorum. Heywood's own theatrical practice, however, had rarely observed prescriptive controls of this kind. Plays like *The Royal King and the Loyal Subject* (*c.* 1602) and *The Rape of Lucrece* (1608) had violently juxtaposed the serious and the farcical, and had also shown a growing fascination with the ways in which each of these tones might collapse into its opposite. This is crucially the case with *The English Traveller*, with its two plots, ostensibly tragic and comic respectively, which *seem* to be self-contained. It is customary, though neither helpful nor accurate, to see the Caroline Heywood limping helplessly after whichever bandwagon happened to be passing; but this drama owes little to Fletcherian tragicomedy with its Guarini-derived sense of providential closure, and its strict (and increasingly influential) separation of the low comic material from the high and grave. *The English Traveller* is rather – like *The Roman Actor* – a play concerned with the instability of generic conventions, and yet it is also one which confidently insists on its capacity to amuse and disturb in the same breath.

The exchange which opens the first scene introduces the protagonists of the serious plot, a story of deception and sexual betrayal which Heywood had not only told but declared to be true in an earlier prose work (*Gunaikeon*, 1624). Two intellectuals in early manhood, Young Geraldine and Dalavill, enter comparing experience acquired through the active life of travel with the knowledge to be gained merely by reading. Dalavill, though effortlessly conversant with the most recent developments in cartography and archaeology, claims to value 'Practicke' over 'Theoricke' and flatters his much travelled companion accordingly:

>   what I
> Haue by relation onely, knowledge by trauell
> Which still makes vp a compleat Gentleman,
> Prooues eminent in you.   ($A4^r$)

These men seem casually familiar with fashionable travel writers like Sandys (*A Relation of a Journey*, 1615) and Moryson (*Itinerary*, 1617) and Heywood may also allow Dalavill a gesture here towards the first or second of the many editions of Henry Peacham's *The Compleat Gentleman* (1622, 1627).[8] In so doing Heywood establishes a rank and a social style for his characters: these are sophisticated if self-conscious young gentlemen, but the only hint of strain between them arises from the way in which the effusive friendliness of Dalavill is met by the rather stiff modesty of Young Geraldine. Heywood, however, is thus far giving little or nothing away in terms of plot and even this minor distinction disappears as 'Roger the Clowne', servant at the

Wincott household towards which they are heading, makes his first appearance.

As so often in Heywood there is a frisson of tension when the witty and articulate servant confronts characters who are of higher social rank and who are insistent upon their status being acknowledged. This is particularly the case in the later works, when 'clowns' who are essentially Elizabethan throwbacks intrude into a rarefied world of Caroline aestheticism, pitting their earthy semantic quibbles against the 'sprezzatura' of their masters: Corydon in *Loves Mistresse* (1634) is a fine example.[9] Yet, in spite of their irreverence, Heywood's clowns rarely exhibit the amoral opportunism or the prurience so common to the Elizabethan tradition.[10] Here, for instance, it is Roger's task to arouse the audience's anticipation of a conventional comedy of cuckoldry. He does so with a proverbial reference to the marriage between the ageing Wincott ('cold Ianuary') and his young wife ('lusty May'). It is noticeable, however, that his remarks are quite free of the goatish voyeurism that had coloured, for example, the presentation of similar tales, from Robert Armin's jests of the 1590s through to Robert Davenport's recent comedy for the same Cockpit theatre, *The City Night-Cap* (1624–5).[11]

The clown invites the young men to dinner and leaves them. Expectations of marital discord are momentarily defused by Dalavill's sensitive encomium of the perfect match between 'age and gouernment' and 'modesty and chaste respect', only to be reanimated by the arrival of the Wincotts themselves, accompanied by Roger and the Wife's sister Prudentilla. So great is old Wincott's affection for Young Geraldine that he makes him an extraordinary offer:

> I would haue you
> Thinke this your home, free as your Fathers house,
> And to command it, as the Master on't   (B1ʳ)

This may have sounded ominous to spectators old enough to remember Heywood's own *A Woman Killed with Kindness* (1603), in which a similar invitation leads to adultery and tragedy; equally it might have evoked a sense of amused anticipation for a younger generation of Cockpit devotees, recalling the supremely misplaced confidence of Lodovico in *The City Night-Cap*. When Wincott goes on to invite Dalavill to stand on a similarly intimate footing in his household it does at least seem clear that he is embarked on a systematic flouting of the most urgent advice that contemporary marriage treatises could offer: 'The mixing of gouernors in an houshold, or subordinating or vniting of two Masters...vnder one roofe, doth fall out most times, to be a matter of much vnquietness to all parties: Youth and Age are so far distant in their constitutions, that they wil hardly accord in their conditions...'[12]

The scene as a whole carefully sustains a generic instability. The tone of Wincott's enthusiastic myopia is curiously at odds with the sophisticated repartee of the younger generation who resume and expand on the opening dialogue about travel. Like Dalavill, Mrs Wincott has been reading 1.3 of Fynes Moryson's *Itinerary* with considerable attention, whereas her husband prefers his stories to be read aloud. Prudentilla, meanwhile, seems more attuned to Thomas Coryate's titillating tales of erotic Venetian encounters (*Coryats Crudities*, 1611), and she turns the conversation to the consideration of female beauty and its regional variations. Her contributions are full of tacit assumptions about the sexual proclivities of young English-men abroad and she flirts elaborately with Young Geraldine. Since the dialogue has established that Mrs Wincott's intimacy with the young traveller has flourished since childhood, her unease about the familiarity with which her sister treats Young Geraldine would appear to be for structurally obvious reasons. And yet Young Geraldine's responses – to all – are consistently chilly and aloof. As Prudentilla is provoked into ridicule of what she perceives as prim posturing her teasing merely prompts him to a more portentous (and Hamlet-like) seriousness:

> I should be loath
> Professe in outward shew to be one Man
> And prooue my selfe another   (B2^r)

The dynamics of the relationships between the genders and the generations have apparently rendered the 'comedy' of cuckoldry inevitable but the individual roles do not yet fit. The carefully polite Dalavill is a largely unknown quantity, but unless a spectator takes the radical view that the gratuitous acquisition of education and 'experience' cultivates only a flair for hypocrisy – and Young Geraldine has not and will not reveal any motive for his journeying – the returned traveller appears to be singularly unsuitable for the mandatory role of seducer.[13]

In order for anything to develop out of this scene some of these characters must prove other than they seem, but beyond an indication that the naive husband is the least capable of duplicity Heywood thwarts an audience's (and a director's) desire for clarification. The scene also closes in bizarre fashion. Hosts and guests depart for dinner and the Clown, alone on stage, steps forward to offer some proverbial wisdom and a little homily on the subject of hospitality: 'as you loue goodnesse, be sure to keepe good meat and drinke in your houses, and so you shall be called good men, and nothing can come on't but good, I warrant you' (B3^r). The last phrase clearly has a double function: in terms of what we have already seen, it serves as a wryly disingenuous hint to the audience that, in fact, *no* good will come of the old man's generosity. The tone is light but the implication clear, that Wincott is a gullible fool whose 'horning', comic or otherwise, we are about to witness.

Roger is also gently but not innocently introducing the controversial topic of hospitality, around which contemporary debate was protracted and acrimonious. The traditional concept that the Clown urges here was frequently invoked by purveyors of nostalgia as a stick with which to chastise the supposedly growing miserliness of the landowning classes, but it was also a concept under sustained attack from those who deemed it a specious substitute for the serious and year-long business of relieving the poor: 'Hospitalitie falsly so called is the keeping of a good table, at which seldome or never any other are entertained then kinsfolks, friends and able neighbours, merry companions, parasites, jesters... This is no hospitalitie, though it be commonly graced with that title, but it is good fellowship or some such like thing...'[14] Heywood teases his audience – they shall be 'called' good men but not necessarily be so – and deftly prepares the way for his subplot. For, as Roger cosily retires to the Wincott kitchen dresser, the rival factions in the debate he alludes to come out fighting.

Two servants of a long absent merchant, Old Lionel, enter exchanging blows and a range of insults which have their origins in the opening scene of the *Mostellaria* of Plautus. Stock situations and characters from Roman comedy would have been familiar to English audiences of all kinds. Those who had attended grammar schools or institutions of higher education would have read and occasionally acted in the Latin plays and, indeed, as *The English Traveller* appeared, Thomas Newman was producing new English acting versions of Terence for schools. Professional playwrights too –

Shakespeare, Jonson and Middleton among them – were indebted to the scenarios of New Comedy, but Heywood was unique in that twice in the 1620s he produced for the commercial stage works which were less adaptations than free translations of Plautine originals. The main plot of *The Captives* (1624) was a rendering of the *Rudens* and here Heywood annexes the whole of the tightly constructed *Mostellaria* for his subplot. At once, however, the distinctive flavour of the 'translation' is apparent; the shape of Plautus's dialogue is precisely preserved but the language is redolent of Nashe at his most idiosyncratic (in *Lenten Stuffe*), or John Taylor, the Water Poet, at his most carnivalesque (in *Iack-a-Lent*).

Reignald, Heywood's version of Plautus's ingenious 'servus' Tranio, is banishing the honest but dull Robin to the countryside. Robin is considerably more hapless than his Roman prototype Grumio and is on the defensive from the first line in which Reignald endows him with the extra and unwanted generic title of 'Corridon'.[15] Robin claims the protection of his seafaring master but Reignald insists 'wee are Lords amongst our Selues' and proclaims himself 'the mighty Lord and Seneschall / Of this great house and Castle' (B3[r]); this is a nice anglicism for which Heywood's rather serious friend Richard Brathwait might have provided a prophetic gloss: 'As every mans house is his Castle, so is his family a private Common-wealth, wherein if due government be not observed, nothing but confusion is to be expected.'[16]

At least as inclined to the homiletic strain as his friend Roger, Reignald is devout in the pursuit and justification of his misrule, and Heywood has invested his trickster with hedonistic traits picked up from Plautine precursors besides Tranio. The exuberant slave Sagaristo in the *Persa*, for example, plays, as does Reignald, on the word 'boues' (oxen) when he characteristically plans that all the money intended by his employers for investment in a cattle market should instead be blown on 'one crowded day of glorious life'.[17]

The *Mostellaria* opens with the clash between City and Country. Heywood faithfully translates this polarisation into his own play, simultaneously extending the analogous contrast between the mercurial role-playing of Reignald and the dour stolidity of Robin. More importantly, he makes the struggle urgently contemporary by locating it as the politically and theologically sensitive opposition between – to borrow Michael Bristol's categorisation – the Carnivalesque and the Lenten.[18] Thus, to Robin's accusation that

Reignald aspires to 'Keepe Christmasse all yeere long, and blot leane
Lent / Out of the Calender' the trickster responds with a sardonic
lecture on labouring in one's calling, concluding 'our seuerall lots are
cast, / And both must be contented' (B3ᵛ).

The modernisation of the discourse is comprehensive and the
anachronisms, often regarded as examples of Heywood's ineptitude,
are purposeful. Heywood offers the audience its conventional
alliances with the festive and the anarchic but by carefully keying the
language into contested areas of Caroline social policy the balance of
the Plautine comic structure is disturbed and those alliances have to
be re-examined. This is also the case as Heywood goes on to subject
Plautus's play to a more explicitly political updating. As the defeated
Robin retreats, his exit line identifies Reignald as the dissolute
courtier: 'Farewell, Musk-Cat'. His insult coincides exactly with the
arrival of the travelling merchant's prodigal son, Young Lionel, self-
proclaimed 'Lord' of this new luxurious court. He thoroughly
approves Robin's banishment:

> Let such keepe the Countrey where their charge is…
> And visit vs when we command them thence,
> Not search into our counsels.   (B4ʳ)

This echoes, in content and form, the repeated attempts of the Crown
to banish the gentry to the countryside. James had issued several
persistently ignored proclamations to this effect, culminating in an
exasperated 'absolute and peremptorie command' in October, 1624;
Charles followed suit in November, 1626, and again a year later,
when 'Noblemen, Knights and Gentlemen of qualitie' were ordered
to 'their severall Countreys to attend their Services there, and to
keepe Hospitality, as appertaineth to their degree and calling'.[19]

It is far from surprising to find such politicised material in plays of
the mid 1620s. Drue at the Fortune, Middleton at the Globe, and
Massinger at the same Cockpit theatre had all been more overtly
provocative than this in the previous couple of years.[20] The effect
here, however, is complex. The confrontation we have just witnessed
between Reignald and Robin was essentially an archetypal one,
reproducing an opposition as old as recorded comedy. Like Chremy-
lus's defeat of the sober logic and grave eloquence of Poverty in the
Plutus of Aristophanes, the more arbitrary the victory – 'Persuade me
you may, but I won't be persuaded!' – the more splendid the sense of
release as the audience enthusiastically endorses the comic hero's

assertion of abundance and physical gratification. But Heywood, despite his veneration for Aristophanes, has never made his comedy this simple and he doesn't now.[21] Reignald's tempting an audience to enjoy a vicarious prodigality and perhaps a secret thrill at hearing the *Homilies* travestied is not quite the same as Young Lionel's justifying his authority with the language of monarchical prerogative.[22] An intriguing complexity begins to emerge: this play does have two comic heroes but Young Lionel, supposed patron of misrule, is not one of them.

Robin's dismissal signifies, to return to Dalechamp's distinction, the victory of 'good fellowship' over 'hospitalitie'. The endless party Reignald envisages promises to be a joyous and expansive affair; Young Lionel, however, is mostly concerned that it should be an expensive one. So anxious is he to throw off all restraints on his profligacy that he wishes his father dead. This impulse derives from his model in the *Mostellaria* (though Philolaches is a little less blunt) but again Heywood has grafted on features from other Plautine protagonists: the ruthlessness of the parricidal Strabax from the *Truculentus* and the exotic aestheticism of Olympio in the *Casina*. As in the main plot, the Plautine adaptation involves the 'vniting of two Masters...vnder one roofe', and as soon as Young Lionel has dispatched Reignald to fetch whatever is 'rare and costly' for the evening's revels the fragility of the accord between them becomes clear.

At this point in Plautus, Philolaches addresses the audience alone, delivering a halting and rueful analogy between his own life and a nobly proportioned house, now ruined by a combination of indolence and a consuming love affair. Heywood follows his source quite closely but does a number of additional things with the soliloquy. Firstly, he makes the speech serve a function structurally similar to Prince Henry's 'I know you all' monologue in *Henry IV, Part 1*: this indulgence in festive misrule is a kind of self-conscious role-playing and, it is suggested, it will be of short duration. Secondly, the tone of the speech, far from being uncertain, recalls that of Mrs Wincott and Dalavill; this is a connoisseur of interior design, who contrives to sound as if he is reading from Henry Wotton's stylish *Elements of Architecture* (1624). The final deviation from the Plautine original is the unctuous way in which Young Lionel seeks to displace all responsibility for his current degradation onto his mistress, Blanda. And, right on cue, as the soliloquy ends, enters the 'Haile, Shower,

Tempest, Storme, and Gust, / That shatter'd hath this building'
(C1^r).

Again, though, Heywood diverges immediately and significantly
from his source, for Blanda is obviously not the vain, sophisticated, if
affectionate courtesan that Philematium had been. She is, rather,
and to the old bawd Scapha's acute irritation, unalterably devoted to
Young Lionel. The prodigal eavesdrops with comically mounting
indignation as the older woman advises Blanda to play the field. With
a pragmatic sense of conviction that the play's resolution will render
prophetic, Scapha warns her young friend: 'Confine thy selfe to one
Garment, and vse no varietie, and see how soone it will Rot, and
turne to Raggs' (c1^v). Although it is clear that the bawd is wasting
her breath, Young Lionel is unable to contain his rage, and steps
forward to wreak his vengeance on Scapha and her 'Erronious
Doctrine':

> Hencefoorth, I will confine thee to one Garment,
> And that shall be a cast one, Like thy selfe,
> Iust, past all Wearing, as thou past all Vse.   (c2^v)

An audience is, of course, expected to laugh at Scapha's discomfiture,
especially when she faints away on hearing the injunction denying
her further alcoholic refreshment. But here, in the opening scene of
the comic subplot, the carefree expansiveness of Reignald's as-
cendancy has been sourced. Despite Blanda's protests on her
companion's behalf, the inclusiveness of the 'fellowship' is to be
strictly circumscribed by the appetites of the young heir, and his
mistress's pleas for leniency are swept aside in the whispered
arrangements that Young Lionel is making for some other 'Wenches'
to be present at the evening's debauch. Act I ends, then, with Blanda,
who has overheard the whispers, being comforted by a cheerful
drunk who is reductively, if accurately named 'Rioter'.

Already, Heywood has disconcertingly transformed essentially
familiar material. There is a pervasive sense in Plautus that the
period of holiday license is coterminous with the duration of the
performance itself. The audience knows that Tranio will only escape
retribution at the hands of the blocking 'senex' who owns the house
by conceding that the next day – the everpresent 'cras' – will see a
complete restoration of hierarchical relationships. When Jonson
borrowed from the same play, the unexpected nature of Face's
eventual triumph had been dependent on the confounding of the

same conventions. But in the subplot of *The English Traveller* the figure that instigates the time of comic inversion is also the one who ensures from the outset that the holiday will be a short one. In both plots rich young people playing mysterious games are forcing an audience to qualify its responses at every step.

In terms of plot the second act arrests such momentum as the first had generated, although the characterisation is developed in intriguing ways. Old Wincott and his wife discuss Dalavill, the former anxious that the newcomer's attentions might obstruct the match he desires between Young Geraldine and his sister-in-law, Prudentilla. Given the hints that the Wife is reserving the young traveller's services for herself, the reasons for her objections to this alliance are apparently obvious, though she nonetheless manages to project a certain moral authority with her short diatribe on the miseries of enforced marriage. Honest Roger interrupts them with a lurid account of the goings on at the Lionel household. To the Clown's tale of a massacre (admirably lifted from Athenaeus), Mrs Wincott responds with cool amusement, her husband with terror. Although Wincott is painfully slow to register that the mutilated limbs are joints of meat, the servant's mockery is characteristically gentle at the moment of illumination: 'Your grauity hath gest aright' (c4^r).

More news of their neighbours' festivities arrives. Reignald and his crew have apparently drunk themselves into an imaginary shipwreck. The details of this escapade had recently appeared in a weighty treatise by Camerarius on the evils of alcohol but even Young Geraldine, after suitable disclaimers about his aptitude for the task, delivers a spirited rendition. This is fine comic writing but this episode too may be obliquely topical. The revellers' tempestuous disarray is quieted by the arrival of a constable wielding his staff of office, a figure the seriously inebriated partygoers proceed to worship as Neptune, arising to calm the seas with his trident. Both the mixing of culinary and militaristic metaphors from Athenaeus, and the allegorically restorative figure of Neptune (King James) had recently featured in Jonson's abortive celebration for the return of those two most famous of English travellers, Charles and Buckingham, from the equally abortive Spanish marriage expedition.[23] One of the preface's promises has, then, been broken. As Young Lionel's friends are depicted as antimasquers, the myth by which they are delivered and controlled is imaged as an absurd drunken fantasy of their own making. The masque, after all, has surreptitiously entered this text.

The same actors now turn abruptly from mirth to matter. Old Wincott retires to bed, Dalavill and Prudentilla exit exchanging titillating whispers and Young Geraldine and the Wife are left alone. The much delayed adulterous coupling now seems inescapable but what actually occurs is more remarkable. The pair rehearse their long-standing mutual attraction, confess that only his still unexplained but now 'vnfortunate' travels prevented their marriage, and vow to resurrect that thwarted engagement as soon after the unwished for but inevitable death of Old Wincott as is decently possible. Once again, the stability of generic conventions is undermined by Heywood's invention of a story that offers neither the relief of lighthearted cuckoldry nor the arousal of tragic passion. This confrontation, despite strenuous protestations of virtue on both sides, does generate considerable emotional tension: the midnight encounter, right up to the final 'fraternal' kiss, could always collapse into the expected sexual betrayal. The fact that it doesn't, moreover, would seem to have edged the narrative into a cul-de-sac.

If, after almost two acts of exposition, the narrative direction remains obscure, the social definition of the protagonists is increasingly clarified. Financial imagery is pervasive in Plautus and so it is in Heywood's adaptation for the subplot; in the main plot it is, and will continue to be obsessive. It obtrudes jarringly into Mrs Wincott's aforementioned panegyric to the unforced love which brings forth 'an Vsurious Crop of timely Fruit' (c3^r). In the exchange with her once and future suitor, the Wife is wistfully remembered by Young Geraldine as 'th' Exchequer' of his love, and she responds that she would indeed have proved a 'trusty Treasurer' (D2^r). Early in the third act Young Geraldine's father reminds his son that loss of reputation might also entail forfeiture of any 'interest that thy Soule might claime aboue, / In yon blest City' (F1^r). So impenetrable is this shared nexus of interests among the landed gentry that Heywood even allows Dalavill a unique and momentary complicity with the audience, when, in a Vice-like aside, he illustrates the inability of this group to think or speak about relationships without resorting to commercial metaphor:

> What strange felicitie these Rich men take,
> To talke of borrowing, lending, and of Vse;
> The vsurers language right.   (E2^v)

The second act concludes with the 'unexpected' return of the last member of this wealthy circle, the prodigal's father Old Lionel. And, as his gulling begins, there appears one striking deviation from the emergent sense in the play that all actions are motivated by self-interest: Reignald decides to protect Young Lionel, prompted purely by 'a seruants loue' (D4^r).

There is, from the opening of the third act, a noticeable acceleration in the presentation of both plots. The resourceful Reignald embarks on a precarious scheme to persuade Old Lionel firstly that his presumably wrecked house is now deserted save for the avenging spirit of the previous owner's murdered guest (another, though this time fictional violation of hospitality). Secondly, when confronted with an unforgiving moneylender demanding repayment, Reignald brilliantly turns Old Lionel's fury at his son's profligate spending into smug satisfaction; shrewdly assessing the merchant's priorities, he improvises the superbly appropriate fantasy that the money has been used to purchase their neighbour Ricott's property.

Meanwhile, the equally ingenious Dalavill insinuates to Old Geraldine (with several reiterations of Iago's 'I thinke they both are honest', E3^{r-v}) that his son's intimacy with Mrs Wincott is incurring widespread notoriety. The old man confronts Young Geraldine who can appease his father only with an assurance to abjure the Wincott household. During this enforced absence Young Geraldine is angered by Mrs Wincott's serving-maid Bess, who attempts to convince him that Dalavill is sleeping with her mistress. It is a thankless task and, despite the girl's intelligently couching her information in the apposite language of her social superiors – 'You beare the name of Land-lord, but another / Inioyes the rent' (F4^v–G1^r) – a hopeless one. Young Geraldine's agitated musings are interrupted by a summons from Old Wincott who urgently requires an explanation of his young friend's truancy.

The messenger once more is honest Roger and Young Geraldine is again perplexed by the servant's indeterminate status, and that he should be so 'well acquainted with his Masters mind' (A4^v). What mystifies Young Geraldine, of course, is precisely what an audience would find most engaging about this structurally vital character. Like most of Heywood's clowns Roger is an enthusiastic drinker, although he is not in the tradition of perpetually drunken cretins (from Hance in *Like Will to Like* to Adam in *A Looking Glasse for London and England*), nor that of perverse theorists like Bosse (*Everie Woman In Her Humor*), who is prone to demonstrations of how drunkenness 'ingenders with two of the morall vertues and sixe of the lyberall sciences'.[24] Instead, on finding Young Geraldine in his favourite Barnet ordinary Roger displays an affectionate intimacy with all the drinking vessels there which is akin to the manner he adopts in his own household. The familiarity with which Roger treats persons of higher rank has, though, a more complex appeal than the gratification of levelling fantasies common to much Elizabethan clowning. When Roger conducts Young Geraldine to his secret midnight rendezvous with Old Wincott the scene closely resembles one in the recent *The City Night-Cap*. But where Davenport's clown Pambo had been playing the nocturnal bawd, assisting in the seduction of his master's wife, Roger is organising an innocent reconciliation between two friends. It is, therefore, rather moving as well as funny when the Clown brings the two deluded and estranged men together, and then leaves them with the instruction 'Talke you by your selues' (G4^v).

The outcome of the conversation that follows is satisfactory to both parties but the upshot of this nightly visitation as a whole proves profoundly shocking to Young Geraldine and only a little less so for the audience. When Wincott retires the young man is restless and decides to pay the Wife a secret visit too. As before, Heywood screws up the emotional tension – Young Geraldine's dark path is illuminated by his 'fiery loue' (H2^r) – only for the passion to explode into anger as he finds Mrs Wincott in bed with Dalavill. Like Frankford in *A Woman Killed with Kindness*, the betrayed man represses his instinct for revenge and he resolves to become the perpetual traveller again. The adulterers emerge in 'Night-tyre', congratulating themselves on the success of their stratagems. It is notable that even in this state of post-coital satisfaction their discourse is still that of financial monopolists, as when Dalavill, with a grimly ironic but precise echo of Wincott's possessive approach to Young Geraldine, boasts to the Wife how he has been 'studdying to engross you to my selfe' (H2^v).

Meanwhile, what the indulgent neighbour Ricott terms the 'golden age' of Reignald's rule is nearing an end. With the previous owner of the house vehemently and understandably denying that he has murdered anyone in it, with Ricott himself refusing to acknowledge payment for the house he hasn't sold, and with the return of the banished Robin, Reignald's inventiveness is finally exhausted. Old Lionel is not the man to repress *his* instincts for vengeance and Reignald's other 'victims' are also mobilising. When the ambush is finally sprung and 'all the hellish rabble are broke loose, / Of Seriants, Sheriffes, and Baliffes' (H3^r), only one dissenting voice is heard amidst the clamour for punishment. Roger has arrived to announce a general summons to the farewell party Wincott is throwing for Young Geraldine and, besides refusing to 'doe the least hurt to my old friend Reignald' (11^v), he attempts to deflect Old Lionel's spleen away from Reignald's fellow revellers by issuing individual invitations to all of them.

The prospect of rapprochement held out by the Clown fades, nonetheless, almost from the moment it is offered. The turning point is the entirely predictable 'reformation' of Young Lionel, an episode that signals, for both plots, the resumption of normal power relations. Just before his son's confession we saw Old Lionel furiously insisting on the details of the sale supposedly struck with the amiable Ricott. In so doing he had redefined justice as financial expediency but at that stage Reignald had still been sufficiently in control to ensure that such acquisitive mania should rebound humiliatingly into the merchant's lap. Now, the conventions of Plautine closure demand that the subversive threat of Reignald is marginalized, but Heywood prolongs the transition from 'misrule' to the gentry's closing of ranks, capturing the process in a striking tableau. Reignald clings tenaciously to the gallery of the theatre, representing an unreachable part of the Lionel household, and claims of the house that 'It hath bin my Harbour long, and now it must bee my Sanctuary' (12^v). As a 'live-in' servant who owes his master the same obedience that offspring owe parents, Reignald is still joyously turning the patriarchal codes which govern such relationships inside out. But this final gesture is suggestive in other ways too. Reignald's conception of the house as a home is quite distinct from Young Lionel's preoccupation with the 'costliest hangings' and 'beautious Symbols' (C1^r) of interiors which bespeak their possessor's social rank. It is this badge of status that Young Lionel has risked losing and so, while his cornered aide still perches aloft, the penitent, in visual contrast, successfully kneels to reclaim his own.

He does so by wisely explaining his misconduct as a long-term investment. Treacherously protesting that 'Best Natures are Soonest wrought on' he disowns the pleasures and companions that have entertained the audience so well as mere 'Shaddowes, Toyes and Dreames' (13^v). This repentance is not the expedient shamming of the Middletonian heir, nor does it involve the gradual awakening of filial affection depicted in Jonson's recent *The Staple of Newes*, and still less does it resemble the marvellously absurd conversion of *Eastward Ho*'s Quicksilver. Rather Young Lionel's return to the real world of business deals and inheritances is unequivocally earnest and utterly depressing. Blanda, whom we have recently seen in a touchingly simple leavetaking with Reignald, is nonchalantly discarded as the negligible price of an assured patrimony. The text pays only sporadic attention to stage directions but this, the fourth act, should surely close with the entire cast of the subplot heading for the Wincott feast, leaving Blanda to exit alone, her loyalty rewarded exactly as Scapha had predicted it would be.

From this moment onwards mercantilism assumes the same kind of control over the action of the play that it has consistently held over the language. Even if we accept that the business world of Plautine Rome is kept strictly outside the space and time of the plays themselves Heywood has another act of his play still to run once he has completed his adaptation of the *Mostellaria* and economic pragmatism invades the final act of *The English Traveller* with such force that the spirit of comedy is almost, but not quite extinguished.[25]

En route for Wincott's feast Old Geraldine tries to dissuade his son from a journey which might jeopardise the young man's position as principal beneficiary of Wincott's will. At the house Mrs Wincott gets Young Geraldine alone and her perversely brilliant performance as the virtuous and concerned friend breaks down his resolution to remain silent. As Wincott and his guests approach, the cumulative force of Young Geraldine's denunciations shatters her resistance and she faints under the weight of her remorse. It should be remembered at this point that Heywood – at least Heywood the overseer of the printed text – has promised us a tragicomedy. Readers – and, I think, audiences – would thus have been entitled to expect the thrills but not the spills of tragedy: protagonists, as Guarini (or Fletcher) would have it, will come near to death but emerge, emboldened or chastened by their experience, to survive the play's denouement in one piece. But Mrs Wincott's collapse, unlike the bawd Scapha's, proves fatal. The extent and the calculated nature of the Wife's betrayals do little to engage an audience's sympathy but her death still comes as a shock. On-stage reactions to her death, however, are shocking in ways that go beyond mere breaches of theatrical convention. Young Lionel's interpretation of Mrs Wincott's swoon is inept, supercilious and therefore not entirely unpredictable:

> A Womans qualme,
> Frailties that are inherent to her sex,
> Soone sicke, and soone recouer'd.   (к3ᵛ)

But after this piece of fatuous misogyny, the summation of the prodigal's 'wit deere bought' (13ʳ), comes Young Geraldine's smug acknowledgement that the Wife's death has granted him 'a free release, / Of all the debts I owed her'. Honest Roger's anguished cry 'My Sweet Mistresse' is the simplest but most eloquent of reproofs to this callousness and it is the Clown who acquires an unusual dignity as he carries the body away.[26]

Heywood's experiments with the proprieties of genre extend to the very last lines of the play. The drama ends, in fact, with a piece of almost conventional clowning but the performance of it belongs to neither Reignald nor Roger. To jest in the presence of death, to turn from spurious lamentation to defiant laughter, had been the prerogative of clowns, particularly in mongrel tragicomedies, at least since the days of Ambidexter in *Cambises* (1561). But here, in an extraordinary final twist, the role becomes Wincott's. Having offered his wife a perfunctory forgiveness he attempts to reconvene his neighbourhood feast. With a grotesque parody of *Hamlet* – which reverses the denunciation of hypocrisy piously intoned by Young Geraldine in the first act – the bereaved widower exhorts his guests to behave like the parricidal prodigals of citizen comedy:

> Wee'le like some Gallants
> That Bury thrifty Fathers, think't no sinne,
> To weare Blacks without, but other Thoughts within.   (к4ʳ)

As the breathless Roger returns from his fruitless pursuit of Dalavill the gentry are settling to the serious business of land distribution. It would be difficult for an audience to escape the feeling that this prestigious social gathering promises to be a distinctly less salubrious event than Reignald's party with its nameless drunk hiccupping on his allusions to the *Metamorphoses*. It is not simply that the cameraderie, the effrontery and even the drunkenness of the clowns and their friends are more entertaining than the pomposity and hypocrisy of the landed families. Like another Plautine trickster, Chrysalus in the *Bacchides*, Reignald had compared himself favourably with Alexander, Agathocles and Caesar; where they commanded only their subjects, 'I my Master, / And euery way his equalls, where I please, / Lead by the nose along' (G3ʳ). But both he and Roger do more than that. When Old Lionel, at one stage in his gulling, is obliged to tell Reignald that 'Thou teachest me Humanitie' (G3^v), he speaks, albeit unwittingly, no more than the truth.

Montaigne, a man much given to discovering absurdity in the solemn and profundity in the comic, once asked what was wrong with a horseboy calling himself Pompey the Great. Berowne and his aristocratic companions found the idea derisory. Webster's Flamineo inverted the proposition, imagining *the* Pompey as a tailor's apprentice. Heywood habitually, but in this play in particular, sided with the essayist. *The English Traveller* uncovers wisdom, generosity and loyalty in the unlikeliest places. The separation of 'low' comedy from 'high' seriousness has been deliberately overturned. The Aristotelian equation of elevated social rank with moral stature, affirmed so forcefully by Heywood the theorist, had never had much appeal for Heywood the dramatist; in this play he relinquishes it for good.

In the 1620s Heywood may have been stung by watching Massinger's deconstruction of the naive optimism about the theatre which he had espoused in the *Apology*, but he did not succumb to Massinger's pessimism. He produced a drama which demanded a careful scrutiny of what comedy was and what it was not. He did, nonetheless, manage to write a play in which the comic spirit and moral stature, haphazardly colliding in Reignald but embodied in Honest Roger, were found to be mutually indispensable. To stand in contrast to his 'clowns' Heywood also delivered a gallery of figures who constitute a self-appointed elite: characters who construct elaborate codes of ethics to mask adultery, pretenders to wit whose sense of comedy (and hospitality) is governed by the drive for gain, people who are cultured but complacent or vicious. By the time he came to publish *The English Traveller*, Heywood felt that the theatre which he had served for so long was being appropriated by just such talentless but condescending aristocrats, and he, like Massinger, reacted angrily.[27] And so it is possible, after all, that the tortuous syntax of the *Apology* did leave at least a trace of what Heywood now conceived to be a viable purpose for clowning and comedy: 'to shew others their slouenly and vnhansome behauiour...'[28] And perhaps that is why in 1633 he chose, hastily but wisely and from a presumably huge stock, *The English Traveller* as the play with which to answer not only Prynne, but also the fashionable and unscrupulous literati of the Caroline court.

NOTES

1 Anne Barton, 'The Distinctive Voice of Massinger', *TLS* (1977), 624.

2 See Martin Garrett, '*A Diamond, Though Set in Horn*': *Philip Massinger's Attitude to Spectacle* (Salzburg, 1984), 70 n. 4; Jonas Barish, *The Antitheatrical Prejudice* (Berkeley, 1981), 117–21.

3 *Witts Recreations* (London, 1640), B8^v.

4 W. W. Greg, *A Bibliography of the English Printed Drama to the Restoration* (Oxford, 1970), III, 1353.

5 *The English Traveller* (London, 1633), A3^r. All references are to this edition. Heywood's 'ghost' did attempt a belated retraction, appearing in conversation with the 'Songster' Thomas Durfey, and insisting that his canon should properly comprise a modest twenty-five 'Dramatic Peeces', but the damage was done. *Visits From The Shades, Part II; or, Dialogues Serious, Comical and Political, Calculated for these Times* (London, 1705), 75. I am grateful to Jeremy Maule for alerting me to this book.

6 A notable exception is Norman Rabkin's characteristically sensitive essay, 'Dramatic Deception in Heywood's *The English Traveller*', *Studies in English Literature*, 1 (1961); our readings of the play, however, have little in common.

7 *Histrio-mastix; The Players Scourge* (London, 1633). Prynne lost his ears for equating actresses with whores – shortly after the queen's debut on the court stage.

8 Peacham concluded his opening chapter, a definition of true nobility, with an attack on the complacency of sections of the traditional aristocracy who resentfully railed at the emergence of a new meritocracy. He insists, 'to these and such I oppose Marius and that stout reply of his in Sallust' and goes on to quote a famous speech which Heywood had translated fourteen years earlier: 'Now...compare me, scarce yet a Gentleman, with their presumptious and proud arrogancie: what they have either heard or read, I have partly seene, partly put in execution, and what they from written volumes have gathered, I have abroad... purchased by experience.' *The Complete Gentleman*, ed. V. B. Heltzel (Ithaca, 1962), 27; *Heywood's Sallust*, Tudor Translations (London, 1924), 210–11.

9 Jaques in *The Captives* (1624), and the clown in *A Maydenhead Well Lost* (c. 1625), are further examples. A fine examination of the clash between Elizabethan and Caroline aesthetics is, of course, Anne Barton's essay, 'Harking Back to Elizabeth: Ben Jonson and Caroline Nostalgia', *ELH*, 48 (1981), 706–31.

10 The unnamed clown of Heywood's early *The Four Prentises of London* (c. 1594), a distinctly unfunny failed murderer and rapist, is the most notable exception to his usual practice; Thersites in *2 The Iron Age* is similarly and indiscriminately vicious but in that play more characteristically Heywoodian comic deflation is performed by Mars's hapless squire Gallus.

11 Robert Armin, *Tarltons Newes out of Purgatorie* (London, 1590), D3^v.

12 William Whately, *A Care-cloth: or a Treatise of the Cumbers and Troubles of Marriage* (London, 1624), no pagination (10th page of the address to the reader). The advice was not new; cf. Edmund Tilney's warning: 'a man may showe his wife, and his sworde to his friende, but not farre to trust them. For if thereby grow vnto him any infamie, let him not blame his wife, but his owne negligence.' *A Briefe and Pleasant Discourse of Duties in Mariage, called the Flower of Friendshippe* (London, 1568), c5^v–c6^r.

13 Such reservations are discussed throughout John Morgan's *Godly Learning: Puritan Attitudes towards Reason, Learning and Education, 1560–1640* (Cambridge, 1986); see particularly ch. 4. The title of the play may have suggested another (misleading) clue as to Young Geraldine's intentions; 'Traveller', with a pun on 'travailer', commonly indicated someone engaged in (usually illicit) sexual activity; see, for instance, Webster's *The White Devil*, 1.2.49, and *The Devil's Law-Case*, 1.2.210–21.

14 Caleb Dalechamp, *Christian Hospitalitie Handled Common-Place-Wise* (London, 1632), 6–7. See also Felicity Heal's comprehensive study, *Hospitality in Early Modern England* (Oxford, 1990). Heywood worried persistently at the issue; see, for instance, *The Late Lancashire Witches* (1634), the prologue addressed to the Earl of Dorset (8352–8362), and the elegy for Sir George Saint Poole (8567–8576), both from *Pleasant Dialogues and Drammas* (1637), ed. W. Bang (Louvain, 1914).

15 The name recalls the treacherous and cowardly shepherd of Book VI of *The Faerie Queene* but Corydons made cameo appearances as guileless rustics from *A Knack to Know an Honest Man* (1594) to the Cockpit's *The Seven Champions of Christendom*.

16 Richard Brathwait, *The English Gentleman* (London, 1630), 155.

17 Line 264. References to Plautus are to the Loeb texts and translations, ed. P. Nixon, 5 vols. (London, 1965).

18 Michael Bristol, *Carnival and Theater: Plebeian Culture and the Structure of Authority in Renaissance England* (London, 1985).

19 *Stuart Royal Proclamations*, eds. J. F. Larkin and P. L. Hughes (Oxford, 1983), II, 571.

20 See Jerzy Limon, *Dangerous Matter: English Drama and Politics in 1623/24* (Cambridge, 1986). Heywood's *A Maydenhead Well Lost* is, I think, indebted to Drue's *The Duchess of Suffolk*.

21 Heywood read Aristophanes in the parallel Greek and Latin text produced by Frischlin: Nicodami Frischlini, *Aristophanes Veteris Comediae* (Frankfurt, 1597). The *Plutus* reference (in Rogers's translation) is to line 600 (Frischlin, 110).

22 Royal interventions in the countryside were contentious, though cultural historians are divided about their motivation. R. Malcolm Smuts improbably claims that they 'reflect a deeply conservative determination to protect the provinces from contamination by corrupt urban and courtly influences'; *Court Culture and the Origins of a Royalist Tradition in Early Stuart England* (Philadelphia, 1987), 263. The more likely, and

diametrically opposed view is argued by Leah Marcus, who suggests that the measures constituted 'the export of a courtly mode to the countryside in a way that imprinted royal power on the rural landscape'; *The Politics of Mirth* (Chicago, 1986), 19.

23 *The Living Librarie...done into English by John Molle Esquire* (London, 1621), 376–7. Heywood could have read the text of *Neptunes Triumph for the Return of Albion* in the quarto of 1624, where he would also have found the Cook's dish featuring Arion escaping on a dolphin's back, which is exactly how one of the drunks visualises himself in the play, fleeing astride his 'gitterne' (D1^r).

24 *Everie Woman In Her Humor* (London, 1609), G4^v–H1^r.

25 Erich Segal's argument that Plautus's comedies are effectively sealed capsules of Saturnalian inversion ('The Business of Roman Comedy' in *Perspectives of Roman Poetry*, ed. G. K. Galinsky (Texas, 1974) has been questioned persuasively by David Konstan, *Roman Comedy* (Ithaca, 1983), 29–31. Segal's thesis clearly fails to account for the vindication of responsible trading and citizenship with which the *Rudens* (and Heywood's 1624 adaptation *The Captives*) is concerned.

26 The clown Piston in Kyd's *Soliman and Perseda* did demonstrate similar qualities despite his insistence throughout the play on his own opportunism; Babulo in Dekker's *Patient Grissil* is likewise devoted to his mistress but also in love with her.

27 See Heywood's *The Hierarchie of the Blessed Angells* (London, 1635), 205, 208; Peter Beal, 'Massinger at Bay: Unpublished Verses in a War of the Theatres', *Yearbook of English Studies*, 10 (1980). The attacks of both Heywood and Massinger were primarily directed at Thomas Carew and William Davenant.

28 *An Apology for Actors* (London, 1612), F3^v–F4^r.

Etherege's She Would If She Could: *comedy, complaisance and anti-climax*

Michael Cordner

The première of George Etherege's second comedy was an unhappy occasion. The triumphant success of its predecessor and the subsequent delay of four years before the unveiling of this sequel heightened expectations in advance of the first performance of *She Would If She Could* on 6 February 1668 at the Duke's Playhouse in Lincoln's Inn Fields. But, in the event, the new play pleased almost no one. Samuel Pepys, who was present at the première, reported how most spectators in the pit agreed with him in blaming 'the play as a silly, dull thing, though there was something very roguish and witty; but the design of the play, and end, mighty insipid'. He did, however, also observe an embryonic group of dissenters from this prevailing view: 'among the rest, here was the Duke of Buckingham today openly sat in the pit; and there I found him with my Lord Buckhurst and Sidly and Etherige the poett – the last of whom I did hear mightily find fault with the Actors, that they were out of humour and had not their parts perfect'.[1]

Dramatists whose plays have just failed are apt to blame the actors' inadequacy for the disaster. But, in this case, others appear to have echoed Etherege's frustration. In 1671, Thomas Shadwell noted how 'imperfect Action [i.e. poor performance], had like to have destroy'd *She would if she could*, which I think (and I have the Authority of some of the best Judges in *England* for't) is the best Comedy that has been written since the Restauration of the Stage: And even that, for the imperfect representation of it at first, received such prejudice, that, had it not been for the favour of the *Court*, in all probability it had never got up again, and it suffers for it; in a great measure to this very day.'[2] So, Etherege's scapegoating of the players has here hardened into established fact, and socially and aesthetically influential opinion – 'some of the best Judges' and 'the favour of the *Court*' – is at work to enthrone *She Would* as the 'best Comedy' written since 1660. Those

'Judges', we may presume, included Buckingham, Sedley and Buckhurst, all of whom had sat with Etherege in his moment of angry disappointment after the premiere. A narrowly constituted élite was seeking to instruct the wider theatre audience in the incorrectness of its taste. Shadwell's remarks suggest that, although they had made real headway by 1671, their work was still far from complete.[3]

The expectations of *She Would*'s original audience must have been partly shaped by memories of *The Comical Revenge*, its enormously popular predecessor of four years earlier. Etherege's first comedy is a bravura piece of playmaking, intertwining and counterbalancing four socially and stylistically disparate plots with an agility astonishing for a début performance. Beside it, *She Would* must have seemed puzzlingly minimalist, with its much smaller cast of characters, narrower linguistic register and relatively uneventful action. Modern attempts to characterise it indeed often begin by listing all the fundamentals of his earlier comic practice which Etherege has here chosen to do without. For its first audience also, it must have been easier to catalogue what had been mislaid during this process of stripping down than to recognise what might have been gained by it.

She Would's 'tissue-thin plot'[4] narrates the progress of the visit to London of Sir Oliver Cockwood and his wife, who are accompanied by Sir Oliver's bosom friend, Sir Joslin Jolly, and the latter's two young kinswomen, Gatty and Ariana. All the country characters see the capital as offering a release from the confinements of rural existence. All, in different ways, find it more difficult than they had anticipated to avail themselves freely of metropolitan liberties. Their fortunes in London intertwine at every point with the peregrinations of Courtall and Freeman, described in the 1668 quarto's dramatis personae as 'two honest gentlemen of the town' (p. 110).[5] By the comedy's end, gallants and country heiresses appear, unsurprisingly, to be moving towards a marriage bargain.

Simple though *She Would*'s materials undeniably are, Etherege's structural ingenuity in their deployment should not be underestimated. His design provocatively combines a courtship narrative with an anatomy of an irretrievably failed marriage. The stories are so closely interwoven as to constitute a single plot. The four characters who may themselves be about to contract new matches thus have before their eyes throughout the play a vision of the kind of domestic hell to which they risk consigning themselves. The audience too is positioned so as to look 'upon this picture, and on this', its perception and judgement of the young quartet's conduct of themselves being significantly focussed and shaped by the simultaneous spectacle of the marital mayhem inflicted on each other by the Cockwoods. It is an elegantly brilliant mingling of plot materials – and one for which Etherege could have found no exact precedent in English comedy of the 1660s or, indeed, earlier. Once devised, however, it is the kind of structural mechanism which is almost fated to prompt imitation-cum-adaptation from other dramatists. Over the next fifty years, a sustained dialogue on marriage and its attendant woes would be conducted in a series of comedies – by such dramatists as Shadwell, Otway, Vanbrugh, Cibber and Farquhar – which are all linked by their use of that close yoking of courtship and marital disharmony actions pioneered by *She Would* in 1668.

Whatever its formal inventiveness, however, 'the design of the play' and its 'end' appeared, as we have already seen, 'mighty insipid' to Pepys and many others at its premiere. The risk of such a response is aired in the dialogue of *She Would* itself. In 3.1, Courtall and Freeman are coping with the discovery that the two pairs of girls they have been hunting together have disappointingly turned out to be one and the same:

COURTALL ...that which troubles me most, is, we lost the hopes of variety, and a single intrigue in love is as dull as a single plot in a play, and will tire a lover worse, than t'other does an audience.
FREEMAN We cannot be long without some underplots in this town, let this be our main design, and if we are anything fortunate in our contrivance, we shall make it a pleasant comedy.
COURTALL Leave all things to me, and hope the best... (lines 112–21)

Such writing positively flaunts the meagreness of the narrative materials from which Etherege is seeking to build a play. It also assumes in at least some of its potential spectators a lively interest in the laws and logics of playmaking and the games which individual dramatists can play in eluding or reinventing the constraints of the conventional rule-book. And, finally, it aligns dramatist, gallant and spectator along a rakish continuum. The playgoer's delight in multiple-plot actions is analogised to the roving gentleman's prefer-ence for pursuing several amours simultaneously; and the playwright, in devising such a 'fortunate...contrivance' as a multiple plot, is similarly seen as playing to his own, and his spectator's, relish for a diversity of pleasurable stimuli. By implication, playwriting and playwatching are as naturally part of a male libertine's round of eroticised urban pleasures as his multiple sexual liaisons. Paradoxically, however, this exchange also reminds the audience that it is precisely this mandatory variousness of stimulus which Etherege's play has so far conspicuously failed to provide. *She Would* seems teasingly to be offering itself to be read as a comedy by a rake playwright which obstinately refuses to deliver the rakish pleasures which might be anticipated from it.

Since Etherege presumably does not wish to convict his comedy of insipidity, the insinuation must be that the discerning gallant – first as dramatist, then as spectator – can ingeniously contrive a connoisseur's delight for himself and his fellows even from the straitened narrative circumstances in which his fictional twins perforce operate in *She Would*. Such an intricate game with the arousal, disappointment and redirection of expectation asks of the audience a highly specialised and self-aware sophistication of response – an ambitious, possibly even an arrogant, demand, and one which was clearly not met by most of those present at the first performance on 6 February 1668.

Twentieth-century commentary has often coped with the quirky elusiveness of the play's tactics by assigning to it a questionable clarity of thematic organisation. Norman Holland, for instance, identified a 'contrast between liberty and restraint' as one of its key motifs and aligned that antithesis with a recurrent opposition between town and country:

'The Town' in the play stands for a place big enough, offering enough opportunities for anonymity, so that social restrictions do not really interfere with natural desires. Conversely, the country stands for a place where close observation makes social restrictions impinge directly on natural desires.[6]

The certainty that 'among the masse of people in *London*, and frequency of Vices of all sorts' an individual's self-indulgence 'might passe in the throng'[7] is often voiced in writing, dramatic and non-dramatic, of the 1660s. That a matching polarisation of town against country is at work in Etherege's text is evident, for example, from Sir Oliver's complaint that in the country 'if a man do but rap out an oath, the people start as if a gun went off' (1.1.93–4) and Lady Cockwood's relish at the prospect of enjoying 'the freedom of this place [i.e. London] again' (1.1.54–5). But Norman Holland is too inclined to take the word for the deed, since anonymity is precisely what neither country spouse can secure during their urban misadventures. Their every move towards adultery is checkmated by the inhibiting proximity of a close acquaintance or relative. The London staged in *She Would* is, in practice, a place small enough for eight principal characters constantly to interfere, by accident and/or design, with each other's indulgence of their 'natural desires'. The play's events do not, in other words, actualise the contrast between urban liberties and country restrictions which some of its dialogue takes for granted.

As a result, Freeman's certainty that 'We cannot be long without some underplots in this town' is mistaken. *She Would* permits its lead gallants only a single 'main design' on which to exercise their talents – and, in addition, one which tends ineluctably towards marriage with two resolutely chaste girls. Even here disappointments are played out. In 4.2, for example, forged letters make the men think that Gatty and Ariana may defy 'the modesty' of 'their sex' (line 108) and surrender to them 'without assault or summons' (lines 286–7), but their resultant cock-a-hoop brashness is rapidly deflated by a bruising encounter with the indignant victims of this slander. Thus, the gallants are not simply denied the variety they covet, but tantalisingly offered the phantom possibility that chastity might accommodatingly be revealed to be mere masquerade, only to have their hopes once again abruptly dashed.

Sir Oliver endures a parallel, but grotesquer, sequence of sexual anti-climaxes. Thus, in 3.3, he dances with a masked woman he imagines to be a whore, drooling over her 'exact and tempting' body (lines 299–300), only to be immediately floored by the revelation that the titillating disguise conceals his own wife, whose comprehensive lack of sexual allure for him he has just been corrosively expounding. This incident epitomises his fortunes in the play as a whole. Although confidently anticipating the 'variety' (3.3.41) London will afford him, he is in the event comprehensively defeated in his attempts to turn the single plot of detested monogamy into an adulterous double action with the help of the fabled whore, Madam Rampant. The latter's climactic encounter with Sir Oliver is frequently anticipated and never accomplished. The comedy's repeated forestalling of her imminent arrival onstage – a game played with ingenious variations right through to the final moments of Act 5[8] – presses home its commitment to disappointment as a central principle of its dramatic action.

Overturning its subjects' most cherished hopes is, of course, one of comedy's favourite stratagems. But *She Would*'s addiction to the humour of anti-climax is, even so, remarkably persistent and emphatic. The parallel between the careers of the gallants and the country buffoon hints that anti-climax ultimately here means matrimony. Sir Oliver, frustrated in his would-be libertinism, must finally return to the marital boredom he etched so vividly in his 1.1 dialogue with Courtall (lines 133ff.). Equally, Courtall's aphorism that 'a single intrigue in love is as dull as a single plot in a play, and will tire a lover worse, than t'other does an audience' cannot but cast a shadow forwards to the concluding marriage negotiations.

Whatever constraints may bind its leading male characters, however, the play's flamboyant title centres attention on those which trammel its female characters.[9] Its most obvious and most unflattering reference is to Lady Cockwood – driven by adulterous cravings, but relentlessly impeded by circumstances and her own inhibitions from satisfying them. But an early exchange between the girls implicitly acknowledges its application to them also:

GATTY ...how I envy that sex! well! we cannot plague 'em enough when we have it in our power for those privileges which custom has allowed 'em above us.

ARIANA The truth is, they can run and ramble here, and there, and everywhere, and we poor fools rather think the better of 'em.

GATTY From one playhouse, to the other playhouse, and if they like neither the play nor the women, they seldom stay any longer than the combing of their periwigs, or a whisper or two with a friend; and then they cock their caps, and out they strut again. (1.2.163–73)

The women confidently demystify the familiar double standard – it is a matter of mere arbitrary 'custom' – but Etherege does not allow them to envision any substantive rebellion against it. Indeed, Ariana's 'we poor fools rather think the better of 'em' toys with the proposition that female folly can be relied upon to accommodate women to custom's inequalities. For some limited periods – 'when we have it in our power' – a mocking revenge may be exacted; but the absolute differentiation between male and female liberties remains for them an unbudgeable fact of their social existence, as their next speeches make clear:

ARIANA But whatsoever we do, prithee now let us resolve to be mighty honest.

GATTY There I agree with thee.

ARIANA And if we find the gallants like lawless subjects, who the more their princes grant, the more they impudently crave –

GATTY We'll become absolute tyrants, and deprive 'em of all the privileges we gave 'em –

ARIANA Upon these conditions I am contented to trail a pike under thee – march along girl. (lines 174–83)

The bold talk of behaving like 'absolute tyrants', with its confident-sounding inversion of the conventional seventeenth-century male/monarch, female/subject analogies, only temporarily masks the girls' acceptance that in the contest between the sexes society decrees that the advantage finally lies with the men. This conclusion is under-scored by their firm identification of the playhouse itself – in which their dialogue is, after all, written to be spoken – as an arena dedicated to the enactment of specifically male freedoms of be-haviour. (Women are present there in this account only to catch the glance of the ranging gallant and possibly detain his interest for some short time.) Their exchanges thus chime revealingly with the automatic assumption of Courtall and Freeman in 3.1 that the natural spectator for the kind of comedy in which the gallants envisage participating is male.

Thus, Etherege gives Gatty and Ariana an eager desire to emulate male freedoms if they could, but also burdens them with the conviction that their society allows them no discreet or safe way of achieving this. In addition, he allows them to waste no time hankering after what they are told is unobtainable, but instead has them calmly resolve to play within the socially prescribed limits for their sex and class. The ease with which he has them accommodate themselves to those limits clearly works to ratify, not problematise, the double standard. As a result, neither of the girls has been positioned by him so as to be able to apply rigorously reformist pressure with conviction to the gallant she may marry. The women's resolution to be 'mighty honest' is an obeisance to social necessity, not a commitment to a moral imperative, while their imaginative sympathies still surreptitiously lie with the liberties permitted to, and enjoyed by, the rakes. They can thus provide the men with congenial sparring partners in their courtship combats, but can never be radically challenging interrogators of the gallants' way of life.

To all of this Lady Cockwood works as a formidable foil. Gatty and Ariana may imagine becoming 'absolute tyrants' if the men overstep the limits of modesty, but Lady Cockwood's behaviour is constantly imaged in terms of an indecorous and grotesque usurpation of power. Her manipulation and subjugation of Sir Oliver, for instance, are monarchical and absolutist. Emboldened by drink, he dares to berate her as 'a very Pharaoh', who 'by wicked policy... would usurp my empire' and is 'every night... a-putting me upon making brick without straw' (2.2.176–9). In a moment of guilt-stricken panic, on the other hand, he cravenly acknowledges the legitimacy of her enforced rule and foresees himself indicted for a 'premunire' (3.3.330), that is, an act in contempt of her royal prerogative. Even as she comprehensively unmans her husband and denudes him of authority, so she proves imperious and authoritarian in her conduct towards her targeted gallant. Courtall, her potential victim, regards her as 'the very spirit of impertinence', who 'would by her good will give her lover no more rest, than a young squire that has newly set up a coach, does his only pair of horses' (1.1.265, 278–81). In a text where the gallants repeatedly chart their erotic quests in analogies drawn from gentlemanly field sports, Lady Cockwood, in her usurping of male initiative, appears to Courtall as a 'ravenous kite' that 'will be here within this half hour to swoop me away' or a 'long-winged devil' that may 'truss me' before rescue intervenes (3.1.65–6, 87–8). The play thus portrays its embodiment of rampant female desire as comically grotesque and incipiently unnerving.

It also condemns her to a permanent, bathetic failure to find sexual fulfilment. Cheated by hostile circumstances, she is also incapacitated by 'a strange infirmity' (2.2.110) of mind. While invincibly addicted to the pursuit of adulterous consummation, she has so totally internalised her society's insistence on the maintenance of the decorums of female honour that she cannot ever admit to herself the nature of the fleshly imperative which drives her. The wild contradictions and extremes of behaviour which result from this furnish a spectator-sport which the play invites its audience to relish. They also generate moments of passionate extravagance which turn genuinely enigmatic. During her frenzied denunciation of Sir Oliver in 3.3, for example, for attempting the crime she had herself also been set on, it is impossible to disentangle premeditation and bad faith from authentic, yet completely self-deceiving, outrage. As Courtall observes, 'Sure she will take up anon, or crack her mind, or else the devil's in't' (3.3.374–5). Sir Oliver's self-prostration in the same scene is similarly ambiguous. Ariana notes, 'How bitterly he weeps!

how sadly he sighs!', and Gatty replies, 'I dare say he counterfeited his sin, and is real in his repentance' (lines 395–7). This total dissolution of self-knowledge and self-control in husband and wife is clearly intended to contrast with 'the skeptical, yet civil power-broking of the young lovers'.[10] Yet the play's notion of clear-eyed prudence for a woman appears to prescribe that Gatty and Ariana must know the limits set down for them and eschew the imperial delusions which are so comprehensively discredited by Lady Cock-wood's cavortings.

I recognise that many recent accounts of the play discern a quite different pattern at work in it – one which compels the rakes to relinquish substantial freedoms as the play proceeds. One of the most challenging of such readings, for instance, proposes that 'To be a rake, especially at the wrong time, is in this play to come close to being a fool', and also that 'As the play proceeds, the audience is shown that those areas which the rake-hero might reasonably expect to control, be they places in town or stage-devices, work against him until the rake must abandon his claim to social control.' In the play's concluding stages, the rake, 'made dupe-like', must as a consequence 'accept his fall into the state of grace', and central to that acceptance is 'his new distrust of himself'.[11] That Courtall and Freeman are at key moments wrongfooted and outwitted by one or more of the women is undeniable. It is also fundamental to my understanding of the play that there is a carefully calculated ill match between the rakes' instinct for variety and the single, marriage-destined action in which they are assigned to perform. None of this, however, makes it apparent to me that, in the longer run, the rake-hero's 'claim to social control' is itself seriously threatened in *She Would*, nor do I easily recognise the alleged 'new distrust of himself' in Courtall's concluding conduct.

A brief excursion into a comparison with other plays of the late 1660s can, I think, help here. Etherege was not the only Court Wit to have a premiere which flopped during the 1667–8 season. The first performance of Sir Charles Sedley's first play, *The Mulberry Garden*, at the King's Playhouse on 18 May 1668, was in many ways a re-run of *She Would*'s three months earlier. Pepys was once again present to report the audience's advance hopes and the ensuing sad anti-climax.[12] The two dramatists were close friends, and Sedley's modern biographer plausibly imagines the plays as being the product of 'some kind of friendly rivalry' between them.[13] A month before the première of *She Would*, Sedley's working title for his own comedy appears to have been *The Wandring Ladies*,[14] a choice which points up the play's similarities in plot, since in both virtuous country ladies, newly arrived in London and eager to enjoy the freedoms the capital offers, find their reputations at risk as a result of the misrepresentation of their conduct by others. In both *She Would* and *The Mulberry Garden*, this crisis breeds an Act 4 confrontation in one of London's pleasure gardens between the ladies and the gallants they blame for their discrediting. Sedley and Etherege were clearly not writing in total ignorance of each other's designs.

An interpretative context for Sedley's comedy is provided by his having designed the leading roles of Wildish and Olivia for the King's Company's star partnership of Charles Hart and Nell Gwyn. This duo had a formidable influence on innovative comic writing in the 1660s, and it might be expected that Sedley would tailor his invention to their established strengths. Their particular specialty was in playing 'witty, amoral, "mad couples"',[15] flamboyant freethinkers, exuberantly out of step with the straitlaced communities in which they find themselves. In early 1668, the finest play yet inspired by their partnership was undoubtedly John Dryden's *Secret Love, Or The Maiden Queen* (1667), in which Hart played the congenitally inconstant Celadon. His mercurial unreliability attracts Florimell (Gwyn's role), but she also sets herself to curb it. Ultimately, that means imposing marriage on him. In the play's early stages, none of his promises to her are fully earnest, his recidivism always pre-destined. Whatever his ruses, however, he can never keep his other loves secret from her, a pattern which climaxes with a joyous set-piece, in which Florimell, disguised as a dashing male courtier in the latest fashionable garb, diverts two girls Celadon is aiming to seduce into her/his own possession and right from under Celadon's nose. This total undermining of male braggadocio epitomises the play's consistent awarding of the superiority in wit to Florimell. In their concluding marriage-bargaining – the first great proviso scene of the post-1660 comedy – they devise agreed liberties to alleviate what each sees as wedlock's most troublesome and deadening constraints. It is clearly, however, Florimell who now has the negotiating initiative. When she asks him, 'is not such a marriage as good as wenching, *Celadon*?', he wistfully replies, 'This is very good, but not so good, *Florimell*' (5.1.560–2).[16]

Florimell's adoption of male dress to invade and colonise the rake's domain finds its corollary – in the play's other, heroic plot – in the Queen of Sicily's eventually confident manipulation of the conventionally male role of monarch. The Queen and Florimell are their respective 'plots' prime movers and most fully realized characters, authoritative, willful, single-minded, sometimes unscrupulous'. Both 'test their lovers without revealing their own feelings, keeping their "secrets" intact'.[17] In the words of Rothstein and Kavenik, 'Dryden's feminizing of *Secret Love* puts women on an equal footing in nature with men'; the obstacles its principal female characters confront are 'the result of social constraints that bind women differently from men, rather than of a difference in nature'.[18] In this play, those constraints are never definitively eroded or defied. Just as Florimell has finally to lure the straying Celadon into the traditional 'safety' of marriage, so the Queen's climactic coup, in relinquishing her 'secret love' and resolving never to marry, is a concession to those 'social constraints that bind women', since her society effectively prescribes that she cannot enjoy power and the fulfilment of her love simultaneously. But the play leaves her supreme over her political world, as it leaves Florimell surefootedly dictating terms to Celadon. No earlier post-1660 play had awarded one woman, let alone two, so pre-eminent a role in its dramatic power-structure.

Echoes of *Secret Love* are discernible in *The Mulberry Garden*. But Sedley decisively redistributes the balance of power between his leading players. Rebuked by Olivia for his libelling of women, Wildish replies, 'Why, Madam, I thought you had understood Raillery', and then explains:

... this is only the way of talking I have got among my Companions, where when we meet over a Bottle of Wine, 'tis held as great a part of wit to rallee women handsomly behind their back, as to flatter 'um to their Faces. (2.1.84–5, 87–91)[19]

So, style and content of discourse become entirely relative to company, the crucial distinctions being largely drawn on gender lines. Wildish's confession is also a challenge. If his language, chameleon-like, adapts itself to the company he is in, does that not reduce all his avowals of love to her to mere compliance with expected norms? Even as he accommodates himself to conventional decorums, he signals clearly, almost insultingly, that this is indeed what he is doing and thus initiates a far more elaborately knowing courtship game than in any earlier Hart/Gwyn pairing.

Although Sedley deals Olivia/Gwyn many telling put-downs and incisive challenges along the way, it is to Wildish/Hart that he awards the agenda-setting role. This is never clearer than in 4.1, a scene which invites comparison with Florimell's routing of Celadon in male disguise. Gwyn is again assigned a comic routine in which she becomes privy to male secrets which she can then use to devastating effect. But, this time, Hart is not the victim of the revelations, but the smug contriver of others' humiliation. Olivia and her sister listen from concealment while Wildish lures Modish and Estridge into boasting that they have enjoyed the two ladies' favours. The dupes are susceptible because of their sense of how kudos is acquired in all-male society: as Modish says, 'it sounds handsomly, to boast some familiarity' (lines 90–1). The incident Wildish stages thus demonstrates brilliantly his claim that company subdues men to its norms, since it is apparent that, without his temptation, neither Modish nor Estridge would have dared contemplate making such an outrageous allegation. It equally proclaims, of course, his capacity, as trickster, to manipulate the workings of company to his advantage and thus makes him an exception to his generalisation, since what distinguishes him from his victims is the difference between craven compliance with social norms and the capacity to use them as a tool for one's own ends.

Wildish's chameleon manipulativeness in this scene finds no equivalent in Olivia's narrower repertoire. Early in the play, she defines the love-game in a way which promises fireworks to follow:

... the great pleasure of Gaming were lost, if we saw one anothers hands; and of Love, if we knew one anothers Hearts: there would be no room for good Play in the One, nor for Address in the other; which are the refin'd parts of both. (1.3.32–7)

But such fine phrase-making does not yield the expected dividends. For much of the play, Olivia's concealment of her true feelings is only nominal; Wildish is placed in no serious doubt. And the combat between them is often not, as the gaming simile here proposes, waged between two equal players. In *Secret Love*, Florimell invaded Celadon's world and unmasked his secrets. In *The Mulberry Garden*, Olivia merely witnesses Wildish's staging of the indiscretions of which he can make two pliable idiots capable. He himself eludes, and defies, unmasking. The Dryden scene feeds off, and celebrates, Gwyn's intense theatricality. Sedley's subdues her and gives centre-stage to

Hart – and to the rake's capacity to remain almost infinitely flexible and manipulative. The two plays thus represent diametrically opposed responses to the challenge of creating a script for the Hart/Gwyn team. Theatrically, Sedley's looks, and proved, the riskier. Cramping the exuberant wildness which was Gwyn's trademark was unlikely to recommend itself readily to an audience which had applauded her recent successes. That Sedley should, even so, have attempted it may simply reflect a misguided desire on his part to ring surprising changes on a renowned stage partnership. But his choice of tactics can clearly also be read as a reaction against Dryden's emphatic favouring of his two leading actresses in the contest between the sexes in *Secret Love*. Sedley and Etherege, writing in knowledge of each other's stage projects, seem to be at one in a desire to set limits to female freedoms.

As we have already seen, *She Would* also contains an Act 4 episode in which a pair of country ladies tongue-lash two gentlemen for having traduced them. In Etherege's version, however, the men under attack are the play's lead gallants, not second-string dupes. They are also innocent of the offence they are charged with. The acrimony is orchestrated by a revengeful Lady Cockwood, who has discovered not only that Courtall does not reciprocate her passion for him, but that he has been concealing from her his designs on Gatty. The matching incident in *The Mulberry Garden*, like the scene of Florimell's male masquerade, finally resolves itself into a relatively simple display-piece in which one character demonstrates at length and without serious opposition the supremacy of his wit over other contenders. Etherege's scene charts a tenser struggle for control, from which, as yet, no certain victor emerges. Lady Cockwood, arriving to relish her handiwork, finds herself at risk of exposure from the gallants' quick-thinking deductions, and only the violent eruption of a drunken Sir Oliver to embroil Courtall in a sword-fight temporarily reprieves her. At the act's end, it remains unsettled whether the advantage will finally lie with her or with Courtall. Sir Oliver earlier pictured his marriage as a state of 'perpetual civil war' (3.3.283). The play's larger community seems at this point to be overtaken by a comparable fate. Yet, at the comedy's end, general reconciliation has been accomplished, and Lady Cockwood is once again 'in charity' with Courtall (5.1.417–18). Etherege here sets himself a larger dramatic problem than Sedley attempted. He solves it, however, by the same means – the improvisatory dexterity of the rake. In the process, he makes Courtall justify the name he bestowed on him.

In 1.1, an astonished and admiring Freeman watches from hiding the suppleness with which his friend adapts himself to dealing in quick and potentially disastrous succession with an unexpected visit from Sentry, Lady Cockwood's servant and confederate, and then the inopportunely overlapping arrival of Sir Oliver. Freeman's applause – 'the scene was very pleasant' (lines 230–1) – pinpoints the theatricality of the actions he has witnessed. He is also awed by the extreme skill of Courtall's performance: 'I admire thy impudence, I could never have had the face to have wheedled the poor knight so' (lines 231–3). Their subsequent exchanges draw from Courtall a revealing definition of gentlemanly conduct. In dealing with, and eluding, Lady Cockwood's advances, he tells Freeman, he has consistently 'carried it so like a gentleman, that she has not had the least suspicion of unkindness' (lines 263–5). A gentleman thus secures his own interests without seeming to rebuff those whose aims threaten to collide with his. Indeed, he always seeks to maintain amity with the latter. To achieve that requires quasi-diplomatic skills of a high order.

As Susan Staves has observed, the flow of books from the presses on conduct and social interaction in the 1660s and 1670s presumed, and fed, a contemporary conviction 'that modes and manners were changing with unusual rapidity'.[20] The exposition of the arts of complaisance in some of these texts could easily be exemplified from Courtall's actions in *She Would*. In this definition, complaisance is fundamentally a political skill, capable of application to either national or domestic challenges. According to a key text of the 1670s (derived in large part from an earlier French source), 'this admirable Art...by a secret and most powerful charm, calms the displeasures of tyrants, disarms or averts the fury of our enemies, & wrests the sword from the hand of vengeance, all this it does by its submissions, and by perswading them that we have devested our own enmity, and changed it into a true friendship'. It asks of its disciples a '*dexterity*, by means whereof we dispatch our affairs with the most happiness, rendring that which is difficult, easie and pleasant, receiving and representing all things without gall or bitterness'. It also requires '*Affability*', which 'consists...principally in the knowledge to give an obliging reception to all persons, to entertain them with freedom and kindness, to salute, honour and respect them, in short, by all outward signs, and Caresses that may assure them of our Courtesie and good will, giving them by these attractive wayes, all the assurance and confidence that may be'.[21]

The advocates of the civil virtues of complaisance tend to presume 'a threatening world in which considerable skill is needed to avoid giving offense'. Among its benefits, 'by making gentlemen slower to take affront, it avoids violence'. It is also a technique to ensure privacy, even secrecy: 'in a world increasingly filled with importuning but apparently genteel strangers, complaisance is a way to avoid unwanted intimate contact with them'.[22] Courtall's handling of the Cockwoods in *She Would*'s early acts illustrates his mastery of the art. Thus, Sir Oliver is convinced of his own intimacy with the gallant, while being allowed to discern no hint of the reserve and disdain with which Courtall actually regards him. Similarly, Lady Cockwood's designs on him are repeatedly disappointed, without her detecting his responsibility for this. She remains convinced that this 'heroic sir' (3.1.198) is as distressed as she is by their failure to consummate. Her emergence as 'Madam Machiavil' (4.2.305) in Act 4 is provoked by her belated recognition of how radically deceptive his anodyne behaviour has been. But, in a neatly punitive irony, her final accommodation with him is founded on her own need for his ready way with a lie. Her declaration of war produces a crisis in which even Sir Oliver is likely to register her double dealing. Only Courtall commands the required fluency in improvisation to rescue her with a comprehensive, fictitious explanation of all incriminating circumstances. He thus demonstrates complaisance's talent for devising 'lenitive Unctions' and 'Insinuating them sweetly into the spirit of those to whom we speak'.[23] In the process, he also covers his own tracks, by obscuring his previous association with Lady Cockwood from the girls. Whatever tactical reverses, therefore, he may have suffered during the action, Courtall's 'impudence' remains as limber in the final scene as when Freeman first admiringly witnessed it in action in 1.1. Etherege also makes that 'impudence' the indispensable constituent of the peacemaking with which *She Would* ends. In teaching him how to 'court all' with such agility, complaisance fulfils its claims to be '*an Art*' which can '*regulate our words and behaviour, in such a manner as may engage the love and respect of those with whom we Converse*'.[24]

Complaisance, with its resources of strategic reticence, is here the monopoly of the male gallant. In this play, it is the men's prerogative to unmask the women's secrets, while much about the rakes' conduct and natures remains opaque to Gatty and Ariana. Etherege decrees a sequence of farcical coincidences in Act 5 which leads to the gallants being concealed in a closet in the Cockwoods' lodgings. There they overhear the girls talking privately. The latter's susceptibility to being wooed into an easy reconciliation with the men is first made clear:

GATTY ...time will make it out, I hope, to the advantage of the gentlemen.
ARIANA I would gladly have it so; for I believe, should they give us a just
    cause, we should find it a hard task to hate them. (lines 331–5)

Gatty then sings a song which she has come to love since meeting Courtall. It confesses to an overwhelming obsession with a man met in her 'rambles' (line 340) in town and concludes:

> My passion shall kill me before I will show it,
> And yet I would give all the world he did know it;
> But oh how I sigh, when I think should he woo me,
> I cannot deny what I know would undo me!   (lines 346–9)

The play's title has a double application here. In the first couplet, female modesty forbids her to voice the passion she wishes to declare. In the second, she imagines how, faced with Courtall's direct wooing, one part of her mind at least would wish, but be unable, to evade admitting her love. That such a weakness would lead to her undoing is the thought on which the song concludes.

    By contriving their overhearing of this, Etherege has stacked the cards massively in the gallants' favour. In 1.2, referring to Lady Cockwood, Gatty wished this curse on herself: 'if she does not dissemble, may I still be discovered when I do' (lines 123–4). In 5.1, her capacity to dissemble in her courtship games with Courtall is taken from her at a stroke. She justifies the boldness of her song to an alarmed Ariana in this way:

I hate to dissemble when I need not; 'twould look as affected in us to be reserved now w'are alone, as for a player to maintain the character she acts in the tiring-room. (lines 351–44)

But such frank speaking is allowable to her only because the two women think they are alone. If *The Mulberry Garden* built a scene around two country ladies overhearing the 'way of talking' native to all-male company, *She Would* reverses the situation to open the girls' privacy to the gallants' surveillance. Gatty's comparison of the girls to players 'in the tiring-room' gains piquancy from the recurrent association of the rakes – as playwrights, spectators and actors – with the world of the playhouse. Thus, in 3.1, they compare the pleasures offered by single and double plots, in 3.3 Courtall casually sends to the theatre for 'masking-habits' to enhance the plot 'design' (lines 242, 245) he is himself now crafting, and in 4.1 Sentry can sufficiently rely on their addictedness to the playhouse to be certain where they will be during performance time (lines 11–12). It is therefore logical that their moment of final empowerment *vis-à-vis* the girls should also be implicitly analogised to their activities as playhouse habitués. In the 1660s theatres, gallants took to themselves total rights of access to actresses' dressing-rooms. Etherege accords the characters he privileges comparable command over the retirement of the girls they pursue.

That there is in *She Would* a male kingdom of discourse the girls never penetrate is equally apparent. In 3.3, the gallants try to appease his wife's fury by explaining that Sir Oliver's lewd swaggering is 'mere raillery, a way of talk, which Sir Oliver being well-bred, has learned among the gay people of the town' (lines 399–401). There are two levels of irony here: Sir Oliver is, in any case, only capable of talk, not action, and his notion of rakishness, with its wild boasts and flamboyant crudeness, is – far from 'being well-bred' – at best a parody of yesterday's theatrical model of the style. In *She Would*, the modern rake cultivates the composure and even affability of manner which complaisance recommends. Far from flaunting his libertine credentials, he aims to be seamlessly absorbed into civil society. His devotion to his own self-interest and empire-building, however, is not diminished by this. Nor is the ruthlessness with which he may treat the women who place themselves at his mercy. Speaking the dialect of their rakish tribe to Freeman in private, Courtall, for example, asserts that 'talk [i.e. boasting of one's dealings with a specific woman] is only allowable at the latter end of an intrigue, and should never be used at the beginning of an amour, for fear of frighting a young lady from her good intentions' (4.2.99–102). The two men may be innocent of slandering Gatty and Ariana, but we are thus instructed that they are indeed capable of similar actions, when it serves their purposes and pleasures. Their power-play also potentially pits them against each other. When Freeman suggests to his friend that he might 'with your good leave...outbid you for her ladyship's favour' (4.2.163–4), the steely limits of complaisance are briefly glimpsed in Courtall's reply:

I should never have consented to that, Frank; though I am a little resty at present, I am not such a jade, but I should strain if another rid against me; I have ere now liked nothing in a woman that I have loved at last in spite only, because another had a mind to her. (lines 165–70)

The mask, thereafter, is immediately reassumed.

The girls are never vouchsafed a comparable revelation. At the comedy's end, they insist on 'a month's experience of your good behaviour' (5.1.567–8) before final agreement. But this is more a sop to their own self-esteem than a real testing of the gallants' mettle. Complaisance is, after all, an art precisely designed to assure others of 'your good behaviour', while you pursue your own agenda which may even be antagonistic to theirs. Etherege has designed the action so that the rakes, while stooping to the possibility of marriage, have in the process conceded nothing of substance to the girls they woo. Crucially, this is a play without a proviso scene. All that the girls propose to test in its imagined sixth act is whether, 'upon serious thoughts' (line 568), the men will still want 'to engage further'. Their right to retreat is therefore freely conceded. It is also clearly presumed that, if they prove resolute, the girls will, of course, take them. In addition, Gatty and Ariana have not been given the nerve or negotiating muscle to imitate Florimell's precedent and insist on a contract which stipulates penalties for post-marital recidivism by the husband. The extent to which the advantage is here being conceded to the men is further confirmed by the fact that Act 5 also marks Freeman's full coming-of-age. Despite Courtall's warning, he makes an abortive move towards adultery with Lady Cockwood and later meets his friend's suspicions about this with the suave and fraudulent explanation that his visit to her had been part of an innocent attempt to 'clear ourselves to the young ladies' (5.1.471). The erstwhile apprentice thus demonstrates that he too has mastered the arts of complaisance.

My exploration of *She Would* began by noting how it seemed to be offering itself to be read as a play by a rake playwright which was refusing to provide its spectators with the expected rakish pleasures. My subsequent interpretation has moved towards a related, but inverse, account of it. In this version, although the comedy may at first glance seem to relate the process whereby two gallants, used to richer liberties, are subdued to the anti-climax of marriage, a closer reading suggests that within theoretically uncongenial narrative circumstances the rakes contrive a showcase for the complaisant dexterities in which they most excel and in the process largely preserve their own freedom of action. Against the odds, therefore, rakish ingenuity proves that it can make 'a pleasant comedy' (3.1.120) for itself even out of a plot which is unrelievedly single.

There remains one final use of anti-climax to be noted in *She Would*. The confinement of Courtall and Freeman to a single plot heads them towards what for the rake, with his devotion to variety, threatens to be the ultimate anticlimax, matrimony. But its final pages defer that closure to beyond the play's own timespan, if ever. Having identified its likely ending as potentially anti-climactic, *She Would* then suavely cheats expectation yet again by preferring a conclusion which, in effect, does not conclude. The Cockwoods and the girls have been assigned fixed positions of passion, but the rakes are not similarly tethered. All their options remain theoretically open. Freezing the action at this point leaves them permanently poised at the moment before a decision which could begin to foreclose on some of those options.

Modern commentary has made much of a response Courtall makes to Sir Joslin:

SIR JOSLIN ...and is it a match, boys?
COURTALL If the heart of man be not very deceitful, 'tis very likely it may be so. (5.1.571–4)

Dale Underwood, for instance, detects here what he notates as the concluding stage of 'the typical curve of the comic hero – from conviction to experience to doubt'.[25] As the preceding pages will have made clear, I see no evidence that this allegedly 'typical curve' is followed by either Courtall or Freeman. Interrogating the 'heart' of either gallant has never been seriously on the agenda in *She Would*. Similarly, imputing self-doubt – or, indeed, bad faith – to Courtall at this point takes us far beyond what the text justifies. All the play presents us with in these concluding moments are further instances of his assuredly complaisant behaviour. That Gatty engages and stimulates him is evident. Anything beyond that remains mere surmise – as is surely teasingly implied by the conditionality of the form in which Courtall's reply to Sir Joslin is cast.

As Ted Cohen has reminded us, jokes possess 'the capacity to form or acknowledge a...community and thereby to establish an intimacy between the teller and the hearer'.[26] Such communities can be generous in the width of their embrace or very selectively constituted.

All joking relationships work to exclude some potential participants who, for one reason or another, are not positioned so as to be able to understand and/or relish the joke. The principle that works for the single joke also applies to the more elaborate procedures of a five-act comic play. A persistent, but unfounded, myth would have it that audiences in the 1660s were overwhelmingly dominated by courtiers and courtly tastes.[27] *She Would*'s difficult progress into acceptance by its early audiences should in itself have suggested some of the problems this mythology left unaddressed. If my analysis of the play is on the right lines, then one deduction to be made from it is that Etherege partly brought that initial failure on his own head, since his play is designed to be fully savoured only by a relatively narrow community of laughers. The 'Model Spectator' anticipated by the text[28] is precisely the élite one defined by that exchange between the gallants in 3.1. If one cannot confidently locate oneself somewhere on that rakish continuum between lead character, author and imagined spectator, then some of the play's more intimate pleasures will always appear elusive, perhaps indeed inaccessible.

All this has one crucial consequence for Etherege's handling of his structural innovation in yoking so closely courtship and marital disharmony actions in a single comedy. One obvious extrapolation from such a fusion is clearly that the spectacle of a marriage on the rocks should spur those premeditating wedlock in the same play into attempting to ensure that their own prospective unions do not reproduce the catastrophes inflicted on themselves by their elders. Etherege's jealous preservation of his rakes' freedom of manoeuvre means that he does not seek to realise this possibility. What a marriage between Courtall and Gatty or Freeman and Ariana might be like is – as the absence of a proviso scene suggests – left essentially unaddressed in *She Would*. A consequence of this is that Etherege has, in effect, bequeathed this as a potentiality of the form to be developed by some of his successors. In doing so, as also in devising other ingenious and pertinent employments to which it can be put, some of them went on to develop very different notions of an Ideal Spectator or Spectators from that which guided the composition of *She Would*.

NOTES

1 Samuel Pepys, *Diary*, eds. Robert Latham and William Matthews (London, 1970–83), IX, 54.

2 Thomas Shadwell, 'Preface to *The Humorists*', *Complete Works*, ed. Montague Summers (London, 1927), I, 183.

3 This concerted advocacy of the play's merits left a clear imprint on late seventeenth- and early eighteenth-century retrospects on early Restoration drama. Gerard Langbaine, for instance, recorded that *She Would* is 'accounted one of the first Rank, by several who are known to be good Judges of Dramatick Poesy', to which select number he now added Shadwell's name (*An Account of the English Dramatick Poets* (Oxford, 1691), 187). For John Dennis in 1702, the play was an example of the unreliability of popular taste, mistreated by 'the People at first, tho at the same time it was esteem'd by the Men of Sense, for the trueness of some of its Characters, and the purity and freeness and easie grace of its Dialogue', a critical judgement fully vindicated, he alleges, by its having been subsequently 'acted with a general applause' (*Critical Works*, ed. Edward Niles Hooker (Baltimore, 1939–43), I, 289). Six years later, however, John Downes put Dennis's claims into due perspective. In the end, he tells us, it 'took well', but always 'inferior to' Etherege's first play (*Roscius Anglicanus* (London, 1708), 29).

4 John Harold Wilson, *The Court Wits of the Restoration: An Introduction* (Princeton, 1948), 152–3.

5 References for *She Would If She Could* are taken from Sir George Etherege, *Plays*, ed. Michael Cordner (Cambridge, 1982).

6 Norman N. Holland, *The First Modern Comedies: The Significance of Etherege, Wycherley, and Congreve* (Cambridge, Mass. 1959), 29.

7 [James Heath], *Flagellum: Or The Life and Death, Birth and Burial of O. Cromwell The late Usurper: Faithfully Described* (3rd edn: London, 1665), 9.

8 On the issues surrounding the staging of Madam Rampant's final near-arrival, see the note to the stage direction at 5.1.552, in my edition of Etherege's *Plays* (Cambridge, 1982), 205.

9 In 1711, the title drew this comment from Richard Steele: 'Other Poets have, here and there, given an Intimation that there is this Design, under all the Disguises and Affectations which a Lady may put on; but no Author, except this, has made sure Work of it, and put the Imaginations of the Audience upon this one Purpose, from the Beginning to the End of the Comedy' (*The Spectator*, ed. Donald F. Bond (Oxford, 1965), I, 217).

10 Michael Neill, 'Heroic Heads and Humble Tails: Sex, Politics, and the Restoration Comic Rake', *The Eighteenth Century*, 24 (1983), 127.

11 Peter Holland, *The Ornament of Action Text and Performance in Restoration Comedy* (Cambridge, 1979), 51, 53.

12 Samuel Pepys, *Diary*, IX, 203.

13 V. De Sola Pinto, *Sir Charles Sedley 1639–1701 A Study in the Life and Literature of the Restoration* (London, 1927), 104.

14 Samuel Pepys, *Diary*, IX, 203.

15 Katharine Eisaman Maus, '"Playhouse Flesh and Blood": Sexual Ideology and the Restoration Actress', *ELH*, 46 (1979), 599.

16 John Dryden, *Works* (Berkeley, Los Angeles, London, 1961–), IX, ed. John Loftis and Vinton A. Dearing, 200.

17 Eric Rothstein and Frances M. Kavenik, *The Designs of Carolean Comedy* (Carbondale and Edwardsville, 1988), 140.

18 Eric Rothstein and Frances M. Kavenik, *The Designs of Carolean Comedy*, 139.

19 References for *The Mulberry Garden* are from Sir Charles Sedley, *Poetical and Dramatic Works*, ed. V. De Sola Pinto (London, 1928), 1.

20 Susan Staves, 'The Secrets of Genteel Identity in *The Man of Mode*: Comedy of Manners vs. the Courtesy Book', *Studies in Eighteenth-Century Culture*, 19 (1989), 120.

21 *The Art of Complaisance Or The Means to oblige in Conversation* (2nd edn: London, 1677), 5, 14, 34. W. Lee Ustick describes the work's provenance in 'The Courtier and the Bookseller: Some Vagaries of Seventeenth-Century Publishing', *Review of English Studies*, 5 (1929), 149–52.

22 Susan Staves, 'The Secrets of Genteel Identity', p. 122.

23 *The Art of Complaisance*, 15.

24 *The Art of Complaisance*, 2.

25 Dale Underwood, *Etherege and the Seventeenth-Century Comedy of Manners* (New Haven, 1957), 61.

26 Ted Cohen, 'Metaphor and the Cultivation of Intimacy', in Sheldon Sacks, ed., *On Metaphor* (Chicago and London, 1978), 9.

27 Recent scholarship has, one hopes, laid this ghost finally to rest. The key texts include Robert D. Hume and A. H. Scouten, '"Restoration Comedy" and its Audiences, 1660–1776', in Robert D. Hume, *The Rakish Stage Studies in English Drama, 1660–1800* (Carbondale and Edwardsville, 1983), 46–81; Harold Love, 'Who were the Restoration Audience?', *Yearbook of English Studies*, 10 (1980), 21–44; Allan R. Botica, *Audience, Playhouse and Play in Restoration Theatre, 1660–1710* (University of Oxford, D.Phil thesis, 1985).

28 On this useful concept, see, for example, Marvin Carlson, 'Theatre Audiences and the Reading of Performance', in Thomas Postlewait and Bruce A. McConachie, eds., *Interpreting the Theatrical Past: Essays in the Historiography of Performance* (Iowa City, 1989), 84.

Rhyming as comedy: body, ghost, and banquet

Gillian Beer

Welcome sweet and sacred cheer,
Welcome deare;
With me, in me, live and dwell:
For thy neatnesse passeth sight,
Thy delight
Passeth tongue to taste or tell.

George Herbert, 'The Banquet'

I

In his essay 'De l'essence du rire' Baudelaire, that master of rhyme, sees comedy as characterised by 'une dualité permanente, la puissance d'être à la fois soi et un autre'.[1] He contrasts the laughter springing from the grotesque with that of comedy of manners and argues that 'the grotesque has something more profound, axiomatic, and primitive that is very much closer to innocent life and absolute joy than is the laughter caused by the comedy of manners'. Within laughter, he suggests, there is always division, violence, the grotesque, 'le vertige de l'hyperbole' (519). 'La joie est *une*. Le rire est l'expression d'un sentiment double, ou contradictoire; et c'est pour cela qu'il y a convulsion' (514). Throughout the essay Baudelaire insists on pantomime and pantaloon, on the demonic and the doubled. Joy is single, but comedy represents the *effort* of incorporation.

Baudelaire is not here discussing rhyme but his argument suggests ways of thinking about it; as split and liaison, for example, as turncoat, jailor, and prisoner on the run. Rhyme suggests pun: dislodged likenesses, delayed differences. Rhyme has repeatedly been written about (as some of my examples will show) as if it were a person, or two persons, not a pair of words. Rhyme is associated with appetites: with digestion and sex. Rhyme figures embodiment, even the act of eating. Rhyme-words couple but resist collapsing into each other. This essay investigates how rhyme gets under the guard of reason and teases words out of their autonomy, doubling, dissolving, and playing across the rim of meaning.

We read forwards; we rhyme backwards. Doubly so: rhyme relies on backward allusion. But rhyme also specialises in the hidden parts of words, not the front they show the world. Rhyme has to do with words' back parts. Initial letters vanish, shift, collapse before our eyes. Rhyme is de-formation; a first, apparently rationally sanctioned word, is tripped and changed (both semantically and aurally) by the rhyme word. For rhyme is always retrospective. It *is* not until it is seconded. The second word invades, splices to itself engrafted signs, charges the boundaries of the single term. Pounce or slide, the second word moves in on the first and tricks it into rhyme, claims kinship against the odds. The kinship is illegitimate according to the rationale of semantics: sound dominates sense. Rhyme is the bar sinister lying athwart meaning in this heraldry, a 'natural' sibling declared through the more primitive life of sound as utterance alone. 'Dedoublement' – endoubling, estrangement, twinning and discon-necting: the first word in the sound pair is tricked, transfigured, ghosted, sometimes grotesque-ed.

Rhyme seems to encourage such animistic metaphor, threatening always to change from letter to creature. Why is this? Perhaps it is connected with the way rhyme threatens the 'organic', the autono-mous body, of the word. Rhyme challenges word bounds, but needs them. Certainly, hints of the body appear in the titles to rhyming dictionaries, from the earliest English one, *Manipulus Vocabulorum* by Peter Levins (1570)[2] to *Verbotomy: or the Anatomy of Words; shewing their component parts; being an elegant specimen of what may be accomplished in the arrangement of Language, whereby more scientific knowledge of its principles may be obtained in a short time, than from any work hitherto printed; such, at least, is the opinion of W. P. Russel, Verbotomist or Word-Dissector* (London, 1805).

'Word-dissectors', haunted by the oddness of their practice, are apt to emphasise the utility or elegance of their craft. Levins, indeed, clothes himself against criticism with a mantle of rhyme, claiming that he cares not for 'either profit or paine, tauntes or disdaine'.[3] Foreigners, children, barbarians and 'ruder writers' may, he asserts, benefit from studying 'the end of words':

Fourthly, whereas the chief grace and facilities of our Englishe tong, doth cheefly consist in long sillable and short, and in the pronouncing and writing of the same, and namely in the end of words, whereunto we have much respect in this little worke, here of it cometh to passe, that as wel children and ruder schoolers, as also the Barbarous countries and ruder writers, may not a little (if they wil enjoy the offered occasion) well and easily correct and amend, both their pen and speache.[4]

Nothing brings out the phonic grotesque in rhymes more than rhyming dictionaries. The running-heads emerge as grunt and exclamation: ule, ose, neh, ack, rch, and ble.[5] Dissected words cry out, enforced numbers wrung. In such dictionaries, start as words will, rear-ends dominate as in some privy farce: 'O ante D. In *odde*'. The rhyming sequences of the dictionary-maker, unmitigated by other language in between, forge manic verses.

A CLODDE, clot, *gleba*, ae.
A CODDE, fish, *capito, onis, hic*.
A CODDE, cushion, *pulvinar, aris, hoc*.
GOD, *Deus dei*.
A RODDE, *virga*, ae.
A SOD, turfe, *cespes, itis, hic*.
A TODDE, weight, *sexdecim pondo*.
A TROD, path, *callis, is, haec*.[6]

The definitions jar unlike against unlike, the rhyme words 'cling' together.

Altogether, the fantastic world of the rhyming dictionary is characterised by words apparently carelessly abutting (though actually ordered by minute alphabetic gradations) and by earnest explanation. Familiar and arcane terms jostle each other and fall nonchalantly into the ear's agreement. The 'ate' words, for example, in Walker's dictionary run in alphabetical order (or disorder) over *eight* pages, of which these runs are samples:

To rate To value; to chide hastily
Rhabarbarate Impregnated with rhubarb
To exhilarate To make cheerful
To separate To divide; disjoin; separate; secede
To celebrate To praise with distinction
To librate To poise; to balance
To odumbrate To shade; to cloud (164)

Or the less-latinate 'en's:

Seven One more than six
Steven A cry or loud clamour
To enliven To make lively or cheerful
Riven Part. of rive
Driven Part. of drive
Oven A place for baking
Cloven Cleft; divided, part
Proven Used in law for proved
Woven Part. pass. of weave
Wen A fleshy execrescence
Yewen Made of yew
Rowen A field kept up till after Michaelmas (300)

Apart from the fascination of out-of-the-way words that the rhymster may be driven to, and the beauty of useless information, the rhyming dictionary makes clear the ordinary caution of poets, their tendency to stay within tightly chosen parameters for rhyme. Few reach out for scrabbler's dream words like *amygdalate*: made of almonds, or *rugose*: full of wrinkles, though that word usefully rhymes with *trunkhose* – large breeches – and *quelque-chose*, to say nothing of close and nose and doze. Rhyming rare words, as in Byron and Browning, is usually understood as the very type of comic rhyme. But it is not with that effect that I am here concerned; rather, with the figuring of rhyme as body, ghost, and phonemes at once.

Poets, these lists suggest, choose few pairs among the plethora of adjunct terms available. There are advantages to this timidity. The canonical anticipated pairs allow apparitions, extra and excluded rhymes, to show through.[7] Rhyme can conjure not only its elected pair but deflected others. It's an effect much enjoyed in obscene songs and graffiti as well as in Joyce and Hopkins, Byron and Edwin Morgan.

At the beginning of his *Dictionary* Walker points out another use for rhyme closely related to these apparitional words: 'one that will most commend it to commercial men... the assistance it affords in deciphering errors in telegrams'. His dictionary, he suggests, can heal 'word-mutilation': 'In a Telegram received, a word appears as "Sterturn"' (lxxi). By the time the merchant has attempted to decipher this, given up, and asked for a repeat from the telegraph company, Walker suggests, 'the London price has declined to $5\frac{1}{2}$ d per pound'. (The solution to the puzzle is that 'the word originally despatched was "Overturn", meaning "*Sell-to-arrive 1,000 bales Tinnivelly Cotton at 5 three quarter pence per pound.*"' (lxxii).) Walker's translation here is as surprising (indeed, sterturning) in its elaborated form as in its initial phonemic error.

Rhyme has the tendency to emphasise either the fortuitous or the wilful in composition. Sounds intervene and challenge the dominance of syntactical order, threading unforeseen words together in patterns that suggest a new taxonomy framed by sounds alone. Some writers of couplets, like Chaucer, ignore the rhyme so far as may be, constraining the choice of line-end words and making rhyme serve only to flex the lines familiarly. Some, like Keats in *Endymion*, make the caesura the sense-break, so that it snakes down the page, a ribbon, while the end-rhymes seem internal and hidden. Many more place the rhyme at line's ending prominently, so emphasising the incongruities between tongue, lip, and eye, the slips between sense and senses that are activated by rhyme.

In this essay I concentrate on rhyme words that lie close together, in couplets or quatrains, since this strongly signalled rhyme draws particular attention to its own potential oddity. That oddity is not peculiar to close-set rhymes, though most insistent there. It also haunts eccentrically the wide-set internal rhymes of a poem like Hardy's 'The Voice' where the ear's memory just barely encompasses the several seconds delay between first and third stanza and the rhymes survive wraith-like, hardly there – as is the remembered woman of the poem. Yet the poet hears her voice.

The opening apostrophe 'Woman much missed' generates no rhyme in the first or second stanzas. Indeed, in the second stanza the internal rhymes all move obsessionally upon the sound 'oo', the word 'you' (my italics):

> Can it be *you* that I hear? Let me *view you*, then,
> Standing as when I *drew* near to the town
> Where *you* would wait for me: yes, as I *knew you* then,
> Even to the original air-*blue* gown!

But in the third stanza that initiating word 'missed', emanating also from the misty landscape, is caught up and prolonged in the neologisms 'listlessness' and 'wistlessness', refusing the easy pathos of 'wistfulness' for an exact and bleak unknowing:

Or is it only the breeze, in its listlessness,
Travelling across the wet mead to me here,
You being ever dissolved to wan wistlessness,
Heard no more again far or near?

Hardy's reached-for rhymes disturb the ordinary bounds of sense and
the physical bounds of the body. Not humorous, certainly, but mis-
shaping the everyday into unforeseen, grotesque intensities. The
body here has dissolved, leaving only wraiths of sound to figure its
absence: sounds prescient, present, past:

Thus I; faltering forward,
Leaves around me falling,
Wind oozing thin through the thorn from norward,
And the woman calling.

II

A distinction is needed, and is not often enough made, between
rhyme's effects in oral and written poetry.[8] Too often the oral is taken
as the primary model for rhyme so that much of the tension in
rhymed *written* poetry is glossed over. In oral poetry the swing of the
song is sprung on rhyming sequences and the ear takes in the logic of
the narrative in great part through the iterations of rhyme. The lines
do not lie upon the page to be surveyed, so line-ending is implied
largely by end-rhyme. The listener is at the ear's mercy and must rely
upon congruities of sound to figure pathways of intent through plot.
Such poetry tends to work with a very limited repertoire of formulaic
rhyme-clusters. Because the ear alone is sorting the sense, familiarity
has a special heuristic value.

Something very different happens with rhyme on the page. Line-
ending provides an architectonics. Rhymes stress across those line
endings. Here the indecisions between eye and ear, the excesses and
insufficiencies of agreement between what's written down and what's
heard in the mind's ear, can become part of the argument. Doubling
occurs when the rhyme-pair matches at one sensory level but not the
other. Shapes remain discrete; sounds cohere ('missed', 'mist', for
example). What is often called perfect rhyme – the full accord of
sound – may yet be tantalisingly discordant to the eye. Even such
crassly familiar rhymes as June/moon get part of their effectiveness
from the eye's resistance to the ear's fulfilment.[9]

So, lodged in written rhyme there is always the potential for argument, even quarrel, as well as coincidence and improbable resolution. Such are, also, characteristics of comedy. Bakhtin in *The Dialogic Imagination* suggests that stylistics has been singularly deaf to dialogue. Rhyme, in its emphasis on return, synchrony, and debate finds a route alternative to serial, or syntax-bound, reading: a peculiar variant of what Bakhtin terms the 'chronotope'.[10] The licensed licence of rhyme certainly displays 'carnivalesque' qualities – tousling language, overturning the hierarchies of signification, locking together terms from disparate linguistic registers. That its anarchy is always underpinned by system does not distinguish it from carnival, whose displays of disorder inhabit a world where there are always still *lords* of misrule, and mornings after.

Is this concatenation of qualities simply a matter of analogy? Or are there inalienable links between rhyming and comedy? Manifestly, rhyme need not be funny: it may indeed intensify mourning with its recollecting pace, as Tennyson's rhyme-scheme in *In Memoriam* plangently demonstrates. The four-line stanza, rhyming abba, endlessly pulls back towards its own beginning, refusing to release poet or reader. That halting, knitting effect is referentially linked to the subject matter. Yet rhyme does offer to the ear an excess of gratification that outgoes grieving.

The mimesis that rhyme performs must be in some measure referential, though not directly so. That is to say, rhyme does not mean itself only: it means the relations and disparities (the gaps and contingencies) between the words that compose it. But it also means more and other than that, because it foregrounds the phonemic *as much as* the unitary quality of words. Rhyme can uncover within a single word skeins of signifying phonemes that form pithy poems when set in sequence, for example, thus:

> friend
> find
> fiend
> rend
> rind
> end

Lyotard in *Discours, figure* notes how little attention the reader pays to the signs on the page, the inscribed marks that compose words.[11] Written rhyme restores them to prominence, in dissonance, in a series of false relations to sound. So rhyme has doubly the nature of arguments or dialogue: in the answering of two words to each other, and in the fracturing of *one* word into two sensory messages (sight and sound) that do not agree.

Take the following passage from Pope's 'Moral Essays: Epistle to Bathurst'. Here we have a set of rhymes all of which fully satisfy the ear but none of which are spelled identically. The pair that I wish to examine is that of 'spare' and 'heir' because in addition to the differently spelt rhyme words it also embeds an eye–ear pun in the word 'heir'. When heard, one word only is indicated, but seen on the page, a shadowy further rhyme word is drawn in which literalises the metaphor:

> Riches, like insects, when conceal'd they lie,
> Wait but for wings, and in their season, fly.
> Who sees pale Mammon pine among his store,
> Sees but a backward steward for the Poor;
> This year a reservoir, to keep and spare,
> The next a Fountain, spouting through his Heir,
> In lavish streams to quench a Country's thirst,
> And men and dogs shall drink him 'till they burst.[12]

The rhyme pair 'spare/Heir' here generates, between sense and sound, a triadic other: 'Hair'. So, not only do we have the abstract succession of the *heir*, but a vigorously concrete image of a baroque fountain with water spouting through its *hair*: an emblem of the lavish display typical of wealth but resisted by the miser. Comedy here is acted out as frugality: the extraordinary concision with which – by means of the one, sparing, rhyme – Pope conjures display sets him in an equivocally dramatic sympathy with the miser he decries. Here the parsimony of the rhyme, and its excess of meaning, itself dramatises as well as represents. To produce an heir requires ejaculation, a fountain at odds with the miser's interests: the 'spare / Heir' rhyme yields multiple oppositions. Rhyme becomes comedy oscillating between manners and the grotesque, a breeding-ground not only semantic but dramatic.

Yet such extensive reading-out should not be understood as settling matters. It neglects at its peril the *disquiet* of eye and ear, the rapid dissolution of significations and the uncertain accord of what's heard, what's seen in rhyme. Rhyme remains longer in the ear than on the eye. Max Ernst's famous answer in his essay 'What is the Mechanism of Collage?' that it is 'The coupling of two realities irreconcilable in appearance upon a plane which apparently does not suit them' has its relevance to rhyme. The stable survey of visual effects in collage is, yet, less volatile, less dissipated, than the sensory and sometimes contradictory in-fluences of sight and sound in rhymes which pass by.[13]

Two of the most influential modern discussions of rhyme have emphasised what is referential and rational in the practice. William Wimsatt in 'One Relation of Rhyme to Reason'[14] begins by asserting rhyme's 'studiously and accurately semantic character' while recognising its 'alogical implication' (153). The force of his argument is to note the degree to which shifts in parts of speech control the degrees of implied difference in rhyming. 'In the broadest sense, difference of meaning in rhyme words includes difference of syntax. In fact, words have no character as rhymes until they become points in a syntactic succession' (156). He rejects a view of rhyme which appraises it 'as a form of phonetic harmony – to be described and appraised in terms of phonetic accuracy, complexity, and variety –' because this has led to recriminations against Pope for his lack of variety. Certainly, the emphasis on resolution, and married interplay, overlooks the degree to which rhyme acts as intervention, interruption, and up-ender.

But in the light of what has happened since Wimsatt wrote, it is possible to see other characteristics than the logical and referential that pre-occupied him, brilliantly as he observed them. To him, rhymes are 'the icon in which the idea is caught' (165). That stasis might be reversed: rhymes are also, as Ben Jonson long before observed, the energisers, the spoilers, who refuse equilibrium:

> Still may syllables jarre with time,
> Still may reason warre with rime,
> Resting never.[15]

Even if we take the initial 'Still' as *rhyme très riche* (in which opposing significations are held within two words that agree absolutely in sight and sound) the sentence overcomes stillness, perdurance, and repetition, to reach 'resting never'.

Donald Wesling gives greater play to the fickle and the chancy in the activity of rhyme, its transgressive irrationality. 'Rhyme is a deception all the more suspect because it gives us pleasure. Our suspicion is necessary; our pleasure is real.'[16] Oddly, by 'deception' he here seems to mean that rhyme suggests a system of connections askance from our habits of mind – not necessarily the same thing. Wesling is determined in his overall argument to track historical shifts in the functions of rhyme, shifts teleologically underpinned by his implicit notions of progress: as when he suggests that we should take seriously 'those metaphors of organic form which are a sign of avant-gardist intentions whatever their national origin' (104). According to his reading the past strains towards the modern – and some past does quite well at getting there. Despite the odd condescension that such an argumentative shape necessitates, Wesling's book is full of excellent observations and pays more attention than Wimsatt can afford to do to the fortuitousness of rhyming sounds.

Most recently and grippingly, in Garrett Stewart's *Reading Voices*,[17] the emphasis has turned to the unboundedness of words, to what Stewart calls 'Rhymed Treason' (and 'recurrent tendings'). Stewart's chief concern is with 'transegmental drift' (the claim on plate tectonics is not coincidental: despite all the lyricism that his theory implies Stewart toys persistently with a counter-scientism). He emphasises overlaps and deliquescences: 'phonemic reading moves beyond – or behind – "style" altogether. Its concern is more with linguistic accident than with aesthetic craft, the lottery of letters and sounds as they pour in and out of lexical molds' (25).

Stewart draws attention to the way the voice draws sounds across the space between words. Some of his examples depend upon an absence of glottal stopping more familiar to an American than an English ear, but perhaps particularly apposite to the earlier examples he selects. He is concerned not only with rhymes but with assonance, and his instances are drawn not only from verse but from prose. He writes brilliantly about Woolf's *The Waves* which shaves and laves words to produce effects like the sonorities of the ocean. In what he writes on rhyme his main concern is with 'transegmental rhymes' that shift across the boundaries of words (doth us / thus; persever / all else ever, 77). Stewart himself emphasises that this extended understanding of rhyme, where words' edges blur, means that no necessary semantic equivalence can be, or in his view, need be, sustained. His concern is with 'the increased textural possibilities provided by such a drift of acoustic iteration' (70). 'Echoes generated in this way are the most purely phonic of all rhymes' (71). 'If the transegmental audition of rhyme seems to open the floodgates of such syntactic as well as phonemic rearrangements, to trigger major ambiguities by the least pull on a single word, this no more certifies than it denies the existence of the widened rhyme in the first place. It needs only to be heard to be believed, not recovered by meaning (any more than does rhyme in general)' (77).

Such a reading certainly undoes the buttons of rhyme. The slack that Stewart uncovers allows a linguistic play almost Swinburnian in its lassitude (and lissomeness). But because his concern is with the drawn out, drawn through, he has rather little to say about *containment*. Though he makes a few remarks on comedy and comic rhyme he produces comedy in his own writing more than he marks it in others (as when he wonderfully declares himself to be concerned with 'utterance on the cusp of mumble').

Rhyme depends for its urgency upon the crammed, not-quite-split-open amphora of the word quite as much as it gains its sinuousness from the subtle liquidity of one word in another. Signs and sounds in contention, in silence, in the reader's head, make for a paradoxical theatre of division and condensation, producing ditties of 'no tone' (or as Stewart might note 'not one'). The activity of rhyme is autocratic as well as misaligned, burlesqueing the government of the body. My observations are concerned with rhyme as dialogue, quarrel, and undersong and with the helpless excess of possibility that poises it always on the brink of comedy.

III

Poets themselves have written winningly against rhyme, from Ben Jonson's 'A Fit of Rhyme Against Rhyme' onwards, taking the chance to pretend contempt and demonstrate command at once. Such poems ironically characterise rhyme's possibilities by inveighing against them. A recent revision of the kind, Charles Tomlinson's poem 'The Chances of Rhyme', opens with an elegant disappointment which we experience as delay. Indeed, so long does the ear's hope survive that the disappointment is more or less inaudible. Will 'meeting' (the end word of the first line) ever be matched? Paradoxically, the *sense* of the substitute word offered gives us assurance where the rhyme could have afforded only evanescence. The first two lines run:

> The chances of rhyme are like the chances of meeting –
> In the finding fortuitous, but once found, binding;

The alliterating f's of the second line prepare us for a rhyme that is not there; *fleetingly* the practised ear half-hears the anticipated rhyme. Instead of the presaged word 'fleeting' to rhyme with 'meeting', we meet instead the word 'binding' which rhymes back subterraneously within its own line to 'finding'. The couplet by evading end-rhyme refuses to clinch itself as couplet, but the 'finding/binding' rhyme skeins sense together. Such reassurance is part of Tomlinson's wager against those

> who confuse the fortuitousness
> Of art with something to be met with only
> At extremity's brink, reducing thus
> Rhyme to a kind of rope's end, a glimpsed grass
> To be snatched at as we plunge past it –

Rhyme here (grass–past) cannot secure itself at the line's end, but the poem ends by pairing the words 'confusion' and 'conclusion'. That these words come at the *ends* of lines dramatises stable concord. Their positioning shifts slightly the semantic register of 'confusion' towards 'con-fusion': things are not *disordered* (confused), simply, but *coming together* (con-fused) to challenge entropy, in endurance, in ending.

> And between
> Rest-in-Peace and precipice,
> Inertia and perversion, come the varieties
> Increase, lease, re-lease (in both
> Senses); and immersion, conversion – of inert
> Mass, that is, into energies to combat confusion.
> Let rhyme be my conclusion.[18]

Again, as in Jonson, the emphasis is on energy, *restlessness*, now reinforced by contemporary understandings that any final equilibration is, according to the laws of thermodynamics, death. In Tomlinson's comedy of survival, rhyme is the principle of energy and of persistent possibility. Tomlinson's exhilarating poem turns rhymes on their axes. Out of the quarrels between words, and within them too, he achieves an extreme argument against extremism, an awakening of the reader to the energies of taken-for-granted conformities. This re-awakening of energies through rhyme is not a modern effect only.

Pope sometimes similarly turns upon the reader's soporific expectations – though here the expectation challenged is that he will always provide regularly turned couplets. He first wakes attention by rhyming 'write by rule' and 'play the fool' and follows that up with one of his favourite contrary sense, lopped, rhymes (disease-ease):

> Call, if you will, bad Rhiming a disease,
> It gives men happiness, or leaves them ease.

But he goes further in his feigned repudiation of verse, bungling his own best skills, acknowledging himself (purportedly) as only fit for 'plain Prose':

> There is a time when Poets will grow dull:
> I'll e'en leave Verses to the Boys at school:
> To Rules of Poetry no more confin'd,
> I learn to smooth and harmonize my Mind,
> Teach ev'ry Thought within its bounds to roll,
> And keep the equal measure of the Soul.[19]

The skill and gall of this passage leave one gasping, worsted by Pope's morose, skittish, eventually divine comedy. First, he fails to find a rhyme, reaching for one as jejune as any schoolboy's: 'dull' and 'school' may do as association but not as rhyme. Then he sneaks in the expected rhyme word, 'rule', but submerges it near the start of the next line and renders it inexact, 'rules'. The plural, and the visual disunity between the words 'school' and 'rules', play havoc with the rules of poetry that he invokes. Then, breathtakingly, the dowdy monosyllabics of 'There is a time when Poets will grow dull' are echoed, and etherialised, in the distilled precision of the last line's equal weighting, no syllable claiming emphasis until the final 'Soul':

> And keep the equal measure of the Soul.

And with that steady endoubling, metrical and spiritual, Pope reclaims the mastery he has just renounced.

Some comic poems thrive on disappointing the ear, rather than the eye. Take this limerick, in which sense and the speaking voice nonchalantly cast aside the formal claims of rhyme:

> There was an old man of St Bees
> Who was stung on the knees by a wasp
> When asked did it hurt
> He said yes it did
> And I'm glad that it wasn't a hornet.

The formal rigour and licensed innuendo of limericks are here both thwarted. The premature sweet rhyme of 'bees' and 'knees' seems to promise a thickly rhyming form. The ear gropes for rhyme and is firmly carried past it into humdrum statement.

This example brings out the degree to which rhyme relies on the pleasures of flouting taxonomies based on meaning, precisely because here, that flouting pleasure is itself *substituted for rhyme*. The triad bees–wasp–hornet is a spurious natural-historical group, its taxonomy springing out of the singular place name St Bees. Logically, St Bees does not 'rhyme' with wasp or hornet: it is purely semantic; it does not sting. So, in rhyme's absence, we begin to understand more precisely what we receive from its presence.

Rhyme imposes a taxonomic order in which likeness of sound predominates over all other categories. This is not to say that sense is discounted. Rhyme is not outside reason: it (in both senses) aggravates reason. But it outgoes reason in that it disturbs established semantic categories and refuses the hierarchies implicit in those groupings. The knotting together of unlike pairs, or triads, is one reason for rhyme's great utility as a mnemonic: concepts or paradoxes that would otherwise be difficult to take in at a single glance yield to rhyme's order.

Rhyme lends itself to two apparently contradictory movements of mind: scepticism and faith. It is no accident that Pope and Byron, on the one hand, and Herbert and Hopkins, on the other, are among the most inventive of all English poets in rhyme. And that leaves aside the notable example of Emily Dickinson. So satire and divine comedy are two modes of thought that rhyme adheres to. In both, its accords are a form of disputation. The anarchic neatness of rhyme can undermine current social orders, substituting the information of the senses, jangled: new fangled.

IV

The disturbing of established categories by rhyme opens it as an instrument towards faith. If it outgoes reason, it can intensify hopes that must evade the controls of rationality. As Seamus Heaney remarks of Herbert in *The Government of the Tongue*:

An unconstrained, undebilitated mind measured itself against impositions and expectations which were both fundamental and contingent to it. Its disciplines, however, proved equal to its challenges, so that a pun on the word choler, meaning both outburst of anger and emblem of submission, could hold the psychic and artistic balance; and a rhyme of 'child' with 'wild' could put the distress of his personal predicament in a divinely ordained perspective.[20]

Herbert's is the divine comedy of rhyme. Here the parts of the rhyming word are searched and secured: letters, phonemes, syllables are delicately shed. He pares words down as they recur, to reveal not contraction but possibility. Again, rhyme becomes an enactment of

the body: something more material than metaphor, as the signs on
the page play out experience, searching for incarnation.

In 'Paradise' God has become the word-dissector: the surgical
rhymester through whose means the human discovers what endures:

> When thou dost greater judgments SPARE,
> And with thy knife but prune and PARE,
> Ev'n fruitfull trees more fruitfull ARE.
>
> Such sharpnes shows the sweetest FREND:
> Such cuttings rather heal then REND:
> And such beginnings touch their END.[21]

The echo-poem 'Heaven' suggests that within the mortal the
immortal is always waiting to be revealed. Echo is not here mere
repetition but promise for the future. Rhyme is thus displayed not as
nostalgia but as leap. The poem opens:

> O who will show me those delights on high?
>   ECHO   I.
> Thou Echo, thou art mortall, all men know.
>   ECHO   No.

It ends:

> Light, joy, and leisure; but shall they persever?
>   ECHO   Ever.

Amusement and relief are simultaneous: as Baudelaire puts it 'Joy is
one'. Rhyme figures the immortal.

Other poems, less knowingly, in their final couplets slough off the
word's first letter to reach a fuller ending. 'Holy Baptisme (I)':

> What ever future sinnes should be miscall,
> Your first acqaintance might discredit all.

'Love I':

>   onely a skarf or glove
> Doth warm our hands, and make them write of love.

'Antiphon(I)':

> Praised be the God alone,
> Who hath made of two folds one.

Most movingly and most appetitively 'Love (III)':

> You must sit down, sayes Love, and taste my meat:
>   So I did sit and eat.

Herbert rhymes across high and low to produce not bathos but intimacy, a humorous living-through instead of the alienated voyeurism of the grotesque. He is the poet of incarnation and it tells in his rhymes. At the end of 'The Dawning' the lines form a carnivalesque of another kind, in which death and life cross over in the materiality of linen, and in the improbable last perfect rhyme, of 'grief' and 'handkerchief':

> Arise, arise;
> And with his buriall-linen drie thine eyes:
> Christ left his grave-clothes, that we might, when grief
> Draws tears, or bloud, not want a handkerchief.

Nursery remedies, the inadequate token, cleanliness against the corruption of the body, are carried here across a semantic extreme which is perfectly poised by the ear. That's the shock: how well these words rhyme.

The comedy of rhyme lies in its refusal of established categories. It repudiates the high and low of sense. It enjoins new intimacies on the ear. Things lie down together. Words strip off. Teasing is part of the enterprise. Rhyme augments sense without simply mimicking it. It is about its own devices. The animistic language which rhyme so often provokes is no irrelevance. The activity of rhyming on the page makes for a physical dialogue in the reader between eye and ear. And rhyming enacts a drama in which words become themselves figures of the body explored, in ribaldry, appetite and incarnation.

NOTES

1 Charles Baudelaire, *Œuvres Complètes* (Paris, 1955), 1, 524. Further page references in text.
2 Peter Levins, *Manipulus Vocabulorum: A Rhyming Dictionary of the English Language* (1570), ed. Henry B. Wheatley, *Early English Texts Society*, 27 (London, 1867).
3 Levins, *Manipulus Vocabulorum*, 7.
4 Levins, *Manipulus Vocabulorum*, 3.
5 Material from J. Walker, *The Rhyming Dictionary of the English Language in which the whole language is arranged according to its terminations* (London, 1890).
6 Levins, *Manipulus Vocabulorum*, 155.
7 For an example of this effect see the discussion, on pp. 190–1, of Charles Tomlinson's poem, 'The Chances of Rhyme'.
8 But for discussion at large of the tensions between eye and ear in nineteenth-century poetry see Eric Griffiths, *The Printed Voice of Victorian*

Poetry (Oxford, 1988). Henry Lanz, *The Physical Basis of Rime: An Essay on the Aesthetics of Sound* (Stanford, 1931) concentrates on physical analysis of vowel sounds and then argues that the decline of rhyme is a sign of a more general decadence.

9 It can be argued, also, that the aural satisfaction will vary in intensity according to whether or not the reader habitually diphthongises 'June' in speech.

10 M. M. Bakhtin, *The Dialogic Imagination*, ed. Michael Holquist (Austin, 1981), 273.

11 Jean-François Lyotard, *Discours, figure* (Paris, 1971).

12 Alexander Pope, *Epistles to Several Persons (Moral Essays)*, ed. F. W. Bateson, Twickenham edn III.ii (London, 1951), 104–5.

13 Peter Didsbury ends his unlined poem, 'A White Wine for Max Ernst': 'The association of two or more apparently alien elements on a plane alien to both is the most potent ignition of poetry.' *The Butchers of Hull* (Newcastle upon Tyne, 1982), 28.

14 W. K. Wimsatt, *The Verbal Icon: Studies in the Meaning of Poetry* (1954; London, 1970), 152–66.

15 C. H. Herford and P. & E. Simpson, eds., *Ben Jonson*, 11 vols. (1925–52), VIII, 184.

16 Donald Wesling, *The Chances of Rhyme: Device and Modernity* (Berkeley, 1980), ix.

17 Garrett Stewart, *Reading Voices: Literature and the Phonotext* (Berkeley, 1990).

18 Wesling quotes this poem in full (131–2) but, disappointingly, scarcely analyses it.

19 Alexander Pope, 'Imitation of the Second Epistle of the Second Book of Horace', *Imitations of Horace*, ed. John Butt, Twickenham edn IV (London, 1939), 179.

20 Seamus Heaney, *The Government of the Tongue* (London, 1988), 96.

21 Quotations from *The Works of George Herbert*, ed. F. E. Hutchinson (Oxford, 1941).

Wordsworthian comedy

Jonathan Wordsworth

And this, said he, putting the remains of a crust into his wallet – and this, should have been thy portion, said he, hadst thou been alive to have shared it with me. I thought by the accent, it had been an apostrophe to his child; but 'twas to his ass... He then took his crust of bread out of his wallet again, as if to eat it; held it some time in his hand – then laid it upon the bit of his ass's bridle – looked wistfully at the little arrangement he had made – and then gave a sigh... Shame on the world! said I to myself – Did we love each other, as this poor soul but loved his ass – 'twould be something. (Sterne, *Sentimental Journey*)

> All by the moonlight river-side
> It gave three miserable groans:
> ''Tis come then to a pretty pass',
> Said Peter to the groaning ass,
> 'But I will bang your bones!' (Wordsworth, *Peter Bell*)

Wordsworthian comedy owes much to Sterne, something to Burns, and a great deal to Wordsworth's own profoundly original genius. It is to be found locally in many places – in the playful moments and delicately shifting tones of *The Prelude*, for instance – but its sustained achievements belong chiefly to the period of *Lyrical Ballads*. The two passages quoted above may help to define its nature and antecedents. Seated in his French postchaise, Yorick sees a man mourning over his dead donkey in a way that is both incongruous and touching; from the event he draws lugubrious pleasure and an impeccable moral. The episode is humorous, but not satirical or mocking. Though permitted his amusement, the reader is asked to feel respect for the emotions that he regards as excessive.

Those who know their Wordsworth well will know that the second quotation is, and is not, the opening of *Peter Bell*. Nobody has ever felt at ease with Wordsworth's stanza – but then they weren't intended to. Up to this stage in the poem, the poet has indulged himself in a whimsical Prologue (a flight of fancy that owes something to Dante, maybe something to Chaucer); now he is making a little comedy out of beginning the story proper *in medias res*. The reference to banging of bones is deliberately uneasy, and duly caused offence. A reviewer in the *British Critic* of June 1819 regarded the phrase as 'inseparably connected with low and ridiculous associations', adding solemnly

we think there can be no doubt, that the poet should have sacrificed the dramatic effect for the sake of excluding such associations, and merely told us in his own person and *in his own language*, that Peter beat the ass very unmercifully.[1]

What Wordsworth thought in 1819 we cannot know; when the poem was written in spring 1798, he would have laughed.

Wordsworthian comedy has both the unforced eccentricity of Sterne, and the controlling self-consciousness. It works through, not despite, 'low and ridiculous associations', and is aware at all times that the author's 'person' and his 'language' are artifacts. As to the 'dramatic effect', it depends upon layers of contrivance that Wordsworth would be most unlikely to sacrifice. His comic masterpiece, *The Idiot Boy*, is an almost faultless work of art, a creation of exquisite tact, at once humorous and deeply moving. *Peter Bell*, its sequel, leaves us at times uncertain how to react. Peter takes pleasure in the banging of bones, Wordsworth seems to do so, ought we to do so too? It is a poem, however, that has been too easily scorned, too often left unread or read very badly. Comparison with the *Ancient Mariner* (though obviously relevant at times) leads to its being seen as a clumsy vying with the supernatural, eccentric in the wrong ways and funny in the wrong places. It may be more useful to see it as poised between *The Idiot Boy* and the 1799 *Prelude*. It is a comedy of the workings of the mind.

Comedy in the early Wordsworth is rare. It would have done no harm to leaven the earnest tones of *Salisbury Plain* or *The Borderers*, but the poet was not in a mood to do so. It is as if there is something in the rhythm, rhyme and vitality of the ballad-form that releases Wordsworth's sense of the incongruous. As he takes the ballad up, in March 1798, there is an expansion of his emotional range that could not have been predicted. New awarenesses are matched by new technique, new dramatic powers. The young farmer, Harry Gill, lies in wait in a Dorsetshire cornfield, intent upon revenge, as his aged and wretched neighbour takes firewood from his hedge:

And once, behind a rick of barley,
Thus looking out did Harry stand
The moon was full and shining clearly,
And crisp with frost the stubble-land) –
He hears a noise, he's all awake!
Again? On tip-toe down the hill
He softly creeps – 'tis Goody Blake!
She's at the hedge of Harry Gill.

Right glad was he when he beheld her!
Stick after stick did Goody pull –
He stood behind a bush of elder,
Till she had filled her apron full.
When with her load she turned about,
The by-road back again to take,
He started forward with a shout,
And sprang upon poor Goody Blake.

And fiercely by the arm he took her,
And by the arm he held her fast,
And fiercely by the arm he shook her,
And cried, 'I've caught you then at last!'   (lines 73–92)[2]

The scene is not played as comedy, but it has the comic speed and
timing, the comic sense of incongruities. Harry's vengeance we see as
monstrous, but its disproportion to the apron-full of sticks would be
funny if it were not painful. Repetition in the last four quoted lines,
and the use of the feminine rhyme, 'took her' / 'shook her', take us
to the very edge of comedy.

Similar in many ways is the recognition-scene as Betty Foy
discovers her lost son, Johnny, at the end of *The Idiot Boy*:

Who's yon, that near the waterfall
(Which thunders down with headlong force
Beneath the moon, yet shining fair)
As careless as if nothing were,
Sits upright on a feeding horse?...

And that's the very pony too!
Where is she, where is Betty Foy?
She hardly can sustain her fears –
The roaring waterfall she hears,
And cannot find her idiot boy.

Your pony's worth his weight in gold;
Then calm your terrors, Betty Foy! –

> She's coming from among the trees,
> And now, all full in view, she sees
> Him whom she loves, her idiot boy.
>
> And Betty sees the pony too!
> Why stand you thus good Betty Foy?
> It is no goblin, 'tis no ghost,
> 'Tis he whom you so long have lost,
> He whom you love, your idiot boy.
>
> She looks again – her arms are up –
> She screams – she cannot move for joy!
> She darts as with a torrent's force,
> She almost has o'erturned the horse,
> And fast she holds her idiot boy.   (lines 357–61, 367–86)

Again we have a moonlit drama of seeking, recognition, pouncing. Harry's vengeful joy becomes the no less obsessive love of Betty for her mongol son. Repetition is used again to magnificent effect, as the clumsiness of love replaces the earlier violence. Incongruity again is central. Instead of the burly young farmer shaking poor Goody, against a backdrop of glistening frost, we have the genius of: 'She darts as with a torrent's force, / She almost has o'erturned the horse'. We may tell ourselves, if we wish, that Betty's love is 'a power like one of Nature's' (1805 *Prelude* xii 312); we may invoke, if we choose, the poet's response to the London beggar of *Prelude* Book vii: 'My mind did at this spectacle turn round / As with the might of waters...' (lines 616–17). But the brilliant *in*appropriateness of Wordsworth's simile is quite as important as its implication of oneness with the natural world. The scene evoked is as present to us as the grip on Goody's arm. Betty stands transfixed, her arms raised. Her mouth is open as she screams. So visual is the poetry, that for an instant (as she darts forward) we see not only Betty, in her ridiculous eagerness, but the torrent to which she is compared. Half woman, half waterfall, she strikes the horse. And that too we see – knocked off balance by the clumsiness of love.

Comedy, like tragedy, is a going too far; it is in its nature excessive. It cannot conform to expectations or to rules. Or perhaps one should say, it can conform only to those it sets up for itself. If Wordsworth, in *Peter Bell*, had told us 'in his own person, and *in his own language*, that Peter beat the ass very unmercifully', it would not have been dramatic effect that was sacrificed, so much as the power of comic incongruity: disparity between associations of beauty and moonlight, on the one hand, and the misery that is so abruptly introduced – 'All by the moonlight river-side / It gave three miserable groans...' – disparity between the unexplainedness of the 'It', and the specific enumeration of groans. Though *Peter Bell* quickly grew too long, it was written for *Lyrical Ballads*, as part of the experiment with conversational styles. 'Low and ridiculous associations' are evoked with evident delight, in the 'pretty pass' and the banging:

> '''Tis come then to a pretty pass',
> Said Peter to the groaning ass,
> 'But I will bang your bones!'

Wordsworth is out to shock, and does so very successfully. In fact he does so twice – the offensive stanza being first singled out to create the comedy of an opening *in medias res*, then returned to its appropriate place in the narrative.

Context changes vitally the stanza's effect. On its first appearance it forms a mock-opening, drawing comments from the audience which the poet has created to hear his tale, and poking fun at literary tradition:

> 'My dearest sir', cried Mistress Swan,
> 'You're got at once into the middle!'
> And little Bess with accents sweeter
> Cried, 'Oh, dear sir, but who is Peter?'
> Said Harry, ''Tis a downright riddle!'   (lines 161–5)

Byron's more sophisticated fooling in the opening canto of *Don Juan* is much to the point:

> Most epic poets plunge in 'medias res,'
>   (Horace makes this the heroic turnpike road)
> And then your hero tells, whene'er you please,
>   What went before – by way of episode,
> While seated after dinner at his ease...   (i, 41–5)[3]

Wordsworth in *Peter Bell* is no epic poet. He does think partly in terms of mock-epic, however, and like Byron he wishes his readers to be aware of his controlling presence as writer within the narrative. As writer. The often boring tendency of critics to create separable 'narrators' – distinguishable from the writer and detachable from the story he tells – is one that Wordsworth tends to encourage. His

1800 note to *The Thorn* offers *carte blanche* for narrator-invention: 'The character which I have here introduced speaking is sufficiently common. The Reader will perhaps have a general notion of it, if he has ever known a man, a Captain of a small trading vessel, for example...' More significant perhaps in the context of *Peter Bell* and *The Idiot Boy* is Wordsworth's praise of Burns in 1817 for constructing out of his own character and situation in society 'a poetic self, introduced as a dramatic personage, for the purpose of inspiriting his incidents, diversifying his pictures, recommending his opinions, and giving point to his sentiments' (*Letter to a Friend of Robert Burns* 24).

Wordsworthian comedy especially is enriched by the presence of the poetic self – the self who is so literal-minded in *We are Seven* and doesn't listen in *The Leech Gatherer*. At times the self will emerge full in view: a *Peter Bell* draft (significantly never a part of the completed text) goes so far as to identify Peter with a 'wild rover' met by the poet himself on the Wye in 1793.[4] More typically, the poetic self is perceived to be distinct from the writer-as-maker by virtue of his relationship within the poem to one or more of the characters. Stanzas 2 and 3 of *The Idiot Boy* offer distinct voices, neither of them the merely bland voice of the maker. First the dynamic self who knows Betty Foy personally, and remonstrates with her, as Burns remonstrates with Tam O'Shanter:[5]

> Why bustle thus about your door?
> What means this bustle, Betty Foy?
> Why are you in this mighty fret,
> And why on horseback have you set
> Him whom you love, your idiot boy?   (lines 7–11)

Then the more writerly self, still questioning Betty's behaviour, but now addressing the reader:

> Beneath the moon that shines so bright,
> Till she is tired, let Betty Foy
> With girt and stirrup fiddle-faddle –
> But wherefore set upon a saddle
> Him whom she loves, her idiot boy?   (lines 12–16)

Wordsworth is to be seen not so much 'recommending his opinions' as establishing his values. The line with which both stanzas end – 'Him whom you love, your idiot boy' / 'Him whom she loves, her idiot boy' – is not in fact a refrain, but rings through both this

opening passage of *The Idiot Boy* and the final recognition-scene
earlier quoted. Through his poetic self Wordsworth first introduces us
to, then sustains in our minds, the conjunction of love and idiocy
which is central to his poem, but which to most of us comes as a shock.
The earnest questioning in stanzas 2 and 3, the indulgent tones ('this
might fret'), the mystification about putting Johnny on a horse, all
combine to ease our acceptance. The rhythm of the repeated line has
a perfect naturalness. Coming as it does in apposition to 'Him whom
she loves', 'her idiot boy' easily becomes the endearment that we are
expecting.[6]

Johnny is a mongol (Down's Syndrome is the euphemism we now
prefer). Not since Henryson's *Testament of Cresseid* (where the heroine
is a prostitute) had any writer taken on the task of establishing
sympathy for a more incongruous hero. Betty's unthinking love was
a problem too. 'Anile dotage', Coleridge called it in *Biographia
Literaria*;[7] but then, he was not in a very sympathetic mood. John
Wilson, as is well known, wrote in 1802 to express his shock that
Betty's love could not be shared. Wordsworth's answer of 7 June is
unworried, but a trifle solemn. Betty's feelings are exalted in his
comment. 'I have...often looked upon the conduct of fathers and
mothers of the lower classes of society towards Idiots as the great
triumph of the human heart'. Johnny is positively hallowed: 'I have
often applied to Idiots, in my own mind, that sublime expression of
scripture... "*their life is hidden with God*"'.[8] To read these lofty ways
of thinking back into *The Idiot Boy* is a mistake. They have their
relevance of course, but they ignore the comedy, and in a way they
rather undervalue Betty. Hers is no effortful 'triumph'. She exists in
her love.

Sending Johnny off to fetch the doctor brings out in Betty an array
of intense emotions – pride that he is to be the hero of the hour; pride
that he can sit on a horse; fear that he will never return; tenderness
that cannot face his going. Though telling him in ludicrous detail
how to achieve his mission, her chief concern even before he goes is to
have him back:

> And Betty o'er and o'er has told
> The boy who is her best delight,
> Both what to follow, what to shun,
> What do, and what to leave undone,
> How turn to left, and how to right.

> And Betty's most especial charge
> Was, 'Johnny! Johnny! mind that you
> Come home again, nor stop at all,
> Come home again, whate'er befall,
> My Johnny do, I pray you do.'
>
> To this did Johnny answer make
> Both with his head and with his hand,
> And proudly shook the bridle too;
> And then his words were not a few,
> Which Betty well could understand!   (lines 62–76)

As Wordsworth was surely aware, Betty and Johnny experience in an extreme form the Shandy brothers' inability to communicate: 'Well might Locke write a chapter upon the imperfections of words'.[9] Sterne has devised a situation that is endlessly amusing because, despite comic variations on the theme, it is endlessly the same. Walter has only to begin a philosophical discourse, and we may be sure that at some crucial point Toby will misunderstand him in terms of warfare and the bowling-green battlefield:

Now, whether we observe it or no, continued my father, in every sound man's head, there is a regular succession of ideas of one sort or other, which follow each other in train just like —— A train of artillery? said my uncle Toby. – A train of fiddle-stick! – quoth my father... (200–1)

Sterne's is the comedy of mutual incomprehension. Walter and Toby are kept apart by their hobbyhorses, each speaking, and hearing, only the language of his obsession. Each is, according to Walter's definition, a 'sound man' with a 'regular succession of ideas'. But succession in this context depends upon association, and association (as Locke makes clear), must always be personal. Turning Locke to comic (and sometimes poignant) advantage, Sterne offers us trains of thought regularly thwarted by trains of artillery. That the brothers Shandy are felt nevertheless to communicate their love depends chiefly on an inchoate language of gesture: Toby lays his hand on Walter's knee, lays down his pipe, whistles *Lillibullero*.

Wordsworth has his language of gesture too – 'She gently pats the pony's side / On which her idiot boy must ride' (lines 79–80) – and it is hard not to think that it comes from Sterne. In *The Idiot Boy*, however, it expresses tenderness within a relationship that must always be one-sided. We are reminded incongruously of *A Sentimental Journey*, and the mourning Frenchman who first saves the crust for his

dead ass, then on second thoughts lays it fancifully and tenderly on
the bit of its bridle. Tacitly acknowledging that she cannot reach into
Johnny's mongol otherworld, Betty pats the pony that will be close to
him as he rides on his mission. Wordsworth, meanwhile, is saying to
us, 'Did we love each other as this poor soul but loves her damaged
child, 'twould be something.'

As descendants of Don Quixote, Johnny and Uncle Toby have in
common the tradition of the holy fool. Johnny, though, can have no
hobbyhorse: obsession is a deviation in the rational mind. His mind
is a law, or lack of a law, to itself. If Betty has a hobbyhorse, it is love.
Or perhaps it is Johnny himself? When all is said and done, there is
something limited about hobbyhorses. Sterne can give them vitality,
just as Jonson and Molière can give vitality to the comedy of
humours; but they have the same drawback. Though maverick by
definition, they depend upon being dependable. The world of
Tristram Shandy is carefully disordered, the world of *The Idiot Boy* is
creative and anarchic, closer in some ways to that of Burns. It is the
comedy of a horse that thinks, a woman that doesn't, a child that
can't – presented by a poet who intervenes as Sterne intervenes, but
who leaves more to the reader's imagination. The idiot boy who
provides the title of the poem is indeed its true subject, but not as the
burring and inarticulate mongol. He is the creation of Betty's love,
and of our own minds, working on numinous hints provided by the
poet:

> There is no need of boot or spur,
> There is no need of whip or wand,
> For Johnny has his holly-bough,
> And with a hurly-burly now
> He shakes the green bough in his hand... (lines 57–61)

> And while the pony moves his legs,
> In Johnny's left hand you may see
> The green bough's motionless and dead;
> The moon that shines above his head
> Is not more still and mute than he. (lines 87–91)

In effect *The Idiot Boy* creates its subject as it goes along. The poem,
we are told, was inspired by the topsy-turvy words, 'The cocks did
crow, to-whoo, to-whoo, / And the sun did shine so cold', ascribed to
Johnny in the final stanza. The comment, it seems, had been made by
a local idiot at Alfoxden, and reported to Wordsworth by Thomas

Poole. It was an exquisite piece of non-sense, a comic inversion of day and night that had, by chance, the quality of pure imagination. Setting out with his conclusion in mind (very much as he had done in *The Ruined Cottage*) Wordsworth created the world, and the mind, to which the idiot's inspired pronouncements could belong:

> while they all were travelling home,
> Cried Betty, 'Tell us, Johnny, do,
> Where all this long night you have been,
> What you have heard, what you have seen –
> And Johnny, mind you tell us true.'
>
> Now Johnny all night long had heard
> The owls in tuneful concert strive;
> No doubt too he the moon had seen,
> For in the moonlight he had been
> From eight o'clock till five.
>
> And thus to Betty's question, he
> Made answer like a traveller bold
> (His very words I give to you):
> 'The cocks did crow to-whoo, to-whoo,
> And the sun did shine so cold.'   (lines 447–61)

'Thus answered Johnny in his glory', Wordsworth adds with splendid inconsequence, 'And that was all his travel's story'.

When, in *Peter Bell*, we come a second time on the stanza about Peter and the groaning ass it is part of a consecutive narrative. Comedy persists, but in a situation that is not on the face of it humorous. Peter has found the ass, 'one beautiful November night', all alone beside 'the rapid River Swale'. It hangs its head over the stream, and is seemingly abandoned. Regarding it as a lawful prize, Peter tries everything in his power to get it to move, and finally attempts to beat it into submission:

> He pulled – the creature did not move!
> Upon his back then Peter leapt,
> And with his staff and heels he plied
> The little beast on either side,
> But still the ass his station kept.
>
> Quoth Peter, 'You're a beast of mettle!
> I see you'll suit me to an ace.'
> And now the ass through his left eye
> On Peter turned most quietly,
> Looked quietly into his face.

'What's this?' cries Peter, brandishing
A new-peeled sapling, white as cream –
The ass knew well what Peter said,
But as before hung down his head
Over the silent stream.   (lines 411–25)

Like Sterne, Wordsworth was fond of donkeys. It is not on record that he ever gave one a macaroon, but he watched them in the woods at Alfoxden, and associated his writing of *Peter Bell* with personal liking. 'I used', he observed in 1842,

to take great delight in noticing the habits, tricks, and physiognomy of asses; and I have no doubt that I was thus put upon writing the poem out of liking for the creature that is so often dreadfully abused. (Fenwick Note)

The ass that Peter so dreadfully abuses is to an extraordinary extent in charge of the story. He acts independently, takes all the decisions that are made, and has the human qualities that the human hero lacks. Like Johnny Foy he is inarticulate, but he knows how to make a point:

Quoth Peter, leaping from the ass,
'There is some plot against me laid' –
Once more the little meadow-ground,
And all the hoary cliffs around,
He cautiously surveyed...

All, all is silent, rocks and woods;
All, all is silent, far and near;
Only the ass, with motion dull,
Upon the pivot of his skull
Turns round his long left ear.

Thought Peter, what can mean all this?
There is some ugly witchcraft here!
Once more the ass, with motion dull,
Upon the pivot of his skull
Turned round his long left ear.   (lines 431–5, 441–50)

Donkeys' ears really do pivot on the skull. But no amount of inspired observation could explain the effect of Wordsworth's lines. Peter and the ass have an uncanny relationship, felt by Peter in terms of plots and witchcraft, perceived by the reader as a reversal of roles – man as brutal, brute as calm, understanding, rational. There is something strangely impressive about the donkey's acceptance of human brutality. Exerting the only power that he understands, Peter brandishes his new-peeled sapling of willow, and we are told:

> The ass knew well what Peter said,
> But as before hung down his head
> Over the silent stream.

It is remarkable that neither Wordsworth himself in the Fenwick Note, nor his reviewers, made any reference to Balaam. Perhaps his story was so well known that its presence in *Peter Bell* was taken for granted:

And Balaam rose up in the morning, and saddled his ass, and went with the princes of Moab.

And God's anger was kindled because he went: and the angel of the Lord stood in the way for an adversary against him....

And the ass saw the angel of the Lord standing in the way, and his sword drawn in his hand: and the ass turned aside out of the way, and went into the field: and Balaam smote the ass, to turn her into the way.

But the angel of the Lord stood in a path of the vineyards, a wall being on this side, and a wall on that side.

And when the ass saw the angel of the Lord, she thrust herself unto the wall, and crushed Balaam's foot against the wall: and he smote her again.

And the angel of the Lord went further, and stood in a narrow place, where was no way to turn either to the right hand or to the left.

And when the ass saw the angel of the Lord, she fell down under Balaam: and Balaam's anger was kindled, and he smote the ass with a staff.

And the Lord opened the mouth of the ass, and she said unto Balaam, What have I done unto thee, that thou hast smitten me these three times?

And Balaam said unto the ass, Because thou hast mocked me: I would there were a sword in mine hand, for now would I kill thee.

And the ass said unto Balaam, Am not I thine ass, upon which thou hast ridden ever since I was thine unto this day? was I ever wont to do so unto thee? And he said, Nay.

Then the Lord opened the eyes of Balaam...and he bowed down his head, and fell flat on his face.

And the angel of the Lord said unto him, Wherefore hast thou smitten thine ass these three times? behold, I went out to withstand thee, because thy way is perverse before me:

And the ass saw me, and turned from me these three times: unless she had turned from me, surely now also I had slain thee, and saved her alive. (*Numbers* xxii, 21–33)

It is a very vivid story, a very famous one, and a very curious one.[10] The running title in the Authorised Version is, 'Balaam's ass saveth him from an angel.' It seems we are to take seriously the angel's statement that because Balaam's life was 'perverse' in the sight of God, he would have been killed but for the ass's devotion. The ass, meanwhile, can perceive a supernatural being, invisible to her master, and makes it clear (when she is permitted to express herself in words) that she is morally his superior. The ass in *Peter Bell* is discovered keeping watch over the body of a drowned master, to whom his devotion is total. He sees no angels; Peter's guilts, however, credit him with uncanny awareness, and he is associated with a series of apparently supernatural events. Though he is never permitted to speak, the pivoting of his long left ear is merely one among his many forms of communication. Insofar as he has a motive, it is to help the dead master and his family, but within the comedy he is destined to bring about Peter's salvation. Throughout, he shows the astonishing independence of spirit that we see in Balaam's ass: 'What have I done unto thee, that thou hast smitten me these three times?'

By comparison, Johnny's horse in *The Idiot Boy* has only a minor part, but it is an important one. 'His steed and he right well agree', we learn in the opening section:

> For of this pony there's a rumour
> That should he lose his eyes and ears,
> And should he live a thousand years,
> He never will be out of humour.
>
> But then he is a horse that thinks...   (lines 117–21)

The idiot boy, hero of the poem, is, in this context, 'poor Johnny' (line 123): the horse it is that thinks. After her sad and beautifully comic exchange with the doctor, Betty, upon the downs, sits down to weep over this 'dear pony'. '"Oh carry back my idiot boy"', she cries, '"And we will ne'er o'erload thee more!"' Instantly her prayer is answered:

> A thought is come into her head:
> The pony he is mild and good,
> And we have always used him well;
> Perhaps he's gone along the dell
> And carried Johnny to the wood.   (lines 309–13)

Wordsworth (the poetic self) intervenes, teasing the reader with improbable adventures that Johnny and his horse may have undertaken: 'And now perhaps he's hunting sheep, / A fierce and dreadful hunter he!' (lines 337–8). Shades of the fiercely gentle

Quixote! But in truth the pony has taken charge, quietly carrying his burden to safety in the wood. As a reward he is 'almost o'erturned' by the torrential force of Betty's love, and the poet comments:

> The little pony glad may be,
> But he is milder far than she,
> You hardly can perceive his joy.   (lines 404–6)

It is comedy of great charm, great tact, that quietly asserts a sense of proportion. The donkey in *Peter Bell* takes the hero on a more searching journey. He is, as Peter says, 'a beast of mettle'. Like Balaam's ass, who crushes his master's foot against a wall to avoid the angel, making further punishment inevitable, he knows what is going on, and takes whatever steps are necessary. His 'three miserable groans' seem something of an indulgence, but correspond to the three unjust beatings that Balaam's ass receives. Wordsworth contrives to make them at once funny and painful, designing for them (as one critic pointed out with amusement) a mock-heroic genealogy:

> Upon the ass the sapling rings;
> Each blow the arm of Peter stings
> Up to the elbow and the shoulder.
>
> At last – poor patient thing! – at last
> His sides they heaved, his belly stirred,
> He gave a groan, and then another
> (Of that which went before, the brother),
> And then he gave a third.   (lines 458–65)

It is this power to create humour while sustaining our awareness of pain that underlies the comedy of Peter's sighting of the drowned man on the river-bed:

> Is it the shadow of the moon?
> Is it the shadow of a cloud?
> Is it a gallows there portrayed?
> Is Peter of himself afraid?
> Is it a coffin or a shroud?…
>
> Is it some party, in a parlour
> Crammed – just as they on earth were crammed –
> Some sipping punch, some sipping tea,
> But, as you by their faces see,
> All silent, and all damned.   (lines 521–5, 531–5)

Wordsworth's imagination has taken off, become, it seems, quite irresponsible. How does a single waterlogged corpse come to be associated with a crammed and damned party, sipping punch in a parlour of Hell? Byron praised the stanza; Shelley based on it the brilliant opening to *Peter Bell the Third*, 'Hell is a city much like London'; Lamb quoted it in *Elia*. None of which answers the question, where does the comedy lie, what is its nature?

We are invited to enter and enjoy a world of comic unreality that is peculiarly Wordsworthian. Burns in *Tam O'Shanter* takes us into a witches' sabbath, where the Devil himself plays the pipes, and light is provided by the dead, candle in hand, in open coffins round the wall. On the altar lie

> A murderer's banes in gibbet airns [irons];
> Twa span-lang, wee, unchristen'd bairns;
> A thief, new-cutted frae the rape [rope],
> Wi' his last gasp his gab [mouth] did gape;
> Five tomahawks, wi' blude red-rusted;
> Five scymitars, wi' murder crusted;
> A garter, which a babe had strangled;
> A knife, a father's throat had mangled...   (lines 131–8)

As poetic self, Burns is encouraging us not so much to suspend disbelief (subtle though Coleridge's definition is), as knowingly to accept the incredible. *Tam O'Shanter* is all of a piece. We take it whole. As Tam bellows out 'Weel done, Cutty-sark!' (line 189) to the young witch dancing in her skimpy shift, we expect the dancers to vanish. But so far from being the creations of his drunken mind, they chase him like a swarm of bees, and Nannie (younger as well as prettier than the rest) almost gets him. As proof that the episode truly took place, the grey mare Maggie leaves her tail in Nannie's grasp.

Wordsworth too thrusts the unreality of his comic world upon us – the genealogy of groans, the underwater gallows, the party in the parlour – but his poetic self is up to different tricks. It is the whimsical Prologue to *Peter Bell* that enables us to place this poetry:

> There's something in a flying horse,
> There's something in a huge balloon,
> But through the clouds I'll never float
> Until I have a little boat
> In shape just like the crescent moon.   (lines 1–5)

Wordsworthian comedy is a voyaging of the mind, an adventure of the imagination, in which the poet permits himself to dispense with the rootedness that Coleridge unkindly called his 'clinging to the palpable'. The parlour stanza represents nothing that a corpse could have looked like, and nothing that would have been in the mind of Peter Bell. It marvellously evokes, however, the imaginative level at which the poetry in its most successful moments confronts experience. 'And now I have a little boat', the Prologue continues,

> In shape just like the crescent moon;
> Fast through the clouds my boat can sail –
> But if perchance your faith should fail,
> Look up, and you shall see me soon!
>
> The woods, my friends, are round you roaring,
> The woods are roaring like a sea...   (lines 6–12)

In a matter of a dozen lines Wordsworth has stated his wish for a space flight, invented himself a flying boat, got into it, taken off, and is addressing from among the clouds an imaginary earth-bound audience amid the roaring woods below. To put it differently, he has introduced to us his poetic self and made clear the terms of his comedy. We are to look up and see the crescent moon as his 'sky-canoe', we are to listen and hear the woods roaring like the sea. If we see merely the moon, hear merely the sounds of our own experience, this poetry is not for us. Similar flights of fancy occur at two points in *The Idiot Boy*, as Betty ('Oh saints, what is become of him'), and the Wordsworthian other self, speculate in improbable terms on Johnny's whereabouts. Betty's fears become a sort of gothic comedy:

> him that wicked pony's carried
> To the dark cave, the goblin's hall,
> Or in the castle he's pursuing,
> Among the ghosts, his own undoing...   (lines 237–40)

By contrast, the narrator (if such he be) is elegantly self-mocking:

> Perhaps – and no unlikely thought –
> He with his pony now doth roam
> The cliffs and peaks so high that are,
> To lay his hands upon a star,
> And in his pocket bring it home.   (lines 327–31)

In each case an actual journey (improbable enough in its own right) is heightened into a fantasy one by a flight of imagination that we may ascribe either to those present within the poem or to the writer himself.

The effect is to drive us back, not to the ordinary, but to the credible extra-ordinary. The pony has not carried Johnny to the goblin's hall, and is no roamer of peaks: he is a woodman's horse, and when he has a rider who cannot guide him, he returns to the wood. It goes without saying that Johnny has nothing to do with ghosts and goblins, and cannot put stars in his pocket (however beautiful the unlikely thought may be). Nor can he do the quite mundane things that Betty proudly sends him off to do at the beginning of the poem – follow directions, control a horse, fetch a doctor. All he can do is be himself. Betty is asked to recognise this, and to some extent she does so: '"Oh Johnny, never mind the doctor! / You've done your best, and that is all"' (lines 407–8). Only the reader's voyage is incomplete. Teased at the very end with the possibility of 'Johnny's glory', he has the task of construing the idiot's, and the poet's, final words:

> 'The cocks did crow, to-whoo, to-whoo,
> And the sun did shine so cold.'
> Thus answered Johnny in his glory,
> And that was all his travel's story.   (lines 460–3)

The boat in whom the poet travels to the skies in the Prologue of *Peter Bell* is a vessel of remarkable independence, capable of indignation, and capable like Balaam's ass of speech. 'Out, out', she says to the poet (apparently dumping him overboard),

> and like a brooding hen
> Beside your sooty hearth-stone cower!
> Go creep along the dirt, and pick
> Your way with your good walking-stick,
> Just three good miles an hour.   (lines 71–5)

The terms are splendidly insulting, suggestive of an earth-bound imagination, with the creativity of a broody hen and the speed of a stout pedestrian. As an alternative (perhaps one should say, as a temptation), the poet is offered not merely the allure of space-travel – 'Come, and above the land of snow / We'll sport amid the boreal morning' (lines 86–7) – but a visit to a 'world of fairy' that seems a blend of Spenser, Plato, and the classical Underworld:

> Or we'll into the world of fairy
> Among the lovely shades of things,
> The shadowy forms of mountains bare
> And streams and bowers and ladies fair,
> The shades of palaces and kings.   (lines 96–100)

The fact that the poet so quickly opts for a return to the 'dear green earth' should not be seen as a rejection of imagination, or even (to use the later distinction) a rejection of fancy. It may be, as is suggested in *Biographia Literaria* chapter xiv, a leaving on one side of Coleridge's world of the supernatural, in order to 'give the charm of novelty to things of every day'. But the most impressive aspect of Coleridge's famous statement is the care with which it is modified. He does not so much oppose the supernatural and the every day as indicate a middleground of imagination and feeling, to be approached from two directions:

it was agreed, that my endeavours should be directed to persons and characters supernatural, or at least romantic; *yet so as to transfer from our inward nature a human interest and a semblance of truth* ... Mr. Wordsworth, on the other hand, was to propose to himself as his object, to give the charm of novelty to things of every day, *and to excite a feeling analogous to the supernatural* ... (ii, 6–7, my italics)

Peter Bell is of course a poem that excites 'feelings analogous to the supernatural' on more than one level. It gives very frequently 'the charm of novelty to the things of every day' – the ass's long left ear, for instance. More significant to the comedy and the unfolding of Wordsworth's plot is the extent to which Peter, as the ass carries him towards the house of its dead owner, creates the supernatural, giving supernatural explanations to events with natural causes:

> And ever where, along the down
> They go with smooth and steady pace
> You see, driven onward by the wind,
> A dancing leaf that's close behind,
> Following them o'er that lonely place.
>
> And Peter hears the rustling leaf,
> And many a time he turns his face,
> Both here and there, ere he can find
> What 'tis which follows close behind
> Along that solitary place.
>
> At last he spies the withered leaf,
> And Peter's in a sore distress:
> 'Where there is not a bush or tree
> The very leaves they follow me,
> So great hath been my wickedness!'   (lines 851–65)

The passage contrives to be at once gently humorous ('And Peter's in a sore distress'), and a little sinister. Four years earlier, Mrs

Radcliffe, in *The Mysteries of Udolpho*, had based her gothic horrors on supernatural events that turned out to have natural explanations; Wordsworth works in a realm where distinctions are less clear. Like the 'steps / Almost as silent as the turf they trod' that come after the child of *Prelude* Book I, the leaf following Peter in the wind retains for the reader something of its eery power despite an invitation to put the experience down to guilt. In the *Prelude* lines, no natural explanation is offered; we have to conclude that the steps exist only in the child's mind. Peter's leaf, though, does exist – we are told that we can see it. Impelled only by the wind, it follows over the treeless downs, staying always close behind and rustling audibly. Analogous to the supernatural it certainly is.

The truth is that spirits of the mind are playing with us. What are spirits of the mind? Do they have an external existence? Are they created by the mind, or do they work upon it? They have very much the same existence, and non-existence, as De Quincey's Dark Interpreter.[11] 'I know you, potent spirits, well', Wordsworth writes,

> How with the feeling and the sense
> Ye play, both with your foes and friends
> (Most fearful work for fearful ends) –
> And this I speak in reverence...
>
> Your presence I have often felt
> In darkness and the stormy night,
> And well I know, if need there be,
> Ye can put forth your agency
> Beneath the sweet moonlight.
>
> Then – coming from the wayward world,
> That powerful world in which ye dwell –
> Come, spirits of the mind, and try
> Tonight beneath the moonlight sky
> What may be done with Peter Bell.   (lines 946–65)

Beside these strange powerful beings, the more famous spirits that Wordsworth created in the early *Prelude* drafts six months later seem decidedly limited. They exist to preside over the young poet's education, and to personify natural forces. They are too austere to take on a life of the mind:

> Ah, not in vain ye spirits of the springs,
> And ye that have your voices in the clouds,
> And ye that are familiars of the lakes
> And standing pools...[12]

By contrast, the spirits of *Peter Bell* are vital and credible. Coming
from a world that is at once 'wayward' and 'powerful', they have a
touch of Shakespeare's Mab or Puck about them. Yet they come with
the guarantee of the poet's own experience: 'Your presence I have
often felt / In darkness and the stormy night'. We are moved
especially by the statement, coming from the poet within his poem,
'And this I speak in reverence'. Where the *Prelude* spirits are little
more than epic machinery, and are resolved in later versions of the
poem into references to Nature, those of *Peter Bell* are among
Wordsworth's most successful imagings of the great theme of his
philosophical verse, the 'ennobling interchange / Of action from
within and from without' (1805 *Prelude* xii, 376–7). Through the
spirits an unexpected relationship between the poet and Peter is
established that will carry us through the remainder of the poem.

As the ass takes Peter forward on his journey the 'spirits of the
mind' play trick after trick. Where the Ancient Mariner performed a
single symbolic act of destructiveness, Peter is a 'wicked man' (with
all the serious and slightly comic associations of that phrase).
Through its connection with Balaam, his beating of the ass takes on
added significance, but it does not in any way equate with the killing
of the albatross. It is one act of cruelty among many. Through the
promptings of the spirits, and the stirrings of memory, others crowd
in upon him as he rides:

> And now the patient ass is come
> To where beneath a mountain cove
> A little chapel stands alone,
> With greenest ivy overgrown
> And tufted with an ivy grove.
>
> A building dying half away
> From human thoughts and purposes,
> It seems – both wall and roof and tower –
> To bow to some transforming power
> And blend with the surrounding trees.
>
> Deep sighing as he passed along,
> Quoth Peter, 'In the shire of Fife,
> 'Twas just in such a place as that
> (Not knowing what I would be at),
> I married my sixth wife.'   (lines 1061–75)

We shall learn more of the sixth wife, the 'sweet and playful
Highland girl', who marries Peter at sixteen, and dies broken-

hearted with her unborn infant, Benoni, 'Child of Sorrow'. Words-worth's comedy does not shy away from pain. For the moment, though, he preserves a balance of moods. The idea of a sixth wife is faintly comic, and Peter's letting himself off the hook – 'Not knowing what I would be at' – enchantingly so. If he does not yet know what he was at, the spirits of the mind will find their way to tell him. Like the chapel, 'dying half away', he yields progressively to a higher 'transforming power':

> And now the spirits of the mind
> Are busy with poor Peter Bell;
> And from the ass's back he sees,
> I think, as ugly images
> As ever eye did see in Hell.
>
> Close by a brake of flowering furze
> He sees himself, as plain as day
> He sees himself – a man in figure
> Just like himself, nor less nor bigger,
> Not five yards from the broad highway. (lines 1146–55)

So far, comedy in the poet's modest refusal to know what goes on in Hell, comedy in Peter's turning out to be himself the hellish image, comedy in the rhymes, 'figure' / 'bigger'. Wordsworth continues:

> And stretched beneath the furze he sees
> The Highland girl – it is no other –
> And hears her crying, as she cried
> The very moment that she died,
> 'My mother! Oh my mother!' (lines 1156–60)

Till the end of the second line, with its feminine rhyme-word ('other'), we sustain the possibility of a comic reading – only to be betrayed, with Peter, into seeing for the first time the pain that his way of life entails. Suddenly he is no longer the comedy ruffian. Even in the beating of the ass we have been permitted to find him likeable. Now he is not. But now he is not on his own. The terrible cry of the Highland girl goes to the heart of human suffering. Cruelty in each and all of us is rebuked.

To some it will seem gratuitous that Peter, having seen his double, and seen himself, should hear the words 'Repeat! Repeat!' echoing from the woods below, where a Methodist is preaching to his flock. The Hardy who had Tess look up at a significant moment to see 'Thou Shalt Not' written on a wall would have been perfectly happy.

The device is clumsy. Perhaps it is also effective. Wordsworth is returning us from the too-sharp pain of the Highland girl to the world of comedy. In his poem he has adopted (perhaps to some extent parodied) the form of the Methodist conversion-narrative. It is appropriate, as well as corny, that Peter should respond eventually to the marvellous bombast of:

> My friends, my brethren, though you've gone
> Through paths of wickedness and woe
> After the Babylonian harlot,
> And though your sins be red as scarlet,
> They shall be white as snow.   (lines 1181–5)

Peter Bell is quite a long poem – longer in fact than anything Wordsworth wrote, bar the full-length *Prelude*, *The Excursion* and *White Doe of Rylstone*. It would take a lot of space to do justice to its eccentric and powerful vision. To the last Wordsworth, though undeniably earnest, handles his material with the eye for incongruity of the great comic writer. The final scenes, and Peter's final change of heart, depend upon a series of misapprehensions as members of the dead man's family one after another take the return of the faithful ass to be the return, alive, of the father:

> Thought Peter, 'tis the poor man's house.
> He listens – not a sound is heard;
> But ere you could count half a score
> It chanced that at the cottage-door
> A little girl appeared.
>
> Towards the chapel she was going
> With hope that she some news might gather;
> She saw the pair, and with a scream
> Cried out, like one that's in a dream,
> 'My father, here's my father!'
>
> The very word was plainly heard,
> Heard plainly by the wretched mother;
> Her joy was like a deep afright,
> And forth she ran into the light –
> And saw it was another.   (lines 1216–30)

There is a perfect naturalness in the way the child's cry, 'My father, here's my father!' picks up the dying words of the Highland girl. There is genius in the line, 'Her joy was like a deep afright.' And there is terrible bathos, pain, humour even of a sort, in the words, 'And saw it was another'.

The poem is played out – has to be played out – on a note of reassurance. Incongruity persists, but of a gently comic variety:

> And Peter Bell, who till that night
> Had been the wildest of his clan,
> Forsook his crimes, forsook his folly,
> And after ten months melancholy
> Became a good and honest man.   (lines 1356–60)

It is the gestation period that sets the seal on Wordsworth's comedy. Like the 'three miserable groans', the 'ten months melancholy' is quietly improbable. Those deeply in pain do not groan a specific number of times, those suffering from acute remorse do not give birth to 'goodness and honesty' after a specific number of months.

NOTES

1 *The Romantics Reviewed: Contemporary Reviews of British Romantic Writers*, ed. Donald H. Reiman, 9 vols. (New York, 1972–), I, 170.
2 Wordsworth quotations are drawn from the forthcoming Longman Annotated Selections, ed. Jonathan Wordsworth, Nicola Trott and Duncan Wu; line-numbers coincide in all cases with the earliest surviving texts.
3 Lord Byron, *The Complete Poetical Works*, ed. Jerome J. McGann and Barry Weller, 6 vols. (Oxford, 1980–91), V, 10.
4 *Peter Bell*, ed. John E. Jordan, Cornell Wordsworth Series (Ithaca, 1985), 370–1.
5
> Ah, *Tam*! Ah, *Tam*! thou'll get thy fairin!
> In hell they'll roast thee like a herrin!
> In vain thy *Kate* awaits thy comin!...   (lines 201–3)

(*The Poems and Songs of Robert Burns*, ed. James Kinsley, 3 vols. (Oxford, 1968), II, 563.)
6 In my discussion both of *The Idiot Boy* and of *Peter Bell* I am endebted (as all should be) to Mary Jacobus' sensitive and detailed criticism of Wordsworth's ballads; see especially, '*The Idiot Boy*', *Bicentenary Wordsworth Studies*, ed. Jonathan Wordsworth (Ithaca, 1970), 238–65, and *Tradition and Experiment in Wordsworth's 'Lyrical Ballads' (1798)* (Oxford, 1976), 250–61 and 262–72.
7 Ed. James Engell and W. Jackson Bate, 2 vols. (Princeton, 1983), II, 48.
8 *The Letters of William and Mary Wordsworth: The Early Years, 1787–1805*, ed. Ernest de Selincourt, rev. Chester L. Shaver (Oxford, 1967), 357.
9 *The Life and Opinions of Tristram Shandy, Gentleman*, ed. Graham Petrie, introd. Christopher Ricks (Harmondsworth, 1967), 354.
10 The connection between Balaam and *Peter Bell* was first pointed out to me by Nicola Trott.

11 Suffering is a mightier agency in the hands of nature, as a Demiurgus creating the intellect, than most people are aware of.
    The truth I heard often in sleep from the lips of the Dark Interpreter. Who is he? He is a shadow reader, but a shadow with whom you must suffer me to make you acquainted.
(Thomas De Quincey, *Confessions of an English Opium Eater and Other Writings*, ed. Aileen Ward (New York, 1966), 187.)

12 *The Prelude 1799, 1805, 1850*, ed. Jonathan Wordsworth, M. H. Abrams and Stephen Gill (New York, 1979), 488.

Apeing romanticism

Jonathan Bate

for
(Let deeper sages the true cause determine)
He had a kind of inclination, or
Weakness, for what most people deem mere vermin –
Live animals.

(Don Juan, x, 50)

Three bears are celebrated in the annals of English literature. One is fictional, one was real, the third may originally have been either but has most frequently been reinvented as a human in animal skin. Each of them is a servant of Thalia. Winnie-the-Pooh is in the great tradition of *Encomium Moriae*: it is through a show of learning that Wol reveals his ignorance, whilst the Bear of self-confessed Little Brain has that true wisdom which Erasmus ascribed to the *infans*. His is comedy's topsy-turvy knowledge. The bear in *The Winter's Tale*, meanwhile, is a sign of comedy's perpetual proximity to tragedy and its fascination with the interplay of art and nature: a bringer of death to Antigonus but of laughter to the theatre-audience, a marker of the play's movement into the register of nature, but a nature complicated by art, for the animal's appearance is testimony to the human skill of either an actor and costume-designer or a trainer at the local pit.[1]

The other bear is part of a life, not a work – but a life that was projected into the works with peculiar magnification and self-consciousness. One of the two things which every schoolboy used to know about Lord Byron is that he kept a bear whilst an undergraduate at Trinity College, Cambridge. The knowledge gives us our first intimation that Byron was someone who, as Keats put it, 'cut a figure'.[2] We attach the lumbering beast to his owner and Milord has already become outrageous, larger-than-life. It is like Falstaff's first larded appearance: he does not have to speak a word – Byron does not have to pen a line of poetry – for us to know that he will fill his

221

world, that he is life itself. 'Is it not *life*, is it not *the thing?*', we say, as Byron did of his own *Don Juan*.[3]

The bear is also the occasion for comedy's necessary diet, the joke. Byron writes from college to Elizabeth Bridget Pigot:

I have got a new friend, the finest in the world, a *tame Bear*, when I brought him here, they asked me what I meant to do with him, and my reply was 'he should *sit* for *a Fellowship*.' – *Sherard* will explain the meaning of the sentence if it is ambiguous. – This answer delighted them not, – we have eternal parties here, and this evening a large assortment of *Jockies*, Gamblers, *Boxers*, *Authors, parsons*, and *poets*, sup with me. – A precious Mixture, but they go on well together, and for me, I am a *spice* of every thing except a Jockey, by the bye, I was dismounted again the other day. – Thank your Brother in my name, for his Treatise. I have written 214 pages of a novel, one poem of 380 Lines, to be published (without my name) in a few weeks, with notes, 560 Lines of Bosworth Field, and 250 Lines of another poem in rhyme, besides half a dozen smaller pieces...[4]

What is the ambiguity of the sentence? Is it merely that Miss Pigot might not be expected to understand the idiom of sitting for a prize Fellowship? E. H. Coleridge thought that there was more to it, for he annotated the passage in his copy of Tom Moore's *Letters and Journals of Lord Byron* to the effect that 'Byron's dirty *double entente* has been quoted seriously as a piece of academic wit'. But Leslie Marchand footnotes his edition with a disappointed and disappointing 'No slang dictionary has yielded a *double entendre* for the phrase "sit for a fellowship."'[5] We don't, however, need a slang dictionary to tell us that a bear adopts a sitting position in order to defecate. The *double entendre* is surely 'shit for a fellowship'. The qualification for becoming a Fellow of Trinity is to produce a load of shit.

This mockery of learning by means of scatological humour places Byron squarely in the tradition of *The Dunciad*. His generative, associative epistolary style maintains the allegiance to Pope. An evening party becomes the locus of writing; the poet mucks in with the gambler, sportsman and parson. Where the Lakers had made the poet into a Solitary, communing with the sublimities of nature, Byron puts him back into a world like that of the Scriblerians. Satire is the mode, rhyming couplets the form. That 'poem of 380 Lines' quickly grew and was published as *English Bards and Scotch Reviewers*, a brief *Dunciad* for the new century. Pope's theme of the degeneration of poetry is updated so that 'MILTON, DRYDEN, POPE, alike forgot, / Resign their hallow'd Bays to WALTER SCOTT'. Southey is mocked for trying to climb too high in his interminable epics, Wordsworth and Coleridge for sinking too low, as one of them 'both by precept and example, shows / That prose is verse, and verse is merely prose' while the other 'soars to elegize an ass' – 'So well the subject suits his noble mind, / He brays the Laureat of the long-ear'd kind!'[6]

English Bards and Scotch Reviewers is Byron's first blast of the trumpet against the monstrous regiment of Romantics. It is a plea for the banishment of idiot boys and Gothic phantasms, the reinstatement of wit and urbanity. In both its model of decline and its anatomy of Romanticism's exotic *matériel*, it anticipates Thomas Love Peacock's analysis in *The Four Ages of Poetry* (1820), though with the difference that Peacock numbers among the visionary company that Byron who, paradoxically, was himself the apogee of the poetic race he deplored:

> Mr Scott digs up the poachers and cattle-stealers of the ancient border. Lord Byron cruizes for thieves and pirates on the shores of the Morea and among the Greek islands. Mr Southey wades through ponderous volumes of travels and old chronicles... Mr Wordsworth picks up village legends from old women and sextons; and Mr Coleridge, to the valuable information acquired from similar sources, superadds the dreams of crazy theologians and the mysticisms of German metaphysics, and favours the world with visions in verse, in which the quadruple elements of sexton, old woman, Jeremy Taylor, and Emanuel Kant, are harmonized into a delicious poetical compound.[7]

Peacock's version of Romanticism is comic for the very reason that the preoccupations enumerated (crime, old age, philosophy) are not comic. It is because of the absence of self-deprecating humour in so many of his poems that Wordsworth is the most parodiable of major English writers: 'Wordsworth in the Lake District – at cross-purposes' is Beerbohm's most accurate caricature. Keats, with his extraordinary intuition, realised that high Romanticism was readily mockable when he wrote in a letter that his greatest ambition was to write fine things which could not be laughed at in any way.[8] Books such as Morse Peckham's *Beyond the Tragic Vision* and George Steiner's *The Death of Tragedy* have shown how the spirit of Romanticism is at odds with that of tragedy. This essay will start from the assumption that the defining texts of English Romanticism, such as Wordsworth's *Prelude* and *Excursion*, Coleridge's *Statesman's Manual* and Shelley's *Prometheus Unbound*, are far from the realm of comedy.

William Hazlitt's *Lectures on the English Comic Writers* (1819) have the distinction of being the first critical history of English comedy. Hazlitt's canonising of Wycherley, Congreve, Vanbrugh and Farquhar as the four great dramatists of the Restoration and Hogarth, Fielding, Smollett and Sterne as the four great comic artists of the Hanoverian age has remained influential to this day (though had later critics paid more attention to his admiration for Mrs Centlivre, some of the recent polemics about the exclusion of women from the canon might have been superfluous). But the lectures themselves are not much read now, a neglect to be regretted since they offer far more than do Hazlitt's readings of Shakespearean comedy, which are so impoverished in comparison with the richness of his work on the tragedies and histories – the reinvention of Shakespeare as a Romantic necessitated a marginalising of his achievement in comedy. Hazlitt on post-Shakespearean comedy is as Hazlitt always is: sometimes infuriatingly wrong-headed, often brilliant and never less than thought-provoking. The opening lecture on comedy in general is full of pith, of discussable formulations such as 'The essence of the laughable then is the incongruous, the disconnecting one idea from another, or the jostling of one feeling against another' and 'Rhymes are sometimes a species of wit, where there is an alternate combination and resolution or decomposition of the elements of sound, contrary to our usual division and classification of them in ordinary speech, not unlike the sudden separation and re-union of the component parts of the machinery in a pantomime'.[9] The very first words of the course offer a crisp inflexion of a traditional idea: 'Man is the only animal that laughs and weeps; for he is the only animal that is struck with the difference between what things are, and what they ought to be' (5). Romanticism at its most characteristic is a poetry of the difference between aspiration and actuality. 'We weep at what thwarts or exceeds our desires', continues Hazlitt: Romanticism aches with desire while always finding itself thwarted in the material world. But its faith in transcendence takes it beyond weeping towards 'Thoughts that do often lie too deep for tears'. That, together with the Romantic's unrelenting egotism, is why, save when aspirations are reined in, as they are by Keats in his *King Lear* sonnet and 'Fall of Hyperion', the movement exists in an uneasy co-relation with tragedy.

But Hazlitt's concern in these lectures is the decline in his own time of comedy, not tragedy; he shares with Byron a certainty that 'The days of Comedy are gone, alas!'[10] To account for the incompatibility between the comic and what we now call the Romantic, he makes a distinction between the sublime and the ludicrous, intensity and relaxation. He anticipates Henri Bergson's insight that *inelasticity* may be a prime source of laughter.[11] When Wordsworth is writing at his best, the intensity is such that you don't notice the inelasticity. But on the mountainous ground of his sublime, a single slip can lead to a terrible fall. Hazlitt argues in his opening lecture that 'the slightest want of unity of impression destroys the sublime; the detection of the smallest incongruity is an infallible ground to rest the ludicrous upon' (23–4). This is what the anti-Romanticist knows. Just how easy it is to render the Romantic sublime ludicrous is apparent from the way in which several of the early nineteenth century's most hilarious achievements turn the most characteristic 'new writing' of Hazlitt's age to bathos: one thinks here of *Northanger Abbey* in relation to *The Mysteries of Udolpho*, *The Vision of Judgment* and Southey's dream-poem *A Vision of Judgement*, *Nightmare Abbey* and virtually the entire canon of Romanticism. 'In serious poetry, which aims at rivetting our affections, every blow must tell home,' Hazlitt claims, 'The missing a single time is fatal, and undoes the spell. We see how difficult it is to sustain a continued flight of impressive sentiment: how easy it must be then to travestie or burlesque it' (24). Byron proved the point with his merciless treatment of the Lake Poets; Hazlitt, like Byron himself, knew when a cliché was a truth more than it was a platitude, and it was with regard to *Don Juan* that he said, 'From the sublime to the ridiculous there is but one step.'[12]

A bear is not, however, the best creature through whom to turn the Lakers and their kind into asses. Byron's brisk assertion that the bear is the finest friend in the world is a satirist's dig at the frequent disloyalties of human friends, but not much more than that. What he needed was an animal that could entertain him while also demonstrating the cant of high Romantic claims about the uniqueness of humankind as manifested in the imaginative sublime. Hazlitt was of the view that 'To explain the nature of laughter and tears, is to account for the condition of human life; for it is in a manner compounded of these two! It is a tragedy or a comedy – sad or merry, as it happens' (5). Byron sometimes falls into line with this view, as when he writes in *Don Juan*, 'And if I laugh at any mortal thing, / 'Tis that I may not weep' (IV, 4), or when in both poems and letters he slips easily – 'as it happens' – from sadness to merriment. But on other occasions he complicates the matter. Had he read Hazlitt's lectures on comedy, as Keats did, he might have dissented from the opening proposition that 'Man is the only animal that laughs.' A good way of laughing at humankind's inflated sense of itself was to accept the possibility that animals might be capable of laughing at us. Byron liked geese, presumably because they cackled, and parrots because they mimicked. But it was not until 1819 in Venice that he acquired for his menagerie the genus that best fitted the bill:

I have got two monkeys, a fox – & two new mastiffs – Mutz is still in high old age. – The Monkeys are charming. – Last month I had a business about a Venetian Girl who wanted to marry me – a circumstance prevented like Dr Blifil's Espousals not only by my previous marriage – but by Mr Allworthy's being acquainted with the existence of Mrs Dr Blifil.[13]

It is clearly the monkeys that have caught his imagination.

The train of thought in this letter, from the monkeys to the business about the Venetian girl, is suggestive. The bear doesn't help us with the second thing that every schoolboy once knew about Byron, which is to say *the thing* that drives the letter on *Don Juan*: 'Could any man have written it – who has not lived in the world? – and tooled in a post-chaise? in a hackney coach? in a Gondola? against a wall? in a court carriage? in a vis a vis? – on a table? – and under it?' But the Monkey, that ancient symbol of randiness, is just the thing here. As Anne Barton saw in her Chatterton Lecture, the comparison between England's two aristocratic poets is no less revealing for having become a cliché: a painting of Byron and his monkey, like that of Rochester and his, would tell us far more about the inner man than does the dressed-up masquerade of the later Lord in Eastern garb. It is by watching a lady of the town fondling her pet monkey – 'Kiss me, thou curious Miniature of Man' – that Rochester's Artemiza

> took this Time to think what Nature meant,
> When this mixt thing into the world she sent,
> So very wise, yet so impertinent.[14]

For Byron, too, the monkey reveals that humankind is a 'mixt thing'. He watches his pair of them: 'all scratching – screaming and fighting – in the highest health and Spirits. – Fletcher is flourishing.'[15] Like Fletcher, they are part of the family; their vigour is an image of the kind of life into which Byron threw himself – only to draw back into periodic hours of idleness. Thus in a later letter, the news that 'the monkeys I have not looked to since the cold weather, as they suffer by being brought up' is swiftly followed by the chill of 'What is the reason that I have been, all my lifetime, more or less *ennuyé?*'[16]

Byron was an acute observer and the remarks about his monkeys in the letters suggest that he would have noticed many of the behavioural traits which Charles Darwin described half a century later in *The Expression of the Emotions in Man and Animals*. The monkey is a sociable creature ('they perfectly understand each other's gestures and expression'); it can express pleasure and affection, but also dejection and anger; if tickled, a 'chuckling or laughing sound is uttered'; it may sulk.[17] It loves to imitate and is of course a troublemaker, as Byron notes in a letter to Tom Moore: 'I have just been scolding my monkey for tearing the seal of her letter, and spoiling a mock book, in which I put rose leaves'.[18] In all these particulars it resembles Byronic more than Wordsworthian man. Oddly, in view of their love of all things 'natural', the Lakers and their followers didn't seem to have a particular affection for animals (though in one of Keats's visions in verse, Hazlitt is memorably glimpsed playing with Miss Edgeworth's cat[19]). Wordsworth's world at its moments of intensity is strangely silent: the vision enters the boy when the owls *don't* reply. Nothing could be further from the chatter, screech and rapid movement of Byron's monkey-house. Wordsworth's Solitary and Wanderer could not be more different from Juan, that 'little curly-headed, good-for-nothing, / And mischief-making monkey from his birth', or Lambro on his travels, during which

> A monkey, a Dutch mastiff, a mackaw,
> > Two parrots, with a Persian cat and kittens,
> He chose from several animals he saw.[20]

Primates also assisted Byron because they embodied a traditional metaphor for artistic imitation. In the section concerning Florentine Renaissance sculpture in *Childe Harold's Pilgrimage* there is a reference to 'the artist and his ape' (IV, 53), and in *Don Juan* the Trimmer poet's mercenary mimicry includes a trip to Italy where 'he'd ape the "Trecentisti"' (III, 86). Having accused the Trimmer, a figure closely related to the turncoat Lakers, of being an ape, Byron promptly apes that apeing in 'The isles of Greece, the isles of Greece!', a lyric so beautiful that we forget it is being sung by a genius of insincerity (our temporary forgetting of the parody is similar to that we undergo when the Italian tenor sings 'Di rigori armato il seno' in *Der Rosenkavalier*). The false poet becomes the poet in general: 'they are such liars, / And take all colours – like the hands of dyers' (III, 87). And if the poet is an ape, who is not? When Byron apes Wordsworth and Southey, he does so partly in order to have fun at their expense, in accordance with the general aim of *Don Juan* to show that it is possible to mix 'fun & poetry'.[21] But he does so also in order to make the more serious point that all of us, including poets, share a lot with the monkeys and should not be ashamed of the fact.

Though he does not seem to have known Hazlitt's lectures on comedy, Byron was certainly familiar with those of the previous year *On the English Poets*.[22] His 'The Blues: A Literary Eclogue', written in 1821 and published two years later in *The Liberal*, is set outside the door as a lecture is being delivered and then in a salon immediately after it. Hazlitt is an original for 'Scamp the Lecturer', 'harassed / With old *schools*, and new *schools*, and no *schools*, and all *schools*'.[23] Though the anti-systematic Byron disliked the idea of thinking in schools, and emphatically dissented from the view that the 'school' of Pope was in any way 'old' or obsolete, he accorded with the argument of Hazlitt's lecture 'On the Living Poets' that the *Lyrical Ballads* represented the manifesto of the 'new school' in poetry and *The Excursion* its capstone. *Don Juan* is among many other things an anti-Romantic manifesto. Its original preface parodies a notorious Wordsworthian 'note or preface (I forget which)'. The mensuration of the pond was vital to Wordsworth's literalising purpose in 'The Thorn', but the labour of the process ('I've measured it from side to side: / 'Tis three feet long, and two feet wide') was too much even for Coleridge. In his defence, Wordsworth was led to expand on the hint in the advertisement to the first edition of *Lyrical Ballads* that the poem was supposed to be spoken by a loquacious narrator, not by the author himself; so it was that the second edition carried the long explanatory note that begins

This Poem ought to have been preceded by an introductory Poem, which I have been prevented from writing by never having felt myself in a mood when it was probable that I should write it well. – The character which I have here introduced speaking is sufficiently common. The Reader will perhaps have a general notion of it, if he has ever known a man, a Captain of a small trading vessel for example, who being past the middle age of life, had retired upon an annuity or small independent income to some village or country town of which he was not a native, or in which he had not been accustomed to live. Such men having little to do become credulous and talkative from indolence...[24]

And so on and so on. A poem he never felt in the mood to write, an elaborate apparatus of detail which for ever postpones the point – Byron, who in his letters liked to give the impression of not caring when he felt too indolent to write and who in his poetry perfected the Shandean art of not coming to the point, could not resist:

The reader, who has acquiesced in Mr W. Wordsworth's supposition that his 'Misery, oh misery' is related by the 'captain of a small etc.', is requested to suppose by a like exertion of imagination that the following epic narrative is told by a Spanish gentleman in a village in the Sierra Morena on the road between Monasterio and Seville, sitting at the door of a *posada* with the Curate of the hamlet on his right hand, a cigar in his mouth, a jug of Malaga or perhaps 'right sherris' before him on a small table, containing the relics of an *olla-podrida*. The time, sunset. At some distance a group of black-eyed peasantry are dancing to the sound of the flute of a Portuguese servant, belonging to two foreign travellers, who have an hour ago dismounted from their horses...[25]

And so on and so on.

This is good clean parody – a feature in the original is made risible by being taken to an extreme – but it is more than that. It is also an implicit questioning of the whole ethos of Romanticism, for it is a celebration of communal merriment, of story-telling for its own sake, of mundanity that is not invested with mysterious power. A small table with sherry on it replaces the bleak pool and thorn that are the external markers of dark human deeds. Like Fielding's Parson Adams, Byron's narrator likes a drink, a smoke and a chance to put his feet up; it is hard to imagine Wordsworth's Wanderer indulging himself thus. A certain amount of eating does go on in *The Excursion*, but the meals are frugal and the conversation is always elevated and purposeful, never Byronically desultory; merriment upon the village green is sometimes observed, but it is always from a distance – when the Poet suggests to his companion that they should linger amidst 'The simple pastimes of the day and place', the Wanderer replies that they must not, for it is necessary to toil on to the Solitary's cottage.[26]

The matter of food, the need for which is part of our animal nature, is of the essence. If we visualise the typical Wordsworthian personae – Wanderer, Solitary, Pastor, narrator of 'The Thorn' – we are likely to find them gaunt. One or two might even have a touch of

Malvolio about them. Byron's narrator, with his 'right sherris', is
ample; he is Falstaff or Toby Belch. The epigraph to cantos six to
eight of *Don Juan*, published in July 1823, is '"Dost thou think,
because thou art virtuous, there shall be no more cakes and ale?" –
"Yes, by St Anne; and Ginger shall be hot i' the mouth too!"' – this
despite the fact that two of these cantos concern the bloody siege of
Ismail. Crucially, Haidée is a practical girl who gives the near-
drowned Juan a breakfast 'of eggs, coffee, bread, and fish' (II, 133)
before she gives him her love. Indeed, there are two meals in the first
dozen stanzas of the young lovers' relationship, for Haidée and her
maid have already 'made a most superior broth, / A thing which
poesy but seldom mentions' (II, 123). Eggs and coffee for breakfast
or small tables with jugs of Malaga wine on them are things that
matter in Byron's world, as rocks and stones and trees are things
that matter in Wordsworth's. 'A thing which poesy but seldom mentions': in an essay called 'Tragedy and the Whole Truth', Aldous
Huxley argued that (pure) tragedy does not tell the whole truth
because in it people weep and grieve, whereas in real life 'even the
most cruelly bereaved must eat', for 'hunger is stronger than sorrow'
and 'its satisfaction takes precedence even of tears'. As an example of
a writer telling the whole truth, Huxley cites the aftermath of Scylla's
attack on Odysseus' ship in Homer, when the survivors expertly prepare and then eat their supper before they weep for their dead companions.[27] Haidée making breakfast – and making a tasty job of it –
on the beach is of those survivors' company; *Don Juan* as a whole tells
this kind of truth, which may not be the 'whole truth' Huxley claims
it to be, but which is a truth that comedy is especially good at telling.

When Haidée is dead, Byron knows at just what moment to turn
away from her grave and the hollow sea's mourning 'o'er the beauty
of the Cyclades', just when to leave his 'sheet of sorrows on the shelf'
(IV, 72–4), and to change tack with Juan bundled below deck, to
hurry his hero towards the harem. Which brings us to sex – another
aspect of our animal, and in particular our simian, nature. There is
love in Wordsworth's poetry, but it is a universal love, working most
characteristically at the abstract level of the marriage between mind
and nature. Falling in love and making love, the matter of comedy,
are profoundly un-Wordsworthian; 'Vaudracour and Julia' is one of
his principal failures. One reason why Shelley is such a fascinatingly
complex figure – and perhaps why Byron tolerated him as he
tolerated no other Romantic – is that in a poem like *Epipsychidion* he

succeeds in embracing both the Wordsworthian marriage with nature and a Byronic celebration of sexual passion. Shelley at once endorses and modifies the Wordsworthian vision: where the Wanderer fuses himself with the universal 'pure principle of love'[28] alone in the mountains, the speaker of *Epipsychidion* does so through his passion for Emily.

Byron's most acute criticism of Wordsworth may therefore be the sequence in which the adolescent Juan falls in love for the first time (I, 90–4): he wanders (a Wordsworthian thing to do), he thinks 'unutterable things' (the negative prefix, the sense of the inarticulable and the word 'things' are all Wordsworthian hallmarks), and the stanza ends with the line 'Unless, like Wordsworth, they prove unintelligible.' The next stanza begins, 'He, Juan, (and not Wordsworth)' – but it is Wordsworth, for the whole panoply of Wordsworthian Romanticism is there ('self-communion with his own high soul', the 'mighty heart', 'He thought about himself, and the whole earth'). Juan seems to be becoming a young Wordsworth, perhaps Keats under the influence of Wordsworth ('He thought of wood nymphs and immortal bowers, / And how the goddesses came down to men, / He miss'd the pathway...'), until the Byronic lower bodily stratum intervenes ('He found how much old Time had been a winner – / He also found that he had lost his dinner'). The most unkindest cut of all is the couplet, 'If *you* think 'twas philosophy that this did, / I can't help thinking puberty assisted': Romanticism's 'Longings sublime, and aspirations high' are reduced to the level of puppy love. There is a serious critique here, and it is the same as Hazlitt's in his review of *The Excursion*: the line 'He thought about himself, and the whole earth' is so similar to Hazlitt's 'The power of his mind preys upon itself. It is as if there were nothing but himself and the universe'[29] that it may well be one of Byron's many loose quotations. The point is that the egotism, the relishing of the solitary self, sits uneasily beside the aspiration towards universal love. By parodying the Wordsworthian vision in the form of adolescent love, Byron is implying that the goal might better be achieved by an adult love which keeps its feet firmly on the ground, its body well fed and its sexual needs satisfied. In *Don Juan* as a whole, the moral education offered by *The Excursion* is replaced by a comic education in the nature of desire.

At the beginning of canto eleven, Byron offers ironic praise of the Berkeleyan idealism that lies behind the Romantic sublime:

What a sublime discovery 'twas to make the
Universe universal Egotism!
That's all ideal – *all ourselves.*   (XI, 2)

The personae of *The Excursion* are ultimately all versions of
Wordsworth himself: this is what Hazlitt saw in his lectures and
Keats crystallised in his astonishingly apt phrase, 'the wordsworthian
or egotistical sublime'.[30] In opposition to egotism Byron sets up a
principle of '*Tuism*' (XVI, 13), but it is emphatically a principle, not a
system. Only in individual human encounters is the principle lived
out, and the encounter which offers the most intimate 'tu' is that
between two lovers in bed. 'Tuism' is saying 'Oh, Thou!' to your
lover, as Juan dreams of saying to Aurora Raby. As her name
suggests, Aurora represents a new dawn for Juan; he loves her as he
has only loved Haidée before, but she is different from Haidée, for she
lives not on a paradisal island but in the fallen world of contemporary
England ('She look'd as if she sat by Eden's door, / And grieved for
those who could return no more' – xv, 45). She seems to be the first
woman with whom Juan could have a truly adult and truly reciprocal
relationship. When the poem breaks off, it is 'her frolic Grace – Fitz-
Fulke' who has turned up in Juan's bedroom (XVI, 123) and in all
probability, to judge from the sheepishness of the morning after, his
bed. But this is a digression: what we are eagerly anticipating is the
consummation of the hero's relationship with Aurora. In this sense
the poem ends as comedy traditionally ends at the moment before the
lovers who are meant for each other climb into bed together:

All tragedies are finish'd by a death,
    All comedies are ended by a marriage,
The future states of both are left to faith.   (III, 9)

It is always fun to speculate about how the poem would have ended
if it could have ended. If Byron were to have carried out his intention
of making Juan the 'cause for a divorce in England',[31] there would
presumably have been a much-publicised affair with Lady Adeline.
Suppose that Aurora then forgave Juan and accepted him in
marriage. Of such forgiveness is comedy made: witness Shakespeare's wronged heroines, Sophie Western and, more poignantly,
the Countess in Mozart/Da Ponte's *Figaro*. The 'future state' of the
marriage would be 'left to faith'.

It is important that Tuism is not a 'system' because the attack on
system is fundamental to Byron's anti-Romanticism. Wordsworth's

philosophical epic, despite its divagatory title, tries to make all things one:

> And Wordsworth, in a rather long 'Excursion',
>   (I think the quarto holds five hundred pages)
> Has given a sample from the vasty version
>   Of his new system to perplex the sages.
>
> (Dedication to *Don Juan*, st. 4)

'When a man talks of system, his case is hopeless', wrote Byron in a letter to Tom Moore apropos of Leigh Hunt's 'cant' about writing poetry according to a system.[32] Juan's sexual adventures make good anti-Romantic copy because they cannot be systematised. In *The Excursion*, you walk a little way and then stop to philosophise for a long, long time; in *Don Juan*, you travel at speed by boat or coach, and are driven from scrape to scrape, bed to bed. Byron's mock-epic keeps on coming; it is insatiable, unstoppable, the very antithesis of Southey's epics, which strive and strive for thousands of lines but never make it, because ultimately they are sterile:

> And then you overstrain yourself, or so,
>   And tumble downward like the flying fish
> Gasping on deck, because you soar too high, Bob,
> And fall, for lack of moisture, quite adry, Bob.
>
> (Dedication, st. 3)

That Southey's verse is like coition without emission (the 'dry bob') implies that sex is a question of style. Wordsworth's verse, especially that of *The Excursion*, is perhaps the chastest, most unyielding in the language; Byron's, especially that of *Don Juan*, is probably the most stylistically promiscuous. What Byron didn't like about *The Excursion* was its single-mindedness, its systematisation and its concomitant lack of stylistic variety: 'A drowsy frowsy poem, call'd the "Excursion", / Writ in a manner which is my aversion' (III, 94). It is not only the aspiration towards solitary communion with nature and the self, but also the style that gets in the way of the spirit of community, that sense of Horatian 'communia dicere' which is Byron's ideal: Wordsworth's drowsy frowsy blank verse 'builds up a formidable dyke / Between his own and others' intellect' (III, 95). The Byron of *Don Juan*, by contrast, is always crossing the dykes on the bridges of his rhymes. Those bridges are built between radically disparate territories; as Hazlitt remarked of the poem, 'the drollery is in the utter discontinuity of ideas and feelings... A classical intoxication is followed by the splashing of soda-water, by frothy effusions of ordinary bile. After the lightning and the hurricane, we are introduced to the interior of the cabin and the contents of wash-hand basins.'[33]

Naturally Byron is unfair to Wordsworth, for the didactic blank verse of 'Despondency Corrected' (*The Excursion*, book 4) was by no means his only medium. Much parodied as it was, the verse of the prologue to *Peter Bell* is both supple and witty – it was on the visit when he heard a recitation of this poem that Hazlitt noticed 'a convulsive inclination to laughter' about Wordsworth's mouth.[34] One even suspects that it may have been because it had an almost Byronic pace and lightness, a breathless self-deprecation which Wordsworth usually lacks, that *Peter Bell* was excoriated so in the Trimmer-poet section of *Don Juan* ('Another outcry for "a little boat", / And drivels seas to keep it well afloat' – III, 98). Byron's talk of 'air-balloons' (I, 92) implies that 'Peter Bell' is so much hot air, whereas in fact it mixes the sublime and the ludicrous with an effect, if not a polish, akin to that of *Don Juan* itself. But fair play is not the issue here; Byron's anti-Romanticism is driven by the perception that the systematising ambitions of *The Excursion*, together with Coleridge's Germanic philosophising ('Explaining metaphysics to the nation – / I wish he would explain his Explanation'[35]), leave no room for play at all. Remembering Freud's view that dream-work and *Witz*-work share the same origin as means of discharging cathexis, we may say that humankind needs both the sublime and the ridiculous. We need willingly to suspend our disbelief in Romanticism's dream of transcendence, but we also need to acknowledge, as Macbeth does tragically and Don Juan comically, that we are 'cabin'd, cribb'd, confin'd'.[36] Macbeth will never be able to rest, since a Fleance will always 'scape; Juan's journey will always restart, even after Haidée's death. Haidée, like Duncan, 'sleeps well' in the grave. But Byron does not allow us to dwell on her, flipping instead to Juan in the cabin: as Bernard Beatty writes, 'The pun on "cabined" is atrocious and funny; hence the tragic allusion is now made to look ridiculous.'[37] The joke effects a discharge of emotional tension in the exact manner of the Freudian paradigm.

Accepting 'the interior of the cabin and the contents of wash-hand basins', as the Byron of *Don Juan* does, is not just a matter of splashing the water around while we wait for death. As M. H. Abrams and others have repeatedly shown, Wordsworthian Romanticism was a profoundly religious phenomenon. The project of *The Recluse*, as outlined in the prospectus published with *The Excursion*, was to rediscover 'Paradise, and groves / Elysian, Fortunate Fields' in the form of 'A simple produce of the common day'. To bring humankind closer to the ape than the angel will at first seem to dampen this ambition. But it need not necessarily be so: confinement within the animal body may afford a kind of grace by returning us to the 'paradise' of the natural.

In an annotation to some letters of Shelley's published in *Fraser's Magazine* in 1860, Thomas Love Peacock wrote: 'Lord Byron told Captain Medwin that a friend of Shelley's had written a novel, of which he had forgotten the name, founded on his bear.' He went on to deny the identification: 'assuredly, when I condensed Lord Monboddo's views of the humanity of the Oran Outang into the character of *Sir Oran Haut-ton*, I thought neither of Lord Byron's bear nor of Caligula's horse. But Lord Byron was much in the habit of fancying that all the world was spinning on his pivot'.[38] But the denial is beside the point; what is significant is that Byron read Peacock's *Melincourt* and imagined that the character of Forester with his noble and companionable ape was open to being read as an image of himself – he specifies the bear because it was his most famous pet and was large and hairy, but he could not have failed to think also of his monkeys.[39] The association suggests that Byron found in the novel an image of his own way of thinking.

The premise of *Melincourt* is Lord Monboddo's view that the orang-utan is not a monkey at all, but rather 'a specimen of the natural and original man'. Buffon's observations of an Oran in Paris, who drank wine but preferred to lace it with milk or tea, were among Peacock's sources, but the great French naturalist is upbraided by Forester for placing the Oran 'among the *singes*, when the very words of his description give him all the characteristics of human nature' (ch. 6). Sir Oran, as Forester points out in a long quotation from Monboddo's *Ancient Metaphysics*, behaves

with dignity and composure, altogether unlike a monkey; from whom he differs likewise in this material respect, that he is capable of great attachment to particular persons, of which the monkey is altogether incapable; and also in this respect, that a monkey never can be so tamed, that we may depend on his not doing mischief when left alone, by breaking glasses or china within his reach; whereas the oran outang is altogether harmless; – who has so much of the docility of a man, that he learns not only to do the common offices of life, but also to play on the flute and French horn; which shows that he must have an idea of melody, and concord of sounds, which no brute animal has; –

and lastly, if joined to all these qualities, he has the organ of pronunciation, and consequently the capacity of speech, though not the actual use of it; if, I say, such an animal be not a man, I should desire to know in what the essence of a man consists, and what it is that distinguishes a natural man from the man of art.

(ch. 6, italics indicating quotation from Monboddo)

Throughout the novel it is man who makes mischief, the orang-outang who behaves with grace, fearlessness and generosity.

As the French modulation of his surname implies, Sir Oran is a supremely *high-toned* creation: Peacock's central comic device is to give the highest characteristics of mankind – affection, tender-heartedness, fierce loyalty, a sense of natural justice, a love of gardening, and, above all, music – not to a well-born human, but to the highest of the apes. If such an inversion had been made in the name of misanthropy, as it is when Swift gives reason to the Houyhnhnms and insults the apes by making man a Yahoo, the mode would have been satire. But it is not, for Sir Oran is the most philanthropic of creatures: he is violent only when Anthelia must be rescued from the corrupt representatives of aristocracy and church, Lord Anophel Achthar and the Reverend Mr Grovelgrub, or when he loses patience with the corruption of electoral manipulation in the borough of Onevote. Finally, he saves Anthelia from being raped by Lord Anophel. Here, his simplicity and integrity are at one level those of Fielding's Tom Jones, with Anthelia standing in for Sophie and Anophel for Lord Fellamar. But the parallel which Peacock makes explicit in the text indicates that the genre of *Melincourt* is pastoral rather than Fielding's comic epic in prose:

They discovered in the progress of time, that he had formed for [Anthelia] the same kind of reverential attachment, as the Satyr in Fletcher forms for the Holy Shepherdess: and Anthelia might have said to him in the words of Clorin:

> – They wrong thee that do call thee rude:
> Though thou be'st outward rough and tawny-hued,
> Thy manners are as gentle and as fair,
> As his who boasts himself born only heir
> To all humanity.   (ch. 42)

Thalia is the Muse of pastoral as well as comedy. Sir Oran, like Fletcher's Satyr and Spenser's Sir Satyrane, is a being who is courtly when one would expect him from his name and nature to be savage. This is pastoral's use of the natural to show up the artifice and corruption of the sophisticated. But where Renaissance pastoral typically treats the sojourn in the green world as but an interlude before it swerves back towards the court (the shepherdess turns out to be a princess in disguise), *Melincourt* seriously believes in Rousseau's and Monboddo's arguments that civilisation is a decline from the original virtues of the natural.

Monboddo's distinctive emphasis is on language. In the passage from *Ancient Metaphysics* quoted above, and at great length in *The Origin and Progress of Language*, from which Peacock takes most elements of Sir Oran's behaviour,[40] Monboddo argues that speech is an artificial, not a natural, faculty and that it is therefore readily associated with the abuses of that decline away from the natural which we call progress. It was this that made his work a gift to Peacock. In his first novel, *Headlong Hall*, Peacock satirised what he took to be the worst excess of language in his age: the cant of fashionable theories about man and society, expressed in convoluted abstractions. But since he wrote in the form of Menippean dialogue, he found himself in the awkward position of using speechifying to debunk speechifying. Thus Mr Jenkison, the moderate man-in-the-middle who compromises between the perfectibilism of Foster and the deteriorationism of Escot, is linguistically no different from either of them. *Melincourt* has its local parodies of the cant of theory, notably in the visit to Coleridge, alias the 'poeticopolitical, rhapsodico-prosaical, deisidaemoniacoparadoxographical, pseudolatreiological, transcendental meteorosophist, Moley Mystic, Esquire, of Cimmerian Lodge' (ch. 31). But at its centre, in place of Jenkison, is Sir Oran. He represents the alternative to theory. He has the capacity for language, but he chooses not to use it. His silence witnesses against cant with all the eloquence of Byron's wit. And when he breaks that silence, whether under the stress of society or solitude, it is not to speak but to harmonise art and nature in the best sound of which humankind is capable. 'His greatest happiness was in listening to the music of her harp and voice: in the absence of which he solaced himself, as usual, with his flute and French horn.'

NOTES

1 Live animals were a feature of the Elizabethan and Jacobean stage, as Richard Beadle shows elsewhere in this volume, but we cannot know whether the bear would have been one such. Mouse, the Clown in *Mucedorus*, wonders whether the bear he meets is a supernatural agency: 'Nay, sure it cannot be a bear, but some devil in the bear's doublet; for

a bear could never have had that agility to have frightened me'
(1.2.2–4). Here 'doublet' strongly suggests a bear-costume and consequently an actor rather than a live animal.

2 *The Letters of John Keats 1814–1821*, ed. H. E. Rollins, 2 vols. (Cambridge,
Mass., 1958), II, 67.

3 *Byron's Letters and Journals*, ed. Leslie Marchand, 12 vols. (London,
1973–82), VI, 232.

4 *Letters and Journals*, I, 135–6.

5 *Letters and Journals*, I, 136n., where E. H. Coleridge's marginalia is also
cited.

6 *English Bards and Scotch Reviewers*, quoted from *The Oxford Authors: Byron*,
ed. Jerome J. McGann (Oxford, 1986), 5–7. Where possible, all
subsequent quotations from Byron's poetry are from this edition, and are
followed by line or canto and stanza reference.

7 'The Four Ages of Poetry', in *The Halliford Edition of the Works of Thomas
Love Peacock*, ed. H. F. B. Brett-Smith and C. E. Jones, 10 vols. (London,
1924–34), VIII, 19–20. Thomas Babington Macaulay provides the best
summary account of the paradox whereby Byron was at once the
quintessence and the antithesis of the new school in poetry: 'During the
twenty years which followed the death of Cowper, the revolution in
English poetry was fully consummated. None of the writers of this
period, not even Sir Walter Scott, contributed so much to the
consummation as Lord Byron. Yet Lord Byron contributed to it
unwillingly, and with constant self-reproach and shame. All his tastes
and inclinations led him to take part with the school of poetry which was
going out against the school which was coming in. Of Pope himself he
spoke with extravagant admiration. He did not venture directly to say
that the little man of Twickenham was a greater poet than Shakespeare
or Milton; but he hinted pretty clearly that he thought so. Of his
contemporaries, scarcely any had so much of his admiration as Mr
Gifford, who, considered as a poet, was merely Pope, without Pope's wit
and fancy, and whose satires are decidedly inferior in vigour and
poignancy to the very imperfect juvenile performance of Lord Byron
himself. He now and then praised Mr Wordsworth and Mr Coleridge,
but ungraciously and without cordiality. When he attacked them he
brought his whole soul to the work' – *Critical and Historical Essays*, 2 vols.
(London, 1907, repr. 1951), II, 632.

8 *Letters*, II, 174.

9 *Lectures on the English Comic Writers* (1819), 'Lecture I – Introductory, On
Wit and Humour', in *The Complete Works of William Hazlitt*, ed.
P. P. Howe, 21 vols. (London, 1930–4), VI, 7, 21. Subsequent quotations
from these lectures are followed in my text by page reference alone.

10 *Don Juan*, XIII, 94.

11 See Bergson, *Laughter: An Essay on the Meaning of the Comic*, trans.
C. Brereton and F. Rothwell (London, 1911), 9–10, 18–29.

12 Essay on Byron in *The Spirit of the Age, Complete Works*, XI, 75. Also quoted in the opening lecture on comedy, immediately before the passages cited in this paragraph.

13 *Letters and Journals*, VI, 108.

14 'A Letter from Artemiza in the Town to Chloe in the Country', passage quoted and discussed by Anne Barton in 'John Wilmot, Earl of Rochester', in *English Poets: British Academy Chatterton Lectures* (Oxford, 1988), 64. For the comparison of Byron and Rochester, see 57–9. The 1974 reprint of Graham Greene's biography, *Lord Rochester's Monkey*, has as frontispiece a fine colour reproduction of the portrait of Rochester and a monkey, attributed to Jacob Huysmans; the book's two epigraphs are a passage from a letter of Rochester's to Henry Savile suggesting that the nonsensicality of human affairs makes it 'a fault to laugh at the monkey we have here, when I compare his condition with mankind', and some lines from the 'Satyr against Reason and Mankind', including 'I'd be a dog, a monkey or a bear, / Or any thing but that vain animal, / Who is so proud of being rational'.

15 *Letters and Journals*, VI, 171.

16 *Letters and Journals*, VIII, 15.

17 Darwin, *The Expression of the Emotions* (1872; repr. Chicago and London, 1965), 60–1, 131–8.

18 *Letters and Journals*, VII, 105.

19 'To J. H. Reynolds Esq.', line 10.

20 *Don Juan*, I, 25; III, 18.

21 *Letters and Journals*, VI, 101.

22 See *Letters and Journals*, VI, 100n.

23 Eclogue 2nd, lines 122–3, in Lord Byron, *The Complete Poetical Works*, vol. VI, ed. Jerome J. McGann and Barry Weller (Oxford, 1991). I cannot agree with McGann's flat assertion in his commentary that 'Scamp is Coleridge' (665). The name fits Hazlitt's public image as much as Coleridge's, as do both Scamp's thinking in 'schools' and his supposed reliance on quotations from *Elegant Extracts*. Frederick Beaty thinks that Scamp is 'probably Hazlitt' – *Byron the Satirist* (DeKalb, Illinois, 1985), 179 – but the character is best seen as a composite representation of Hazlitt and Coleridge.

24 Wordsworth and Coleridge, *Lyrical Ballads*, ed. R. L. Brett and A. R. Jones (London, 1963, repr. 1968), 288.

25 Preface to Cantos I and II, in *Don Juan*, ed. T. G. Steffan, E. Steffan and W. W. Pratt (Harmondsworth, 1973; text based on Steffan and Pratt's *Variorum Edition*), 38.

26 Wordsworth, *The Excursion* (1814), book II, lines 111–63.

27 Huxley, 'Tragedy and the Whole Truth', in his *Music at Night and other Essays* (London, 1931), 3–18 (7).

28 *The Excursion*, IV, 1213.

29 'Observations on Mr Wordsworth's Poem The Excursion', in *The Round Table, Complete Works*, IV, 113. This review, probably known to Byron

from its first publication in Leigh Hunt's *Examiner*, is the seminal critique of Romanticism's 'intense intellectual egotism [which] swallows up every thing'. Byron was also familiar with the similar account of Wordsworth in Hazlitt's lecture 'On the Living Poets'.

30 *Letters*, I, 387.

31 *Letters and Journals*, VIII, 78.

32 *Letters and Journals*, VI, 46.

33 *Spirit of the Age* essay on Byron, *Complete Works*, XI, 75.

34 'My first Acquaintance with Poets', *Complete Works*, XVII, 118. This essay first appeared in *The Liberal*, no. III, immediately after Byron's 'The Blues', an ironic juxtaposition if Hazlitt is indeed Scamp.

35 Dedication, stanza 2. For a reading of *Don Juan* as a critique of Coleridgean 'method', see Jerome J. McGann, *Don Juan in Context* (Chicago, 1976), 107–9.

36 *Macbeth*, 3.4.24; *Don Juan*, IV, 75.

37 *Don Juan and Other Poems: A Critical Study* (Harmondsworth, 1987), 93.

38 *Works of Thomas Love Peacock*, VIII, 500–1. Quotations from *Melincourt* itself (originally publ. 1817) are from this edn, but are followed in my text by chapter reference. Byron's original remark – 'There was, by the bye, rather a witty satire founded on my bear' – is recorded in Medwin's *Conversations of Lord Byron*, ed. Ernest J. Lovell Jr (Princeton, 1966), 67.

39 Byron read and admired *Melincourt* in 1820 or 1821, after obtaining his pet monkeys – for his admiration, see Shelley's letter to Peacock of 10[?] Aug. 1821, in *Letters of P. B. Shelley*, ed. F. L. Jones, 2 vols. (Oxford, 1964), II, 331. The Shelleys asked Maria Gisborne to bring them copies of *Headlong Hall* and *Melincourt* in July 1820. Peacock was on Byron's mind in June 1821: on the 22nd he included in a letter to Tom Moore the epigram, 'The world is a bundle of hay, / Mankind are the asses who pull; / Each tugs it a different way, / And the greatest of all is John Bull' (*Letters and Journals*, VIII, 141), which looks as if it is adapted from Mr Derrydown's stave in ch. 16 of *Melincourt* on the theme 'Every man for himself': 'This world is a well-furnished table, / Where guests are promiscuously set: / We all fare as well as we're able, / And scramble for what we can get' (the parallel is not recorded by the editors of either *Letters and Journals* or *Complete Poetical Works*). A letter of 29 June 1821 refers to Peacock as 'a very clever fellow' (VIII, 145).

40 For example his ability to fell a tree, which gives the means of his first rescue of Anthelia, and his tears: in chap. 33, when he can't find Anthelia, 'throwing himself into a chair [he] began to shed tears in great abundance' – Monboddo reports a gentleman who attested 'that an oran outang on board his ship conceived such an affection for the cook, that when upon some occasion he left the ship to go ashore, the gentleman saw the oran outang shed tears in great abundance' (*Origin and Progress of Language*, bk. II, ch. 4, cited by Peacock in a note to ch. 6 of *Melincourt*).

A complete history of comic noses

John Kerrigan

Early in 1895 the consulting rooms of Sigmund Freud became the scene of a drama as learnedly comic and painful as anything in *Tristram Shandy*. Volume III of that novel – a favourite, as it happens, of Freud's[1] – describes how Dr Slop, using new-fangled forceps to deliver the hero, so badly crushes his nose that reconstruction must be attempted using whalebone and cotton thread. Dismal for any infant, this mishap strikes Tristram's father as a catastrophe, for he has hobby-horsed his way through a library of works on noses and been persuaded by Erasmus, Paraeus et al. that a firm upstanding proboscis is a mark of human worth. Over several generations, he believes, the success of male Shandeans has run in proportion to nasal length – an innuendo pointed up by the narrator's insistence, 'by the word *Nose*…I mean a Nose, and nothing more, or less'.[2] Certainly sexual associations underlie the treatment handed out by Freud. Encouraged by Wilhelm Fliess to believe that the pathology of the nose mirrored that of the genitals, and that the hysteria of his patient, Emma Eckstein, could thus be surgically resolved, Freud permitted Dr Fliess to cut out part of her nose. Unfortunately the surgeon, with Sloppian incompetence, left half a metre of gauze in the nose and it began to fester. Only when another specialist, under Freud's anxious supervision, pulled out the bloody and purulent thread, like a train of handkerchiefs from a conjurer's hat, did Eckstein's health improve.[3]

The analogy with conjuring will not seem extravagant when one recalls the scenes of folk theatre which lie behind Slop's depradations. There is the doctor of the Mummers Play who turns up to revive the corpse carrying a bagful of tools or bottle of 'hokey-pokey', and extracts a magic tooth or funny bone to bring the patient back to life. As close is Dottore Gratiano, fount of legal and medical jargon in *commedia dell'arte*, who wears a mask which consists of nothing but a

241

majestic nose. This organ is poked into other people's business, snobbishly stuck up in the air, and led about metaphorically between the *zanni*'s fingers and thumbs. In other words, its physicality merges into the patter of comic fantasy. What happens to the *dottore* is bound up with the idioms 'naso in aria' and 'prendere per il naso'. Many European languages are rich in nasal phrasing. Lichtenberg would not quip, 'Long before the French Revolution he had hoisted his tricolour nose',[4] were this not so in German. Nabokov shows that Gogol's imagination was fired by the 'hundreds of Russian proverbs and sayings that revolve around the nose.'[5] A train of highly verbal comedy, running from Rabelais to *Cyrano de Bergerac*, delights in the organ's linguistic brio, its capacity to detach itself from the visage and wander about as a quibbling signifier. Yet the nose's ability to be at once out-of-joint, kept to a grindstone, browned by sycophancy and rubbed in its mistakes would not be so comic were its underlying thereness ('as plain as the nose on your face') not also highly ambivalent. Time and again the question is whether the nose should be 'on your face', given its link with low bodily functions.

Genital noses were rampant long before Freud and Fliess. When Tristram Shandy protested that a nose was a nose was a nose, early readers knew better. Physicians and physiognomists such as Laurent Joubert and della Porta had said, 'the nose corresponds to the rod'.[6] The parodic psalm, 'Ad formam nasi cognoscitur, ad te levavi', is a phallic joke in Rabelais, but Richard Sanders' *Physiognomie* (1653) quotes it as a contribution to science.[7] For Renaissance doctors, however, the nose was more than a 'verga' hung between the balls of the eyes. A breast dripping 'mucous slime',[8] it was the anus of the brain: a 'gutter', as Du Bartas put it, 'Through which the heavier excrements do finde / Evacuating passages'.[9] It hardly needs Bakhtin to tell us that such grotesquerie has comic potential. Whether long and flaring (the Shandean ideal), gross and hairy (as on the face of Chaucer's Miller), or clownishly red and bibulous, the comic nose is an index of appetitive and excremental indulgence. Moreover it makes this statement in proximity to the seat of reason. Perversely situated by God just below that pineal gland which Descartes took to be the home of the soul, the nose perkily reminds us of other organs of discharge elsewhere shrouded in clothes. Not that polite society likes the nose itself to be naked in action. As Desdemona discovers, a handkerchief is not just to be sneezed at. Distinctly resembling underwear – frilly for ladies, plain for gents – this item covers the shame of having anything so basic as a nose. Othello's rant about the 'Handkerchief...Noses, ears'[10] could not speak so thematically of disguise and unhinged pudency, of not seeing what is under your very eyes, if Shakespeare had taken Rymer's advice and had Desdemona lose a garter.

Yet the comic power of noses is not limited to their advertising what lies behind zips and plackets. Palpable tokens of difference, their reputation for intimate disclosure is inseparable from the notion that each of us bears one appropriate to our deepest natures. In origin this belief is ancient. Indeed its earliest exposition, in the pseudo-Aristotelian *Physiognomonica*, harks back to a time before the growth of cities. People who 'have thick extremities to the nostrils are lazy; witness cattle', the treatise says:

> Those that have a thickening at the end of the nose are insensitive; witness the boar. Those that have a sharp nose-tip are prone to anger; witness the dog. Those that have a circular nose-tip, but a flat one, are magnanimous; witness the lions. Those that have a thin nose-tip are bird-like; but when it is somewhat hooked and rises straight from the forehead they are shameless; witness ravens...[11]

It is right that, in reading this, Corbaccio and Volpone, Mickey Mouse and Aristophanes' Hoopoe should come to mind together. The *Physiognomonica* lays the foundation of a long history of thought about human nature. Endorsed by such authorities as Polemo of Laodicea and Adamantius,[12] it was known during the Middle Ages and widely read after the Renaissance. In della Porta's *De humana physiognomonia* and the post-Cartesian work of Charles Le Brun, various kinds of humanity are illustrated in conjunction with the heads of animals. This mode of analysis would be modified by Lavater towards the end of the eighteenth century,[13] but the Europe of Darwin and Haeckel saw a revival of animal paradigms. Even now, more than heraldic shorthand makes cartoonists depict Boris Yeltsin as a bear.

From the outset, moreover, difficulties with this model paradoxically aided comedy. As Victorian phrenologists liked to show, with much calibrating of skulls and snouts, Greek statues make distance from animal types a measure of human excellence. In the masks of classical comedy, as categorised by Pollux (*Onomastikon*, IV.143–54), patricians have blandly regular features while amusing slaves are endowed with snubs. Already adumbrated here is the division of roles by nose-type which would assist the production of English-speaking clowns from Tarlton to W. C. Fields and Benny Hill. The great Elizabethan jester had only to show his flat-nosed face to make the groundlings wriggle with mirth. Nothing similar is recorded of Alleyn, or could be expected of Michael Pennington. Unlikeness to animals at one end of the socio-generic spectrum generates laughter at the other. The graph of comic energy not only runs across the range of animal types but towards and away from it. Further, as even pseudo-Aristotle must have noticed, not everyone with a thick nose is condemned to bovine behaviour. By his own, or at least Plato's, admission, deep-brained Socrates (for instance) had the snub and spread nostrils associated with low characters in comedy. Not surprisingly, several passages show the philosopher contemplating, and making comic capital out of, the ambiguities of appearance.[14] But then, one way for commentators to make sense of this nose was to emphasise the *eiron* in Socrates, to bring out (in the manner of Erasmus) his tendency to clown his way towards truth. So strong was the grip of pseudo-Aristotle, however, and so exalted the standing of Socrates, that not even this tactic seemed persuasive, until Rabelais solved the problem by announcing that his nose had been pointed after all.[15]

Resistance to the reading of faces could take on more extreme forms. Associated in post-Reformation England with palmistry and other Godless modes of prediction, it was forbidden by Act of Parliament[16] – a fact which helps explain the comic risk and mischief of fortune-telling in *The Gypsies Metamorphosed*. Superstitious belief in metoposcopy declined in the seventeenth century, but a hard core of nasological credulity, though damaged by Baconian science, proved remarkably resilient. Asking, in 1763, why '*index animi vultus* is in every man's mouth', John Clubbe compared the success of 'Urinal Quacks and Conjurers', and blamed 'a difficulty of access and a parade of hard words'. As a satirical alternative he argued for the construction of a machine which would literally weigh human worth.[17] Significantly, however, the engraving which shows this device in action cannot resist distinguishing the person of 'absolute Levity' by giving him a clown's red nose. So strong was the pull of Kames's dictum, 'The character of a man may be read in his face',[18] that the keenest wits of the age were infected by the orthodoxy they mocked. Even Lichtenberg, who memorably parodied Lavater by deducing people's moral qualities from the shape of the pigtails on their wigs,[19] was unable rigorously to disentangle his favoured science of expression, pathognomy, from the pseudo-Aristotelian line. Throughout the eighteenth century noses were a measure of human value. In *The History of Ancient Art* Winkelmann declared that the ideal face was three noses long and two in breadth. Lavater maintained that it was impossible for a beautiful face to sustain an ugly nose, and that a handsome organ indicated 'an extraordinary character'. His *Essays on Physiognomy* (1775–8), first translated into English by the comic playwright Thomas Holcroft, insist that, far from being excremental, the nose is 'the foundation or abutment of the brain', and a fine specimen 'of more worth than a kingdom'.[20]

As the nose became culturally prominent, urgent questions arose. If a snub-featured person was servile, did his character shape the nose or the nose determine his character? The latter sounds preposterous, the former merely bizarre, but during the Victorian period the prestige of physiognomy was such that trust in appearances went into overdrive and noses took command. According to McDowall's *The Mind in the Face* (1882), Wellington 'could scarcely have won Waterloo but for his nasal organ of fighting type and colossal size'.[21] Superior noses were straight and capacious because this facilitated ventilation and did not kink the olfactory nerve-threads. Such beliefs self-fulfillingly diminished a badly-nosed man's chances in life. Darwin was almost denied a place on *The Beagle* because his nose betrayed a lack of fortitude. Criminal types were identified by the shape of ear and nose.[22] The great size of Victorian coat lapels is clearly relevant here. This was a good period in which to be born with a Roman nose, but a turned-up (or 'celestial') one was worth burying in a muffler. The use of physiognomy by novelists reinforced the prejudice. Some, including Charlotte Brontë, were unnervingly hospitable to Lavater. Others, such as George Eliot, mistrusted his insidious determinism. As for comic authors: physiognomy was almost irresistible, because any absurdity attached to the science was digested by a mode of writing which, meanwhile, could heavily capitalise on its compact and reader-involving conventions. Though English cartoonists were not always as physiognomically resourceful as those of Daumier's France, Dickens (above all) found illustrators well able to catch the spirit of his noses. Hablôt K. Browne, an early collaborator, was simply known as 'Phiz'. Cruikshank's contributions to *Oliver Twist* were celebrated by the nasologist 'Eden Warwick' as well as by John Ruskin.

Undeterred by circular argument, Warwick says in *Nasology* (1848) that the 'characteristic Snubs and Celestials' given to the Artful Dodger's gang 'have been verified by the applauses of all'.[23] Yet if noses were plainly veracious, and applaudable as such, Warwick would not need to begin his treatise 'by vindicating the Nose from the charge of being too ridiculous an organ to be seriously discoursed upon' (4). His defensiveness helps prove that, throughout recorded history, and even at the height of its power, the English literary nose has been buffeted by cross-currents of comedy. For Warwick, by contrast, what 'history' shows is that every man gets the nose he deserves, and that the national organ responds to changes in social tone. Hence, 'during the time of Charles I and the Protectorate, the Romano-Cogitative was almost universal... The Noses of the time are remarkably broad and thick, a circumstance which can only be attributed to the serious religious and political questions which then agitated the minds of all men. With the careless dissipated days of the second Charles came in the thin, long Greek, or Greco-Roman Nose' (97). Warwick's is comedy of a peculiar sort. Wary of appearing ridiculous, he makes himself the more absurd by acknowledging that he might be funny. Here he is, for instance, on snubs:

Perhaps the reader expects that we are going to be very funny on the subject of these noses. But we are not; – far from it. A Snub Nose is to us a subject of most melancholy contemplation. We behold in it a proof of the degeneracy of the human race. We feel that such was not the shape of Adam's Nose; that the original type has been departed from; that the depravity of man's heart has extended itself to his features, and that, to parody Cowper's line, purloined, by the bye, from Cowley: – 'God made the *Roman*, and man made the *Snub*.' (174)

When Warwick deplores 'the depravity of man's heart' he mostly does mean 'man'. Nasal types have always divided by gender, and, despite the efforts of Fliess to assert the bisexuality of all persons on the grounds that male nose-bleeds are a form of menstruation, distinctions continue to hold. Recent research at St Andrews, using computer-manipulated photographs, found that a male face was judged 'sexy' when it had 'large, rugged features, such as big nostrils and a strong nose', while 'The "hyperfemale" turned out to have large, bright eyes and a slightly upturned, button-shaped nose.'[24] For Warwick, with typical condescension, 'the Celestial Nose feminine' was attractive so long as it showed 'no tendency to cogitativeness, lest it should look as if its owner thought' (205). Women with pensive noses have a way of looking absurd. Of course, a diminutive organ would not be felicitous. That is why Pascal said that, if Cleopatra's nose had been 'plus court', the face of the world would have been changed.[25] Even so, the prevailing bias is against quasi-phallic length. What could be funnier – for some – than that loathly lady ballad in which no man (of any trade) can bear to marry *The Long-Nos'd Lass* (1685–8)?[26] At least Rostand's Cyrano makes up for his protuberance by courage and intellectual flair. Christian might be better-nosed, but he cannot write seductively to Roxane. To find a feminine analogue of this situation, one needs to go to medieval Japan. And even there, in *The Tale of Genji*, the reclusive daughter of Prince Hitachi has the kind of nose which makes it inevitable that the letters with which she tantalises the hero should have been written by her waiting woman. When Genji finally gains access, the social and creative incapacities which he will discover are signified all in an instant: 'the nose. That nose now dominated the scene. It was like that of the beast on which Samantabhadra rides, long, pendulous and red. A frightful nose.'[27]

Eden Warwick's own views easily stretched as far as Japan. One of his funniest, yet most depressing, claims is that the Indo-Germanic nose began life in ancient India, then passed to Europe, is currently migrating to America, and will finally reach Eastern Asia (158–61, 239–41). On completing its circumnavigation, this ideal nose will usher in an apocalyptic 'consummation of all things' (159). It is, of course, 'Indo-Germanic' which sets up troubling vibrations. Ever since pseudo-Aristotle, races have been physiognomically stereotyped. Herodotus' unfriendly remarks about Persian and Tartar noses are widely reported in Renaissance and eighteenth-century treatises. Yet Victorian physiognomy draws on racial theories which are potentially far more dangerous. There is a definite change in temperature between the observations of Lavater and Warwick's hysterical warning that 'the σιμοì, or flat-nosed nations' of the East 'are gathering force' to sweep across Europe (229). Noses demonstrate to Warwick that there are superior, and slave, races: 'the low development of the Negro mind and his miserable nasal conformation... are worthy of each other' (251). Predictably, this made noses fluctuate in response to political prejudice. Warwick's second edition, *Notes on Noses* (1852), shows the potato famine and land unrest leading him to find the '*depressed noses*' of 'the Negro type' on Irish faces, even though, four years earlier, in *Nasology*, the Irish organ had a 'Romano-Greek profile'.[28] At this point, comic noses lead – through such curious taxonomies as Risley's 'Orbito-Nasal Index'[29] – towards the cartooning of Jews on Nazi propaganda posters. Only now, as the nasometry of the Reich dwindles to a painful memory, can its absurdity yield a comedy not used to mobilise hate. Just how hard this is to manage, even so, is shown by the reception of *Maus* (1986), the controversial American cartoon book which depicts Poles as pigs, the SS as cats and Jews as twitchy-nosed mice. Art Spiegelman's almost pseudo-Aristotelian typology runs the risk of replicating the racism he satirises. A happier route to laughter lies through finding disruptive exceptions to so-called biological 'laws'. Thus, in *Mendelssohn is on the Roof* (1960) the Czech novelist Jiří Weil[30] describes how, during the Nazi occupation of Prague, monuments to Jewish achievement were ordered to be destroyed. Two workmen are sent out on to the roof of the national theatre to take down the bust of Mendelssohn. Unsure which composer is which, they set to work with a ruler and pick the one with the biggest nose. The bust is, inevitably, that of Wagner.

Laurence Olivier often recalled the 'very special word of advice' which Elsie Fogarty gave him after his audition for a scholarship at the Central School of Speech Training and Dramatic Art.[31] '"You have weakness... *here*",' she said, 'and placed the tip of her little finger on my forehead... and slid it down to rest in the deep hollow of my brow-line and the top of my nose.' Whether on account of its psychological truth, or of the actor's suggestibility, this advice became the focus of inhibitions which lasted until Olivier 'discovered the protective shelter of nose-putty and enjoyed a pleasurable sense of relief and relaxation when some character part called for a sculptural addition to my face... In respect of the prophetic insight of Elsie's gesture,' he adds, 'I would ask my critics to look back in benign remembrance on the staggering array of false noses that have been remarked upon me.' Accepting his invitation, one is struck by how often the nose-putty came out not just for character roles, and for beaky grotesques like Richard III, but for romantic leads, as in the 1935 *Romeo and Juliet*. Olivier's career demonstrates the lasting power of masks as psychological prostheses in Western theatre. In his built-out, self-sustaining noses one recognises the same kind of launching pad for the projection of identity as had been provided by the linen and paste shells of Menandrian comedy and the half-vizards of *commedia dell'arte* – so different in their provisionality and individuation from the solid, hieratic, expressively open masks of Japanese Noh. One is also prompted to respect the courage of the actor when, noticing, in the spirit of Jiří Weil, that 'the so-called Jewish nose was to be seen more frequently on Gentile faces than on Jewish ones',[32] he played Shylock for Jonathan Miller unsculpted about the nose.

Whether the masks of *commedia dell'arte* to any extent derive from those of classical drama remains debatable. What is not in doubt is that ancient mosaics and wall-paintings show theatrically characterful noses on more than comic servants. Hetairai and old women have pointed nose-masks and snubs. Especially in Old and Middle comedy, gaping nostrils appear on male characters.[33] In Pollux's catalogue of masks the toady and parasite are hook-nosed, while the female slave known as the 'shorn poppet' adds a slightly snub nose to her short hair and scarlet chiton. If the surviving terracotta statuettes can be trusted, actors playing Maccus in the Roman Atellanae could have formidably obtrusive probosci. Yet these are thin pickings when compared with *commedia dell'arte*. Pantalone, Pulchinello, the Capitano and, of course, Dottore Gratiano: all had prominent, often hooked noses, as did Scapino, Brighella and Pasquariello. Some variants bore positively monstrous constructions; the Neapolitan doctor, Caviello, seems to wear spectacles chiefly to be able to see to the end of his organ. Such exaggerated features must have contributed to performance style. David Wiles is surely right to correlate the curved gestures of Arlecchino in Rousseau's *Chacoon for Harlequin* (*c*. 1733) with his arched brows, rounded beard – and, we might add, discreet, snub nose.[34] Pantalone, by contrast, was led by his hooked beak (originally paired with a false phallus) into angular body language. As for the *zanni*, their noses were able to work in different ways. Carlo Boso, who leads a modern *commedia* troupe, reports that 'The beak-nosed *zanni* looks stupid when the mask is presented frontally, but aggressive when the mask is seen in profile.'[35]

The actor who puts on a huge nose to play Richard III draws strength from a self-concealing outness which experiments with humiliation. It is a paradox of grotesque masking that it energises performance by making the actor a focus of ridicule. The buoyancy of a comic-nosed Olivier must derive not only from his concealment of a felt deficiency but from his sense of relief at not actually being visaged as he is masked. The pleasures of comedy have always involved more than the Hobbesian delight of having our normality confirmed by others' deformities. Yet it is significant that early defenders of *commedia dell'arte* felt obliged to address this moral crux. Andrea Perrucci, for example, concedes that the form makes use of lameness, baldness and bizarre noses, but says that 'these defects, counterfeited by the use of masks and by the actors' skill, although in real life they would be pitiful and apt to arouse commiseration, become in the world of fiction simply laughable'.[36] Such a decisive boundary around 'the world of fiction' is hard to accept, given the festive associations of *commedia*. The masks of Arlecchino and Coviello milled about in carnival crowds as well as facing them from scaffolds. Professional troupes performed to audiences masked for the occasion. Nor were the half-vizards, worn on and off-stage, straightforwardly concealing. Tooled and detailed in fine leather, they resembled the patina of ceruse and rouge on faces spangled with beauty spots. The similarity between masks and cosmetics was not first noticed at the Renaissance. Meg Twycross and Sarah Carpenter have shown that, in medieval drama, meshes across the face, vizards and applications of soot or pigment merge to such an extent that 'face' and 'mascarure' describe both masks and painted features.[37] During the neoclassical period of Perrucci, however, the tendency for an actor's visage to be regarded as a signifying (rather than disclosing) locus brought masks into a peculiarly close equivalence with the face's intelligible surface.

What would happen to such an actor if his mask got stuck in place? The question sounds absurd until one thinks of Cyrano. Cursed with the nose of Giangurgolo, the captain of *commedia*, he attempts to be less conspicuous by concealing his native tenderness behind the rodomontade expected of his nose. The eloquence spurred by his visage thus carries a tragic burden. Musing on Princess Hitachi in the company of a young friend, Genji uses face-paint to explore a similar alienation:

He went and looked at himself in the mirror and as though dissatisfied with his own fresh complexion, he suddenly put on his own nose a dab of red ... His handsome face had in an instant become ridiculous and repulsive. At first the child laughed. 'Should you go on liking me if I were always as ugly as this?' he asked. Suddenly she began to be afraid that the paint would not come off. 'Oh, why did you do it?' she cried. 'How horrible!'[38]

When we are cool towards a character, noses which don't belong generate *Schadenfreude* far more freely than, say, a cauliflower ear.[39]

But comic noses on sympathetic faces easily modulate from the touchingly sad – think of Edward Lear's Dong – to the 'horrible!' The subject of H. G. Wells' short story, 'The Man with a Nose', for instance, denounces his face as 'a hen-house built behind a portico.... Bah! The thing is not a nose at all, but a bit of primordial chaos clapped on to my face.' Comedy is awkwardly painful here because long subjection has not crushed a wit which is far more perceptive about carnival-time[40] and deformation than Perrucci:

'This nose, I say then, makes me think of the false noses of Carnival times. Your dullest man has but to stick one on, and lo! mirth, wit, and jollity. They are enough to make anything funny... Think of going love-making, or addressing a public meeting, or dying gloriously, in a nose like mine! Angelina laughs in your face, the public laughs, the executioner at your martyrdom can hardly light the faggots for laughing... The bitter tragedy of it is that it is so comic.'

Except in one particular, the spread of *commedia dell'arte* across Renaissance Europe had a limited impact in England.[41] But that exception is important: from the masked visage of Pulchinella, the misshapen and amoral *zanni*, was born large-nosed Mr Punch. A star in puppet theatre since at least 1662, when an Italian Pollicinella was witnessed by Samuel Pepys, this club-wielding subversive won huge affection from popular audiences. Crucial to his success was a continuity with Pulchinella which lay not just in his hunch-back, clownish attire and red-tipped nose[42] but in what those appearances facilitated. For Punch retained and developed the enabling outness of the mask. As the puppeteer and historian George Speaight notes, 'The puppet is, indeed, the complete mask – the mask from which the human actor has withdrawn.'[43] If the vizard of *commedia dell'arte* fascinates by blurring back into the visage of an actor who is, in his half-concealedness, oddly congruent with the audience, Punch shows how far a nose can go when a performer projects it beyond his inhibitions into a riotous play of mischief: beating Judy and dropping the baby, wrestling with a crocodile for sausages, resisting the Doctor, hanging Jack Ketch and, at least in some versions, baffling the devil. Peter Barnes's *Red Noses* (1985) concerns a group of drifters who, during the Black Death, form a comedy troupe which laughs its way through the plague, opposing the greed of the corpse-gatherers and suaver cupidity of the church. Flote's company is collectively able to ease the anguish of some auditors, but Barnes is also interested in the liberation of individual performers from their fears and hangups.

One character in particular, Brother Frapper, is crippled by a stutter which even behind the shield of acting makes him deliver would-be comic lines with excruciating slowness. Then he goes one better than putting on a red nose: he learns to manipulate a puppet and, through its extension of the mask, becomes unstoppably fluent.

What kind of voice should this puppet have? Clearly that of Frapper's nose. Throughout the early modern period we hear of Punch 'speaking in his nose'.[44] This high-pitched twang seems at first to have been produced by a clip on the puppet-master's nostrils. Later reports describe a swatchel lodged in the roof of his mouth. From the audience's point of view, however, it continued to be a nose that spoke. 'Punchinello', we are told in 1786, 'speaks with a squeaking voice that seems to come out at his nose.'[45] This was a reasonable deduction to make given that, since a puppeteer's fingers and thumbs could not control Punch's jaws as well as his head and arms, his wooden face never included a moveable mouth. But a description given by Swift suggests that the voice also devolved to the nose because of the quintessential Punchness of that feature:

> Observe, the audience is in pain,
> While Punch is hid behind the scene,
> But when they hear his rusty voice,
> With what impatience they rejoice....
> If Punch, to stir their fancy, shows
> In at the door his monstrous nose,
> Then sudden draws it back again,
> O what a pleasure mixed with pain![46]

This nose was so successful that, during the eighteenth century, it grew larger and more scarlet. As it expanded, however, the tool became a handle. Punch, according to Swift, 'In every action thrusts his nose' (line 109). Once thrust, it could be seized by the Beadle, the Crocodile and, in some productions, Toby the dog. The florid nose became a sign of such tenderness as Punch possessed. It could even lead him, occasionally, into an appreciation of others' features. In 'Papernose Woodenhead's' script of 1854, Punch compliments Judy, 'Ain't she a beauty? There's a nose!'[47]

'Woodenhead' is the sobriquet of Robert Brough: journalist, burlesquer and radical author of 'Songs of the Governing Classes'. Victorian intellectuals and artists such as John Payne Collier and Cruikshank made invaluable records of the Punch and Judy show at a time when it remained close to its Italian origins. The involvement of Brough, however, shows that more than antiquarian interests were engaged. Papier-maché nosed Punch had political vitality. In some Victorian productions, the final phase of the show, where the hero sees off the Policeman, the Doctor, the Publican, the Beadle, and any other respectable puppet sent to curb him, was extremely protracted. But the idea of resistance to authority was always integral to Punch, and the repetitive mode of his triumphs was consistent with their formulaic nature. A single Punch and Judy play was performed over and over, uniting young and old in admiration of the irrepressible hero. Even those productions which had Punch dragged off to hell could not prevent audiences from knowing that the unregenerate would be back. Like Marlowe's no doubt huge-nosed Barabas, flung over the city walls as a corpse only to jump up alive, Punch has the perennial appeal of the comic who won't lie down and die. He must have renewed the resilience of those ragged, impoverished audiences observed by Mayhew in the East End.[48] Like riotous drinkers in Whitechapel gin shops, Punch asserted his freedom in a ritual of recreational violence. 'Punch…is a carefree independent fellow', recalled the veteran puppeteer John Stafford (1902–81): 'He doesn't want security or comfort; he just wants to live his own life, think what he likes, and sing in the streets. And the only reason he gets into trouble is because so many people try to stop him doing just this.'[49]

Despite the efforts of 'Professor' Stafford and others, anarchic violence drained from Punch during the early twentieth century. With the bland help of Walt Disney he even began to be ousted from the popular mind by Pinocchio.[50] Far from taking pleasure in his extended nose, this wretched marionette is grateful to the Good Fairy for arranging to have it shortened. Even worse, his long nose is a punishment for telling the sort of fibs which a comic hero should be proud of. *Pinocchio* shows us the comic nose being hi-jacked by bourgeois morality. Hence its tiresome stress on the proper use of money. Squandering twopence to see Punch in a puppet show, Pinocchio is blamed for leaving his father in destitution. An exemplar of the parable of the talents updated for the age of stockmarkets, he is ruined when he tries to increase his capital by burying it in the Field of Miracles. It is true that *Pinocchio* makes much of man's inhumanity to donkeys, and is ecologically sound about crickets. But no child of spirit should be expected to stomach a tale which so transparently uses comic noses to persuade it to work hard at school and be grateful to its parents. The ultimate insult comes in the closing pages when

Pinocchio is rewarded for his docility by turning into a little boy. True comedy makes the child in us want to turn into Mr Punch. Where can he be found, now that puppet plays are often innocuous? Despite its suspect complicity with the media-trash it satirises, *Spitting Image* seems the best antidote to the moralism of *Pinocchio*. With its gallery of grotesque noses, its rottweiler version of Toby (waving a string of sausages) and utter contempt for anyone in power, this is the closest approximation which mass culture offers to Punch's radical gusto.

After this it comes as no surprise to learn that subversive Cromwell was red-nosed. Now better known for his warts, Oliver's 'copper nose' was mocked by contemporaries. It was also cited in Parliament (1659) as bearing on his likely appearance in puppet-plays 'thirty year hence'.[51] The problem was roseate acne, a condition which cannot have been helped by the nervous strain under which Cromwell laboured before taking political decisions. But for royalists the high colour of this organ confirmed the commonplace that a red-nosed person was 'no lover of peace or unity'.[52] What made the feature embarrassing for a puritan leader was the link between copper noses and clownage which ran through alcoholic excess. Like the beer-gut of a twentieth-century slob, the early modern red nose was a boozer's badge of pride. One reason for the success of the Elizabethan actor William Elderton[53] was that his large, florid nose was (like that of Bardolph) his C. V., an illuminated sign of good cheer. Elderton's clownish drinking attracted much admiring comment, and his own contribution to nasal comedy, *A New Merry Newes* (1606), turns on the conceit that the gods require co-operation between the vintners and the coppersmiths to stoke up ruddy noses. An early section of this performance piece, 'The Vintners Supplication', is a loving survey of London taverns, 'The Myter in Cheape, and then the Bull head, / And many like places to make Noses red' (A3ᵛ). Still more explicitly, 'the Commission sent to the Copper-smiths' reports that 'England, France' and other places as far as 'Candy' boast

> As goodly red noses and faces as can be.
> With pimple and pumple to furnish the place,
> To set forth the glory of the nose and the face...

According to this commission – a pleasing fantasy for topers – any vintner who sees a passer-by 'with copper or brasse, / In any part of his nose' must instantly rush out with a 'quart' of ale or 'cup of good wine' to sustain that beacon of good fellowship (A4^v–5^r).

A New Merry Newes goes on to describe the arms and oath of the coppersmiths. Elderton says that the company's annual feast should be preceded by a procession of 'Nose autem', 'Nose Gloriare', 'Libra Nose', 'Ne Nose', 'Salua Nose', 'Iustifica Nose', 'Letifica Nose' and 'O Beata Nose'. Jokes like these now pall, but they must have been enlivened by the sight or recollection of Elderton's visage (for example, 'my nose' [A6^v]). As for the actor, he can only have been encouraged in his repetitiveness by an extreme version of the Olivier paradox: possessed of a disfiguring nose, he could, in playing the clown, make it a mark, or mask, of performance. In action the nose became tractable, more apt to amuse than self-lacerate. Comic noses, even when real, make good props (in every sense) for reasons implicit in the derivation of 'mask' from Arabic *maskhara^h*, 'clown'. Certainly clowns had exuberant snouts long before the red-nosed Auguste became a fixture of late nineteenth-century circuses. The medieval antic, for instance, often sported a beak-like proboscis in addition to his coxcomb. Both suggested sexual potency, still associated with the word 'cock'. Nasal tissue can be flared and extended, is phallically hard yet soft. A clownishly uninhibited organ flushes red to indicate appetite. When he dallies with his bauble and teases ladies with his clap-stick, the fool's nose goes before him as a banner of hot blood. This nose refuses to conform to the pallid order of the face. Irregular to the point of seeming 'a bit of primordial chaos', it is always a measure of being-as-potential. Hence the pathos of Shakespeare's Yorick, his flowing wit and Rhenish reduced to noseless death. There is a fine moment in Cyrano's delirium – cut in the sentimental Depardieu film[54] – when Rostand's hero mocks his final antagonist: 'He's coming. I already feel stone boots…lead gloves…yes, I see him, with his noseless face, daring to look at my nose!'[55] This is the comic nose at its most sublime, spurred by painful conspicuousness into deriding death. The noses of Punch and the Auguste, of Cyrano and William Elderton, are not comic merely because they deviate from human norms, but because their distinctiveness and capacity for self-delight are polarised against the noseless skull which we all fear to become.

Yet if that were the end of the story, comic noses would stick up and out for life with tedious cheerfulness. In fact, as we have seen,

Cyrano's bragging eloquence seeks to camouflage his nose, while his courage in the face of death draws on undercurrents of self-disgust which make him long for unnosed extinction. Comedy is not just attracted to the red, the warty and prominent. It takes pleasure in the heaps of noses chopped off by John Gay's Mohocks, in the blank on the face of Gogol's (and Shostakovitch's)[56] Kovalyov when he wakes up to find his nose gone. The moral of Poe's tale, 'Lionizing', is that 'in Fum-Fudge the greatness of a lion is in proportion to the size of his proboscis – but, good heavens! there is no competing with a lion who has no proboscis at all.' Nasal jokes often depend on substitution, decay or absence. Even that ancient and almost universal genre, 'the nose riddle', deals in puzzles far more interesting than the 'answer' that underpins them: 'Between two lakes there stands a hill' (Yakut), 'It is a mountain ridge, but it has two harbours' (Malay), 'Something descending comes from the hill' (Makua).[57] When Pamphagus is told by Cocles, in Erasmus' celebrated dialogue,[58] that the former's nose could be used as 'a lamp extinguisher' or 'wedge for splitting wood', that 'If you act as a herald, it will be your trumpet; if you sound the call to battle, a bugle; if you dig, a spade; if you reap, a scythe; if you go to sea, an anchor', the extended riddle structure amuses by copious variation rather than its motivating solution. And if we return to Cyrano in the light of Erasmus, we find, in his famous Act I tirade, not only confirmation of Aristotle's view that riddles and metaphors lie together near the root of creativity, but a self-goading mode of dialogue in which the nose is puzzled away. 'Is it limp and dangling, like an elephant's trunk', Cyrano asks, 'Or hooked like an owl's beak?' Far worse: 'When it bleeds, it must be like the Red Sea!... Is that a conch, and are you Triton risen from the sea?... That don't look like no nose to me. It's either a big cucumber or a little watermelon.... The enemy is charging! Aim your cannon' (38–41). With protean quickness the nose is exaggerated into something always other. The wish is virtually realised that it be any of all these things and not a nose.

The comic value of an absent nose is most evidenced in English by William Davenant. Scourged with syphilis in 1630, he turned, before his friends' eyes, into something like Yorick's skull. Even after he was cured, his face remained decayed. In the frontispiece of *Hesperides* (1648), a version of Herrick's profile, mounted above Latin verses and following a title-page citation from *Amores*, displays a magnificent nose. Davenant's *Works* (1673), by contrast, are prefixed by the poxy features of a shrivel-nosed bard. Both poets wittily knew that their icons would be referred to Ovid. Though the latter's inherited cognomen does not seem to have been played on in antiquity, after the Renaissance it became the basis of innumerable Holofernes-type jokes: 'Ovidius Naso was the man. And why indeed "Naso", but for smelling out the odoriferous flowers of fancy.'[59] Anne Barton has written perceptively about the pull of comedy towards cratylism: its liking for names which express the nature of the bearer.[60] Ovid's afterlife confirms this, since, as his name was put to comic use, the qualities it implied were projected back upon 'Ovid'. For seventeenth-century wits Davenant's nose gave a fresh twist to this comedy. According to *Certain Verses* published after the appearance of *Gondibert*, Davenant had 'an old grudg…With *Ovid*, because his Sirname was *Naso*'.[61] Clearly his face bore, in the words of *Finnegans Wake*, 'The nose of the man who was nought like the nasoes'.[62] Writing might fill up the blank, as when it is teasingly said that *Gondibert's* 'long Preface shows, / What ere we want, our Book has nose.' But once the punning started, Davenant's own name began to unravel. Dubbed 'our Anti-*Naso*' in lines '*Upon the Continuation of* GONDIBERT', the poet is also called '*Daphne*'. The point was not just that this name chimed with the first syllable of Dav-enant, but that, in Ovid's *Metamorphoses*, Daphne turned into laurel. In Suckling's 'The Wits' (1637), Davenant had been denied the court position occupied by the ailing Jonson because the company 'in all their Records' could not find 'one Laureat without a nose'.[63] By the time '*Upon the Continuation*' was written the poet had, in fact, become Poet Laureate. '*Denham* come help me to laugh / at old *Daph*', one dig at the establishment butt begins. Another, '*The Poet is angry…*', is as quibblingly dense as any riddle: '*Daphne*, in scorn, not knows me. In all shows / More know *Jack puddin* then *Jack pudding* knows.'

Davenant's missing nose led his whole name into comedy. '*In Daphnen Causedicum*' makes much of the '*Will*' he shared with the Shakespeare whose illegitimate son he claimed to be. Alluding to a trial in which Davenant stood accused of treason (presumably following the Army Plot, 1641), it says:

> In answer to which by a speech *Will* showes,
> Alas, that his words are drawn through his nose.
> Through his nose it was the witnesses cry'd,
> But *Will* has none, so again they ly'd.

Thus with a lost nose the fame he bears,
To have won both his enemies ears,
And now by his Poetry sure *Will* knows
How to turn those ears again into nose.

This has fun with the cropping of ears for libel and with the
rhinoplastic surgery (pioneered by Tagliacozzi) which would be a
target of English comedy from Butler to Sterne.[64] What braces the
wit, however, is an underlying tension between phallic Will and
noseless Daph. '*Virgill* thou hast no Wit', one tribute declares, 'and
Naso is / More short of *Will* then is *Wills* Nose of his'. The balance of
'Wit' and '*Will*' points up a risible antithesis between lusty '*Will*'
and anti-Naso's impotent non-'nose'. 'Will Davenant' is membered
and castrated, each name cancelling the other. One contribution to
Certain Verses wonders at '*the Authors writing his name, (as in the Title of
his Booke) D'Avenant*', because nobody knew where 'Avenant' might
be: '*Thus Will intending D'Avenant* to grace / Has made a Notch in's
name, like that in's face.' Such jokes are crypto-deconstructive,
splitting the signifier and fragmenting it into quibbles spun away
from reference in a play of Joycean wit. The double games with 'Will
D'Avenant' recall Derrida's entertaining forays upon 'Francis
Ponge'. In *Signéponge* that poet's Christian name is said to be
masculine, Frank and assertive, while his surname is split into the
yielding, absorbent femininity of a sponge.[65] Da, we might recall, is
Indo-European for 'to divide'. Literally split by its apostrophe, D'a,
becoming D'aph, is (to play out the play) the cut or notch which
makes the masculine feminine, opening a lack which frees signification.

If the speculative confidence of the theory were not itself so
laughable, a Lacanian sort of comedy could be found in this history of
a name destabilised by a phallic signifier (the graphic non-nose)
which was always palpably absent. Study of the links between names
and noses was not, though, pioneered by psychoanalysis. Credit for
that, once again, must go to Walter Shandy. According to 'the
Shandean System', names like 'Andrew' and 'Dinah' have 'a strange
kind of magic bias' which, as surely as nasal length, shapes the fate of
their owners (77ff.). The naming joke at the heart of Sterne's novel is
that Walter seeks to compensate for his newborn son's crushed nose
by auspiciously calling him 'Trismegistus', only for a domestic
blunder to give him a label (i.e. 'Tristram') which Walter has shown
to be ill-fated (81). Features tagged on by nature and culture,

supplementary yet prominent, noses and names, like other chance endowments, do indeed influence lives. If you want to work in the Belfast shipyards it is prudent not to be christened 'Seamus'. Truck drivers called 'Algernon' are no more abundant than red-nosed beauty queens. Raised to a higher hobby-horsical power, these are Walter Shandy's concerns, and he finds them richly illustrated in 'Slawkenbergius's Tale'. This narrative, reproduced (from Latin) in the novel, describes the arrival of a huge-nosed stranger in Strasburg, to the general distraction of the town and its consequent invasion by the French. Much bawdy amusement is provided by the sensitivity and length of the nose. But Sterne is more interested in subjectivity and rationalisation than he is in absolute size. Taking a hint from Shakespeare (where the fairy queen stirs dreams by riding over noses),[66] he writes: 'Queen Mab, like an elf as she was, had taken the stranger's nose, and without reduction of its bulk, had that night been at the pains of slitting and dividing it into as many noses of different cuts and fashions, as there were heads in Strasburg to hold them' (257). Among the learned, it is disputed whether God could make an impossibly large nose (the view of the 'Nosarians') or whether his power 'extends only to all possible things' – as held by Lutheran 'Antinosarians' (26off.). This argument quickly gravitates to naming. For antinosarians hold that Luther was not born on 22 October 1483, and thus astrologically destined to 'die cursing and blaspheming', but 'in 84...on the 10th of November, the eve of Martinmas day, from whence he had the name of Martin'. Finding 'two of his strangest hypotheses together – his NAMES and his NOSES', Walter triumphantly tells Uncle Toby: 'Now you see... "that Christian names are not such indifferent things"; – had Luther here been called by any other name but Martin, he would have been damned to all eternity' (264–5).

The labours of Queen Mab, slitting and dividing the nose without any diminution of its bulk, correlate, in their dream-like way, with comic cuts and splits in a nasally motivated name like 'Will Davenant'. Time and again, noses are comically pierced, squashed and chopped. Open an old collection like *A Banquet of Jests*, and you find a typical joke begin, 'A Country-man standing at a mark, an arrow lighted on his nose and spitted it through.'[67] Amelia's 'lovely Nose... *beat all to pieces*' in a carriage accident provoked such mirth in Fielding's readers that he was forced, in the second edition of his novel, to emphasise that a surgeon had reconstructed her features.[68]

What most amuses children, when 'Sing a Song of Sixpence' is recited, is learning ('twixt finger and thumb) how a blackbird 'pecked off' the maid's 'nose'. More quirkily, Peter Greenaway's film, *The Belly of an Architect*, solves an archaeological mystery by showing us the man who goes round Rome chipping noses off old statues. Sterne's sense of humour can be similarly educated but robust, as when he describes the fenestral loss of the tip of Tristram's unnameable: an event already determined, a Shandean might think, by the natal wounding of his nose. But the particular merit of Sterne, at this late stage of argument, is the way his comic physicality operates as much on the stuff of discourse as on the noses (and genitals) it represents. So, when Walter reads Erasmus's dialogue of Pamphagus and Cocles, he probes for 'the mystic and the allegoric sense' (235). This means looking for truths buried in or behind the text, scratching at words with a pen-knife, notching and dividing, to release meaning from gaps. 'I've got within a single letter, brother Toby, cried my father', wielding his blade, 'of Erasmus his mystic meaning...I've done it...I have mended the sense. – But you have marred a word, replied my uncle Toby. – My father put on his spectacles – bit his lip, – and tore out the leaf in a passion' (235–6).

Walter's literal deconstruction of the claim that Pamphagus' *naso* 'will do excellently well, *ad excitandum focum* (to stir up the fire)' serves, in its bawdy way, to remind us that nasal jokes often spark across languages. The organ's comic potency is enhanced by the Indo-European rootedness of its own name, securing it a pivotal role in translingual games. Hence, to some extent, its success in psychoanalysis. Freud's seminal paper on 'Fetishism' (1927), for example, starts from a patient whose obsession with a 'sort of "shine on the nose"' becomes explicable when this '*Glanz auf der Nase*' is related to the English spoken in his childhood. With 'nose' held as a constant, the object of attraction turns out (Freud argues) to have been 'in reality a "*glance* at the nose"'. The nose was thus the fetish, which, incidentally, he endowed at will with the luminous shine which was not perceptible to others.'[69] Of course, the name of the nose can itself undergo comic distortion. One thinks of that episode in *Biographia Literaria* – no doubt improved in the telling – where a government agent with a 'Bardolph nose' takes himself to be the 'Spy Nozy' referred to in Wordsworth and Coleridge's conversations about a certain Dutch philosopher.[70] When a character like Nosey Flynn, in *Ulysses*, is given a comic identity by the name of his snot-dripping snout, he, in the eye of the reader, blurs into his nose. But comedy is not deterred by that. In Gogol's 'The Nose', Kovalyov pursues a state councillor endowed with no proper name (or nature) other than that of the protagonist's 'nose'. This returns us, however, to Queen Mab. For the title of Gogol's tale, 'Nos' was initially the other way round: 'Son', 'The Dream'.

Put through several revisions, each more flatly surreal, 'The Nose' lost the dream frame which had rationalised its extreme recycling of nasal comedy. The barber who might be responsible for chopping off Kovalyov's organ, and who finds it in his breakfast roll, derives (like his shrewish wife) from the coarse-nosed puppets of folk theatre.[71] The influence of Sterne on Gogol's nasal quibbles and 'nomenclatorial orgies'[72] is a commonplace of scholarship. More largely, the post-Lavaterian tendency of noses to physiognomic independence, that trend epitomised in England by Eden Warwick's *Nasology*, encouraged Kovalyov's organ to cut loose and become a wandering sign suggestive (as psychoanalysts note)[73] of castration. That the tale shows the marks of trauma is indisputable. Gogol was deeply troubled by his own long, pointed organ, and his repeated references to nipped noses, snoring noses, stuck-out noses and snuff ('the final cause', Coleridge suggests, 'of the human nose'),[74] make him a prose Olivier or Elderton: displaying and exaggerating, while wishing away, his proboscis. His interest in snuff is significant, though, because Gogol, more than earlier comic writers, thought of the nose as not just to be poked into the world and looked at but as having sensuous uses. As Nabokov deduces from his letters, 'The flowers of Italy... filled him with a fierce desire to be changed into a Nose: to lack everything else such as eyes, arms, legs, and to be nothing but one huge Nose, "with nostrils the size of two goodly pails so that I might inhale all possible vernal perfumes".'[75] This, again, has a history. In *Le Miasme et la jonquille* (1982), Alain Corbin shows that, 'From about the middle of the eighteenth century, odors simply began to be more keenly smelled',[76] and that, during the period of Gogol, strong odours became associated with supposedly animal activities, with sexuality, in particular, and disgust. The nineteenth-century individualist demanded a sphere free of others' smells, and showed his social conscience by fitting good sanitation. Gogol's noses are of their time in combining a prickly sensitivity to otherness with a rapacious appetite for experience. Of course, macabre comedy can be extracted from earlier olfaction – as in Patrick Süskind's novel, *Das Parfum*

(1985), about murder in the Enlightenment – but it was during Gogol's lifetime that noses developed full acuteness as instruments of knowledge. 'Gogol's long, sensitive nose', writes Nabokov, 'discovered new smells in literature... As a Russian saying goes "the man with the longest nose sees further"'; and Gogol saw with his nostrils.'[77]

When he invokes this 'saying', with its linguistic short-circuiting of the senses, Nabokov shows critical acumen. For noses ultimately attracted Gogol by virtue of an overdetermination and instability which they share, in a heightened form, with those other bodily grounded significances which perception reads into objects. Even when not dreaming, most of us see our noses: they are the only organs to be permanently lodged in the field of sight. But, as a result, we never see them as squarely as we think we do our hands or feet. Gogol's Agafya Fedosyevena 'had three warts on her nose... and it was about as difficult to make out where her waist was as trying to see one's own nose without a mirror'.[78] Short of installing closed circuit television, the only way of looking at one's nose is indeed reflectively reversed. Yet the back-to-front 'nos' is a 'son': a nose at the level of our dreams. As plastic surgeons know, people neither accurately judge their noses nor choose new profiles which accord with nature. They misconstrue real organs as absurdly as they imagine ideal ones. Now that the great and famous have 'nose jobs' performed as often as they change their hair-styles, jests about this are plentiful. The bridge of Michael Jackson's nose, like that of Tristram at Dr Slop's hands, is a (just about) standing joke.[79] Nothing could be more © 1987 than that the hero of *Roxanne*, Schepisi's up-date of *Cyrano*, should have a droll scene with his doctor exploring the prospects of surgery. Exactly the same psychology operates, though, long before Gogol and Sterne. In *Thomas of Reading* (1598–9), for instance, Deloney describes how Sir William Ferrers, rejected by fair Margaret on the pretext of his having an 'ill-fauoured great nose', becomes obsessed with the vileness of his perfectly normal organ until cured by a physician using a concealed bladder of sheep's gore to 'bleed' his nose.[80] This is a morbid instance of something shared by all who manage to stay one nose ahead of Davenant. The final appeal of noses to comedy is that in what we make of them is shown how seamlessly imaginative is the world we inhabit, how fantastic are our relations even with those parts of it which are us.

NOTES

1 Wolfgang Iser, tr. David Henry Wilson, *Laurence Sterne: Tristram Shandy* (Cambridge, 1988), 110.

2 *The Life and Opinions of Tristram Shandy, Gentleman*, ed. Graham Petrie, introd. Christopher Ricks (Harmondsworth, 1967), 225; further references in the text.

3 For sceptical commentary, with contexts, see Frank J. Sulloway, *Freud, Biologist of the Mind: Beyond the Psychoanalytic Legend* (London, 1979), chs. 5–6, J. M. Masson, *The Assault on Truth: Freud's Suppression of the Seduction Theory*, rev. edn (Harmondsworth, 1985), ch. 3.

4 Albert Leitzmann, ed., *George Christoph Lichtenbergs Aphorismen*, 3 vols. (Berlin, 1902–8), III, 455.

5 *Nikolai Gogol* (London, 1947), 10.

6 'Del Naso', in Giovan Battista della Porta, *De humana physiognomonia* (1586, &c.); cf. Alfred David, 'An Iconography of Noses: Directions in the History of a Physical Stereotype', in Jane Chance and R. O. Wells, Jr, *Mapping the Cosmos* (Houston, 1985), 76–97, 82.

7 François Rabelais, tr. J. M. Cohen, *The Histories of Gargantua and Pantagruel* (Harmondsworth, 1955), 127 ('By the shape of his nose he is known, / I have lifted up mine eyes to thee', cf. Ps. 121), Richard Sanders, *Physiognomie, and Chiromancie, Metoposcopie, &c.* (1653), 174.

8 Helkiah Crooke, Μικροκοσμογραφια: *A Description of the Body of Man*, 2nd edn (1631), 527.

9 Quoted by Sanders, *Physiognomie*, 174.

10 4.1.37–42; all quotations from *The Riverside Shakespeare*, ed. G. Blakemore Evans et al. (Boston, 1974).

11 Aristotle, tr. W. S. Hett, *Minor Works*, Loeb Classical Library (London, 1936), 121.

12 On its classical currency and influence see Elizabeth C. Evans, 'Physiognomics in the Ancient World', *Transactions of the American Philosophical Society*, n.s. 59:5 (1969).

13 See, e.g., Graeme Tytler, *Physiognomy in the European Novel: Faces and Fortunes* (Princeton, 1982), esp. chs. 2–3.

14 E.g., *Symposium* 215b, *Theaetetus* 143d–144e.

15 See Paul Barolsky's lively pages, in *Michelangelo's Nose: A Myth and its Maker* (Pennsylvania, 1990), 4–5, though his link with 'the nose of Falstaff, "sharp as a pen"' (*Henry V* 2.3.16) mistakes a sign of age (e.g., Robert Gomersal, 'Upon Our Vain Flattery of Ourselves...', line 21) for one of wit.

16 Act 39 Elizabeth c. 4 (1597–8).

17 *Physiognomy* (London, 1763), 5, 7.

18 Quoted by F. Price, 'Imagining Faces: The Later Eighteenth-Century Sentimental Heroine and the Legible, Universal Language of Physiognomy', *British Journal for Eighteenth-Century Studies*, 6 (1983), 1–16, p. 3.

19 For discussion see E. H. Gombrich, 'On Physiognomic Perception', in *Meditations on a Hobby Horse and other Essays on the Theory of Art*, 3rd edn (London, 1978), 45–55.

20 *Essays on Physiognomy... Abridged from Mr Holcrofts Translation* (1793), 60–1.

21 Quoted by Mary Cowling, *The Artist as Anthropologist: The Representation of Type and Character in Victorian Art* (Cambridge, 1989), 149.

22 See, e.g., Daniel Pick, *Faces of Degeneration: A European Disorder, c. 1848–c. 1918* (Cambridge, 1989), 135.

23 Eden Warwick [= George Jabet], *Nasology: Or, Hints Towards a Classification of Noses* (London, 1848), 177; further references in the text. Cf., e.g., Alexander Walker, *Physiognomy Founded on Physiology* (London, 1834), 256–64, 'Notes on Noses', *Illustrated London News*, 28 May 1842, Joseph Simms, *Physiognomy Illustrated: Or, Nature's Revelations of Character*, 8th edn (New York, 1887), e.g., 134–45, 217–18, John William Taylor, *Noses, and What They Indicate* (London, 1892), Arthur Cheetham, *Noses, and How to Read Them: A Lecture* (Rhyl, 1893).

24 Steve Connor, 'Which is the truest of them all? Him with the funny face', *The Independent*, 22 December 1991.

25 *Pensées* fr. 413, in *Œuvres complètes*, ed. Louis Lafuma, pref. Henri Gouhier (Paris, 1963), 549.

26 For an accessible text see John Ashton, coll. and ill., Humour, Wit and Satire of the Seventeenth Century (1883; New York, 1968), 53–5.

27 Murasaki Shikibu, tr. Edward G. Seidensticker (Harmondsworth, 1981), 124. Samantabhadra's steed is a white elephant with a red trunk.

28 *Notes on Noses* (London, 1852), 132, Warwick's italics; *Nasology*, 226.

29 Sir Herbert Risley, director of ethnography for India, correlated nasal types with the hierarchy of castes; see *The People of India* (Calcutta, 1908), esp. Appendix IV.

30 Tr. Marie Winn, pref. Philip Roth (London, 1992), ch. 1.

31 *Confessions of an Actor* (London, 1982), 23–4.

32 Laurence Olivier, *On Acting* (London, 1986), 123.

33 See T. B. L. Webster, *Monuments Illustrating New Comedy*, 2nd edn, *Institute of Classical Studies Bulletin*, Supp. 24 (London, 1969) and *Monuments Illustrating Old and Middle Comedy*, 3rd edn, rev. J. R. Green, *Institute of Classical Studies Bulletin*, Supp. 39 (London, 1978).

34 *The Masks of Menander* (Cambridge, 1991), 125.

35 Quoted by Wiles, *Masks of Menander*, 126.

36 *Dell'arte rappresentiva* (1699), tr. and quoted by Allardyce Nicoll, *The World of Harlequin: A Critical Study of the Commedia dell'Arte* (Cambridge, 1963), 149–50.

37 'Masks in Medieval English Theatre (1 & 2)', *Medieval English Theatre*, 3 (1981), 7–44, 69–113, 'Materials and Methods of Mask-making', *Medieval English Theatre*, 4 (1982), 28–47.

38 This time quoting Arthur Waley's tr. (London, 1935), 127.

39 E.g., the wicked princess in Hutton Warwick, *The Nose Tree* (London, 1981).
40 The temporal aspect is explored by Edmund Leach, 'Time and False Noses', in *Rethinking Anthropology* (London, 1961), 132–6.
41 For an inventive exception see Jonson's '*the Nosed*', in *Time Vindicated to Himself and to His Honors* (1623).
42 See Rochester's 'My Lord All-Pride', lines 13–18, for early evidence of this feature.
43 *The History of the English Puppet Theatre*, 2nd edn (London, 1990), 11.
44 Also a trait of puritan preachers (e.g., *Hudibras* I.I.228), giving an edged aptness to Zeal of the Land Busy's quarrel with the puppets.
45 Joseph Baretti, *Tolondron: Speeches to John Bowle about his Edition of Don Quixote*, quoted by Speaight, *English Puppet Theatre*, 172.
46 'Mad Mullinix and Timothy', lines 83–6, 93–6, in Pat Rogers, ed., *Jonathan Swift: The Complete Poems* (Harmondsworth, 1983).
47 Quoted by Speaight, *English Puppet Theatre*, 190.
48 The entire discussion of Punch in *London Labour and the London Poor*, 4 vols. (1861–2; rpt. New York, 1968), III, 43–60 is of interest.
49 Quoted by Michael Byrom, *Punch and Judy: Its Origin and Evolution*, rev. edn (Norwich, 1988), x.
50 'Carlo Collodi''s *Avventure di Pinocchio: storia di un burattino* was rapidly and widely translated after publication in 1883.
51 *The Lord Henry Cromwell's Speech in the House* (1659), quoted by Speaight, *English Puppet Theatre*, 71.
52 Sanders, *Physiognomie*, 175.
53 See Hyder E. Rollins, 'William Elderton: Elizabethan Actor and Ballad-Writer', *Studies in Philology*, 17 (1920), 199–245. Richard Rowland kindly drew my attention to Elderton, and this article.
54 Directed by Jean-Paul Rappeneau (1990).
55 Tr. Lowell Bair (Harmondsworth, 1972), 206.
56 There is a vivid Chant du Monde recording of *The Nose* (1934), performed by the soloists, chorus and orchestra of the Théâtre Musical de Chambre de Moscou, dir. Guennadi Rojdestvenski (1975). Cf. Chris Hurford's sparky dramatic update of Gogol, *The Nose: A Farce*, produced at the Edinburgh Festival, The White Bear, London and the British Council Festival, Göttingen (1990–1).
57 Quoted by Patrick Sims-Williams, 'Riddling Treatment of the "Watchman Device" in *Branwen* and *Togail Bruidne Da Derga*', *Studia Celtica*, 12/13 (1977–8), 83–117, 102.
58 'In Pursuit of Benefices', in *Colloquies*, tr. Craig R. Thompson (Chicago, 1965), 7–11. Erasmus was no doubt encouraged by the *Greek Anthology* epigram on Proclus' sneeze (tr. in, e.g., Sir Thomas Browne, *Pseudodoxia Epidemica* IV.ix, and *Witts Recreations* [1640], no. 101).
59 *Love's Labour's Lost* 4.2.123–5.
60 *The Names of Comedy* (Oxford, 1990), esp. 14–15.

61 *Certain Verses Written by Several of the Author's Friends: To be Re-printed with the Second Edition of 'Gondibert'* (1653); quoting from David F. Gladish, ed., *Sir William Davenant's 'Gondibert'* (Oxford, 1971), Appendix ii.

62 James Joyce, *Finnegans Wake*, 3rd edn (London, 1964), 403.

63 For further quotation and analysis see Mary Edmond, *Rare Sir William Davenant* (Manchester, 1987), 73.

64 *Hudibras* 1.1.179–84, *Tristram Shandy*, 239.

65 Jacques Derrida, tr. Richard Rand, *Signéponge/Signsponge* (New York, 1984), esp. 66–9.

66 *Romeo and Juliet* 1.4.53–88.

67 *A Banquet of Jests New and Old*, enlgd edn (1657), 210. (For large, red and wry noses see 91, 96, 114.)

68 Cf. Geoffrey Day, *From Fiction to the Novel* (London, 1987), 64–8.

69 *The Standard Edition of the Complete Psychological Works of Sigmund Freud*, ed. and tr. James Strachey et al., 24 vols. (London, 1966–74), XXI, 147–57, p. 152.

70 Ed. James Engell and W. Jackson Bate, 2 vols. (Princeton, 1983), I, 193–4 and 193 n. 3.

71 See V. V. Gippius, tr. Robert A. Maguire, *Gogol* (Ann Arbor, 1981), 31–2 and, generally, Catriona Kelly, *Petrushka: The Russian Carnival Puppet Theatre* (Cambridge, 1990), ch. 2.

72 Nabokov, *Nikolai Gogol*, 89.

73 See, e.g., Ivan Yermakov, 'The Nose', in Robert A. Maguire, ed. and tr., *Gogol from the Twentieth Century: Eleven Essays* (Princeton, 1974), 156–98.

74 *Table Talk*, ed. Carl Woodring, 2 vols. (Princeton, 1990), I, 36; 7 January–13 February 1823.

75 *Nikolai Gogol*, 124.

76 Tr. Miriam L. Kochan, Roy Porter and Christopher Prendergast, *The Foul and the Fragrant: Odor and the French Social Imagination* (Leamington Spa, 1986), 56.

77 *Nikolai Gogol*, 11.

78 Nikolai Gogol, 'How Ivan Ivanovich quarrelled with Ivan Nikiforovich', in *Diary of a Madman and Other Stories*, tr. Ronald Wilks (Harmondsworth, 1972), 126.

79 E.g., *The Sun*, 30 July 1992: 'The world's most famous nose came to Britain yesterday – followed by super-star Michael Jackson ... Some fans said his nose was "as normal as anyone else's" – but others were shocked by the white cake of make-up he was wearing ...'

80 Francis Oscar Mann, ed., *The Works of Thomas Deloney* (Oxford, 1912), 251–4.

Noël Coward and comic geometry

Peter Holland

When Sir William Davenant turned his attention to adapting Shakespeare's *The Tempest* for his own theatre company, he found a play that seemed in need of something more. As Dryden, who was invited by Davenant to collaborate with him on the project, noted in his preface, Davenant,

as he was a man of quick and piercing imagination, soon found that somewhat might be added to the Design of *Shakespear*... and therefore... he design'd the Counterpart to *Shakespear*'s Plot, namely that of a Man who had never seen a Woman; that by this means those two Characters of Innocence and Love might the more illustrate and commend each other.[1]

It was to Davenant's 'invention' as well that Dryden ascribed the 'Comical parts of the Saylors'[2], adding to Trinculo and Stephano two more, Mustacho and Ventoso, thereby making their debate on rule and rebellion all the more satisfyingly comic by being doubled.

Of course addition may be the first mathematical task one learns but it is not an easy one to control; it must have been difficult for Davenant to know when to stop, especially with a second, younger and far more talented writer, Dryden, now adding his own imagination and invention. Having added Hippolito, the man who has never seen a woman, to balance Miranda, either Davenant or Dryden must have noticed that any love-plot involving the young-sters was now bound to be out of balance: if Miranda and Ferdinand are still destined for each other, there is no one for Hippolito. Hence the happy expedient was lighted upon to give Miranda a sister, Dorinda, as naive as Hippolito, his natural dramatic match.

But now that Ferdinand, as heir to the dukedom of Savoy, and Hippolito, as heir to the dukedom of Mantua, have dynastic marriages built into the list of characters, Davenant and Dryden must have wondered whether it might be funnier if the competing comic dukes of the island, the sailors, also thought of marrying and whether decorum might not be better preserved and comedy increased if their aspirations were directed at someone other than Miranda. Another brilliant solution was found: give Caliban a sister, Sycorax, someone only he would describe as 'beautiful and bright as the full Moon' (2.3.201). And if Caliban has a sister why should Ariel be left on his own? Hence, at the end, Ariel now tells Prospero of 'a gentle Spirit for my Love, / Who twice seven years hath waited for my Freedom' (5.2.256–7) and who can duly appear to dance a saraband with him as a final entertainment. At which point in this imaginary account of their process of composition and addition, even Davenant and Dryden had had enough of elementary mathematics.

Extreme though Davenant's solutions here may seem they were at least more harmonious and consistent than his earlier creation of a play he called *The Law Against Lovers* out of two of the nine Shakespeare plays to which he had been granted the acting rights in December 1660, *Much Ado About Nothing* and *Measure for Measure*. This extravagant use of resources, making one play out of two, is in many ways the inverse of his method with *The Tempest*, making the simplicity of the original into an endlessly duplicated, mirrored perspective. The set for the island designed for the spectacular operatic adaptation of the Davenant–Dryden text in 1674 provided a fine visual metaphor for the text's games with parallels and reflections:

'Tis compos'd of three Walks of Cypress-trees, each Side-walk leads to a Cave, in one of which *Prospero* keeps his Daughters, in the other *Hippolito*: The Middle-Walk is of great depth, and leads to an open part of the Island.[3]

But, in adding Hippolito and Dorinda to Shakespeare's Ferdinand and Miranda, Davenant and Dryden incorporated into their play a fundamental comic pattern, the quadrilateral of lovers as I shall dub it. As a pattern it is as tense with the potential of comic energy as any dramatist could want. The audience of this adaptation would, I think it reasonable to presume, quickly realise that the right pairings, Miranda–Ferdinand and Dorinda–Hippolito, will emerge at the end of the evening but along the way there is ample scope for confusion: hence, for instance, Hippolito's pure innocence expressed as uncivilised, uncontrolled appetite leads him to desire Miranda and Ferdinand's anxious ship-wrecked state of love leads him to misinterpret Miranda's solicitude on Hippolito's behalf as a rejection.

The possibilities are many and the conventional comic invention of the dramatists is able to generate adequately the potential for comic activity inherent in the situation.

Of course the pattern of two pairs of lovers would be fundamental to the forms of Restoration comedy from Etherege's *She Would If She Could* (1668) onwards but it was to be used surprisingly rarely for the comic possibilities of cross-wooing. The lovers usually manage to pair up quickly and easily, the problems posed not by their confusions over which young man or woman they may be in love with but by the complicating interferences of other, often older, lovers. For a paradigmatic display of the virtuoso handling of the energies within the comic quadrilateral, Shakespeare's *A Midsummer Night's Dream* serves as the obvious example. One might even see in it something approaching a source for Davenant's and Dryden's comic quadrilateral in *The Tempest*. Though the direction of desire for Hermia and Helena does not alter, the play sets up pattern after pattern of desire unfulfilled, with the love-drugs providing their own means of reformulating the object of desire. The play seems provocatively to suggest that the progress of its action can be best mapped in a succession of neat diagrams of the four lovers with arrows of desire, obviously to be borrowed from Cupid, marking the routes of passion and frustration. The premise of the women's constancy limits the full range of this comic geometry but the invention within that restriction is unequalled in its freshness. It even includes its own version of an opt-out clause as, for instance, Helena, confronted by what she perceives as a conspiracy of mockery between Lysander and Demetrius, finds herself increasingly unwilling to love anyone.

Shakespeare's exploration of comic geometry in *A Midsummer Night's Dream* may be diagrammatic but it is never clinical or scientific: the Puck's actions that produce the redrawings of the initial pattern are error, not design. Yet the potential of the comic quadrilateral seems to encourage a form of authoritarian experimentation. One of the more improbable lines of connection running from the Dryden–Davenant *Tempest* would move towards Marivaux and Mozart. Marivaux's one-act play *La Dispute* (1744) shows the enactment of a *philosophe*'s experiment, eighteen years in preparation, designed to prove whether Man or Woman were responsible for the first inconstancy or infidelity. Since in order to know which gender can be blamed 'il faudrait avoir assisté au commencement du monde et de la société',[4] a Prince's father arranged for four children, two boys and two girls, to be brought up in total isolation from each other and from the rest of the world but for two black servants. Now the Prince, engaged in the same debate as his father, sets the experiment in motion, watching from a gallery as the young meet each other for the first time. Like much laboratory work, the results are inconclusive, though the rats placed in this particular maze duly go through the expected gyrations of desire and jealousy, forming and transforming the potentials inherent in their unstable quadrilateral. The Prince and Hermiane who began the play in agreement, defending women against the united front offered by a male court, end in dispute. The last line of the play, given to Hermiane, almost removes the play from the realm of comedy, as if the dispute over gender has become a dispute over genre: 'Croyez-moi, nous n'avons pas lieu de plaisanter. Partons'.[5] Timberlake Wertenbaker translates this finely in her version of the play as 'Believe me, your Highness, this is no laughing matter. Let's go.' and then adds an unnerving final line for the Prince: 'Yes, let us go back to the court, and try once again to resolve this dispute'.[6] In a brutal and extreme production by Patrice Chéreau for the Théâtre Nationale Populaire in 1976, a production usually credited with rediscovering the play, Marivaux's laboratory took on overtones of the Marquis de Sade and the pseudo-science of Nazi eugenic experimentation.[7]

The lovers' quadrilateral as cynically controlled scientific experiment reaches its finest formulation in Mozart's *Così Fan Tutte* where the terms of the two young men's wager with Don Alfonso enable him, as Mozart's representation of embittered misogynistic rationalism, to control the action, turning it into a demonstration of female inconstancy, at least as far as his view of events is concerned. The design is as patterned as in a play by Marivaux; indeed, Andrew Steptoe has recently diagrammatised the opera's outline in explicit comparison with Marivaux's *Le Jeu de l'amour et du hasard*.[8] The opera's final sextet may praise the man guided by reason but the perfunctory nature of the women's apology for 'inconstancy' and the impossibility of envisioning the future of these uncoupled couples blurs the evaluation of the experiment.

Such scientists, Marivaux's Prince and Mozart's Don Alfonso, are embedded within their plays, substituting for the dramatist. Unlike them, Davenant's Prospero does not use the availability of his innocents to engineer the investigation of infidelity and jealousy, however much he may treat the shipwrecked lords as material for experiment; Davenant and Dryden conduct the experiment on the innocents, Prospero's actions towards them merely helping the action along.

These two models for exploring the comic quadrilateral, the scientist within the drama and the dramatist outside the drama, represent versions of the amused detachment of observation of a spectacle that the form encourages: as the Puck says,

> Shall we their fond pageant see?
> Lord, what fools these mortals be! $\qquad$ (3.2.114–15)[9]

In Noël Coward's two finest versions of the comic quadrilateral the exploration of the potentialities is as rigorous as in Marivaux. In *Hay Fever*, written in 1924,[10] the lovers' quadrilateral begins to appear more like an eightsome reel. As each of the four members of the Bliss family, David and Judith and their children Simon and Sorel, prove to have invited a guest down for the weekend, without having bothered to inform the others, and, as some at least of the possible repairings and, more explicitly, recouplings are explored, it becomes apparent that the central comic quadrilateral is that of the family, not of the lovers. The weekend guests are nothing more than pawns in the family's inexhaustible delight in social games and the pleasurable tensions between the family members are resources for the pleasures of play-acting. There can be no true lovers' quadrilateral since no love matters a fraction as much as the family's joy in its own quadrilateral form. *Hay Fever* ridicules mercilessly the desires of those who wish to establish new pairings while leaving ambivalent the audience's admiration and loathing for the Bliss family. This celebration of the family over love is deliberately perverse, for, when comedy sees the family as opposed to new pairings, it identifies the family as a block to be overcome, the dramatic action providing the mechanism for the outwitting and defeat of, for example, Egeus' refusal to allow Hermia to marry Lysander. Coward's reformulation is innovative and joyfully bizarre.

By the end of the play, the four outsiders, exhausted and maddened by the game-playing and performances that constitute the quotidian behaviour of the family together, have no solution other than to escape:

During this scene, MYRA, JACKIE, RICHARD *and* SANDY *creep downstairs with their bags, unperceived by the family. They make for the front door... The universal pandemonium is suddenly broken by the front door slamming. There is dead silence for the moment, then the noise of a car is heard.*[11]

As so often in Coward, the play ends when some of the players creep out, abandoning the stage-space. The escape of the guests leaves the Bliss family triumphant in their condemnation of the others' manners:

SOREL: They've all gone!
JUDITH *(sitting down)*: How very rude!
DAVID *(also sitting down)*: People really do behave in the most extraordinary manner these days – [12]

In *Private Lives* (written in 1929), it is Amanda and Elyot who at the end '*go smilingly out of the door, with their suitcases*'.[13] For all its opulence of epigrammatic brilliance, *Private Lives* is almost ascetic in its exploration of the lovers' quadrilateral. The diagram allows only one permutation, a re-establishment of a pattern that preceded the play, just as Demetrius loved Helena before he turned his attention to Hermia. Amanda and Elyot were married and were in love; they are now divorced, have re-married but are still in love with each other. The play does not have any interest in the potential relationship between their discarded spouses, Victor and Sybil, who join forces only in order to pursue their errant other halves. It is the spectacle of Victor and Sybil fighting that provides the cover for the others' final escape. The action of the play amounts to little more than the attempts of Amanda and Elyot to disencumber themselves from the human baggage of their second marriages in order to create a space to explore the possibility of harmony within the tensions of their own relationship. The comic quadrilateral is here no more than pretext for a central agon. As in *Hay Fever*, *Private Lives* celebrates a pre-existent form, here a dissolved marriage rather than the family, an indestructible unit that the comedy has to rediscover and accept. Divorce and remarriage have changed nothing; the play has, in effect, to turn the clock back, a manœuvre that comedy has rarely been prepared to value highly.

If the Davenant–Dryden solution to what they perceived as the inadequacies of *The Tempest* was comedy by addition it is a form that has an honourable history. Shakespeare's *The Comedy of Errors*, after all, finds the form of its action by doubling the twins of Plautus' *Menaechmi*, recognising that the additional pair more than doubles the potential for the misunderstandings of farce. Yet Shakespeare's form has an internal limit, a logical framework for its additions complexly built into its narrative; Egeon's narrative exposition is a precondition of such comedy, even if some versions of the form choose to suppress such exposition until later in the play. I would wish to argue that the comic logic of *The Comedy of Errors* is endemic to the forms of New Comedy, a coherence premised emphatically on comic probability and on the causative, plotted inter-relationships which establish the dramatic boundaries to the accumulation of characters.

Old Comedy has no such prescribed limits. Nothing intrinsic to the development of something one might dub 'plot' defines how many characters should turn up trying to gain citizenship in Cloud-Cuckoo-Land. In the work of its most brilliant English exponent, nothing limits the number of clients facing Jonson's alchemists or pursuing Volpone's legacies other than Jonson's own virtuosity. Indeed *The Alchemist* repeatedly mentions other customers who seem to be clustering unseen around the door: the 'Good wiues' (1.3.1) and 'fish-wife' (1.4.1), 'your giantesse, / The bawd of *Lambeth*' (1.4.2–3), the 'waiting maid' (5.4.110) and 'saylors wife' (5.4.115) and all those visitors Lovewit's neighbours so eagerly describe:

> Ladies, and gentlewomen. Citizens wiues.
> And knights. In coches. Yes, & oyster-women.
> Beside other gallants. Sailors wiues. *Tabacco*-men.
> Another *Pimlico*! (5.1.3–6)[14]

The limitation of the onstage customers, the visible clients, to Dapper, Drugger, Sir Epicure and Surly, Kastril and Dame Pliant, Tribulation and Ananias, is an arbitrary decision of Jonson's controlled only by his own sense of how many characters he can manage to juggle at any one time. The list is already spectacularly long, the juggling already extreme in its display of its own talent, the action already as frenetic as any play can reasonably manage to contain. To imagine Jonson adding even one more client is to risk turning the juggling into a parade of objects tossed into the air rather than a mesmerisingly interweaving network. If each client poses for the alchemical trio a slightly different problem, a different scenario that needs to be set up and sustained, the basic problem of satisfying each visitor while always ensuring that any one playlet does not destroy another remains the same.

Superficially simple, such comic form requires immense skills, like all the best juggling. But where Jonson's alchemists, like Volpone, positively encourage their visitors, the Aristophanic form tends to see the visitors as inherently troublesome, needing endlessly to be chased away, rather than invited in, the problem faced with such exquisite torture by Jonson's Morose. In Molière's *Les Fâcheux*, the drama pursues the Aristophanic model as Eraste too attempts to free himself from the endless stream of annoying individuals troubling his peace:

> Sous quel astre, bon Dieu! faut-il que je sois né,
> Pour être de fâcheux toujours assassiné![15]

Coward's version of Eraste in *Present Laughter* (written in 1939) is Garry Essendine, unmistakably a self-portrait, the star whose flat is invaded by his managers, his wife Liz, a succession of his lovers and, the real penalty of his stardom, the threatening demands of a procession of various would-bes, actresses and writers. Some of these categories of trouble-makers overlap: one discarded lover, Daphne, turns out to be a would-be actress whom he is obliged to audition in the presence of her aunt Lady Saltburn. By the end of the play, with people stuffed into every available adjacent room to the living-room which constitutes the play's single set, Garry and Liz 'tiptoe out together'.[16]

The escape exit as a means of resolving the play may by now be beginning to appear a little predictable as Coward's method of ending his comedies, as if Coward's formula for drama is nothing more than fulfilling the demands of that phase of comedy so neatly defined by Northrop Frye as one 'in which the hero does not transform a humourous society but simply escapes or runs away from it, leaving its structure as it was before'.[17] But it should by now be equally predictable that the nature of the escaping group is a little odd. For, as one might expect, Garry and Liz are not a conventional married couple at all. Liz, as Garry's devoted secretary puts it, 'gave up being Garry's wife' (155) or, as Liz herself describes it, 'I upped and left him years ago', though the two 'never quite got round' to divorcing (156). Liz's attitude to Garry's affairs is that he is now too old at forty for such frenetic philandering: 'in my humble opinion all this casual scampering about is rather undignified' (160). Her attitude is explicitly not derived from a moral judgement: 'I'm merely basing my little homily on reason, dignity, position and, let's face it, age' (160).

When at the end of the play Liz announces to Garry that she has decided to come back to him – a decision, incidentally, which he is powerless to resist – the re-establishment of the marriage is based on business interests, what she identifies as 'the good of the firm' (246). One might expect to see such an attitude to marriage defined as cynical, mercenary, even inappropriate. But Coward's play argues that it is logical, necessary, even desirable. Garry, cocooned in his indulgence in his own vulnerability, needs protecting from himself and Liz is the efficient means of providing that protection. With sexual fidelity redefined as irrelevant to the play's morality, marriage as a locus for the acceptable social expression of sexual desire is replaced by marriage as the locus for the acceptable social expression of self-protection of the artist. All social forms take second place to the egotistic rights of the star.

The clarity of *Present Laughter*'s attitude towards marriage as convenience is, to say the least, unusual. Marriage is, after all, comedy's most normative close. Multiple and dubious though the marriages in a comedy may be, the institution of marriage is hardly called into question but viewed as a social necessity, the means of continuation of the family unit as the basic unit of social structure. Even in comedies where marriages are shown to be foolish or dangerous patterns, as, for instance, in Congreve's *The Double Dealer*, the union of young lovers, Cynthia and Mellefont, is inconceivable without marriage. While Cynthia perceives with frightened clarity that 'tho' Marriage makes man and Wife One Flesh, it leaves 'em still two Fools' her only suggestion for avoiding this fate is to ask Mellefont 'What think you of drawing Stakes, and giving over in time?'[18] When, as her fears increase later in the play, she begins a promise to Mellefont, he assumes she is offering elopement, 'To run most wilfully and unreasonably away with me this moment and be Married', but all she is prepared to promise is 'Never to Marry any Body else' (44). As he recognises, 'That's but a kind of Negative Consent', but it is consent to the significance of marriage nonetheless.

If the audience are encouraged to entertain doubts about the future success of, say, Touchstone's marriage to Audrey, then that anxiety does not significantly undercut or subvert the future of Rosalind and Orlando. Marriage as the most likely form of resolution of the tensions of the comic action is not itself under threat. The audience at comedy accepts marriage as the inevitable, necessary and appropriate solution; it is not in any way threatened by a play's advocacy of marriage. Even a play like Farquhar's *The Beaux' Stratagem*, for all its dazzling advocacy of the advantages of divorce by mutual consent, does not encourage consideration of another form of social partnership to replace marriage, only consideration of the degree of permanence marriage is accorded within the society. *Present Laughter* offers, albeit only in passing, a wry reinterpretation of marriage's social function and in doing so redefines something of comedy's conventional attachment to marriage as resolution.

Present Laughter is Coward's only successful exploration in comedy of the accumulative mathematics of Aristophanic form. More often the model underpins his work in revue where the accumulation of loosely interconnected sketches is the premise of the entertainment's form. But the Aristophanic form is also a comic mathematics that resists geometry. It identifies, in the way that the comic quadrilateral does not, a number of characters as effectively parallel, defining them as multiple representations of a single dramatic purpose. Any functionalist attitude to comic form is bound to see these figures as effectively indistinguishable. I do not mean for a moment that Jonson does not characterise with great brilliance the nature of a Dapper or a Drugger but rather that the differentiation has no necessary link to their function in the action. Each object juggled may be very different – indeed the more different the better the juggling – but each is in the end only an object thrown up and caught in turn.

Coward, whatever his other talents, lacked the necessary dramatic skills to make such a form a desirable option. But his revaluation of the social and comic function of marriage is part of Coward's extraordinary examination of the comic potential of another and far simpler geometric form, the triangle. In a series of plays, culminating in the triumphant subversion of comic and social forms in *Design for Living*, Coward redefined comic form through considering ways to stabilise the triangle.

For the triangle as a comic form had always seemed to be an unstable model for desire. Davenant and Dryden needed a fourth young innocent to enable the pattern of their version of *The Tempest* to be resolved. In a culture dominated by the notion of the pair, the triangle is without social justification. In *The Merchant of Venice*, for instance, the pattern of desire involving Antonio, Bassanio and Portia is only resolvable by redefining Antonio's position as external to the social form of marriage. From being lover he must become, at most, friend, for the dramatic structure cannot tolerate his homosexual desire for Bassanio within its patterns of triumphant heterosexuality. Throughout the play the terms on which the redefinition of his relationship with Bassanio will be based are renegotiated. His 'death-speech' defines his love almost as a threat to Portia for he directs his valuation of that love towards her: 'bid her be judge / Whether Bassanio had not once a love' (4.1.273–4). By the end it is in Belmont, on Portia's territory and effectively on her terms, that the triangle is resolved; it is from Portia that Antonio gains both 'life and living' (5.1.286). The difficulty so many recent productions have had in deciding how Antonio will leave the stage at the very end reflects directors' awareness of his extraneousness in the dance of the couples in Belmont.

In its unstable state, in the apparent impossibility of finding a social form that will accommodate it, the triangle more readily suggests tragedy. If *A Midsummer Night's Dream* derived its lovers' plot in some way from the Palamon–Arcite–Emelye triangle of Chaucer's *Knight's Tale*, then it needed to square off its source's triangle, add its second female lover, in order to turn Chaucer's tragic narrative into the material of comedy. In the long sequence of Amphitryon plays, one might see the transformation from tragedy into the generic ambivalence of tragi-comedy, the transition from, say, Aeschylus' *Alkmene* to Plautus' *Amphitruo*, as marked by the uneasy balancing of a triangle by an additional quadrilateral. Where Aeschylus' play and other classical tragedies on the myth almost certainly focused on Amphitryon–Alkmene–Zeus, Plautus adds the unquestionably comic form generated by Sosia–Mercury–Amphitryon–Zeus.[19]

As early as 1923, in *Fallen Angels*, Coward posed his own comic version of the problematic triangle. Julia and Jane, married to two ciphers aptly named Fred and Willy, are unexpectedly confronted, when their husbands go off for a day, with the reappearance in their lives of the archetypal amorous Frenchman, Maurice Duclos, a man with whom, as they quickly discover, they each had had an affair before their marriages, 'the one Grand Passion in both our lives'.[20] It has to be said, in passing, that naming characters is not Coward's most inventive talent.

With Maurice expected at any moment the women's friendship is untenable at the prospect of sexual excitement. By Act 2, barely able to control themselves, the two women settle down to wait, having agreed it would be safest 'for him to arrive unexpectedly and discover us quietly dining together in charming domestic surroundings' (200). As Maurice's arrival becomes later and the women become drunker as they eat an over-elaborate meal, mutual recriminations and anxious jealousies become uncontrollable. The act, a virtuoso duologue, ends with Jane and Julia hurling threats at each other and with Maurice still to appear.

If at this point Maurice Duclos begins to look promisingly like a prototype for Godot, Act 3 is a disappointment. As Coward freely acknowledged, the play 'needed a stronger last act'.[21] The return of the husbands and the eventual appearance of Maurice lead to various misunderstandings and embarrassments, none of which have a fraction of the verve and momentum of Act 2. But at the end, having convinced Fred and Willy that neither woman had had an affair with Maurice, the two women leave with him, ostensibly to help choose his curtains for the flat above which he has rented. As the two husbands *'gaze at one another with stricken faces'* Maurice can be heard singing *'with great feeling'* the last phrase of the song the two women associate with him: *' Je t'aime – je t'aime – je t'aime'*.

Fallen Angels is far from being even a good play but its plot, in particular the 'idea of two gently nurtured young women playing a drinking scene together'[22] outraged the custodians of public decency: on one night a Mrs Hornibrook who had recently resigned from the London Council for the Promotion of Public Morality 'stood up in a box and began to speak against the play, but her words were drowned by the orchestra, which began to play "I want to be Happy"'.[23] The reviews were, in Coward's description, 'vituperative to the point of incoherence'.[24] Looking back on it, Coward affected to be amused by the attack on it in the press as 'amoral, disgusting, vulgar and an insult to British womanhood' and defended it as 'of course none of these things'.[25] But in the comfortable exit of the two women arm-in-arm with M. Duclos and the clear implication that their affairs with him before marriage are to be resumed, now adulterously, one might at least see something a little heterodox. As the reviewer in *Punch* carefully judged,

An unpleasant subject, you may say? Well, not edifying or elevating, certainly, but Mr Noël Coward has written it so gaily and wittily and they play it so lightly and briskly that it is relieved of all offensiveness.[26]

More to my point is the women's final acceptance of each other's desire for Maurice and the replacement of their desperate jealousy by the mutual trust necessary to cover up the past and, presumably, the future. As a device it is reminiscent of the pact of Horner's mistresses in the later stages of Wycherley's *The Country Wife* but here it is restricted to the creation of a triangle which can maintain its own controlled equilibrium. In the end it is the relationship between the two women that matters for the continuation of the action beyond the limits of the play and beyond the limits of acceptable norms of social behaviour, far more than the relation of either woman to their lover. It is, as it were, in the base-line of this particular triangle that the dramatic and comic interest lies.

In *The Marquise* (written in 1926), Coward explores the problem of the triangle again, though without conspicuous success. The play's success in the theatre was entirely the result of the performance of Marie Tempest in the title-role. As Coward himself honestly admitted, her performance covered a multitude of sins in the play's form:

I might, if I could only forget her eating an orange and watching Raoul and Esteban fighting a duel, realise how weak and meretricious the last act is.[27]

The Marquise shares with *Fallen Angels* the concept of the re-appearance of a previous sexual problem into a situation that had achieved a comfortable social equilibrium. The play opens at the celebrations for the impending marriage of Adrienne, daughter of the Comte Raoul de Vriaac, to Miguel, son of Raoul's old friend Esteban, el Duco de Santaguano. Coward's attempts at names for a comedy set in the eighteenth century are no better than his names for one set in the twentieth. The appearance of the Marquise Eloise de Kestournel leads to the revelation that both Raoul and Esteban had had affairs with her years before, unbeknown to each other, that Adrienne and Miguel are both her children, that, as a result, the impending marriage is incestuous and hence that Adrienne is free to marry the man she really loves, Jacques Rijar, her father's secretary. This could, of course, equally serve as the plot for a romantic tragedy.

Coward is not really interested in the plot of the young lovers, a triangle quickly resolved to the satisfaction of all three. More intriguing and more problematic is the triangle of the parents. When it becomes clear that Eloise has had no lovers other than Raoul and Esteban and that she has never been married, the possibility of a future is foreshadowed:

Many men since then have made love to me, but none have won me. I preferred to preserve my integrity and wait, and now – now – I have come back, and God help you both... one of you is going to house, feed, protect and adore me until the day I die.[28]

The resolution of this triangle is, once confronted, swiftly and honourably achieved: much to Esteban's relief, Eloise chooses Raoul who is still desperately in love with her and is able at last to admit it openly to her. *The Marquise* is a glib play with a facile, sentimental ending. But Coward's awareness of its meretriciousness suggests his awareness that the triangle deserves a different solution, that what he dubbed 'a brittle modern comedy'[29] might have deserved a better ending. At the end of this play, significantly, no one makes an escape through the front door.

Design for Living was written in 1932. It was first performed in America the following year and filmed by Paramount, in an adapted version by Ben Hecht, the same year. The Lord Chamberlain's anxiety about its representation of heterosexual promiscuity prevented a London production until 1939. In 1934, in a Broadway revue called *Life Begins at 8.40*, Bert Lahr and Ray Bolger performed a sketch called 'C'est La Vie'.[30] The scene is a bridge over the Seine; Pierre and Jacques, both suicidal, discover they have been spurned by the same woman. When she arrives she announces 'I tell you I do not love you because I love you each so much and if I tell one, I hurt the other.' But now, after seeing the film version of *Design for Living*, she has the answer:

LAHR Is it where the woman and the two men love each other and the other each?
LUELLA But yes. And they live happily together after, for evermore. And I think to myself – Pierre, Jacques, me, why not we so?

The two men start a song:

> We're living in the smart upper sets,
> Let other lovers sing their duets.
> Duets are made by the bourgeoisie – oh,
> But only God can make a trio.

But, as they dance past the woman, now perched on the wall, 'they push her off the bridge'.

The sketch neatly identifies the social exclusivity of Coward's world, its 'smart upper sets', though I find in its transposition of Coward's Anglophone lovers to France an intriguing assumption that sexual sophistication is a French prerogative. For Coward's play is concerned with the boundaries of sexuality and the diagrammatic plotting of *Design for Living* does result in an extraordinary and unprecedented redefinition of the possibilities of the comic triangle, a discovery of a stable sexual equilibrium for three people. In *Design for Living* Gilda does not need to be pushed off a bridge.

The play's sequence of geometric forms is part of its careful exposition of the difficulties of its own continuation. As each step in the action is established, the audience, like the characters, is left wondering what on earth could constitute a next step, whether there could be a solution. In Act 1, Gilda is living with Otto but, while he is away, she has been sleeping with Leo, their best friend. As Gilda and Leo ponder what they are to do, Leo defines the problem:

It doesn't matter who loves who the most; you can't line up things like that mathematically. We all love each other a lot, far too much, and we've made a bloody mess of it!³¹

In Act 2, Gilda is now living with Leo but, while he is away, she sleeps with Otto. Even at this stage of the plot's complexity Otto is smugly comfortable, content to dub the trio morally heterodox: 'Our lives are diametrically opposed to ordinary social conventions' (64). Though, as Otto says, any religious group could call them 'loose-living, irreligious, unmoral degenerates... But the whole point is, it's none of their business' (65).

Otto's assessment of the triangle is perceptive, even if Gilda rightly defines his rhapsodic style here as soap-box ranting:

A gay, ironic chance threw the three of us together and tied our lives in a tight knot at the outset. To deny it would be ridiculous, and to unravel it impossible. Therefore, the only thing left is to enjoy it thoroughly, every rich moment of it, every thrilling second – (65)

At the end of Act 2 she leaves both of them and runs off with good, sober, sensible and completely unexciting Ernest. In a long duologue, Leo and Otto become maudlin drunk and end up sobbing helplessly in each other's arms, as they contemplate a future together without Gilda: 'we're going to be awfully – awfully – lonely' (92).

The diagram looks complete, a satisfactory solution no nearer being achieved. In Act 3 Gilda has now married Ernest and is living with him in his penthouse flat in New York. Gilda has changed; she is, as Coward's stage-direction makes clear,

more still and sure than before. A certain amount of vitality has gone from her, but, in its place, there is an aloof poise quite in keeping with her dress and surroundings. (93)

Gilda, once the expression of gilded youth, now seems gilded in another sense, fixed and sprayed into place with a sheen of style that has suppressed what the play had not so far been able to contain.

The inevitable reappearance of Otto and Leo still does not suggest a solution and Gilda rushes out. Again Coward seems to be toying with his conventional solution of escape. But there is one final scene, the morning after. Gilda, returning, admits defeat and announces she is leaving Ernest and going away with Leo and Otto, who sit smugly triumphant, wearing Ernest's pyjamas. Ernest is now pushed into expressing, over and over again, the conventional moral responses to the establishment of the trio: 'I gather the fact that I'm your husband is not of the faintest importance to you?' (120), 'I see a ruthless egotism, an utter disregard for anyone's feelings but your own' (120) or 'Your values are false and distorted... From the point of view of anyone who has the slightest sense of decency' (122). But, finally losing his temper, he announces 'I never could understand this disgusting three-sided erotic hotch-potch!' (123) and, calling them 'unscrupulous, worthless degenerates', he *stamps out of the room*'. Where Gilda had earlier threatened to leave, it is finally Ernest who abandons his own apartment. It is then Ernest who makes the necessary escape, leaving the three others screaming with hysterical laughter:

they break down utterly and roar with laughter. They groan and weep with laughter; *their laughter is still echoing from the walls as* – THE CURTAIN FALLS (124)

This laughter is no longer the laughter of wit; indeed the whole play seems marked by its lack of that epigrammatic, lapidary poise of Coward's normal comic style. As Brooks Atkinson, reviewing the American production, noted,

Unfortunately for the uses of artificial comedy, establishing this triangular situation involves considerable sobriety. All through the first act Mr Coward writes as earnestly as a psychologist... When *Design for Living* sounds serious, you wish impatiently that Mr Coward would cut the cackle...[32]

Instead the exploration of this logic has produced a different cackle in this final laughter. Recognising its multiplicity of potential meanings, Coward tried protectively to define his own understanding of its meaning:

Different minds found different meanings in this laughter. Some considered it to be directed against Ernest... If so, it was certainly cruel, and in the worst possible taste. Some saw in it a lascivious anticipation of a sort of triangular, carnal frolic... I as author, however, prefer to think that Gilda and Otto and Leo were laughing at themselves.[33]

This sounds like special pleading. It is Ernest's fall over some packing-cases that provokes the outburst and the laughter has a childish merciless glee at the sight of someone's pain. The trio have taken on a new hardness, almost a new viciousness, in their harsh rejection of Ernest and his very slightly Puritanical values. His humiliation, the traditional comic humiliation of the individual who refuses to celebrate the comic virtues, cannot here result in any easy acquiescence in the model the end of the play adumbrates. The ending is designed to outrage the audience nearly as much as it upsets Ernest. The new triangle is both the product of incontrovertible logic and distinctly unpalatable and abnormal. Ernest is not wrong to find the trio twisted, degenerate and altogether peculiar. For the play's joyful fantasy of sexual equilibrium is comfortably exclusive both of Ernest's representation of conventional social behaviour and of any extrapolable application.

It is also based on the exploration of Leo's and Otto's relationship in their drinking scene at the end of Act 2. It is a difficult scene to analyse. I find in it an admission and approval of the men's bisexuality. It is as close as Coward dared dramatise in 1933 to a male relationship which goes beyond vague notions of friendship and is instead quite explicitly emotional and sexual. Alan Sinfield, in an outstanding study of Coward's representation of homosexuality, prefers to see the relationship as 'homosocial, effecting a male bonding via their desire for Gilda',[34] using the term developed by Eve Kosofsky Sedgwick,[35] while acknowledging that 'homosexual love... may still be implicit'. But his argument suggests that, since the focus of the men's relationship is Gilda this 'effects an apparent exclusion of homosexuality'.[36] Yet, if the crucial point is their bisexuality, Gilda must be part of that focus.

James Agate, in an irritable review of the 1939 London production, suggested that

The play might make easier watching if Mr Coward, normally so nattily minded, were less vague in his use of the word 'love', to which he gives a plurality of meanings.[37]

But the example, a speech by Leo, which Agate uses and which he compares to the multiple modes of love in Dickens's *Nicholas Nickleby*, deliberately refuses to differentiate between the types of love in the different relationships of desire it so neatly states: 'I love you. You love me. You love Otto. I love Otto. Otto loves you. Otto loves me. There now! Start to unravel from there' (21). This is love as mathematics, the harmony of desire in this triangle is perfect geometry. For this trio of lovers it is precisely the equivalence, in nature and power, of the forms of desire that contributes both to the creation of the muddle and to the possibility of its resolution.

For the triangle is a deliberately restrictive model. *Design for Living* is not what John Lahr sees it as being, a 'homosexual daydream of sexual abundance'.[38] The activities of 'these poor wincing worms in a winecup', as Sean O'Casey called them,[39] do not involve others other than by discarding them. There is no need for Coward, like some twentieth-century Davenant, to invent a second woman so that a bisexual Gilda could explore all the permutations, as if the comedy were only a free variation on the Kama Sutra. There is in the triangle an ideal form of sufficiency for the three lovers.

But Coward also recognises that the balance of *Design for Living* is exceptional; he is not establishing a framework for the future of socio-sexual relationships. The play's incorporation of its own anxiety at the wish-fulfilled world it has somehow managed to create is oddly Aristophanic. It does not know and cannot imagine what to do with the trio, anymore than Athens would know what to do with Cloud-Cuckoo-Land or a returned Aeschylus. Yet its solution, in the clear logic of its development from a premise it cannot even enunciate until late in the play, is as subversive as anything in Aristophanes. As introverted and delightfully anti-social as the end is, it nonetheless threatens the limitations of conventional sexual behaviour, denying the binary limitations of the couple by accepting this extreme example of the supreme adequacy of the 'mariage à trois' for Gilda, Leo and Otto. But the balanced triangle is restricted to that quintessentially Coward world, a fantasy of social elitism, the only one in which, Judge Brack notwithstanding, people do do such things.

Design for Living has the virtues and vices of a thesis-play. If it lacks the satisfactions of the surface brilliancies of Coward's style at its best, it replaces them with a serious-minded and revelatory exploration of comic form. It considers and turns into form ideas that comedy had never before managed to resolve.

One might have thought the problem of the triangle was at last solved but I offer one last rotation of the geometric form. In *Fallen Angels* the resolution of the triangle depended on Julia and Jane without rancour accepting their half-shares in Maurice. At the end of Joe Orton's *Entertaining Mr Sloane*, Kath and Ed, brother and sister, need to resolve how to deal with their shares in Sloane. Ed proposes an elegant solution to be formalised by contract: 'You've had him six months; I'll have him the next six'.[40] The scheme allows for occasional visits to Kath during Ed's half-year: 'I've got no objections if he visits you from time to time. Briefly. We could put it in the contract' (97). Kath is delighted:

KATH Perfect, Eddie. It's very clever of you to have thought of such a lovely idea!
ED Put it down to my experience at the conference table. (97)

It is a device typical of Orton's metamorphoses of classical myth. Sloane, as a latter-day Proserpina, will divide his time between two hells, spending half of each year with Kath, the play's Ceres, both Sloane's substitute mother ('mamma' as Kath recurrently calls herself) and his pregnant lover. The agreement is, as it were, a comic punishment for Sloane's murder of Kemp, imprisonment transformed into many hours of community service in the siblings' beds. Again, as with *Design for Living*, bisexuality is the necessary premise for the solution but one that, now imposed on Sloane, humiliates him for the sexual charm he had depended on earlier. He will no longer have any choice about his sexuality and his sexual performance.

Ed's plan is tidy, with all the elegance of a good contract and the narrative balance of myth. But it also provides an aesthetically pleasing resolution with all the satisfaction of a mathematical model, this triangle established on the firm base-line of the legal agreement of siblings. In his fascination with such geometrical forms in comedy, the discovery of solutions where none seemed possible, Joe Orton stands as Coward's true heir. For both the patterns invented by Davenant and Dryden would have seemed superfluous. In their delight in the simplest forms of comic geometry, Coward and Orton seem almost Puritan.

NOTES

1 John Dryden, *The Works*, ed. H. T. Swedenberg et al. (Berkeley, 1956–   ), x, 4 (roman/italic reversed).
2 John Dryden, *The Works*, x, 4.

3 C. Spencer, ed., *Five Restoration Adaptations of Shakespeare* (Urbana, 1965), 121 (roman/italic reversed).

4 Pierre Carlet de Marivaux, *Théâtre complet*, ed. Bernard Dort (Paris, 1964), 522.

5 Ibid., p. 530.

6 Pierre Marivaux, *Three Plays*, trans. Timberlake Wertenbaker (Bath, 1989) 174.

7 The production is briefly outlined by Claude Schumacher in his introduction to Pierre Marivaux, *Plays* (1988), xxvii–xxviii.

8 Andrew Steptoe, *The Mozart–Da Ponte Operas* (Oxford, 1988), 133–4.

9 All quotations from Shakespeare are taken from *The Complete Works*, ed. Stanley Wells and Gary Taylor (Oxford, 1986).

10 All dates are taken from Raymond Mander and Joe Mitchenson, *Theatrical Companion to Coward* (1957).

11 Noël Coward, *Plays: One* (1979), 92–3.

12 Coward, *Plays: One*, 93.

13 Noël Coward, *Plays: Two* (1979), 90.

14 All quotations from Ben Jonson, *The Works*, eds. C. H. Herford and P. & E. Simpson (Oxford, 1925–52), v. I have omitted the speech-prefixes from the neighbours' hubbub. See also R. L. Smallwood '"Here in the Friars": Immediacy and Theatricality in *The Alchemist*', *RES*, n.s. 32 (1980), 142–60, especially p. 150.

15 *Les Fâcheux*, lines 1–2 in Molière, *Oeuvres Complètes*, ed. P.-A. Touchard (Paris, 1962), 162.

16 Noël Coward, *Plays: Four* (1979), 247.

17 Northrop Frye, *Anatomy of Criticism* (Princeton, New Jersey, 1957), 180.

18 William Congreve, *The Double-Dealer* (1694), 18.

19 On the early history of Amphitryon on stage see James H. Mantinband and Charles E. Passage, *Amphitryon: Three Plays in New Verse Translations* (Chapel Hill, N.C., 1974), 10–16.

20 Noël Coward, *Plays: One*, 189.

21 Noël Coward, *Play Parade*, ii (revised edn, 1950), vii–viii.

22 Noël Coward, *Autobiography* (1986), 145.

23 Quoted by Mander and Mitchenson, *Theatrical Companion to Coward*, 145.

24 Coward, *Autobiography*, 145.

25 *Play Parade*, ii, vii.

26 Quoted by Mander and Mitchenson, *Theatrical Companion to Coward*, 65.

27 Noël Coward, *Play Parade*, iii (1950), xv.

28 Coward, *Plays: Two*, 272.

29 Coward, *Play Parade*, iii, xv.

30 I owe my account of this to John Lahr, *Notes on a Cowardly Lion* (rev. edn, New York, 1984), 136–7.

31 Noël Coward, *Plays: Three* (1979), 20.

32 Quoted by Mander and Mitchenson, *Theatrical Companion to Coward*, 179.

33 Noël Coward, *Play Parade*, [I] (1934), xviii.
34 Alan Sinfield, 'Private Lives/Public Theater: Noel Coward and the Politics of Homosexual Representation', *Representations* 36 (1991), 43–63, p. 47.
35 See *Between Men: English Literature and Male Homosocial Desire* (New York, 1985), esp. 1–5.
36 Sinfield, 47.
37 James Agate, *Red Letter Nights* (1944), 247.
38 John Lahr, *Coward the Playwright* (1982), 82.
39 Sean O'Casey's phrase for the trio in 'Coward Codology: II. Design for Dying' in *The Flying Wasp* (1937), 152.
40 Joe Orton, *Entertaining Mr Sloane* (1973), 96.

Ludwig Wittgenstein and the comedy of errors

Eric Griffiths

Wittgenstein told Russell that William James's *The Varieties of Religious Experience* profited his soul:

> This book does me a *lot* of good. I don't mean to say that I will be a saint soon, but I am not sure that it does not improve me a little in a way which I would like to improve *very much*: namely I think that it helps me to get rid of the *Sorge* (in the sense in which Goethe used the word in the 2nd part of Faust).[1]

This is an early reference to James, from whom Wittgenstein continued to quote throughout his career; the letter already shows him concerned with what 'good' a philosophical book may do a person, though unsure how to measure that good (in consecutive sentences, it is both 'a *lot*' and 'a little'). The uncertainty in measuring is not just muddle; it can't be written off as a result of a novice in English fumbling the verbs 'to do someone good' and 'to improve someone'. The uncertainty is permanent and not confined to English; expert speakers declare 'a little of what you fancy does you good' though they might not claim that, *ipso facto*, such a fancied little 'improves you'; a 'good laugh makes you feel better' but better than what, and do we laugh in order to better ourselves? Much the same point could be made, replacing 'good laugh' with 'good philosophical argument', or the equivalent of either phrase in an other language.

The idea that philosophy might do someone good has long amused comedians, from *The Clouds* to *Beyond the Fringe*. A characteristically sharp and well-informed sketch by Jonathan Miller and Alan Bennett ends:

> JON ... the burden is fair and square on your shoulders to explain to me the exact relevance philosophy *does* have to everyday life.

288

ALAN Yes, I can do this quite easily. This morning I went into a shop, and a shop assistant was having an argument with a customer. The shop assistant said 'yes' – 'yes', you see – and the customer said 'What do you mean, "yes"?' – and the shop assistant said, 'I mean "yes".'

JON This is very exciting indeed.

ALAN Here is a splendid example in everyday life where two very ordinary people are asking each other what are in essence philosophical questions – 'What do you mean, "yes"?' – 'I mean "yes"' – and where I, as a philosopher, could help them.

JON And did you?

ALAN Well no – they were in rather a hurry...[2]

And, on those dots, a black-out. Scathingly though the writing evokes fatuous, professional philosophers – Alan's confidence that he can 'quite easily' explain what, for instance, Kant couldn't, the petering out of his confidence into 'Well no' and 'rather', Jon's 'This is very exciting indeed' which will raise a laugh whether he plays the line bored or enthused, the flicker of disdain for 'very ordinary people' which comes over the 'ordinary language' philosopher – the jokes are instinct (as working jokes have to be) with the manner of what they contemn. They also raise philosophical questions. The lines call up a form of life (someone who understands them will be able to specify, without having seen them performed, how their speakers should sit, furrow their brows, and which sort of jacket they wear), but it is ponderable how so few words can do this so well. The sketch is called 'Words... and Things' and was written in the early 1960s. Willard van Orman Quine published *Word and Object* in 1961. Were there an allusion here, it would be an in-joke of the university-educated; the dots between 'Words' and 'Things', dots which make 'Things' hover between the metaphysical and the matey ('Just drop your things in the hall and come and have a drink'), perform a rangier, more inquiring, comic turn in the area of overlap between what we say and how we talk when we reflect on what we have just said.

Trying to explain, not 'exactly' but more clearly, what he meant by 'Sorge', Wittgenstein had recourse to German drama. That might surprise believers in one legend of what Russell, Moore and Wittgenstein got up to early this century, a legend which feeds the parody in Bennett and Miller's recessing of 'yes' further and yet further into quotation-marks as they pursue exact definition. With all its virtues, the second part of *Faust* is not the first place to look for unambiguous formulation of the meaning of terms. Wittgenstein was thinking of the 'Midnight' scene from the last act of *Faust*, II. Four weird sisters – Lack, Guilt, Deprivation, and 'Sorge' – loom over Faust's palace which the first three cannot enter because he is a rich man; only 'Sorge' ('anxiety', 'care') can assail Faust, or the similarly well-off young Wittgenstein. She creeps through his keyhole, and into his inner ear. Though he is an enlightened man, he still toils in superstitious fears; to his assurance that he is worldly wise, and that nothing can be known of the other worldly, she replies with a nagging evocation of dreadful imminences: insatiability amid abundance, a life beset by dilemma, when existence has become a mere rehearsal for hell.[3] One line from this scene of inward wrangling particularly haunted Wittgenstein, Sorge's 'ewiges Düstre steigt herunter' ['eternal gloom comes down from above']. In 1946–7, he gave it as an example of the difficulty with which we distinguish literal and figurative senses when talking about psychological states (*RPP* I, 133; I, 151–2). This difficulty makes itself felt in Goethe's scene, where Faust twice uses the word 'düstre' before Sorge utters it. Once, he qualifies the rhyme of 'Not' and 'Tod' ['Deprivation' and 'Death'] as 'düstres', which could be translated as 'sad' or 'ominous', but when he talks of his magical studies as research 'im Düstern', he means 'things of darkness' in a sense which cannot untendentiously be called literal or figurative. So, Sorge's picture of his future as 'ewiges Düstre' may threaten either depression or stormy weather or both. A similar ambiguity looms over her 'herunter' ['downward'], for Faust has previously given the vertical axis a symbolic force when he scorns to look 'upward' or seek his own image 'above the clouds'. It is as if she said 'You may be right that man will find nothing "up there", but beware lest something "up there", the "ewiges Düstre", find you.' Her 'ewiges' also retorts on his confident saying that it is a waste of time to wander in thought through 'eternity'; she threatens not just 'eternal gloom' but the 'gloom of eternity'. Even the man who lives in the clear light of rational day, who says at one moment that his bugbears are merely 'Unsinn' ['nonsense'], may at the next be overshadowed by her, because 'Dämonen... wird man schwerlich los, / Das geistig-strenge Band ist nicht zu trennen' ['one rids oneself of demons only with difficulty, this knot is as tight as the spirit itself, and can't be cut through']. The sense in which Goethe uses 'Sorge', then, might be brought out as 'religious dread, persisting beyond reason'.[4]

Wittgenstein in 1912 shows that dexterity with examples which characterises his later work. The perpetual fretfulness of Sorge finds abiding shape in Goethe's scene: the protagonists' back-chat twists words about, now in one direction, now another, as worlds and otherworlds contend within Faust. He speaks mostly in decasyllabic couplets to which she replies with trochaic tetrameter couplets that jingle against his adult measures with a shade of infantilism he yet cannot outgrow. She and Faust formally alternate, and would be theatrically visible as two distinct figures, but when the scene impresses itself on us we become aware of them as composing together a unity, the staging of a mind at odds with itself, an arena of disquiet. Evidently, for a complex though frequently occurring cultural state like this, an instance as refined as Goethe's dramaturgy was needed, but it was not complexity alone which took Wittgenstein to drama to say just what he meant. A late remark recommends dramatic setting for the understanding of any meaningful utterance: 'The contexts of a sentence are best portrayed in a play. Therefore the best example for a sentence with a particular meaning is a quotation from a play' (*LW* 1.6). He complains of philosophers and logicians that they are not dramatic enough: 'In philosophy, sentences like "This is not green" are discussed without giving the specific conditions under which one might use them,' or 'Logicians use examples which no one would ever think of using in any other connection. Whoever says "Socrates is a man"? I am not criticizing this because it does not occur in practical life. What I am criticizing is the fact that logicians do not give these examples any life. We must invent a surrounding for our examples' (*Ambrose* 120; 124).

The concept of a 'surrounding' ['Umgebung'] makes many appearances in Wittgenstein's second period of philosophical work. It is a vague concept, but then, as he said, '"Concept" is a vague concept' (*RFM* 433). Elizabeth Anscombe suggests what the word involves when she emphasises that consideration of 'linguistic practice' entails for Wittgenstein attention to extra-linguistic activities: 'It is important that it includes activities *other* than the production of language, into which a use of language is interwoven. For example, activities of measuring, of weighing, of giving and receiving and putting into special places, of moving about in a huge variety of ways...'.[5] He thinks of 'surroundings' when describing the character of a musical phrase (*RPP* I, 85; *CV* 51), when remarking how odd a ritual gesture would seem if isolated from the rest of the

ceremony to which it belongs (*PI* 153), or in showing how the same
smile might look now malicious, now benign (*PI* 145). 'Surrounding'
is, in fact, a colloquial expansion of Frege's 'context' ['Zusammen-
hang']; the word's gestural amplitude and looseness – imagine how
we indicate 'put it somewhere over there' with our hands – are
typical of what vexes some in his later work, and of what could more
admiringly be regarded as a signature-tune of his genius.[6] Over and
again, his approach to a philosophical problem is to give various
surroundings to his examples in the hope of disentangling what
seemed a single perplexity into a number of interconnected,
unpuzzlingly interconnected, human activities (see, for instance, the
discussion of what two shades of a colour have in common with each
other, *BB* 132–5). This procedure carries his conviction that 'To get
clear about philosophical problems, it is useful to become conscious of
the apparently unimportant details of the particular situation in
which we are inclined to make a certain metaphysical assertion'
(*BB* 66). An equivalent method for literary critics might be to remind
ourselves of the theatrical setting of words we pore over in a script,
when we ask, say, 'What is it about Hamlet's soliloquies that makes
them sound so intimate?' without giving weight to the possibility
that his being alone on the stage before us may play a part in that
effect. Such surroundings are 'the circumstances which form the
theatre of our performance in language' ('...Umstände, die den
Schauplatz unseres Sprachspiels bilden', *PI* 72: my translation).
When we forget where our words belong, we get into difficulties; this
is the point of his celebrated aphorism 'philosophical problems arise
when language *goes on holiday*' (*PI* 19). Such problems occur, like
lager-loutishness, when we are freed from our tasks in those ordinary
surroundings which mostly keep us sensible.

Thus, he will remark that 'The puzzles about time are due to an
analogy between time and motion. There is an analogy, but we press
it too far; we are tempted by it to talk nonsense. We say time "flows",
and then ask where to and what from, and so on...' (*Lee* 60), or 'one
of the great sources of philosophical bewilderment: a substantive
makes us look for a thing that corresponds to it' (*BB* 1), or again
'Where our language suggests a body and there is none: there, we
should like to say, is a *spirit*' (*PI* 18). Given such an account of how we
go philosophically wrong, it looks as if it might be quite easy to keep
our thinking permanently straight, just by noting when words
prompt us to false moves; there is at times a temptation to read the

Investigations as a conceptual miracle-diet which offers a way, quickly and with little effort, to lose heaps of unsightly, erroneous analogy. Neither Wittgenstein's temperament nor his conception of philosophy (in so far as these can be distinguished from each other) would have permitted him to make such an offer. As a manuscript note puts it, 'We are misled by false analogies & cannot extricate ourselves. This is the *morbus philosophicus*.'[7] One reason why we cannot extricate ourselves is that there is no litmus test for when an analogy is false (cf. *BB* 28). He was particularly fond of Tolstoy's tale 'The Three Hermits', in which a Bishop calls on three old men who are in the habit of praying to God in the words 'Three are ye, three are we, have mercy upon us.' On hearing their formula, the Bishop smiles, remarks 'You have evidently heard something about the Holy Trinity', and teaches them the Lord's Prayer. He then sails off to continue his diocesan visitation, only to find the three hermits running after him across the waters of the lake to apologise for having forgotten the words he taught them and to ask for renewed instructions: 'The Bishop crossed himself, and leaning over the ship's side, said: "Your own prayer will reach the Lord, men of God. It is not for me to teach you. Pray for us sinners."'[8] Wittgenstein would not have thought the hermits were misled by an analogy in their prayer, though he probably sympathised with the implicit Tolstoyan moral that credal formulae matter less than holiness of life in common. He might have said that the hermits had given their analogy an application by their life together, shown what could be done with it, whereas philosophical analogies are often aimless marshlights, as, for instance, when we transfer 'physical' vocabulary to a 'spiritual' realm where that vocabulary no longer has a grammar because the 'linguistic practice' which surrounds words for bodies (weighing them, bumping into them, measuring distances between them) has no place there.

The concept of 'depth', in its regular migrations between differently measured realms, may misguide us, especially in applications such as 'deep thought' or 'deep feeling'. The ocean-floor may unpredictably and deeply shelve but 'What is a *deep* feeling? Could someone have a feeling of ardent love or hope for the space of one second – *no matter what* preceded or followed this second? – What is happening now has significance – in these surroundings' (*PI* 153). Shakespeare is adept at creating moments in his comedies when a character or an exchange seems for a moment to have vastly extended its reach, as if the set before which the action is played had been suddenly back-lit, turned out to be a gauze, and revealed for a while unsuspected vistas of implication. When Helena is left breathless after chasing Demetrius through the wood, one line of her lament stands out from the rest of her complaint: 'The more my prayer, the lesser is my grace.'[9] For the space of little more than one second, she sounds like a theologian of a Protestant cast; the more she petitions her god, the less he favours her, because her supplications express what she wants rather than seek to realise what he wills. The fleeting, implied simile between the soul's pursuit of the divine and her unreciprocated sexual desire lifts the play momentarily, like a shuttle-cock, into a realm of conceptual punning. It is seductive to regard such moments as somehow key, hints of a teaching above or beneath or behind the charm of the play's evident surface. Yet a line like Helena's carries its charge just by not being on a level with what surrounds it; if we meditate on the single line, we can no more fathom its nature than we could find out what a 'deep feeling' means by isolating from its surroundings in a person's life some intense moment, and studying that alone.

More generally, a critic trying to explain the 'depth' of a Shakespearean comedy may be attracted by phrases such as 'personal identity', 'illusion and reality', or 'sexual difference'. These locutions form part of a recognised philosophical vocabulary; we accredit philosophy as a realm of 'deep thought', and suppose that if we can show that a play has for a 'theme' a consideration like one of these we shall have gone some way into its depths. At least two problems arise from this supposition. First, the integrity of the individual work dissipates – all too many plays prove to be about illusion and reality; secondly, we use the word 'theme' and its cognates so loosely that our explanation yields less than we had hoped. In Shakespeare's English, a 'theme' was a prescribed topic for rhetorical elaboration; we can untendentiously identify the 'theme' of the *Diabelli Variations*. Neither case provides a satisfying model for our sense of the way a Shakespearean comedy grows to deep meaning. We have been led astray by the belief that if a play is deep, it must be deep in the way a philosophical argument is deep, but that belief is itself an instance of a trouble in our philosophising: 'When words in our ordinary language have prima facie analogous grammars we are inclined to try to interpret them analogously; i.e. we try to make the analogy hold throughout' (*BB* 7). Early in *The Comedy of Errors*, there are two

profoundly exquisite speeches which seem to have something to do
with each other. Antipholus of Syracuse knows why he is so sad:

> I to the world am like a drop of water,
> That in the ocean seeks another drop,
> Who, falling there to find his fellow forth
> (Unseen, inquisitive), confounds himself.
> So I, to find a mother and a brother,
> In quest of them (unhappy), ah, lose myself. (1.2.30ff.)

A little later, Adriana rebukes him in similar words for making her
miserable:

> How comes it now, my husband, O, how comes it,
> That thou art then estranged from thyself?
> Thyself I call it, being strange to me,
> That undividable, incorporate,
> Am better than thy dear self's better part.
> Ah, do not tear away thyself from me;
> For know, my love, as easy mayst thou fall
> A drop of water in the breaking gulf,
> And take unmingled thence that drop again,
> Without addition or diminishing,
> As take from me thyself and not me too. (2.2.119ff.)

They are joined in details as small as the learned placing of the echoic
phrases 'unseen, inquisitive' and 'undividable, incorporate'. Her
words answer to his, though she did not hear his speech; the
characters sound wholly in tune with each other, and that harmony
underscores her insistence on their nearness of soul. He was talking
about his lost twin; when she then speaks of marriage as a twinning,
it is as if Aristophanes's story in *The Symposium* of human love as a
search for re-union with the lost half of an original pair had been
proved true. Yet she is not his wife, and knows her husband less well
than she thinks if she can mistake his brother for him. The poignant
abstraction of both speeches may derive in part from reminiscences of
Plato, though it is not a philosopher but a comic dramatist who
speaks the relevant passage in *The Symposium*. If there is an allusion to
Aristophanes's speech hereabouts, it is an allusion wrily kinked by
the fact that Adriana gets Antipholus wrong, gets the wrong
Antipholus, as if Shakespeare admired his predecessor's fictional
theory, warmed to it, but kept his cool and observed that it is
sometimes when we speak most passionately of neighbourhood or
kinship with an other that we are most likely to be making a bish,

about ourself or someone else. A sense of these speeches' depth arises equally from their ordinary but intricate relation to their surround-ings, from the fact that Shakespeare has brought loss at sea to the forefront of his play, so that Egeon has spoken of 'unjust divorce' in a shipwreck (1.1.104) before Adriana imagines a married couple indivisible as drops in the ocean, though she fears Antipholus might try to separate from her with a 'deep-divorcing vow' (2.2.138). Such thoughts come naturally to those whose business is with ships, as naturally as a merchant's wife like Adriana moves from a minor irritation about a trinket, a 'gold chain' she has been promised, to jewels of the soul such as reputation and marital honour (2.1.6off.) Not that the metaphors simply encode material realities but rather the converse: 'The *facts* of human natural history that throw light on our problem are difficult for us to find out, for our talk *passes them by*, it is occupied with other things. (In the same way we tell someone: 'Go into the shop and buy...' – not: 'Put your left foot in front of your right foot etc. etc., then put coins down on the counter, etc. etc.')' (*RPP* I, 17).

For much of the time in *The Comedy of Errors*, the talk passes by the narratively crucial fact of Egeon's impending death, as in our lives we mostly bypass thought of our own mortality. Time moves at several speeds in the play – the suspenseful procrastination of Egeon's doom, the farcical bustle which overtakes his wait and helps us forget it. This comic timing of our capacity for reflection makes the play 'deep'; equally, it is an element in the 'depth' of Helena's 'The more my prayer...' that she is breathless saying it and rushes on to other matters. The brisk tempo assists us to see the place of our reflections in 'human natural history' (we have to scan quickly to take the panorama), to see how many concerns overlap in them, under what pressures they take shape. A play returns us to the surroundings of our thought, and this may be one reason why Wittgenstein said the best example for a sentence with a particular meaning is a quotation from a play. Doing philosophy, we are attracted by the notion that if we could only make ourselves think slowly enough, deal with the issues one at a time, we could make headway, maybe arrive at a solution, but philosophical problems are 'undividable' one from another, and, taken singly, they assume a chimerically unfathomable 'depth'. In criticism, we are similarly drawn to conceptually ringing, single lines such as Helena's and feel that, if we could only get to the bottom of them, we would be out of the wood. On the other hand, it would be wrong to make out that we always think straight when we don't 'stop to think' or that perplexity is something only philosophers endure and from which 'very ordinary people' are, in their hurry, free. Just as it would be wrong to deny that there are these lustrous, swift enigmas in *A Midsummer Night's Dream* and *The Comedy of Errors*. At times we wish to believe one or the other of these things (and over time it may happen that we wish to believe both); it is as if we wanted to mislead ourselves.

Gordon Baker has acutely said that, eager though Wittgenstein was to 'eliminate obstacles' from our seeing philosophical issues aright, he acknowledged that 'what distorts our vision is as much defects of the *will* as it is defects of the intellect'.[10] Many features of the work bear out this claim. There is, for instance, Wittgenstein's deployment, in an unsystematic, conversational manner, of words such as 'Tendenz' ['tendency'] and 'Trieb' ['drive'], which probably came to him through a familiarity with Freud's theories of desire. Facing a problem, we often feel in advance of presented evidence or articulated reasons that its solution must lie in this direction rather than in that; such a feeling, Wittgenstein usually calls an 'inclination' ['Neigung'], and these inclinations are frequently the objects of his most inquiring description (see, for examples, *RPP* I, 2, 4, 65, 71). A small, recurrent phrase in his prose – 'man möchte sagen' / 'we would like to say' – marks, like a cairn, an underlaid inclination, as at a climatic remark during the sustained discussion of aspect-seeing in the *Investigations*:

Now, when I know my acquaintance in a crowd, perhaps after looking in his direction for quite a while, – is this a special sort of seeing? Is it a case of both seeing and thinking? or an amalgam of the two, as I should almost like to say ['wie ich beinahe sagen möchte']?

  The question is: *why* does one want to say this? (*PI* 197)

Not that Wittgenstein's reply to such a '*why*' is of the form of an in-depth explanation; rather, he describes our concepts of 'sight' and 'thought' and shows how they may overlap at such a moment of recognition. Nor is there more than a superficial resemblance between his inching through these matters and the sweep of Nietzsche who conflates 'what we are inclined to say' with 'what we can give a philosophical justification for saying', a conflation Wittgenstein rejects: 'What we are "tempted to say" ['zu sagen versucht sind']…is, of course, not philosophy; but it is its raw material.'

(*PI* 91) Nonetheless, the fact that Wittgenstein confesses in his notebooks an inclination to lie and an inclination to jealousy (*CV* 37 and *RPP* II, 34) with the same words as he will examine an inclination to this or that philosophical view reveals the living intentness of his thought. And, though it is only a verbal coincidence, it is felicitous that the German for the philosophical temptations which assail us, 'Versuchungen', should be close to the investigations, 'Untersuchungen', with which he combated them (Cf. *CV* 81). He wrote of himself: 'Working in philosophy – like work in architecture in many respects – is really more a working on oneself. On one's own interpretation. On one's way of seeing things. (And what one expects of them.)' (*CV* 16).

The temptations of philosophy, for those who are truly susceptible to them, do not differ from other kinds of temptation: having resisted them does not guarantee they will not recur. A man thoroughly convinced of the untenability of Cartesian dualism may still have spasms in which he thinks of his own body as distinct from his self, when ill, say, or frustrated at his inability to thread a needle. Of such troubles, Wittgenstein observed: 'One must put up with them: the worst thing a person can do is rebel against them. They too come in attacks, brought on by inner and outer causes. One must then say: "Still another attack".'[11] Though he himself struggled hard to free himself from an equally precarious dualism in the philosophy of language, from the attempt to distinguish an 'inner' act of 'meaning' something and the 'outer' act of uttering words 'with' that meaning, the later writings revert chronically to just such a picture, not that they credit it but that it has not been wiped out, just partly overpainted. 'Ever and again comes the thought,' as *Zettel* wearily remarks, 'that what we see of a sign is only the outside of something within, in which the real operations of sense and meaning go on.' (*Z* 25; this is one aspect of the experience of 'a picture forcing itself on us', about which see *PI* 48, 55, 204; *RPP* I, 6, 52, 185.)

It may help at this point to make a distinction which our language does not draw clearly. I shall distinguish between a 'mistake' and an 'error' (the conceptual distinction is to be found in Wittgenstein, though it would be contrary to the principled style of his later writings to press the words 'Fehler' and 'Irrtum' into the service of a fabricated terminology as I shall, for a while, press their English equivalents). The distinction is rough but ready for action, and can be sketched like this: there might be a person who always wrote the name 'Wittgenstein' 'Wittgenstien'; this could be either a mistake or an error. To tell the difference, try pointing out the correct spelling and see what happens. If the person speedily relinquishes 'Wittgenstien' (after double-checking with a few reputable authorities), it was a mistake; if, however, the spelling is defended with claims such as that the general English rule '"i" before "e" except after "c"' *ought* to apply to German too or that there is no such thing as 'correct' spelling, no authority with whom to double-check, then we confront an error. Almost any mistake may become an error, if persisted in with sufficient stubbornness or ingenuity, or if such weight has accrued to it that to give it up has become more than its holder can manage. A mistake, in my sense, 'doesn't only have a cause, it also has a ground... that is, roughly: when someone makes a mistake, this can be fitted into what he knows aright' (*OC* 11), as the merely mistaken speller shares common notions of orthography which quickly bring about a rectification. An error, on the other hand, may be fiercely maintained because, if the person were convinced of his being in error, he would lose not merely one bit of knowledge but perhaps also his sense of what it is for him to 'know' anything – such is the case when we reject the suggestion that we might be wrong to trust the report of previous generations that the earth has existed throughout the last hundred years: '...mayn't they [previous generations] be wrong? – "Nonsense!" one will say. "How should all these people be wrong?" – But is that an argument? Is it not simply the rejection of an idea? And perhaps the determination of a concept? For if I speak of a possible mistake here, this changes the role of "mistake" and "truth" in our lives' (*OC* 20–1).

Wittgenstein responded to *The Golden Bough* with such ferocious penetration because he detested Frazer's manner of treating magical rites and beliefs as if they were only mistaken scientific hypotheses, as if, so to speak, primitive tribes were already measuring with our rulers though doing it not very well. But a rain-dance need not be an attempted weather-forecast, nor even the expression of a wish to be able to forecast the weather. Such practices may seem to us wrong, but the kind of wrongness they have is that of an error and not a mistake. In dealing with them, actually or in contemplation, 'We must start out from the sphere of error and carry error over into truth. That is, we must discover the source of error, or hearing of the truth will profit us nothing... To convince somebody that he is in error, it is not enough to state the truth, but rather we must find the *path* from

error to truth' (*RFGB* 1; my translation). We must find the sense of
the error, the inclination which perhaps speaks in it, and to do that
requires of us acquaintance with the surroundings in which believing
and acting like this have their life. Error too has not only a cause but
grounds which it inhabits, and these grounds are not opinions which
may shift at the drop of an argument; they are a world: '...I did not
get my picture of the world by satisfying myself of its correctness; nor
do I have it because I am satisfied of its correctness. No: it is the
inherited background against which I distinguish between true and
false' (*OC* 15).[12] Which does not mean that I cannot come to change
my picture of the world, but that such a change occurs by many
piece-meal alterations (none of which may have had so entire a
change in view), as a baby learns to move its muscles, takes lurching
steps, until one day we say that it can walk. The encounter with a
culture quite different from our own may leave us standing, like
Wordsworth in face of the blind beggar, 'as if admonished from
another world'; that we feel admonished, rather than just blankly
apart, though, shows that we can find something of ourselves and for
ourselves in that other world, as Wittgenstein said that, when we
study the magical picture of the world, it is the discovery of 'what
connects this picture with our own feelings and thoughts' that 'gives
the contemplation its depth' (*RFGB* 13). We cannot simply decide to
step out of our frame of reference (cf. *PI* 230) any more than some
other creature could decide to step into it, and yet from where we
stand we can discern more than just the fact that we are standing
here. Philosophically speaking, there may be little or nothing to say
about that 'more'; this does not entail that the words 'The *edifice of
your pride* has to be dismantled. And that is terribly hard work.'
(*CV* 26) have no sense, nor that it is not required of us in such a
situation to act so as to give them meaning. So to act is 'to carry error
over into truth', as in the story of the good shepherd who sought the
lost sheep and brought it home.[13]

Such a pastoral care for what has gone astray sounds unlike the
neat confidences of some philosophers: Alan Bennett's 'Yes, I can do
this quite easily'. Wittgenstein on Frazer, or on the technical
assurances of some of his contemporaries – their semantic hygiene,
their hopes for a 'scientific' method in philosophy – speaks rather in
the voice of Lafew: 'we have our philosophical persons, to make
modern and familiar things supernatural and causeless. Hence is it
that we make trifles of terrors, ensconcing ourselves into seeming

knowledge, when we should submit ourselves to an unknown fear.' (*All's Well That Ends Well*, 2.3.1ff.) Indeed, the shape of *All's Well* – elements of its plot which seem both *passé* and fresh, the mobility of its verse – gives a comic form to Wittgensteinian 'Sorge' and shows how repeatedly we are assailed by longings we thought superseded. A positivistic sense of the play turns it into a parable of Bertram's mistakes, and how he is rid of them. But the play tells rather the story of error's reluctance in several people, especially Helena: 'Thus Indian-like, / Religious in mine error, I adore / The sun, that looks upon his worshipper, / But knows of him no more' (1.3.204–7, cf. 1.1.228–9). Helena is 'undone' by her love (1.1.84), Bertram 'undone' by his marriage (2.3.267 and 3.2.20), Parolles 'undone' (4.3.323), all but his scarf. Yet each of them finds a way to build on this deathlike wreckage of the edifice of his or her pride. Looked at one way, *All's Well* just transfers Bertram from Parolles to Helena, from the mistaken laddishness and social self-esteem which attracts him to his male companion to the beginnings of a true value for his wife. We need to recognise that Helena and Parolles are not only opposites but alike, a recognition Shakespeare underlines by comparing Helena's desperate project of curing the King (everybody, including the King, says it's hopeless) with Parolles' equally rash feint at service to the state, 'this business which he knows is not to be done' (3.6.86–7). So too, eventually, Parolles comes to something like the state of rueful self-acceptance in error from which Helena begins. The lords talk as if self-improvement follows from self-knowledge: 'Is it possible he should know what he is, and be that he is?' (4.1.44–5); it is even as if growth in self-knowledge were a matter of acquiring information. To which Parolles gives the permanent, comically and philosophically resilient, reply: 'Simply the thing I am / Shall make me live' (4.3.333–4). The play carries error over into truth; it converts the 'wondrous cold' (3.6.113) sense of what it is to look upon yourself as a 'thing', isolate and abjected, into the 'wondrous kind' (5.3.309) acknowledgment of mutual human failing. Such a change is more than a change of mind, nor can it be brought about by argument alone (though argument may play a part); it does not happen once for all, but, like a play, is essentially rehearsed and reperformed; people do not always agree on what they have witnessed when they have seen such a change.

Philosophy has little to say in such circumstances, as Bertram has little to say in the new ruins of his former life at the end of *All's Well*, because 'in philosophy we do not draw conclusions. "But it must be like this" is not a philosophical proposition. Philosophy only states what everyone admits' (*PI* 156). In this respect, philosophy resembles comedy. Comedy can in effect 'say' something only by provoking laughter (or other, similar response of assent – a smile, a shrug of the shoulders, contentedness with how a plot pans out, and so on), and 'laughing at the same jokes is evidence of far-reaching psychical conformity'.[14] The main reason why philosophers have often been the butts of comedy is that few of them have so sternly limited themselves to 'what everyone admits' as Wittgenstein wished they would; they can therefore be represented as Aristophanes represents Socrates. Truly laughable though such guying is, it remains on the outside of philosophical activity. Aristophanes's jokes assert common sense against Socratic flightiness, and that is a quite proper thing to do, though it does not constitute a reply to philosophy, for 'Philosophy can be said to consist of three activities: to see the commonsense answer, to get yourself so deeply into the problem that the commonsense answer is unbearable, and to get from that situation back to the commonsense answer. One must not in philosophy attempt to short-circuit problems' (*Ambrose* 109; cf. *BB* 58–9). We remember from *The Clouds* mostly its quips, but the comic understanding of philosophical activity really takes the form of a farcical imbroglio, not of a one-liner; where Aristophanes most keenly and funnily challenges philosophy is in Strepsiades's ambitions for his son (and it was as a corrupter of youth that Socrates, like a comedian, 'died the death'). A father's ambitions for his son are not defeated easily, not even by a good 'put-down'. The same holds for a son's ambitions for his father.

One, perhaps small but still authentic, distinction of Wittgenstein is that he is a philosopher of genius who understands, depicts (and suffers under) an inward sense of what is funny in philosophising. Particularly his own, as a comically doleful manuscript note puts it: 'A person with "common sense" who reads one of the earlier philosophers, thinks (and not without justification): "Sheer nonsense!" When he hears me, he thinks: "Just insipid commonplaces!" Again, with justification. And thus the look of philosophy has changed.'[15] This view of philosophy as a 'synopsis of trivialities' (*Lee* 26), constant in Wittgenstein from the *Tractatus* to the *Investigations*, though put with a less amiable irony in the earlier work, shows how native to him was the thought in the 1912 letter which I began by quoting – the thought that William James improved him both 'a *lot*' and 'a little', for in the perpetual aspect-shift which makes philosophy look now a cure and now the disease itself lie the grandeur and the humour of Wittgenstein's engagement with his own life-work (he tried to give up philosophy as intently as Tolstoy tried to give up smoking).

The motto of the *Investigations* is taken from Nestroy's comedy, *Der Schützling*: 'Above all, it is in the nature of progress that it looks much greater than it really is.'[16] More of the remark's context helps in seeing the point of Wittgenstein's choice: 'There are so many methods of rooting things up and weeding them out, and yet so little of the wickedness in the world has been uprooted, so little of its evil weeded out, that it is very clear people may invent a host of methods but they still haven't found the right one.'[17] Wittgenstein was extremely fertile in inventing methods for posing and revolving conceptual questions, but because philosophy is a 'working on oneself' and teaches only what everybody admits, he claims for himself no great advance or break-through. He thought of philosophy as a form of intellectual housework – 'In philosophy we are... tidying up a room, in the process of which we have to touch everything a dozen times. The only way to do philosophy is to do everything twice' (*Lee* 24) – and like a housewife's his work is never done. (I do not mean that he did not bring any of the writings of the second period to a state he thought fit for publication, but that the 'finished' form he was searching for would itself have involved that incessant recursion which the 'Preface' to the *Investigations* describes.) In this respect too, his philosophising resembles comic practice as another of his preferred authors, Lichtenberg, portrayed it: 'Comedy does not effect direct improvement, and perhaps satire does not do so either: I mean one does not abandon the vices they render ludicrous. What they can do, however, is to enlarge our horizon and increase the number of fixed points from which we can orientate ourselves in all the eventualities of life more quickly'[18] (Cf. *CV* 61). For comedy and Wittgensteinian philosophy turn principally on error, and error, like Faust's 'Dämonen' is something of which we are rid, if at all, only with difficulty. Indeed, Wittgenstein wrote that of an error 'it is never right to say simply: "no, that is false, it must be abandoned"'.[19] Even for Parolles a place has to be found.

Norman Malcolm notes that 'Wittgenstein once said that a serious and good philosophical work could be written that would consist

entirely of *jokes* (without being facetious) '; he further records that his
laughter was normally 'moderate and brief: I could hardly conceive
of him laughing to the point of tears'.[20] There is actually one story
about Wittgenstein laughing immoderately, at a skit written by Paul
Engelmann's brother, in which Tolstoy was grossly caricatured

...as a kind of spectacular monster under the name of 'Lew Fux
Nikolajewitsch Tollhaus' ['Tollhaus' is German for 'madhouse'], led like a
bear on a chain. The most offensive aspect of that satire, of course, was its
lampooning of Wittgenstein's ideological convictions. But when my brother
read the uncensored text of the satire to the devout Tolstoy-admirer
Wittgenstein... the reaction was unexpected. Wittgenstein slipped from the
sofa and, shaken by spasms of uncontrollable laughter, literally rolled on the
carpet.[21]

We may agree with Engelmann in finding this scene 'grotesque', but
not because it is odd that an admirer of Tolstoy should laugh at jokes
about him. On the contrary. As a church is the place where we would
expect to find gargoyles, so it is the disciple who is most receptive to
jokes about the teacher, and has the best right to hear them, for in
laughing at his hero, he laughs also at his own hero-worship, and thus
exercises an essential comic skill by turning himself into the
protagonist of his own amusement.[22] Adapting Wittgenstein's aphorism about philosophical problems and the daily surroundings of
language, we could say that comedy arises when ethical attitudes go
on holiday, and that here too we need to consider the jobs these
attitudes normally do if we are to understand what happens when
they are given time off. There is an analogy with the role of
philosophical scepticism, as Jonathan Lear describes it: '...the
skeptic's success depends on his zeroing in on those beliefs which we
cannot prove or refute. His importance depends on those beliefs'
being important to us.'[23] While it may be true that there are things
too sacred or tender for us to laugh at, it is also true that there are
things, as it were, *beneath* laughter (there are few jokes about regular
breathing). Philosophising for Wittgenstein appeared under the
aspect-shift of mattering 'a *lot*' and 'a little', and thus provided a
perfect subject for humour; his own aspirations in and for philosophy
looked that way to him too: 'don't think that I believe that my ideas
are very important but I cannot help feeling that they might help
people to avoid *some* errors. Or am I mistaken?... I have of course no
judgment at all as to whether my ideas are worth preserving after my
death or not. And perhaps it is ridiculous of me even to consider this

question at all. But if this is ridiculous please try to excuse this foolishness of mine because it is not a superficial foolishness but the deepest of which I am capable.'[24] His words double-take about their own importance; a comic contortionist could not tie himself into more intriguing knots: 'but I cannot help... Or am I mistaken?... I have of course no judgment at all... And perhaps... But if...' The Erasmian turn of thought, 'the deepest [foolishness] of which I am capable', was native to his mind. In the notebooks he wrote 'Our greatest stupidities may be very wise' and 'If people did not sometimes do silly things, nothing intelligent would ever get done' and 'Never stay up on the barren heights of cleverness, but come down into the green valleys of silliness' (*CV* 39, 50, 76); two of his students remember his advising them how to behave in philosophical discussion: 'Don't try to be intelligent; say it; then let intelligence into the room'.[25] He took his own advice, for that last quotation amply describes the shape of many of the remarks in the *Investigations*, those dialogues with himself before one half of which he might have written, as Erasmus did at the beginning of the *Praise of Folly*, 'Folly speaks:', though Wittgenstein might have joked that it is not always clear *which* half.

'The deepest foolishness of which I am capable': Wittgenstein is a 'deep' thinker, but how do we fathom philosophical 'depth'?

The problems arising through a misinterpretation of our forms of language have the character of *depth*. They are deep disquietudes; their roots are as deep in us as the forms of our language and their significance is as great as the importance of our language. – Let us ask ourselves: why do we feel a grammatical joke to be *deep*? (And that is what the depth of philosophy is.) (*PI* 47)

Throughout his later work, he maintains that it is a characteristic 'inclination' of philosophy to misconstrue its own depth, as if this depth were created by 'some tremendously subtle and mysterious matter which we must investigate' whereas it occurs 'because in *this* spot a great many misleading forms of expression intersect';[26] that is, the 'depth' arises as it does in stereoscopic toys, by the super-imposition of two or more images, each flat in itself. Many philosophical problems stem from unrecognized puns; hence the possibility of writing a serious work of philosophy consisting entirely of jokes. Jokes have the advantage that in telling them we overtly abstract from the surroundings of such serious linguistic practices as giving information, and so are less likely to fall victim to that disorientation which Wittgenstein thought endemic in philosophising. We stand in certain ways, adopt facial expressions and tones of voice, employ set, introductory phrases such as 'Have you heard the one about...?' to signal that what follows is a joke. (Many jokes, if told without these signals, if narrated as accounts of actual happenings, would provoke grave reactions – indignation or even horror.) A joke, or a play, offers us the 'dual control' over our sayings and deeds which a driving-instructor has in his specially designed car; we abstract from behaviour when we tell a joke, but that abstraction is itself a way of behaving; a play moves faster than we can think, but in so doing shows us how we think, and needs us to replay it. Nor is it true that jokes work only once; it is the old jokes we go back to, as we return to old habits, old arguments.

Sending Russell a copy of the typescript now known as the 'Blue Book', Wittgenstein wrote: 'two years ago I held some lectures in Cambridge and dictated some notes to my pupils so that they might have something to carry home with them, in their hands if not in their brains' (*BB* v). The donnish zeugma – two senses of 'carry', two senses of 'in' – is not much of a joke, and yet it contains 'a whole cloud of philosophy condensed into a drop of grammar' (*PI* 222). The 'Blue Book' itself devotes a great deal of time to that 'cloud of philosophy', in which an 'inner', 'mental' realm is conjured up on the model of the physical world and our language for it. If we always kept in mind what the joke shows, he would not have needed to dictate the notes; on the other hand, someone who has read the notes better appreciates how 'rich' the joke is.

Wittgensteinian humour more typically stems from his extended sense of 'grammar' (the sense given in Professor Anscombe's account of 'linguistic practice'). Thus: 'Suppose that I were a doctor and a patient came to me, showed me his hand and said: "This thing that looks like a hand isn't just a superb imitation – it really is a hand" and went on to talk about his injury – should I really take this as a piece of information, even though a superfluous one?' (*OC* 60). If we laugh at the idea of a patient's feeling the need to say this, we are also laughing at that radical scepticism which imagines everything can at any time be doubted, whereas doubt too has surroundings in which it makes sense, and becomes senseless outside them. Or again: 'The law of excluded middle does not say, as its form suggests: There are only these two possibilities. Yes and No, and no third one. But rather:

"Yes" and "No" divide the field of possibilities into two parts. – And that of course need not be so. ("Have you stopped beating your wife?")' (*RPP* I, 55). He recalls the old chestnut to good effect for the awkwardness of applying the law of excluded middle to the possible replies to the question – the law apparently restricts the answers to either 'Yes, I have' or 'No, I haven't' – shows, amongst other things, that a law which governs the logic of some propositions may seriously skew our understanding of the logic of utterances of those propositions. Moore's paradox of assertion demonstrates a related point: though the propositions 'There is a fire in this room' and 'I don't believe there is a fire in this room' do not contradict each other, there is an absurdity about asserting 'There is a fire in this room and I don't believe there is'.[27] Wittgenstein wrote the absurdity large, and produced a joke, which also shows that the absurdity of the assertion is not, as Moore had originally said, 'psychological': 'Imagine an announcer in a railway station, who announces a train according to schedule, but – perhaps groundlessly – is convinced that it won't arrive. He might announce: "Train No.... will arrive at...o'clock. Personally I don't believe it"' (*RPP* 93). No facts about the announcer's 'state of mind' (his love-life, for example) affect the deep foolishness of this imagining, nor would it much matter whether trains generally run on time. The example sketches the grammatical relations of 'announce' and 'personally'. The joke takes us, as Wittgenstein said it was his ambition in philosophy to take us, 'from a piece of disguised nonsense to something that is patent nonsense' (*PI* 133). So too, when asked by colleagues in Trinity College, to give an instance of the relations between 'surface grammar' and 'depth grammar', he is said to have replied: 'Is "Should one say 'Father, Son and Holy Ghost *is* one God' or 'Father, Son and Holy Ghost *are* one God" a question about surface grammar or about depth grammar?'.[28] He gave a life to his logical example by asking it in his real surroundings – asking about the Trinity in Trinity. There lives no record of reply.

These are jokes which serve as philosophical examples, but the relation may be worked the other way round: philosophy can illustrate a joke. In Chaplin's *Modern Times* (1936), the 'little man', after much suffering, gets a job in a shipyard where he hopes to make good at last. The foreman assigns him his first task; the inter-title reads: 'Find me a wedge like this!' We see him examine several pieces of wood, and offer them to the foreman who angrily rejects them, pointing to the wedge he holds in his hand as if to say 'No, no, can't you *see*, like *this*.' Chaplin wanders off, comes upon an identically triangular wedge, removes it, and heads off back to the foreman. Unfortunately, this wedge was serving as one of the chocks which kept the uncompleted ship on the slipway, and we see the vast hull slide away behind him and sink, while he, his sense of a job well done crumbling in his hands, holds out his wedge to the astounded and furious crew of shipbuilders. Compare: 'A language-game: to bring something *else*; to bring the *same*... But then how does he know what he is to bring the next time as "the same" – with what justice can I say that he has brought the right thing or the wrong?' (*RFM* 406). Chaplin's sequence gives a paradigm of Wittgenstein's discussion of rule-following, one of the principal themes of the later philosophy; it also suggests why Wittgenstein often resorted to instances of commands between builders when talking about rules and meaning, the relevant surroundings hereabouts are so sharply consequential. But what does this coincidence of Chaplin and Wittgenstein show? It is a speculation, a pleasant one, that the Hollywood-movie-loving Wittgenstein saw *Modern Times* and found in his laughter at it some inspiration. It does not seem important that a conference of Wittgensteinians would respond knowingly to the episode. After all, nobody supposes Chaplin needed to read Wittgenstein before he could invent the story of the disastrous wedge, nor that Wittgenstein must have been prompted to thought by *Modern Times*. Evidently not, and that is the point. Chaplin's joke has no more and no less depth than Wittgenstein's remarks on following a rule. The moment in the film and the years of philosophising have the equal depth of a grammatical joke, and that *is* the depth of philosophy. That the truth of each translates into the language of the other shows that here at least Wittgenstein has done what he strove to do – say only what everybody admits. 'Imagine...', he often says, but some might doubt whether we can imagine what we asks. In this case, there is no doubt; Chaplin shows the imagining can be done, Wittgenstein, that it is worth thinking about.

'Talking back', in the sense of 'making a riposte', as two comedians in a double-act talk back at each other, multiplying the funniness of each individual remark by the perpetual capping and trouncing of the exchange, is Wittgenstein's preferred form of philosophical investigation. The 'deep thinker' and the 'man in the street', 'common sense' and 'philosophical problem', are held permanently fact to face on the stage of his writing, like Faust and 'Sorge', but, in his later work, with a refreshed accommodation to each other. One example from the many:

"What the names in language signify must ['muß'] be indestructible; for it must ['muß'] be possible to describe the state of affairs in which everything destructible is destroyed. And this description will contain words; and what corresponds to these cannot then be destroyed ['darf dann nicht zerstört sein'], for otherwise the words would have no meaning." I must not ['darf...nicht'] saw off the branch on which I am sitting. (*PI* 27)

Much in this altitudinous passage hangs on the German modal verbs 'müßen' and 'dürfen'. The person who speaks within inverted commas is in the grip of a way of thinking about how language manages to speak of the world (that person might be called 'the Wittgenstein who wrote the *Tractatus*'; another of his aliases is 'Cratylus'). His train of thought goes: a word has a meaning rather as a person has a name; all words are really names; names mean the person or thing they name, they are like identity-tags round the necks of their referents; but if that is so, what can we do with an identity-tag when the person or thing it belongs to is no more? – nothing; therefore, names do not name what they appear to name (perishable individuals), they must name something which cannot be destroyed because it must be possible to 'describe the state of affairs in which everything destructible is destroyed' (and there must be such a state, for if there were not, how could the distinction 'destructible' / 'indestructible' have an employment?) The person who speaks the laconic sentence outside inverted commas could be called 'the Wittgenstein who is writing this remark'. He has, I think, been watching animated cartoons. In a lightning comparison, he sees the frantic and strained argumentation that has gone before as resembling the behaviour of, say, Tom chasing Jerry: Tom catches Jerry on a high branch, saws through the branch, leaps down to catch Jerry on the next limb below (and so on) until – still high above ground-level – Jerry makes one of his conventional escapes, expected by everyone but Tom who, not noticing his absence, nor aware that the branch on which he now stands is his last remaining support, saws through it, stands happy for an instant, about at last to triumph over his enemy, about to eat, come to his metaphysical goal, and then finds himself about to plummet (perhaps he makes that most risibly philosophical of all cartoon moves, putting his own hands under his own feet to 'make sure' he really is groundless), and falls out of sight.

Whether or not the notion came to Wittgenstein from cartoons, this passage makes one of those 'beautiful similes'[29] with which he frequently replied to misleading analogies: the 'hardness of the logical must' (*PI* 129; cf. *PI* 45) is for a moment implicitly compared with the exigencies of an empirical situation, being stuck up a tree and depending for support on a single branch. The simile is underlined by a contrast between the lexis of 'abstract' thought and down-to-earthiness, between 'muß' and 'darf', where, as used here the first tries to express logical necessity and the second delivers a 'tip' – the last sentence quoted might better be translated as 'I'd be well advised not to saw through the branch on which I'm sitting'. The two idioms behave with regard to each other like the standard comic pair of dreamy master and clued-up servant; in this instance, the servant gets the better of the exchange, as is traditional. From which a comedian might be inclined to draw a parable, flattering to his profession, of the respective standings of philosophy and his own jocular common sense. Yet what matters about the comic master/ servant pair is not that one of them tends to win their battles of wit but the permanence of their reciprocity, the fact that they are *traditionally* related to each other; the servant gets the pay-off but does not leave his service. Many a joke, as many a philosophical problem, 'we must first get familiar with, by running into it countless times. We then come to recognize its flavour.'[30] When we have come to such a recognition, we may be less inclined to believe that one of the partners in the double-act must be dominant, just as we may recognise that it is neither the case that the ordinary surroundings of our linguistic practices always cause our philosophical views, nor that those views lay down permanent laws for practice, but rather that 'where that practice and these views go together, the practice does not spring from the view, but both of them are there' (*RFGB* 2).

So cosy a picture of the home-life of the Queen of Sciences is not what we would expect from the Sorge-ful Wittgenstein, but the picture is not as cosy as it looks. For concomitant with his non-revisionary characterisation of the task of philosophy is his despondency, indeed grief, over how little philosophising can help a person or a society towards reform. His advice to the philosopher in him and us – 'Say what you choose, so long as it does not prevent you from seeing the facts' – sounds permissive, even blithe, but it had a sombre rider – (And when you see them there is a good deal that you will not say)' (*PI* 37). 'Now God delay our rebellion! As we are ourselves, what things we are!' (*All's Well*, 4.3.19–20): the attendant lord speaks for the supervising philosopher – their attitudes ride in tandem. Human thought is not much to write home about, but philosophy has no place else to lay its head.

Norman Malcolm records that Wittgenstein 'did not have a "sense of humour" if one means by this a humorous view of the world and of oneself. His outlook was grim. He was always troubled about his own life and was often close to despair. He was dismayed by the insincerity, vanity and coldness of the human heart. He thought that all of us greatly needed help (and perhaps himself most of all) if we were to become more honest and more loving.'[31] These words bespeak a close acquaintance with Wittgenstein; they are hard to challenge as biographical testimony, but it is possible to wonder whether Professor Malcolm was right to think that by 'sense of humour' we mean always and only 'a humorous view of the world and of oneself'. In the fifth act of Corneille's *L'illusion comique*, for instance, we watch a pair of young lovers who have evaded in time-honoured fashion paternal veto on their union; they are now richly dressed and seem socially well-connected. But their marriage, to which we had long with them looked forward, has foundered in recrimination and infidelity; the young man is murdered to avenge the man he has cuckolded, and his bride dies of sorrow. Only after witnessing this catastrophe do we discover that the lovers have taken jobs as actors, and that we have been seeing them at work in a romantic tragedy. So pleasant a reassurance that there is 'no harm done' is a comic convention, but just in the measure that we recognise it as such (having seen it countless times before), we are not inclined to credit it as a picture of how our world is but rather take it as something which, having seen the facts of that world, we would like to say but cannot, except as a joke. Corneille shifts our sense of the gravity of this closing scene back and forth, as the aspects of an ambiguous figure may alternate under our gaze; such potential for 'shift' constitutes the realism of his intricately artificial play. Though we are left finally with the comic aspect of events, we have still heard how young love can go sour, seen hearts harden; the end of *L'illusion comique*, as of many romantic comedies, is not more than a happy beginning.

Wittgenstein considered our ability thus to vary the aspect under which the world appears to us as a more important element of humour than the light-heartedness which Malcolm seems to mean:

Humour is not a mood but a way of looking at the world. So if it is correct
to say that humour was stamped out in Nazi Germany, that does not mean
that people were not in good spirits, or anything of that sort, but something
much deeper and more important. (*CV* 78)

The word translated here as 'stamped out' is 'vertilgt', which
appears in the context of the quotation from Nestroy Wittgenstein
chose some time after 1947 as the motto for *Philosophical Investigations*
(the remark about Nazi Germany is from 1948): 'Ausrottungs- und
Vertilgungs-mittel', which I rendered above as 'methods of rooting
things up and weeding them out'. The Nazis were indeed prolific of
eradications; that fact too is a surrounding of Wittgenstein's work
which should not be forgotten if we are to recognise the honest
anguish with which he carried on philosophising, aware that doing so
might bring little improvement where there was need of help.

We know that he saw and enjoyed at least one classic theatrical
comedy, Molière's *Le malade imaginaire*. It was staged by his friend,
Paul Engelmann, in Olmütz during the first war. Engelmann had
'scruples of conscience about staging such a show while the war with
all its horrors continued. I was torn by bitter inner struggles, for I was
passionately drawn to a venture which my pacifist urges condemned
as frivolous. I was then, as later, myself a great hypochondriac, and
– as usual in such cases – it was hard to draw a borderline between
my real, and by no means trifling, complaints and my imaginary
ailments.[32] Drawing such a borderline is both ethically and philosophically hard, as Wittgenstein's career attests and *All's Well* stages,
for while it may be that 'in philosophy we are deceived by an
illusion', nonetheless 'the illusion too is something & I must get it
clearly in view before I can say that it is only an illusion'.[33] Molière is
a great habitué of that borderline, nowhere more so than in his last
play. An audience laughing at Argan may communally admit that,
in his case, the fear of death has become absurd, but they are not
likely for ever to have disembarrassed themselves of such a fear just by
laughing at it. Punch-lines are only a version of *elenchus*; it is not in
comedy any more than in philosophy that we look for what we find
'clinching'. Even Argan's credulity about medical science and its
pseudo-explanatory terms like the 'virtus dormitiva', a credulity
similar in many respects to the fond trust in science against which
Wittgenstein raged, is not something easy to laugh ourselves out of,
for it is pervasively part of the language of the play, and that
language repeats a picture of the world to us at every turn, speaks to

our inclinations. Thus, the vocabulary of erotic pastoral with its 'peine mortelle' and 'mortelle douleur' sounds differently in Argan's sickroom; his readiness to submit to the 'ordonnances' of his doctors twins with his parental insistence that he has a right to 'ordonner' whatever he wants; and everywhere misleadingly analogous expressions – 'sang-froid', 'vous n'aurez pas ce coeur-là' – intersect, until it seems there is no cure for his manner of seeing things.[34] The complications mount up 'farcically', as we say, but farce is also a form of philosophical entanglement, where error piles on error inextricably: 'A philosophical trouble is an obsession, which once removed it seems impossible that it should ever have had power over us. It seems trivial' (*Ambrose* 98). Laughter says we believe we see our way out, but that belief does not itself provide a method of removal from these toils, or of carrying Argan over from error into truth. This is the point of the moment in *Le malade imaginaire*, 3.3 when Béralde urges Argan that it would do him good to see one of Molière's satirical comedies against doctors. Yet Argan is already *in* such a comedy, and that comedy has been swallowed by his errors (as Molière, who created the role of Argan, was consumed by his own creation, vomiting blood during the fourth performance of the play's final ballet and dying, in the legend, in the wings that same night). Here comedy is as powerless as philosophy against error, because Argan would give his life rather than give up his belief that he can prevent himself from dying. As Kafka puts the sad fact when describing Josef K's last, illusioned grasp at hope, 'Logic is certainly unshakeable, but even logic can't withstand a man who wants to go on living.'[35]

Engelmann was right to worry whether he should stage a comedy in the middle of a war, though, as the phenomenon of 'wartime humour', of joking in trenches, shows, surroundings of dire need evoke laughter, even from those who suffer most. Affliction calls for relief, and settles for comic relief if it can get nothing better. It is not only heartening to reflect on how long our species' sense of humour has managed to continue playing over our history of indifference to the sufferings we cause. Jokes and arguments, comedy and philosophy, 'keep us going', as we say; they do not, cannot, ask whether we should be kept going. A comedian can say no more about that than a philosopher: 'We can only *describe* and say, human life is like that... One would like to say ['Man möchte sagen']: This is what took place here; laugh, if you can' (*RFGB* 3).

NOTES

1 Letter to Russell, 22/6/1912, in *Letters to Russell, Keynes and Moore*, ed. G. H. von Wright (Oxford, 1974), 10. References to works by Wittgenstein in what follows appear in the main text, according to this system of abbreviation: *Philosophische Untersuchungen*, trans. as *Philosophical Investigations* by G. E. M. Anscombe (Oxford, 1953; third edn, 1967): *PI*; *Bemerkungen über die Grundlagen der Mathematik*, trans. as *Remarks on the Foundations of Mathematics* by G. E. M. Anscombe (Oxford, 1956; third, rev. edn, 1978): *RFM*; *The Blue and Brown Books* (Oxford, 1958; second edn, 1969); *BB*; *Zettel*, trans. as *Zettel* by G. E. M. Anscombe (Oxford, 1967): *Z*; *Über Gewißheit*, trans. as *On Certainty* by D. Paul and G. E. M. Anscombe (Oxford, 1969, corr. repr., 1974): *OC*; *Wittgenstein's Lectures: Cambridge 1932–1935* ed. Alice Ambrose (Oxford, 1979): *Ambrose*; *Bemerkungen über Frazer's 'Golden Bough'*, trans as *Remarks on Frazer's 'Golden Bough'* by A. C. Miles and R. Rhees (Retford, 1979): *RFGB*; *Bemerkungen über die Philosophie der Psychologie*, trans. as *Remarks on the Philosophy of Psychology* by G. E. M. Anscombe, C. G. Luckhardt and M. A. E. Aue, 2 vols. (Oxford, 1980): *RPP*; *Wittgenstein's Lectures: Cambridge 1930–1932*, ed. Desmond Lee (Oxford, 1980): *Lee*; *Vermischte Bemerkungen*, trans. as *Culture and Value* by P. Winch (Oxford, 1980): *CV*; *Letzte Schriften über die Philosophie der Psychologie*, trans. as *Last Writings on the Philosophy of Psychology* by C. G. Luckhardt and M. A. E. Aue, 2 vols. (Oxford, 1982): *LW*. I have accepted these standard translations on all but a few occasions signalled in the text. All other translations from foreign languages are my own except where noted.
2 I quote from the script given in *The Complete Beyond the Fringe* (London, 1987), 51–2.
3 All paraphrases and quotations are from *Faust*, II, lines 11384–510; I have used the text of the edition by Erich Trunz et al., 14 vols (Hamburg, 1948–1960) where the scene appears in volume III, 343–9.
4 I know no discussion of what this scene meant to Wittgenstein. Both Ray Monk (*Ludwig Wittgenstein: The Duty of Genius* (London, 1990)) and Brian McGuinness (*Wittgenstein: A Life*, vol I (London, 1988)) quote the letter; neither considers the Goethe in detail. McGuinness's suggestion (156) that 'Sorge' means 'sense of futility' cannot be right. Russell may have understood the allusion, though he was far from such 'Sorge' himself; see *The Autobiography of Bertrand Russell, 1872–1914* (London, 1967), 41: 'Throughout the long period of religious doubt, I had been rendered very unhappy by the gradual loss of belief, but when the process was completed, I found to my surprise that I was quite glad to be done with the whole subject.'
5 'The Question of Linguistic Idealism', in *Essays in Honour of G. H. von Wright*, ed. J. Hintikka (Minnesota, 1976), 194.
6 I an indebted to the discussion of Fregean contextualism in G. P. Baker

and P. M. S. Hacker's *Wittgenstein: Meaning and Understanding* (Oxford, 1980; 2 vol. reprint, 1984), I, 145–71.

7 MS 110, quoted in Garth Hallett: *A Companion to Wittgenstein's 'Philosophical Investigations'* (Ithaca, 1977), 336.

8 'The Three Hermits' (1886), trans. Louise and Aylmer Maude, in *Twenty-Three Tales* (London, 1906; repr. 1967), 198, 201. Wittgenstein's admiration for the tale – 'My favourite' – is attested by M. O'C. Drury. 'Some Notes on Conversations with Wittgenstein', in *Ludwig Wittgenstein: Personal Recollections*, ed. R. Rhees (Oxford, 1981), 101.

9 *A Midsummer Night's Dream* 2.2.89. All quotations and references follow *The Riverside Shakespeare*, ed. G. Blakemore Evans et al. (Boston, 1974).

10 'Following Wittgenstein: *Some Signposts for Philosophical Investigations* §§ 143–242', in S. H. Holtzman and C. M. Leech, eds, *Wittgenstein: To Follow a Rule* (London, 1981), 58.

11 MS 138, quoted in Hallett, *Companion*, 336.

12 I touch here on one of the most contentious areas of Wittgenstein's work, his notion of a 'form of life'. There has been a lot of debate about the application of this notion to the social sciences. I am broadly in sympathy with the line of thought suggested in Simon Blackburn's 'Rule-Following and Moral Realism', in Holtzman and Leech, *Wittgenstein*.

13 Jonathan Lear discusses these matters in his 'Leaving the World Alone', *Journal of Philosophy*, 79 (1982) 382–403.

14 Freud, *Der Witz und seine Beziehung zum Unbewußten* (1905), trans. as *Jokes and Their Relation to the Unconscious* by James Strachey (1960, repr. Harmondsworth, 1976), 203–4. Wittgenstein would have queried that 'psychical', and a 'far-reaching…conformity' does not go as far as 'what everyone admits'.

15 MS 219, quoted in Hallett, *Companion* 225.

16 It is wrong of Wittgenstein's translators not to have translated this motto in the German/English text, and still more wrong of his editors to have omitted it from the 1972 English edition. Perhaps they had textual reasons for their omission of which I am unaware.

17 *Der Schützling*, Act 4, Scene 10. I translate from the text of *Johann Nestroy, Sämtliche Werke*, eds. F. Brükner and O. Kommel, 14 vols. (Vienna, 1924–30), VII, 216. It is fair to record that he also considered, amongst other possibilities, an epigraph from a tragedy, *King Lear*: 'I'll teach you differences', and then added, while laughing, 'The remark "You'd be surprised" wouldn't be a bad motto either'; see Drury, 'Some Notes', 171.

18 Lichtenberg, Notebook D 1773–1775, trans. as *Aphorisms* by R. J. Hollingdale (Harmondsworth, 1990), 53; there are similarities between Lichtenberg's remark and the role played by 'Übersicht' in the later Wittgenstein – see the helpful chapter in Baker and Hacker, *Wittgenstein*, 295–311.

19 MS 112, quoted in Hallett, *Companion*, 336.

20 Norman Malcolm, *Ludwig Wittgenstein: A Memoir* (1958), 29.

21 Paul Engelmann, *Letters from Ludwig Wittgenstein with a Memoir*, ed. B. F. McGuinness, trans. by L Furtmüller (Oxford, 1967), 66.

22 Cf. Baudelaire: 'A man who has fallen over doesn't laugh at his own fall, unless he happens to be a philosopher, a man who by long practice has acquired the power of quickly splitting himself in two and being present as a detached spectator at the phenomena of his own "I"', *De l'essence du rire* (1855) in *Curiosités esthétiques...*, ed. Henri Lemaitre (Paris, 1962), 251.

23 Lear, 'Leaving the World Alone', 397.

24 Letter to Russell, 20/9/13, in von Wright, ed., *Letters*, 28. The tone and shape of this passage look forward to the Preface to the *Investigations*.

25 D. A. T. Gasking and A. C. Jackson, 'Ludwig Wittgenstein', *Australasian Journal of Philosophy*, 29:2 (1951), repr. in K. T. Fann, ed., *Ludwig Wittgenstein: The Man and His Philosophy* (New York, 1967), 53.

26 MS 228, quoted Hallett, *Companion*, 64.

27 See Wittgenstein's letter to Moore on the subject, October 1944, in von Wright, ed., *Letters*, 177.

28 Godfrey Vesey, 'Locke and Wittgenstein on Language and Reality', in H. Lewis, ed., *Contemporary British Philosophy*, 4th series (1976), 263. A similar question might be asked about Jonathan Lear's phrase 'by the time the *Investigations* was written' (Lear, 'Leaving the World Alone', 385): 'should we say "by the time the *Investigations* was written" or "by the time the *Investigations* were written"?' Different senses of 'the time' and of what it was to write what we now call 'the *Investigations*' turn around the choice between singular and plural, and turn even more sharply around our not knowing which to choose.

29 Letter to Moore, Oct. 1936, in von Wright, ed., *Letters*, 167.

30 Wittgenstein, MS 109, quoted Hallett, *Companion*, 64.

31 Malcolm, *Ludwig Wittgenstein*, 74.

32 Engelmann, *Letters*, 68–9. Wittgenstein recalled the performance a decade later; see his letter to Engelmann of 31/3/1927, *Letters*, 5.

33 Wittgenstein, MS 110, quoted in Hallett, *Companion*, 127.

34 *Le malade imaginaire* (1673); I quote from the text of the *Oeuvres complètes*, ed. Georges Couton 2 vols. (Paris, 1971), II, respectively 1092, 1137, 1105, 1100, 1107, 1109.

35 *Der Proceß* (1925); I translate from the edition of Malcolm Pasley (Frankfurt a.M., 1990), 312.

Index